The Contested Homeland

ERLINDA GONZALES-BERRY

The Contested

ALBUQUERQUE

AND DAVID R. MACIEL

Homeland

A Chicano History of New Mexico

UNIVERSITY OF NEW MEXICO PRESS

Library of Congress Cataloging-in-Publication Data

The contested homeland : a Chicano history of New Mexico /
[edited by] David Maciel and Erlinda Gonzales-Berry.—1st ed.
    p.   cm.
Includes index.
  ISBN 0-8263-2198-4 (alk. paper)—ISBN 0-8263-2199-2
(pbk. : alk. paper)
    1. Mexican Americans—New Mexico—History.   2. New
Mexico—History—1848–   3.   New Mexico—Ethnic relations.
I. Maciel, David R.   I. Gonzales-Berry, Erlinda, 1942–
III. Title.
F805.M5 C66 2000
978.9′0046872—dc21   99-050412

To all those
men and women
of the
Alianza Federal de Mercedes
who struggled
with such courage
and commitment for
"the contested homeland"

Contents

Illustrations following page 142

Acknowledgments

The idea for this anthology originated in the editors' desire to address the serious gap in historical and cultural studies of the Chicano community of New Mexico. Yet, in the process of elaboration and completion of the manuscript, it became much more than what had been set forth in its initial purpose. And as with all collective projects, it owes many intellectual debts.

First and foremost, the contributors themselves merit special gratitude. They all worked within the parameters set forth by the editors and ably completed their original and well-researched chapters in a prompt and professional manner. In addition, since they are all experienced scholars of Nuevo Mexicano history and culture, they also were in a position to offer insights and commentary on the entire project.

In the preparation of the submitted manuscript, the staff of the Department of Chicano/Chicana Studies at California State University at Dominguez Hills (Virginia Rodríguez, administrative assistant, and Alfonso González and Claudia Rodríguez, student assistants) labored long and hard to correct, check, and format the entire book. One could have not asked for more professional or dedicated assistance. Evelyn A. Schlatter, the managing editor of the *New Mexico Historical Review,* shared her considerable editorial skills with us. She meticulously read, corrected, and edited the entire manuscript in its final version. Her efforts, displaying great care and sensitivity for the material, certainly improved the text.

David V. Holtby, the editor and associate director of the University of New Mexico Press, exemplified the ideal editor. He was a firm and committed supporter of this project from its origins to its final resolution. Over the course of the project, he became an integral part of the design and content of the volume. The book is surely enhanced by his experience and suggestions. One would be hard pressed to work with a better editor.

To the authors of the few existing studies of the Nuevomexicano homeland who opened up a fascinating and complex history, we owe great respect
and admiration. We learned much from their works. Certain senior colleagues
and friends merit special recognition for their contributions to this project.
Richard Etulain, director of the Center for the American West of the University of New Mexico, close friend, and colleague of many years, offered important constructive suggestions during every stage of the project. His generosity with ideas and time is forever appreciated. In a similar vein we thank
three other colleagues: Juan Gómez-Quiñones, Richard I. Griego, and Richard Griswold del Castillo. Each carefully read portions of the manuscript and
provided invaluable insights that enhanced the text.

We also acknowledge with special fondness our former colleagues at the
University of New Mexico. Both volume editors arrived as faculty members
to UNM in the fall of 1979, and both left UNM in 1997. During that memo-
rable interval, we were fortunate and privileged to have worked alongside
gifted scholars and close friends who shared much with us. Such interactions
made us better observers and scholars of the Nuevo Mexico experience. And
although we have physically left *la tierra del encanto*, spiritually and on a personal
level, Nuevo México and its Nuevomexicano history, society, and culture are
ever present in our minds and souls.

The Contested Homeland

Introduction

Nowhere in the United States has the presence of Chicanos and Chicanas been more evident than in New Mexico. Since the territorial period (1848) and after statehood (1912) they have represented a larger percentage of the total population than in any other state. Nuevomexicanos comprised the first major settlement in the northern periphery of Mexico, and they have remained a vital, culturally identifiable group for several centuries. A substantial number of families can trace their ancestry to seventeenth-century settlers, many of whom belonged to the colonial oligarchy of the province. Numerous villages and cities, among them Mora, Los Lunas, Madrid, Los Padillas, and Los Griegos, carry the names of these early settlers, and pride in Spanish descent runs deep. Identification with a Spanish past is clearly stronger in New Mexico than in other regions that have a strong Chicano presence.

Early in its development there emerged in New Mexico an influential and well-to-do Hispanic elite that set the structural and social parameters of the region. This group managed to retain its privilege and after 1848, it shared power with Anglo-Americans. In no other region in the country has a Chicano elite wielded as much power and influence as in New Mexico. In all walks of life—politics, education, labor, business, and cultural production—this elite has functioned as an influential pressure group that has greatly impacted the institutions and social interactions in the state. Self-determination, resistance, and cultural maintenance are repeated themes in the Nuevomexicano historical experience and legacy. From the Anglo-American invasion of 1846 to the end of the millennium, the Nuevomexicano community has struggled valiantly and with a certain degree of success to maintain its traditions, language, land holdings, political participation, ethnic identity, and individual way of life. Either collectively or individually, using legal or extralegal measures, Nuevomexicanos have struggled against the forces of colonialism, ethno-centrism, racism, and sexism throughout their history. Because of their num-bers, class composition, percentage of the population, and extensive political representation and experience, they have more than survived or endured. They have triumphed and still maintain a dominant Nuevomexicano presence and influence in all facets and regions of the state. In fact, Anglos frequently have had to adjust their assumptions and practices to local ways.

Nuevomexicanos have the highest level of education among all Chi-canos in the United States. Their active participation in public life is borne out in a number of ways: New Mexico has had four Nuevomexicano elected governors since achieving statehood in 1912. It was the first state in the Union to be represented by a Hispano senator. Octaviano Larrazolo, Dennis Chávez, and Joseph Montoya were also elected to the prestigious national office. In state politics, Nuevomexicanos have always held critical posts, be it in Dem-ocratic or Republican administrations, and in local politics, particularly in the northern counties, they are a major political force. The significant political participation of Chicanos in New Mexico, unlike in other regions, is not re-stricted to the Democratic Party. Although they have had a highly visible pres-ence among the Democrats since the nineteenth century, they have also exhib-ited strong and influential involvement in the Republican Party. This tradition has been constant and follows family party loyalties and interpersonal ties. In no other state can the Republican Party boast of a similar base of Chicana and Chicano voters. One other significant dimension of the Nuevomexicano po-litical experience is the major role and participation of Nuevomexicanas in all levels of state and national politics.

Politics is but one aspect of the Nuevomexicano experience. Chicana and Chicano workers have made significant contributions in the economic life of the state and its labor history. In the colonial and territorial period, Nuevo-mexicano laborers worked the land and began ranching and sheep-shearing in-dustries. The discovery of valuable minerals led to the development of mining as an important component of the economic and labor life of the entire state. Cities such as Socorro, Gallup, Silver City, Raton, and Roswell have been im-portant mining centers, and often more than 50 percent of the work force in this industry has been of Mexican origin.

Length of continuous residency, land ownership, and participation in the public affairs of the state have given Nuevomexicanos a strong sense of place and identity. Because their roots run deep in the soil, Nuevomexicanos have been able to sustain vital cultural traditions and to adapt their traditions to conditions of cultural contact with preexisting Native cultures and also with an external culture that has sought to establish hegemony over Native cultures. The strength of the Nuevomexicano culture has allowed it simultaneously to resist and adapt to change. It is this flexibility that has resulted in the vital hybrid nature of Nuevomexicano culture. Religious practices have been preserved, and the Spanish language has sustained a strong oral tradition. But even as older elements have remained, new ones have been added and hybrid forms have emerged. Nowhere is this more evident than in the traditional arts. The baroque style of colonial *santos* and classic patterns of furniture and tinwork, for example, have given way to new configurations that reflect technological advances, new products, and the idiosyncratic vision of artists who have access to traditional forms and scholarship on tradition as well as to contemporary artistic developments. What could be more hybrid than a low-rider with its slick metallic paint job forming the canvas for an airbrushed image of the Virgin of Guadalupe? A veritable *retablo* on gold-leaf wheels! Then there is the hybridity manifest in the favorite mode of the Nuevomexicano for ending a telephone discussion: *Bueno, bye.*

There are important variants of the Nuevomexicano experience within the state based upon generational, class, gender, and regional differences. Much of the scholarly attention on New Mexico tends to focus on northern New Mexico, but the southern portion of the state has a rich history and a strong Chicano presence. While northern New Mexico has historically been marked by geographical isolation from Mexico, southern New Mexico has been more closely linked to it. Nuevomexicanos and Mexican immigrants in this region find employment in the transportation, agricultural, mining, and service industries. Cities such as Las Cruces, Silver City, Deming, Hatch, and Garfield have had predominantly Mexican-origin populations from their founding to the present. Because of the region's proximity to the U.S.-Mexico border, its cultural patterns, language preference, and orientation are also very Mexicano. Here Mexican immigration has been constant within every generation, and the service, agricultural, and construction industries rely heavily on Mexican legal and, more recently, undocumented labor. Although the roots of many Chicanos and Chicanas in this region are also colonial, for this segment of the population, ties to Mexico have been and continue to be strong and ever present.

Central and northern New Mexico are heavily Nuevomexicano, and many counties, cities and towns—Socorro, Mora, Santa Fe, Las Vegas, Raton, Taos, and Española, for example—are predominantly Chicano. The northern area of the state is best defined as a regional culture with its unique characteristics shaped by contact with settled indigenous cultures, distance from the root culture, numerical majority in the face of external occupation, and the imposition of a foreign hegemonic culture. Over the centuries northern Nuevomexicanos have developed a strong sense of identity as a people inhabiting a place of their own—a place Richard Nostrand has called a *homeland*—made theirs though length of residence and perseverance despite scant material resources and, as with their kinfolk in the south, conditions of exploitation and discrimination. The heavy representation of Nuevomexicanos in jails and prisons in the state is but one manifestation of the latter.

Lest we give the idea that the ability to endure and to conserve colonial cultural values has contributed to the formation of a static culture, we turn now to the tremendous changes taking place in Nuevomexicano culture and social structures. These are due primarily to demographic shifts brought about by migration of new populations from other sections of the United States as well as Mexico. The migratory stream from Mexico, which historically has stopped short in the southern part of the state, is currently moving to the northern section of the state. The impact of Mexican immigration is apparent in businesses, in education, in language, in the media, in the configuration of neighborhoods, and in emerging conflicts between established Hispano populations and recent arrivals from Mexico.

But even as New Mexico becomes more latinized through immigration from Mexico and other Latin American countries, the Euro-American population has also been increasing through migration, shifting the societal and political influence of Nuevomexicanos. The coming of the railroads, land graft, and expanding cattle empires in the latter half of the nineteenth century brought the first influx of Anglo settlers into New Mexico. World War II and its effects brought the second wave of migrants. The making of the atomic bomb and the expansion of the military-scientific complex and of the security forces assigned to the state for protection, as well as the industrial and urban growth that followed, have been instrumental in the accelerated growth of the state during the second half of the twentieth century.

The most recent migration of Euro-Americans is linked to the "discovery" of the so-called mystique of New Mexico by affluent sectors from both west and east. A considerable number of Anglos have come seeking privacy, a better quality of life, traditional charm, and a lower cost of living. After Robert Redford descended on New Mexico to film *The Milagro Beanfield War,* his colleagues not only shared his fascination with New Mexico, but also began purchasing homes and land. Santa Fe is perhaps the best example of the effects of Anglo migration because, thanks to the compressed time frame in which this influx has taken place, it is so patently visible, as is the displacement of the working-class Nuevomexicano population and the resulting decline in their standard of living. In fact, some have characterized the heart of the city as a fortified enclave of outsiders circled by locals who inhabit its periphery. Furthermore, greater competition for jobs and the battle for cultural ownership are beginning to create social conflicts, thereby putting to the test the long-standing romantic notion of tricultural harmony in the "City Beautiful." The changes currently taking place as a result of these demographic shifts will soon provide the grist for a follow-up to this anthology.

Two other concurrent demographic trends have recently appeared. One is the outmigration of young Nuevomexicanos who leave to attend universities elsewhere, or who leave in search of better employment opportunities and do not return. The effects of this tendency are somewhat offset by the fact that the Nuevomexicano community is largely a young population whose childbearing years still lie ahead of them.

One final theme that deserves attention, given that it has been so universally misunderstood, is the question of Nuevomexicano identity. Let there be no doubt that Nuevomexicanos have always been very sure of their identity as a people who for centuries have occupied a particular region which they have come to see as their homeland, albeit a contested one. However, a peculiar practice, lasting for almost a century, of insisting on being called Spanish Americans and reacting adversely to being labeled Mexicans has earned them the scorn of their Mexican-descent kin in other regions of the country. Put off by the elitist and frankly racist nature of this tendency, given that it exalts the European provenance of the group at the expense of Mexican (read: indigenous) roots, critics have also understood its function as a tactic employed to assuage racism's harsh effects. However, they have not always been clear about the origins of this phenomenon. Most scholars have attributed the practice to a desire of Nuevomexicanos—in light of the strong nativist reaction displayed toward Mexican immigrants—to disassociate themselves from the poor masses who fled Mexico during the revolution of 1910–1921. While there is certainly some truth to this claim, this period does not mark the beginning of the phenomenon, as a number of scholars (e.g., Rodolfo Acuña and Nancie González) have suggested.

To find the roots of Nuevomexicanos' proclivity for attempting to distance themselves from a discourse of colonial domination that attached a stigma to the term "Mexican," we must examine the record of the struggle for statehood and the campaign to attract Anglo-American immigration to New Mexico in the late nineteenth century. As early as 1882, Le Baron Bradford Prince, an influential statesman and entrepreneur in the territory, declared—for the benefit of statehood opponents in Washington who viewed Nuevomexicanos through a lens that rendered people of racial backgrounds other than Caucasian unfit for citizenship in the zealously guarded "American" Union—that Nuevomexicanos were unequivocally descendants of Spanish dons and conquerors. The Spanish American mantra was chanted over and over in defense of the Nuevomexicano community and in an effort to emphasize its European lineage. Understanding the advantage that said filiation bestowed upon them, Nuevomexicanos were forced to perform this privileged identity as a necessary maneuver to end the drawn-out struggle for statehood. That this was for the benefit of Euro-Americans who were in a position to make judgments regarding eligibility of Nuevomexicanos for citizenship is attested to by the fact that, in their native language, the majority of Nuevomexicanos dispensed with the performance, calling themselves simply Mexicanos and the language they spoke not Spanish, but Mexicano. The point here is that while the dialog in this performance was articulated by Nuevomexicano actors, the script was written primarily by Anglo directors.

The unfortunate aspect of this charade is that later generations came to believe that the performance was the real thing, rather than just one element of a complex equation. The encapsulation of the history of the region in the popular historical discourse of the "Spanish Borderlands"—a discourse that eschewed the issue of cultural hybridity resulting from cross-fertilization between Native peoples and Spanish or Mexican explorers and settlers—further complicated the confusion regarding Nuevomexicano identity.

We had to wait until the advent of the Chicano movement and the revisionary research and literature it would produce to understand the complexity of Nuevomexicano history and identity formation. This understanding involved not only recognizing the experiential and cultural links to the Mexican nation, but also reinscribing the lost memory of those Native ancestors who were forced with cross and sword to perform an identity called Hispanidad. To recognize the *genízaro* (detribalized nomad Indians incorporated into Nuevomexicano culture) roots of countless Nuevomexicanos is to understand how far the myth of *pureza de sangre* (in this case, pure Spanish blood) has strayed from history. Regarding this facet of the identity question, Richard Nostrand made the significant observation that Nuevomexicanos are "by and large mestizo, different from Mexican Americans only because of a great nomad Indian admixture."[1] Use of the label *genízaro*, discouraged during the Mexican period, when all caste labels were forbidden, virtually disappeared from cultural memory. In recent decades, however, it has been restored in the writings of contemporary Nuevomexicano scholars and writers.

It would, of course, be naive for us to overcompensate by claiming a mestizo heritage for all Nuevomexicanos. The fact that there was indeed a caste-determined pecking order in the colonies would encourage some—particularly those of the elite class—to avoid "miscegenation." As such, there are certainly families that can trace their genealogies directly to Spain with no detours via Native chambers in "new" or "old" Mexico. Since this is the class that set the pace for interaction with Euro-Americans and subsequently carved out the space for claiming Nuevomexicanos' rightful civil status, it stands to reason that their pedigreed identity would be held as the filiational ideal. That certain facets of Nuevomexicano culture remained visibly Hispanic (e.g., oral genres, religious practices, and numerous archaic linguistic features of peninsular Spanish) also contributed to the conflation of Nuevomexicano and Spanish cultures, so much so that even today one finds people who call dishes of distinctly indigenous provenance "Spanish food."

The term Chicano, popularized in the 1960s and 1970s, exploded the conceit and cleared a path for linking Nuevomexicanos to their kin in California, Texas, Illinois, and elsewhere, but it failed to take root in the arid landscape of Nuevo México. In more recent times, the more popular term, Hispanic, coin of the governmental realm, has gradually replaced the entrenched preference for the label Spanish American. Its Spanish version, Hispano—used primarily by the elite class in the past—is rapidly displacing Mexicano. For this text, we have used numerous identity labels—Nuevomexicano, Chicano, Mexican American, Mexicano, and Hispano—interchangeably, but we have favored the term Nuevomexicano.[2] When all is said and done, this is the label that best identifies a culture and a people whose roots reach deep into the brown earth of their homeland and across its cultural borderlands. Recently arrived kinfolk from the south will eventually lay claim to their Nuevomexicano identity, as third and fourth generations have done in the past.

To conclude this introduction, we would like to call attention to the fact that given the complex, fascinating, and critical role Nuevomexicanos have played in the historical and cultural development of the state, one would expect the existence of an extensive historiography. This is not so. For the most part, studies on the Hispano community of New Mexico are just now beginning to emerge. There is much more published creative writing by Nuevomexicanos and Nuevomexicanas, a trend that has grown out of a strong oral tradition and an equally strong literary tradition nourished by the development of the Spanish-language press in the late nineteenth and early twentieth centuries and solidified by established writers such as Eusebio Chacón, Manuel C. de Baca, Felipe M. Chacón, Fray Angélico Chávez, Fabiola Cabeza de Baca, Nina Otero-Warren, and Cleofas Jaramillo. All literary genres are represented in this trend, and the list of established and up-and-coming writers includes, among others, Sabine Ulibarrí, Rudolfo Anaya, Denise Chavez, Demetria Martínez, Jimmy Santiago Baca, E. A. Mares, Leroy Quintana, Leo Romero, Estevan Arellano, and Orlando Romero.

The scholarly materials on the Nuevomexicano experience that do exist have been written largely by social scientists, anthropologists, sociologists, and political scientists. These tend to be local or regional studies of specific towns or areas. Next in line would be cultural studies that have focused on the artistic, literary, and cultural production of Nuevomexicanos. The University of New Mexico Press's Pasó por Aquí series, edited by Erlinda Gonzales-Berry and Genaro M. Padilla, has been particularly significant in this regard. Two recent publications in this series that merit recognition are Gabriel Meléndez's *So All Is Not Forgotten* and Doris Meyer's *Speaking for Themselves.*

Excluding the extensive writing on the Spanish period, particularly writing from the pens of "Spanish Borderlands" scholars, the least represented discipline in Nuevomexicano scholarship is history. It is acknowledged that the vast majority of historical studies on the Chicano people have focused on the states of California and Texas. Since most Chicano and Chicana historians have been trained in graduate programs of universities in these two states, there is some logic to this situation. Yet the importance and uniqueness of the Nuevomexicano experience certainly merit extensive scholarly inquiry.

From the Mexican period to the post—Chicano movement era, substantive historical interpretations are scarce, though we would single out Sarah Deutsch's work on Cordova, New Mexico; Richard Nostrand's cultural history; and the award-winning study by Ramón Gutiérrez, *When Jesus Came, the Corn Mothers Went Away,* as notable exceptions. The most extensive historical source materials are articles found in such journals as the *New Mexico Historical Review,* scattered book chapters, and unpublished dissertations by Robert Rosenbaum, Tobías Durán, Anselmo Arrellano, Deena González, and John Nieto-Phillips. The Nuevomexicano historical legacy very much remains to be researched and published.

We offer this collection as one step in addressing the historiographic omission of the Nuevomexicano experience. Beyond filling a gap, our goal is to provide information and analysis on Nuevo México from the perspective of scholars engaged in the study of the topic from a Chicano perspective. What this means, in essence, is that we offer a collection of scholarly essays by both established and promising young scholars who, through a variety of methods and interpretive frameworks, have inscribed the effects of and reaction to structures of power and domination on the ethnically identifiable group of people who call themselves Nuevomexicanos and who self-consciously inhabit a place they call their homeland.

NOTES

1. Richard L. Nostrand, *The Hispano Homeland* (Norman: University of Oklahoma Press, 1992), 24.

2. With regard to the problem of the gender-marked nature of Spanish labels, we have struggled with how to avoid the sexist nature of the language's grammatical conventions but lamentably have found no way to satisfactorily deal with this dilemma. The a/o form is discouraged by the Press. Because gender-marked repetition (e.g., Chicanos and Chicanas) tends to be burdensome, we have not employed it consistently. Its occasional use is, however, meant to remind the reader that we are aware of the problem and certainly are not speaking only of the male half of the population.

Part I

The Nineteenth Century: Overview

Nuevomexicano history developed with a most particular set of characteristics. Its origins date to the clash of civilizations of Spain and the Native Americans residing along the Rio Grande and beyond. After discovering that a unique urban, sedentary indigenous population (the Pueblos) existed, Spanish administrators decided to settle and colonize the area that is now central and northern New Mexico. They expected to secure Indian labor and also to protect the northern border of the recently occupied land. After a period of Native American and Spanish conflict, the territory of Nuevo México (the *provincia interna*) became a major Spanish outpost and later the most heavily populated province of the northern reaches of the Spanish American empire.[1]

Remote and removed from other settlements of northern and central New Spain, Nuevo Mexico evolved with a unique pattern of social, cultural, and political traditions that would condition and shape its history and society. In 300 years of Spanish rule, New Mexico developed fairly autonomously from the central government and in a self-sufficient manner. In addition, strong bonds with Pueblo communities developed in the face of threats from nomadic indigenous groups, bonds that were to seal interdependent modes of living and instill in Nuevomexicanos a profound spiritual relationship to the land. The forced entry of *genízaros,* or detribalized Plains Indians, into the Hispano structural and social fabric would also inscribe strong traces of their cultural ways upon Nuevomexicano culture.[2]

The early nineteenth century brought about the crisis of Spain in America. Demanding their independence from the colonial order and from the Spanish empire, the residents of the Americas, after a costly ten-year struggle, successfully severed their political ties with Spain. In 1821, the former New Spain became an independent nation—Mexico. Nuevo México diverted then to Mexican authority and influence. Although the independence struggle had not been fought in the far north, Nuevomexicanos felt a New World consciousness and anticipated their new status with optimism and a positive attitude toward the incipient nation. As nationhood began to consolidate, a complex relationship between Nuevo México and the central authority in Mexico emerged. Nationalistically and spiritually, Nuevomexicanos certainly perceived themselves as an integral part of the Mexican nation. Padre José Antonio Martínez had studied for the priesthood in Durango, Mexico, where his thinking was greatly influenced by the discursive practices of Miguel Hidalgo, the Mexican religious leader who set the stage for Mexico's War of Independence. Upon his return to New Mexico, Padre Martínez disseminated the emerging discourse of Mexican national identity to his parishioners and to other priests. But the distance between New Mexico and the cities of authority, Guadalajara and Mexico City, was great, in terms of both geography and priority. Communications and official links were weak and erratic throughout the Mexican period.[3]

Mexico's quest for nationhood was a difficult one. In attempting to define its political structures along with other priorities, the new government was forced to relegate the further settlement and development of the north. The elite in central Mexico were engulfed by an endless series of power conflicts, which led to instability and inertia. Critical issues such as economic development, societal needs, and the process of instilling a strong sense of nationalism did not receive proper resolution in the decades that followed independence.

Distant from such conflicts, Nuevomexicanos continued to develop more or less autonomously. Their distance from the central authority in Mexico City led them to become reliant on each other. The appearance in 1834 of the first Spanish-language paper, produced in Taos by Padre Martínez, contributed to the formation of a sense of homeland and cultural identity. As such, the years of the Mexican period (1821–1847) for Nuevo México are marked by the consolidation of particular traditions, values, and social patterns that have endured over time.

Confronting their isolation and neglect during this period, Nuevomexicanos began expanding their horizons and seeking out trading and mercantile possibilities beyond Mexico's borders. They established economic links with peoples and groups that the Spanish empire had kept at bay with its zealously guarded border. Nuevomexicanos also began to envision their own independence: the Chimayó rebellion in 1837, led by Pueblo Indians, *genízaros*, and Hispanos, resulted in the beheading of Albino Pérez, who had been sent from Mexico to govern the province. But once the grassroots rebellion was squelched, the stage was set for the American occupation.[4]

While Mexico underwent a multitude of changes and faced deeply rooted problems in its quest for nationhood, the United States began a century of expansionism fueled by the ideology of Manifest Destiny. The desire to acquire the Southwest and Far West, particularly the ports of California, prompted the United States to attempt to purchase the northern half of the territory of Mexico. When all such efforts proved unsuccessful, the United States contrived a conflict, which led to the inevitable war with Mexico.[5]

Resistance to American occupation was not restricted to the interior of Mexico. When the forces of Colonel Watts Kearny attempted to secure New Mexico in its westward march, Nuevomexicanos initially appeared to acquiesce, leading some historians to view the event as a bloodless conquest. Yet, the 1847 Taos and Mora revolts of Mexicans and Indians against the American forces of occupation belie the passivity attributed to Nuevomexicanos.

The Taos resistance was met with swift and harsh retaliation by the invading military forces, causing considerable resentment and anger among the Nuevomexicano population. The rebels were apprehended and tried on charges of murder and treason. They questioned the charges, but to no avail. As many as thirty Nuevomexicanos were executed, others were severely flogged, and ill will ran high against the Anglo invaders.[6]

This fierce and costly conflict would forever mark U.S.-Mexican relations. After Mexico's defeat and the occupation of its capital and country, a peace agreement was signed. The Treaty of Guadalupe Hidalgo ceded 51.2 percent of Mexico's territory to the United States. The United States not only "incorporated" the desired territory, but it also gained a Mexican-origin population of more than 100,000, 60 percent of whom resided in New Mexico.

When peace came and the new situation became a reality, Nuevomexicanos were faced with the task of dealing with their legal status and social position in the country that had incorporated them as a part of the spoils of war. Even before hostilities came to an end, Nuevomexicanos were assured by the conquering forces that they came as friends and that with the signing of the new peace accord they would be party to "all the rights of citizens of the United States." Yet, these promises would prove to be false both in practice and in spirit. Soon after the annexation, patterns of domination and prejudice emerged that would characterize Chicano-Anglo relations well into the twentieth century. As George Sánchez stated in his classic study *Forgotten People*: "that treaty [of Guadalupe Hidalgo], in setting forth the boundaries of the territory acquired and in making casual provision for the citizenship of individuals, failed to recognize the major issues involved, in the incorporation of people into a new culture. In the march of imperialism a people were forgotten, cast aside as the by-product of territorial aggrandizement."[7]

In their unfolding subordinated condition in the second half of the nineteenth century, Nuevomexicanos faced their fate with dignity, a strong sense of place, and contestatory cultural practices that manifested an entrenched will to endure. For some time after the takeover, however, changes were minimal, and statehood for New Mexico was postponed for sixty years. While the reasons for admitting New Mexico to the Union were complex, the record clearly shows that Easterners were opposed to granting full civil rights to a people who, in addition to being "illiterate" in English, possessed too "foreign" a culture and were of mixed racial background. In addition, the Roman Catholic religion practiced by a huge majority of Nuevomexicanos was a major concern.[8]

Anglo-American migration to New Mexico was not significant prior to the 1880s, but this was to change with the arrival of the railroad. That event, more than any other, promoted Anglo-American migration and signaled a new era for the state. The construction of railroad lines in New Mexico brought to the region numerous fortune hunters, civil bureaucrats, military personnel, ranchers, fugitives, and questionable characters who became willing players in a saga whose main theme became the wresting of land and power from the dominated Mexican population.

As an initial step in the shift of power, these adventurers placed themselves in positions of influence and policy making, displacing the Nuevomexicanos. This process altered the administration of legal claims to the detriment of Nuevomexicanos. In due time, many administrative and official positions in both territorial and federal government offices were in the hands of a coalition called the Santa Fe Ring. This unscrupulous and ruthless alliance of lawyers, politicians, and ranchers made use of their offices and the legal system they controlled to achieve political and economic dominance in the region.

The Santa Fe Ring was greatly responsible for the unleashing of the most intense conflict of New Mexico in the second half of the nineteenth century. Known as the Lincoln County War, this range conflict was fought to determine political control and the ownership of land in the region.[9] Without proper assistance and the support of the protectors of justice, Nuevomexicano ranchers and farmers would figure prominently among the greatest and ultimate losers in the conflict. Much of the land that exchanged hands because of the Lincoln County War was Nuevomexicano property. This story has yet to be fully told. Ironically, one champion of Chicanos in the conflict was the notorious and legendary William Bonney, better known as Billy the Kid, or, as Nuevomexicanos called him, "El Chivito."

Eager to consolidate its power, the recently arrived Euro-American population engaged in classic patterns of colonial domination, relegating the native Nuevomexicano population to second-class status. Negative representational practices justified the exploitation of Nuevomexicanos and impeded harmonious accommodation. Antagonism between the two groups resulted in a social order characterized by separatism and segregation that affected and conditioned most societal and governmental institutions. Discrimination, prejudice, and disdain were not, however, the only attitudes governing interactions between the Nuevomexicano community and the growing Anglo population. Conflict of varied degrees and in many arenas became a daily occurrence, as did resistance and the employment of survival strategies on the part of Nuevomexicanos. The most intense Anglo-Chicano conflicts were played out in struggles for domination of economic enterprises, for representation and control in politics, and for cultural hegemony.

New Mexico was sheep country before the arrival of Euro-Americans, with individual Nuevomexicano families owning as many as 2 million head of sheep. Realizing the grazing potential of lands in New Mexico, vast herds of cattle were introduced by Texans shortly after New Mexico became an American territory. The cattle population rose from 90,000 in 1860 to 1 million by 1910. The competition for the rangelands intensified, and the need for additional land owned by Nuevomexicanos became of paramount urgency for Anglos. As expansionism prevailed and more Americans arrived in the region, they quickly foresaw the vast potential for building capital through land ownership. Besides ranching and grazing, they realized the importance of such lands for transportation, commerce, and real estate profit. Hence, a systematic campaign to acquire the lands of the less powerful and less affluent was placed in motion.

No single conflict proved as significant and detrimental to Nuevomexicanos as that related to land ownership. Land had been the most abundant and valuable commodity in the northern reaches of the Spanish empire. The authorities who issued land titles to those sent to colonize this region were not concerned with detailed boundaries in the titles. Descriptions of property boundaries, called *diseños,* included such landmarks as a stream, a stamped tree, a cow skull, or "the skirt of a mountain." Since ownership was respected and bound by tradition and honor, boundaries and titles were often neither exact nor guarded and filed. Legal titles with all the proper documentation were seldom needed, much less required.[10]

Conflicts over land were exacerbated by fundamental differences in attitudes and in land-use practices. Nuevomexicanos emphasized use and occupancy rather than ownership. In addition, there was an established tradition of communal land for the common good and the collective use of an entire community. Such practices were alien to Euro-Americans. A series of legal and extralegal tactics were thus employed to take over huge Nuevomexicano landholdings. After Nuevomexicano lands were singled out, claimants were notified to present their titles for scrutiny and verification. Not all Nuevomexicanos responded to the call. At times timidity, confusion, or the lack of familiarity with the U.S. legal system and its agents deterred them from protecting their interests. At other times language and unfamiliar procedures created even more difficulties.

In 1854 new regulations concerning land ownership were passed by territorial authorities, stipulating that the expenses of establishing titles and boundaries be assumed by the owners themselves rather than the U.S. government. Numerous Nuevomexicanos flatly refused to comply and bring their papers for examination into the courts; others did not have the resources to pay the assigned legal fees. Nuevomexicanos were subsequently removed from their land.

The introduction of a system of taxation by Anglo authorities further accelerated loss of land by Nuevomexicanos. The new tax laws were based on the erroneous presumption that land had been used for commercial enterprises, as was the case in the United States. Yet the fact remained that the traditional economy of Nuevomexicanos was largely based on subsistence agriculture and stock (particularly sheep) raising, rather than on commercial endeavors.

The payment of land taxes was another burden. Most Nuevomexicanos did not have the resources to pay them. They often became delinquent, making their lands subject to seizure by eager authorities. Irrigation projects at times imposed cash necessities that led to further loss of Nuevomexicanos' land. The arbitrary creation of forest reserves by the U.S. federal government in the newly created territory also withdrew extensive portions of land for the public domain. The Santa Fe National Forest was created in 1892 and the Cibola and Carson National Forests in 1906. All were established in a large measure at the expense of Nuevomexicano landowners.

The end result was the usurpation of millions of acres (close to 80 percent of all Nuevomexicano landholdings) by unscrupulous entrepreneurs and the government. Not just individuals but entire villages were affected.[11] With the loss of land came displacement and the onset of erosion of the traditional way of life.

The numerical ratio of Nuevomexicanos to Euro-Americans in the state has been a critical factor in determining the uniqueness of the relationship and in separating this particular case study from that of any other regional Chicano-Anglo relationship in the Southwest. It has also been a major determinant in shaping the economic, political, social, and cultural interactions between the two groups.

Despite many instances of conflict, accommodation for Nuevomexicanos finally was made possible by their significant political influence, their economic base as landholders, and a highly self-conscious sense of ethnic identity and pride. Gradually Nuevomexicanos began to send their children to public schools. Though the process was gradual, those who had the opportunity to attend the more elite sectarian schools, such as St. Michael's College in Santa Fe, the University of Notre Dame, or other colleges in the East, learned English and paved the road for coexistence.

The degree and rate of assimilation to Anglo society, on the other hand, was slow or nonexistent throughout the territorial period and even afterward.

The Nuevomexicano community, particularly in the north, retained its ethnic distinctiveness, reflecting its deep roots in the area and an unshakable pride in its ancestry and cultural legacy. Unlike the Californio landowning class, Nuevomexicanos, both the elite and the masses, stood strong and successfully resisted assimilative influences well into the twentieth century. Additional factors that contributed to Chicano resistance to assimilation were their pride as the original settlers of the region; their antagonism to Euro-Americans, whom they viewed as intruders and usurpers; and their continued geographic cohesiveness. In addition, their strong sense of place led them to view New Mexico as the occupied homeland. This ideological positioning made cultural preservation rather than assimilation a strong base for their social and political agendas.

Anglo colonialism was also met with resistance and vigorous patterns of contestation. From the beginning of Anglo occupation, Nuevomexicanos fought in the political arena to preserve their rights and privileges. More dramatic forms of resistance were carried out in the extralegal activities of individual endeavors or collective movements. Paramount among these was the Movimiento del Pueblo in and around Las Vegas, led by a clandestine group that called itself Las Gorras Blancas.[12]

Cultural forms of expression, such as oral genres ridiculing the newcomers, were a popular form of contestatory behavior. These were particularly evident in the blossoming of the Spanish-language press, which served as an avenue for the emergence of a highly visible and sophisticated level of creative writing. The press played an important role in nurturing the Spanish language and in contributing to the development of native-language literacy. Worth noting is the fact that the owners and editors of the newspapers were not only members of an emerging literati, but in many cases also political leaders at the local and state levels. Thus, a coalescing of cultural expression and sociopolitical concerns flourished, in what, from today's standpoint, can assuredly be viewed as a self-conscious struggle for cultural hegemony.[13]

The Americanizing influence of the Catholic church was resisted by the nonsanctioned religious group known informally as Los Penitentes. For decades this religious brotherhood had met the religious needs of isolated villages that did not have the luxury of a full-time priest. Their folk religious practices were proscribed by the church to such a degree that the Penitentes had no choice but to take their organization underground. Their relegation to outlaw status only made them more cohesive and strengthened their resolve to protect the cultural legacy of their villages. (It is curious to note that as the Euro-American presence increased, the brotherhood's hand-carved religious icons, particularly those representing a crucified Christ, also grew in size. It was as if the image of *Cristo* were being raised as a giant amulet to ward off the evil portended by the ways of the strangers among them.) Beyond ministering to spiritual needs, the brotherhood served as an important social force by contributing to the material well-being of their communities and, not infrequently, by orchestrating their political activities.[14]

There was one important difference between the Nuevomexicanos and Euro-Americans. The former had been for the most part a settled, fairly homogeneous resident community. On the other hand, the latter were, in large measure, a mobile, transient, and diverse population. A good number of Anglos who arrived in the territory in search of political office, commercial success, government offices, or the territory's healthful climate were temporary rather than permanent residents.

Even with the influx of Euro-Americans, the Nuevomexicano community still outnumbered Anglos and remained the largest ethnic bloc in the territory. Yet maintaining numerical superiority would not have been a major advantage had Nuevomexicanos not been able to successfully combat Anglo policies and actions in the political arena. They became a formidable force, consistently outvoting the Anglo community and dominating many key elective offices from 1850 to 1911. The lack of English language skills did not impede participation in the political process. In fact, Spanish was used freely in the courts and in legislative sessions for half a century, and laws were printed in both Spanish and English. Many Nuevomexicanos excelled in territorial politics. Miguel Antonio Otero held the office of governor for nine years (1897–1906). Hispanos held the office of state superintendent of schools until 1905, and Salomón Luna and Octaviano Larrazolo, among many others, became exceptional politicians.[15]

Scholars writing on this period have described Nuevomexicanos as excellent politicians who "throw a personal passion into the performance of their functions; they shame their adversaries for there is nothing perfunctory, nothing cold-blooded about their politics." Another observer wrote, "[T]he Spanish-American takes readily and seems to derive intense enjoyment from the drama of political campaigns." A third comment on this theme was articulated by the ex-governor W. H. H. Davis, who described Nuevomexicano politicians as "keen, cunning men[,] in politics quite a match for the Americans."[16]

The Nuevomexicano community did not evolve similarly throughout Nuevo México. Although its presence and importance was dominant in the economic, political, social, and cultural life of the territory, its influence and power, nonetheless, were more representative in some regions than others. Nuevomexicanos were most successful at protecting their culture and institutions in the Rio Grande Valley of northern New Mexico. There Mexican or Chicano culture had its deepest roots and was best prepared to resist the imposition of Anglo cultural aggression. In the Rio Grande Valley, Nuevomexicanos remained the numerically dominant group throughout the nineteenth century, conditioning Euro-Americans to be on the defensive. Anglo newcomers, frequently hostile and prejudiced toward the Mexican-origin population on first encounter, with time—and when they were outnumbered—tended to become tolerant of and even made efforts to appreciate Nuevomexicano culture and society. In north central New Mexico, mixed marriages between the two groups were common. Euro-American businessmen and professionals learned Spanish and formed partnerships with Nuevomexicanos. Accommodation between the two groups became the norm.[17]

Southern New Mexico, which borders Mexico and Texas, developed differently from other regions of the state. This area far more than all others reflected its closeness to Mexico. Las Cruces, from its founding to the present, has had a population which was overwhelmingly of Mexican origin (as high as 70 percent of the total number of city residents), with profound ties with El Paso, Texas, and Ciudad Juárez, Mexico. In addition, recent research has shown (see Martín González de la Vara's essay in this volume) that shortly after the American occupation of New Mexico, there was internal migration of Nuevomexicanos from central and northern New Mexico to the south. No doubt they sought a setting more Mexican than that which was developing with the influx of Euro-Americans.

The economic bases of southern New Mexico have traditionally been agriculture, mining, ranching, and transportation. All require a readily available and abundant labor force that has been for the most part Mexican. Yet, the power and political base was always in the hands of a small but powerful Anglo elite.

Southeastern New Mexico evolved differently. The area came to be dominated by Anglo ranchers by the 1890s, and to be known as "Little Texas." Anglo settlers in this section of the territory took pride in its "development, enlightenment, progress and power," which resulted, one local paper boasted, from "the magic wand of the Anglo-Saxon," as opposed to the culture of the "'greaser' [who] is too lazy to keep up; and smells too badly to be endured." [18] Anglo residents of this area attempted to annex themselves to Texas. Failing this, in 1906 Anglos in Eddy County resorted to more sophisticated, Southern-inspired techniques for excluding Chicanos from the electoral process: an all-white primary election and a poll tax. Each attempt met with violent objections from Nuevomexicanos and moderate Anglos and was defeated.

Following suit, in the southwestern corner of the state, a mining region, Euro-Americans had become the majority group by the 1870s. There, too, they displayed an aversion to the political and cultural influence of Nuevomexicanos, in spite of the fact that the majority of the labor force of the mines was of Mexican origin. In the 1870s, Grant County attempted to annex itself to Arizona in order, as one newspaper put it, to be better represented by an "American" legislature.

By the 1890s, Nuevomexicanos no longer dominated all of New Mexico, but they did retain control of the north central portion, and they continued to outnumber Euro-Americans in the territory's total population. But even as Anglo influence increased, assimilation was not a position chosen by Nuevomexicanos. Few Nuevomexicanos, even those from the elite sectors, opted to break entirely from their traditions, values, identity, and language for personal betterment. In fact, the Nuevomexicano community had endured, maintained its culture, and carved out spaces of influence as best it could. Certainly, with the coming of Euro-Americans and the institutions they imposed, segments of the community had lost much. Yet, more than in any other part not only of the Southwest but of the entire nation, Nuevomexicanos were able to preserve their autochthonous traditions, social networks, language, and political involvement. In many instances, Nuevomexicanos were more than a match for Anglo-American colonialism. The chapters that follow detail this history and legacy in greater detail.

NOTES

1. Marc Simmons has published extensively on the colonial period of New Mexico as have other historians and writers. His *Spanish Government in New Mexico* (Albuquerque: University of New Mexico Press, 1990) is a solid contemporary study.

2. Ramón Gutiérrez's award-winning *When Jesus Came, the Corn Mothers Went Away: Marriage, Sexuality, and Power in New Mexico, 1500–1846* (Stanford: Stanford University Press, 1992), is a provocative and authoritative narrative of colonial New Mexico and its society and interethnic relations.

3. See the excellent initial two chapters of the monumental study by Juan Gómez-Quiñones, *Roots of Chicano Politics* (Albuquerque: University of New Mexico Press, 1994), 1–191, for detail and interpretation.

4. Myra Ellen Jenkins and Albert H. Schroeder, *A Brief History of New Mexico* (Albuquerque: University of New Mexico Press, 1974), examine the Mexican period in a satisfactory although superficial manner. To date, the most exhaustive study of this period and themes is David J. Weber, *The Mexican Frontier, 1821–1846: The American Southwest under Mexico* (Albuquerque: University of New Mexico Press, 1982).

5. The historiography of the U.S.-Mexican War is extensive but uneven. One study that stands out is Gene M. Brack, *Mexico Views Manifest Destiny, 1821–1846* (Albuquerque: University of New Mexico Press, 1975), 115–35.

6. A complete narrative of these events and their significance is found in Alvin R. Sunseri, *Seeds of Discord: New Mexico in the Aftermath of the American Conquest, 1846–1861* (Chicago: Nelson Hall, 1979).

7. George Sanchez, *Forgotten People: A Study of New Mexicans* (Albuquerque: University of New Mexico Press, 1940), 12.

8. Robert W. Larson's scholarly study *New Mexico's Quest for Statehood* (Albuquerque: University of New Mexico Press, 1968) continues to be the standard work on the subject.

9. Robert M. Utley, *High Noon in Lincoln: Violence on the Western Frontier* (Albuquerque: University of New Mexico Press, 1987), is a fine synthesis of this critical era and conflict.

10. Howard R. Lamar has provided an insightful analysis of these issues in "Land Policy in the Spanish Southwest, 1846–1891: A Study in Contrast," *Journal of Economic History* 22, no. 4 (Dec. 1962): 140–153.

11. David J. Weber, *Foreigners in Their Native Land* (Albuquerque: University of New Mexico Press, 1973), 156–57.

12. Robert J. Rosenbaum's superb unpublished "Mexicano versus Americano: A Study of Hispanic American Resistance to Anglo Control in New Mexico Territory, 1870–1900" (Ph.D. diss., University of Texas, 1982), is still the most outstanding study of the Gorras Blancas and northern Nuevomexicano resistance.

13. Recently two complementary book-length studies have covered this important theme in detail: A. Gabriel Meléndez, *So All Is Not Lost: The Poetics of Print in Nuevomexicano Communities, 1834–1958* (Albuquerque: University of New Mexico Press, 1997), and Doris Meyer, *Speaking for Themselves: Neomexicano Cultural Identity and the Spanish Language Press, 1880–1920* (Albuquerque: University of New Mexico Press, 1996).

14. Gómez-Quiñones, 236–37.

15. These statements are cited in the very able chapter by Martín González de la Vara, "La historia política de los chicanos de Nuevo México, 1848–1912," in *El México olvidado: la historia del pueblo chicano*, ed. David R. Maciel (Ciudad Juárez: Universidad Autónoma de Ciudad Juárez and University of Texas at El Paso, 1996), 226–34.

16. See Carolyn Zeleny's well-researched and interpretative "Relations between the Spanish-Americans and Anglo-Americans in New Mexico: A Study of Conflict and Accommodation in a Dual-Ethnic Relationship" (Ph.D. diss., Yale University, 1944). It is still a valuable and insightful study of ethnic conflict and resolution.

17. Ibid, 231.

18. Ibid.

Chapter One

CARLOS R. HERRERA

New Mexico Resistance to U.S. Occupation during the Mexican-American War of 1846–1848

In the absence of primary sources, the writing of history proves to be a difficult task. The quest for historical truth often results in misinterpretations of past events and the mythologization of historical figures. This mishandling of the past is unfortunate, since it tends to silence the voices of certain individuals or groups who participate in the making of history. Such was the case for New Mexicans with regard to the U.S.-Mexican War of 1846–48.

In the past, traditional accounts of this war focused more on the U.S. view of causes and outcomes, while the Mexican perspective was usually played down or ignored altogether. Through the predominant use of U.S. primary sources, writers of these histories promoted the myth that New Mexicans offered little or no resistance to U.S. occupation of their homeland. These authors also reinforced the belief that the superiority of U.S. military and social institutions allowed for this "passive conquest" of New Mexico.

Modern scholars are rethinking the U.S.-Mexican War; they conclude that traditional histories of this conflict need to be revised. For Hispanic New Mexicans, and for Mexican Americans as a whole, such revision is vital because it allows them to claim an equal voice in a past they share with their fellow Americans. To deny this voice is to misconstrue the historical role people of Mexican origin played on the North American continent, a role that predates the creation of the United States by some 250 years.

DEBUNKING THE "PASSIVE NEW MEXICANS" MYTH:
REVISIONIST HISTORY AND THE U.S.-MEXICAN WAR

Revisionist histories of the war in New Mexico seem to agree that a limited supply of Mexican documents influenced the reliance on popularized versions of the conflict. Martín González de la Vara wrote that early accounts of the war included diaries of U.S. merchants such as Josiah Gregg, who profited from commerce on the Santa Fe Trail. Gregg's *Commerce of the Prairies* served as a travel guide for Americans who saw in the west a vehicle for adventure and economic gain. According to González de la Vara, Gregg argued that New Mexicans welcomed the annexation of their territory as far south as the state of Durango. While most New Mexicans enjoyed the opportunity to trade for manufactured goods, most also opposed the idea of conquest by the United States.[1]

Historians made ample use of travel diaries such as Gregg's in their interpretations of the U.S.-Mexican War. Rodolfo Acuña described these accounts of the war as "[t]he distortion of history."[2] He argued that the supposed passivity of New Mexico's Mexican citizens during the war is erroneous. Acuña's view is supported by U.S. military documents, which clearly state that armed rebellion and resistance to occupation occurred in New Mexico throughout the war. For example, on February 26, 1847, Colonel Sterling Price wrote to U.S. Secretary of War William L. Marcy claiming, "The opinion that the New Mexicans are favorably inclined to the United States Government is entirely erroneous."[3] Price concluded that New Mexicans were not happy with U.S. occupation and that insurrection by the citizens was a real threat.

The perceived scarcity of Mexican sources contributed to the selective use of U.S. documents, which implied that New Mexicans offered little or no resistance to U.S. occupation of the border. A lack of sources, however, does not fully explain why the Mexican voice was silenced regarding this important event in U.S.-Mexican relations. What other forces could influence such a slanted analysis of the war? In *My History, Not Yours: The Formation of Mexican American Autobiography*, Genaro Padilla sheds some light on this issue. Padilla wrote that after the 1846 Bear-Flag Revolt in California, Mariano Guadalupe Vallejo, a prominent Californio, was encouraged by Hubert Howe Bancroft to write a history of the territory. Vallejo agreed after some initial resistance, but was outraged to discover that Bancroft refused to publish his work. Bancroft chose instead to select bits and pieces of Vallejo's history to supplement his own; in so doing, he relegated the latter's viewpoint to a secondary status. According to Padilla, Bancroft tried to justify his actions by claiming that Vallejo had agreed to relinquish the story, and that therefore it belonged to him.[4]

Bancroft's historical imperialism ensured that his account of California's past would outlive Vallejo's. But why would Bancroft silence the Californio's voice? It would appear that, as with most historians of the epic genre, the business of history dictated the nature of his work. For Bancroft, history was a commodity to be exploited for profit; he knew that, like other goods, its marketability depended on the consumer. In order to sell his history, Bancroft had to make it appealing and exciting to the American reading public. His work thus expressed a dichotomy of "good" versus "evil" characters competing with each other on the western frontier. In this hostile environment, the good guy always defeated the bad, and therefore justified his or her dominion over the latter.[5] Bancroft thus silenced Vallejo's history because it did not portray the U.S. conquest of the west in a positive light. In so doing, he exiled the Californio's literary voice to the dusty shelves of the library that bears his name.

Bancroft's effort to romanticize the U.S.-Mexican War went hand in hand with perceptions most Americans had of themselves as a nation in the nineteenth century. The 1800s proved an age when citizens of the U.S. regarded themselves the custodians of democracy in all the Americas. In their eyes and minds, Americans regarded it their duty to spread the ideals of the Declaration of Independence, and of their Constitution, from coast to coast. As a nation, the United States considered this goal its manifest destiny, a principle adopted by the citizenry to justify the territorial conquest of Mexico's northern frontier. Political, economic, and military victories achieved against Mexico came to be identified and associated with the supposed superiority of U.S. society and its institutions. In addition, the more the United States succeeded in expanding its influence and hegemony throughout all of Latin America, the more its citizens were convinced that the ideal of manifest destiny was justified.

In his book *Mexicano Resistance in the Southwest: "The Sacred Right of Self Preservation,"* Robert J. Rosenbaum argued that the United States used its self-perceived superiority to explain the conquest of New Mexico. Rosenbaum supported the idea that a perceived lack of Mexican documents reinforced the belief that New Mexicans offered little or no resistance to U.S. occupation of their homeland.[6] He suggested that some historians chose to focus their analysis on the speed by which U.S. forces took New Mexico during the war and concluded that Americans then added this rapid-victory theory to their annals of apologetic arguments that supported the "manifest right" of conquest. According to Rosenbaum, "Speed dominated the Anglo American perception because it justifies the war and, by extension, United States expansion . . . rapid victory implies little or no resistance."[7]

U.S. attitudes such as those identified by Rosenbaum were used not only to promote the superiority of the United States, but also to influence racist ideologies toward all Mexicans of the border region. In his book *To the Halls of the Montezumas: The Mexican War in the American Imagination,* Robert W. Johannsen described U.S. perceptions of Mexicans before, during, and after the war. He demonstrated how the American public had adopted the principle of manifest destiny and used it as a rallying cry for justified imperialism. According to Johannsen, Americans learned to believe that the speed by which conquest was achieved during the war demonstrated the superiority of Anglo culture and the innate racial inferiority of Mexicans.[8] In New Mexico, Americans misperceived, or misrepresented, the reality of local resistance, which in turn reinforced their view that New Mexicans not only were passive but also welcomed occupation.

In light of impediments such as Bancroft's relationship with Vallejo, a perceived scarcity of documentation, and racist ideologies, can a New Mexican voice to U.S. occupation be identified? Rosenbaum, Padilla, and other scholars of the border region write that New Mexicans were anything but passive during the war of 1846. They argue that many Nuevomexicanos opposed U.S. aggression, and that their resistance was manifested in various ways. Padilla, for example, suggested that Vallejo's history served not only as a means of preserving a nostalgic memory of Mexican culture, but also as a form of struggle against Anglo-American domination. He argued that Mexicanos avoided total destruction of their heritage by preserving the traditional past through literature. In this respect, the Mexican literary voice of the nineteenth century served as a form of cultural resistance.[9] This body of work exists on paper and therefore refutes the argument that documentation on the war by Mexicans is nonexistent.

Like Padilla, Rosenbaum wrote that New Mexican opposition to U.S. occupation assumed various forms throughout the war. He identified four modes of resistance, the most common of which was "withdrawal," or the act of ignoring the fact of conquest. Rosenbaum argued that this type of behavior was not difficult for New Mexicans, most of whom simply avoided contact with Americans in their daily lives. He concluded that this form of resistance was most prevalent among rural New Mexicans, who did not live in areas of high population density and therefore were seldom forced into contact with Americans.

Rosenbaum argued that New Mexico's elite class preferred "accommodation" as a form of cultural resistance. This group held on to their Mexican heritage, but they did interact with their new U.S. neighbors in order to maintain their wealth and status in society. Other New Mexicans preferred to "assimilate" within the new "democratic order," to become a part of it and use it for the benefit of the Mexican populace. Finally, Rosenbaum argued that many New Mexicans took up arms during the war to resist the invading U.S. army.[10]

Rosenbaum concluded that assimilation proved the rarest form of opposition to U.S. territorial and cultural hegemony in New Mexico. He refutes Josiah Gregg's claim that all Nuevomexicanos welcomed annexation to the United States. Rosenbaum's modes of New Mexican resistance can be readily identified within the narrative of the war itself, and so it is to these that we now turn.

THE WAR NARRATIVE: NEW MEXICANS DEFEND
THEIR HOMELAND AND CULTURAL HERITAGE

The causes of the U.S.-Mexican War are open to interpretation. For Americans, the issue at hand involved the disputed boundary that separated Texas from Mexico. The United States claimed that its borders extended to the Rio Grande, refusing to accept Mexico's view that the Texas border was located farther north, at the Nueces River. Most Americans embraced the war, for it reinforced the economic aspects of manifest destiny. For them, the occupation and conquest of Mexico represented an attempt to acquire the bountiful riches of the west. In so doing, Americans believed their government would ensure the availability of natural resources needed for the nation's growing industry and land-hungry population. Most Americans in the 1840s thus openly supported a national policy of expansion and found a champion of this ideal in James K. Polk, who ascended to the presidency of the United States in 1845.

For Mexicans, the dispute over national frontiers represented only one cause of the war. As a nation, Mexico also expressed concern over the issue of U.S. imperialism; the country had experienced this process in the past. No Mexican could forget the disgrace of having lost Texas to U.S. insurgents in the 1830s. In was in this period too that various U.S. presidents had offered to buy New Mexico and California. Mexico's government regarded these offers as insults, but also as a sign that the United States was determined to take Mexican lands. For Mexicans, defense against U.S. expansion proved to be a matter of not only of territorial survival but also of patriotism and national honor.

Open hostility between Mexico and the United States occurred early in 1846. President Polk ordered U.S. troops, under the command of Zachary Taylor, into the disputed territory between the Rio Grande and the Nueces. Here, Taylor met resistance from Mexican forces. Polk accused Mexico of initiating the conflict and claimed that a state of war existed between the two neighbors. He called his countrymen to arms by convincing Congress to formally declare war on Mexico on May 13, 1846.

United States forces under Brigadier General Stephen W. Kearny entered New Mexico in August 1846.[11] Kearny had orders to take New Mexico with a minimum of military force.[12] This campaign of "peaceful persuasion" may explain in part the biased military accounts of conquest reported to Washington and to the American public. The army leadership, in order to gain approval, recognition, and possible promotion, felt it necessary to convince their superiors that orders were being carried out. American officers thus initiated the myth of New Mexican passivity and fueled the American imagination regarding the military's superiority.

In New Mexico, Governor Manuel Armijo formed a force to oppose the invaders just outside the capital of Santa Fe. But the governor disbanded the army when he recognized that his troops were poorly trained and not sufficient in number to withstand the U.S. military. Armijo fled to Chihuahua, claiming that he needed to recruit more troops for the defense of New Mexico. In his absence, Lieutenant Governor Juan Bautista Vigil y Alarid assumed the leadership of his people.[13]

Armijo's motives for not initiating an armed defense are vague at best, but they did contribute to the myth of nonresistance. Prior to the conquest, Kearny had contacted the governor through an agent and insisted that New Mexico accept a peaceful occupation. The agent, James Magoffin, claimed to have convinced both Armijo and his second in command, Diego de Archuleta, not to resist. Of the two New Mexicans, Archuleta seemed to prefer a fight rather than capitulation. Magoffin, however, claimed:

> El coronel Archuleta hubiera peleado; yo lo calmé . . . el pelear estaba en él . . . y hubiese salido antes llevándose a Armijo con él si no hubiese sido por mis gestiones.[14]

> [Colonel Archuleta would have fought; I appeased him . . . the will to fight was within him . . . and he would have done so, encouraging Armijo to follow him had it not been for my gestures.]

It has been argued that Archuleta agreed to surrender the defense of New Mexico because of an alleged bribe offered by Magoffin; the offer consisted of all the land in New Mexico west of the Rio Grande. Archuleta did go on to fight the Americans, but his motives for so doing are also clouded in mystery. It is probable that the New Mexican took up arms as a form of resistance to U.S. imperialism. Yet again, it has been argued that Archuleta rebelled only after it became clear that Magoffin would not offer a bribe.[15] His patriotism notwithstanding, Don Diego did participate in a failed plot, which had been scheduled for December 1846, to overthrow Kearny's appointed government of occupation.

The results of Armijo's and Archuleta's actions imply that these men preferred withdrawal and accommodation as means of resistance. In the case of Armijo, this view is supported by his family's involvement with American merchants in the Santa Fe trade. The governor's retreat to Chihuahua, however, was not in keeping with previous efforts on his part to resist U.S. expansion into New Mexico. In 1841, Armijo had successfully repelled a Texan invasion by calling on all Nuevomexicanos, including naturalized foreigners, to defend the territory against its enemies.[16] According to their leader, General Hugh McLeod, the Texans, who numbered 300 strong, had come to New Mexico to "engage in peaceful trade." McLeod's excuse did not convince New Mexicans that Texas's intentions were peaceful and purely commercial; Nuevomexicanos truly believed they were about to be invaded. After the capture of his troops, McLeod complained of the cruel treatment his men had received at the hands of New Mexicans. Bancroft, however, wrote that the Texans "were simply armed invaders, who might expect to be attacked, and if defeated, to be treated by the Mexicans as rebels, or at best . . . as prisoners of war." [17]

Confrontations with foreigners such as McLeod and company prepared New Mexicans for an eventual assault on their homeland by U.S. forces. When the invasion occurred in August 1846, it did not take the Nuevomexicanos by surprise.[18] On the 18th of that month, Brigadier General Stephen W. Kearny and the U.S. army of occupation entered Santa Fe. Upon his arrival in New Mexico's capital, the general proclaimed:

> We come as friends, to better your condition and make you a part of the Republic of the United States. We mean not to murder you or rob you of your property. Your families shall be free of molestation; your women secure from violence. . . . I hereby proclaim that, being in possession of Santa Fe, I am therefore in possession of all New Mexico.[19]

Kearny's speech of occupation included a rejection of the Armijo government and the granting of U.S. citizenship to all New Mexicans. The general demanded that those people who had taken up arms against his forces should lay them down and return to their homes. Kearny claimed that acts of violence against U.S. troops would be considered traitorous.[20] With these words, the leader of the invading American forces himself made reference to a New Mexican armed rebellion.

On August 19, 1846, Kearny received an oath of allegiance from Vigil y Alarid. He insisted that the governor's pledge represented the collective voice of all New Mexicans. The general was wrong on this account, because not every New Mexican had accepted American occupation. Vigil y Alarid himself expressed resistance when he responded to the ramifications of conquest, claiming that New Mexico could expect good things under the United States, but that the local populace showed little joy at having been occupied. In addition, Vigil y Alarid concluded that Mexico's internal problems had weakened the nation's ability to support the northern territory.[21]

Governor Vigil y Alarid accepted New Mexico's capitulation to Kearny. Even so, Padilla argues, the governor's words were an encoded warning for New Mexicans to resist cultural annihilation. In short, in Vigil y Alarid's response to occupation, he used accommodation as a form of resistance. By agreeing to take an oath of allegiance, he accepted U.S. rule in order to ensure that New Mexican culture would be preserved.[22]

In September, Kearny established a territorial government and appointed Charles Bent as governor.[23] Kearny's attention in the war shifted next to the conquest of California. In his absence, the military command of New Mexico changed hands several times. Along with Bent's appointment as governor, Donaciano Vigil was chosen to serve as secretary, and Manuel Otero was named territorial judge.

Vigil y Alarid's role in the war perhaps best illustrates the use of accommodation as a form of resistance. In June 1846, just months prior the conquest, Vigil y Alarid petitioned New Mexican officials to seek permission from Mexico City to allow the free trade of guns with American merchants. He expressed concern that local Indian groups had been buying weapons from these traders since the 1820s, and that this weakened New Mexico's defensive posture. Vigil y Alarid justified his request by claiming that military aid from the capital could not be expected, and thus, New Mexicans should be allowed to buy weapons from the Americans. Like Armijo, Vigil y Alarid participated in the Santa Fe trade, and so his petition for free trade of arms may have been based on personal goals. By opening up the economic frontier, he hoped to increase his own business interests.[24]

Donaciano Vigil expressed such concern over New Mexico's weak defenses that when the United States' threat of invasion became a reality, he advised Governor Armijo not to resist. Ironically, four days after his September appointment as territorial secretary, Vigil wrote to the president of Mexico and blamed Armijo for the loss of New Mexico. When the United States' occupation proved inevitable, he welcomed U.S. intervention.[25]

It seems easy to judge Vigil as a blatant opportunist, ready to shift allegiances by denouncing Armijo and then accepting a position within the U.S. military government. His actions, however, might be better explained as a resort to accommodation in an atmosphere of perceived Mexican futility. Vigil was convinced that New Mexico could not defeat the United States, and his willingness to ally himself with the enemy may have been a way of helping his people survive the aftermath of conquest.

Not all New Mexicans shared Vigil's views. After Kearny's departure for California, a group of merchant, political, and clerical elites began to meet secretly in Santa Fe to plan a general uprising.[26] In October, the insurgents wrote to the Mexican government and expressed their intention to rebel against the United States. The rebel leaders Tomás Ortiz and Diego de Archuleta had scheduled the uprising for December 19; they changed the date to the 24th, however, in order to attract more support around the territory. In the interim, the group created its own government, with Ortiz being named governor and Archuleta commander of the army.[27]

It has been suggested that the reasons for the December Plot involved discontent among the rebels regarding the administration of their homeland. The group felt that the government of occupation would not be able to provide defense against warring Indians, protection of personal property, and a long-term peace.[28] This argument is questionable if one considers that only four and a half months had passed between the conquest and the scheduled date for the uprising. This does not seem to be enough time for Bent's government to have fulfilled the desires of the rebels. It seems more likely that the insurgents detested the idea of conquest and planned to revolt in order to regain control of their homeland. The December rebellion, however, was thwarted when news of the plot was leaked to Secretary Donaciano Vigil, who then proceeded to arrest most of the conspirators.[29]

Ortiz and Archuleta managed to escape capture. Still, Governor Bent declared that the December uprising had been put down and that New Mexico was now under the rule of the United States. The governor also claimed that the territory had a free government, even though neither he nor the other officials of occupation had been formally elected. Bent criticized Ortiz and Archuleta as jealous men who resented not having received positions within the new government. He ordered the people to remain passive and not to follow any future conspirators.[30] The governor himself refutes the theory that

New Mexicans had not resisted the conquest of their homeland. In the aftermath of their failed revolution, some of the December rebels did shy away
from further acts of insurrection. Still, no one in New Mexico could ignore
the fact that Bent's proclamation indicated that armed rebellion was possible
in the territory.

The governor's demand that New Mexicans accept occupation fell on
deaf ears, and soon after his proclamation, a revolt erupted at Taos that cost
Bent his life. Convinced that peace in New Mexico had been achieved, Bent
left Santa Fe for Taos but refused an escort for his journey home. The governor's decision proved fatal:

> Near dawn on 19 January 1847, a band of Mexicans and Indians led by
> Pablo Montoya, "the self-styled Santa Anna of the north," and Toma-
> sito, the leader of the Taos Indians, crept through the silent, star-lit
> streets, converging on the governor's house.[31]

Bent lost his life at the hands of this allied force of Mexican and Indian rebels.
The governor's assassination, however, has prompted mixed explanations.
Some claimed that Tomasito and the Taos Indians killed Bent because the latter refused to release two of their people from jail.[32] Taos Indians did participate in the attack on Bent's home, but it has been argued that the real leaders
of this revolt were Manuel Cortez and Pablo Montoya.[33] Their leadership
notwithstanding, all of the rebels agreed that a major cause of the Taos uprising involved the abusive behavior of U.S. troops. One group in particular, the
Missouri Volunteers, incurred the wrath of most New Mexicans because of
the ill-treatment and disrespect they had expressed toward the local populace.

The Missouri regiment had been created specifically for the conquest of
New Mexico and placed under the command of E. W. D. Newby. The official
role of these troops was to ensure that rebellion did not occur in New Mexico. Their acts of cruelty, however, only fueled anti-American sentiments in
the territory. On one occasion, the Missourians tied an Indian to a horse-
drawn ambulance and forced him to run as the vehicle sped away from his
pueblo, all the while encouraging him on by lashing a whip across his body.[34]
Prior to his assassination, Governor Bent expressed concern regarding the
atrocities committed by the Volunteers. He concluded that the regiment's
unacceptable behavior in the territory might actually cause the insurrection
they had been sent to New Mexico to prevent:

> In consequence of the numerous complaints of the insubordination and
> after offensive and abusive conduct of the troops under our command,

my duty compels me to call on you to interpose your authority and compel the soldiers to respect the rights of the inhabitants. These outrages are becoming so frequent that I apprehend consequences may result sooner or later if measures are not taken to prevent them.[35]

Although the Taos revolt has been considered a massacre, unconnected in any way to the December Plot, it can be defined as representing part of a larger armed resistance conducted by New Mexicans against the United States. Still, some historians have rejected the idea that an organized rebellion manifested itself in New Mexico because a lack of documentary evidence did not support this view. Revisionist scholars disagree. González de la Vara, for example, wrote that on January 20, 1847, General Jesús Tafoya circulated a formal declaration of war against the United States in the Rio Arriba region. The general urged New Mexican officials to rebel against the government of occupation and to recruit troops for a general uprising. On the same day, the commanding officer of the U.S. Army, Sterling Price, intercepted documents in the Rio Abajo territory that hinted of a possible insurrection. In response, Price led a force of 353 men, who were supported by four twelve-pound howitzer cannons, to subdue Tafoya and his rebel forces at Taos. The armies faced off at La Cañada.[36]

At the Battle of La Cañada, 500 New Mexicans joined the resistance against U.S. occupation of their homeland. Although they outnumbered the enemy, the Hispanos could not mount an effective defense against the American howitzers. Tafoya was killed during the battle, and the day's victory went to Commander Price. In February, 600–700 New Mexicans met U.S. forces at El Embudo Pass and forced the Americans into a hasty retreat toward Taos. Price reached the pueblo and found it heavily fortified. He shelled Taos for two days and forced the defenders to withdraw to the pueblo church, which was destroyed as a result of the ensuing battle. American forces breached Mexican defenses, and the Hispanos in turn sued for peace by handing over their leader, Pablo Montoya. In the first two months of 1847, approximately 200 New Mexicans died in battle against U.S. forces under Sterling Price.[37]

Pablo Montoya was hanged after the Battle of Taos. Other rebels were tried, convicted of treason against the United States, and executed. One Hispano defendant, Antonio María Trujillo, rejected the legitimacy of the Taos trials. He argued that Commander Price had no juridical right to prosecute the rebels for treason since they did not consider themselves citizens of the United States. Trujillo insisted that he and his fellow insurgents were Mexican patriots, and that the rebellion at Taos was a justifiable defense of their homeland.[38] In Washington, President Polk's political opposition began to question the legality of the Taos trials as well as the government of occupation Kearny had appointed in the region. After consideration, the president declared that the territorial government in New Mexico was legitimate, but he concluded that the granting of citizenship to the Mexican inhabitants was illegal since only Congress could perform such an act. Trujillo was acquitted of the charge of treason. The government of occupation, however, was allowed to continue. Donaciano Vigil replaced Bent as governor, but real power remained in the hands of the U.S. military command.[39]

On January 20, 1847, Manuel Cortez carried news of the Taos rebellion to his native Mora. Here, he acquired support from most of the region's communities and organized a second armed front against the United States; only the towns of Las Vegas and Queoloti refused to join Cortez's resistance. The rebellion in Mora started with the assassination of Lawrence Waldo and a group of U.S. merchants who were traveling to Missouri. En route to the east, the traders encountered Cortez and a group of Hispano rebels. The Americans were ordered to surrender their arms, but Superintendent of Teamsters Romulus E. Culver refused. The merchants eventually gave up their weapons, but the Mexicans decided to kill the Americans nonetheless and dumped their bodies in a nearby ravine.[40]

News of the Taos and Mora uprisings spread to Santa Fe. On January 25, eighty U.S. troops under the command of Israel R. Hendley arrived at Mora to confront the insurgents. Cortez's troops entrenched themselves in the local fort and fought the Americans for three hours. During the battle, Hendley received a bullet wound to his groin that ruptured a major artery, and he subsequently bled to death. With the demise of their leader, U.S. troops retreated to the town of Las Vegas to reorganize. Reinforcements arrived, and on February 1, 1847, 200 U.S. troops returned to Mora under the command of Jesse I. Morin. Rather than face superior numbers, Cortez and most of his followers fled to the surrounding mountains. From here, the insurgents continued to resist U.S. occupation of their homeland through the use of guerrilla warfare. Back at Mora, Morin ordered the execution of those rebels that had been captured. This done, the commander then ordered the destruction of Mora and the burning of wheat fields that surrounded the town. The bodies of the slain Americans were recovered, and U.S. troops began the march back to Santa Fe.[41]

The Mora uprising is still considered an act of patriotism by some of the region's inhabitants, although the rebellion has received little attention from historians. As with the Taos revolt, it is easy to conclude that, due to a lack of documentary evidence, the Mora insurrection was an isolated incident rather than an organized Hispano resistance. Careful analysis of U.S. sources and military accounts, however, does indicate that the two rebellions were part of a larger New Mexican movement to reject U.S. occupation of their homeland. How can one claim that the Taos revolt was an act of revenge on the part of irate Indians and Mexicans when hundreds of their comrades died while opposing the American forces? As for Mora, the fact that all the communities of the region but two supported the revolt indicates that this uprising was not simply the result of mob hysteria. The fortification of Mora prior to Hendley's arrival also supports the view that Hispanos expected a fight and had planned for it. In this light, the Taos and Mora rebellions cannot be considered spontaneous and unrelated events. Although no central authority administered either insurrection, they did result from similar causes: resentment of abusive acts performed by U.S. troops and an overwhelming desire to resist conquest.

After the destruction of Mora, Cortez recruited Indian allies in order to raid American camps. U.S. troops countered these attacks with their own assaults on New Mexican settlements, often killing citizens. Throughout the spring and summer months of 1847, minor skirmishes and confrontations occurred at sites such as Cañon del Rio Rojo, Los Pias, and Loquesta. Colonel Price faced off against dissidents in northern New Mexico and claimed that the Hispanos "by day were innocent citizens, but by night rode as guerrilla raiders with the fugitive outlaw, Manuel Cortez." [42] Again, we see in Price's official documentation of the war indications that Hispanos in New Mexico resisted U.S. conquest and occupation of their homeland.

By August 1847, Washington, D.C., had decided that total control of New Mexico had been achieved. Price disagreed. The colonel entrenched his forces at Santa Fe when he received news that Mexican officials had organized a large army in Chihuahua with plans to reconquer New Mexico. Price requested reinforcements but was ordered instead to initiate an invasion of Chihuahua with what forces he had at his disposal. [43]

E. W. D. Newby, the leader of the infamous Missouri Volunteers, eventually replaced Colonel Price as commanding officer in New Mexico. In September 1847, he claimed to have more troops than he needed to defend the territory against Mexican rebels. However, he changed his mind when he too received news of a Mexican army being mobilized in Chihuahua and Durango. Rumors of this alleged force fueled the American's imagination when, on December 29, 1847, one U.S. Lieutenant Armstrong reported he had intercepted documents from the Ministry of War in Mexico City that outlined a plan to organize all of New Mexico's rebel forces under the command of Manuel

Cortez. The Mexican army of reconquest never materialized, however, because in February 1848 the United States and Mexico signed the Treaty of Guadalupe Hidalgo. The treaty ended the U.S.-Mexican War and formalized the conditions and consequences of peace. For Mexicans of the far north, however, the fighting did not end in February. In March 1848, Colonel Price engaged Mexican troops in a final battle at Santa Cruz de Rosalía, which was located near Chihuahua.[44]

Back in New Mexico, Commander Newby found himself confronted with a military problem that existed even before the conquest: Indian raiders had begun to attack both U.S. and Mexican settlements. On April 4, 1848, Newby reversed an order that called for the confiscation of Mexican firearms. The commander demanded that New Mexicans assist in the defense of their homeland, and he denounced any Hispanos who engaged in the trade of arms with Indians.[45]

In June 1848, the U.S. War Department concluded that Newby's troops had fulfilled their purpose in the region and ordered that the Missouri Volunteers depart New Mexico. In August, Colonel Price returned to New Mexico to carry out the expulsion of the hated regiment. The Volunteers left the newly conquered territory, but some 300–400 new recruits soon arrived in New Mexico to replace them. On August 9, Brevet Lieutenant Colonel John McRae assumed military leadership from Price. McRae also replaced Donaciano Vigil as governor, although the latter continued to serve as secretary.[46] The governor's arrival in the territory signaled a new phase in Anglo-Hispano relations.

With the conquest finalized, McRae and Vigil moved to consolidate and assimilate New Mexicans into the new political order. With a deep sense of regret, government officials in Mexico City debated the fate of all Mexicans who remained in the ceded territory. Many regarded the loss of land and the abandonment of compatriots a national disgrace. Mexico's president, Manuel de la Peña y Peña, best expressed this sentiment when he stated:

> Yo no quiero ocultar la verdad en momentos tan solemnes—decía el presidente de la Peña y Peña después de la firma del tratado—ni mucho menos el sentimiento profundo que me causa la separación de la unión nacional de los mexicanos de la Alta California y del Nuevo México; y quiero dejar consignado un testimonio con que mi administración ha visto a aquellos ciudadanos. Puedo aseguraros, señores, que su suerte futura ha sido la dificultad más grave que he tenido para la negociación; y que si hubiera sido posible se habría ampliado la cesión territorial, con la condición de dejar libres a las poblaciones mexicanas.[47]

[I do not wish to conceal the truth in such solemn times, President de la Peña y Peña said after the signing of the treaty, nor much less the profound sentiment which the separation of Mexicans in Alta California and New Mexico from the national union has caused me; and I wish to leave in writing a testimony of my administration's perception of those citizens. I can assure you, sirs, that their future has been the gravest difficulty I have had in the negotiations; and that, had it been possible, the territorial cession would have been extended with the condition that these Mexican populations be set free.]

Most Hispanos accommodated to the consequences of their conquest. Still, many rejected the U.S. occupation of their homeland. The Treaty of Guadalupe Hidalgo had granted those Mexicans who resided in the ceded territory the option to accept U.S. citizenship or to relocate south of the newly drawn international boundary. And even though the treaty suggested that property rights would be respected, hundreds of New Mexicans embarked upon the latter course of action. Ironically, these individuals became known as "repatriated" Mexicans, even though in their minds and hearts they had never left Mexico. For those Hispanos who abandoned their New Mexico homes, the choice of repatriation represented yet another form of resistance to conquest.

The process of relocation proved a difficult task. Mexican officials responded to the displacement of New Mexicans by making land available for them in Chihuahua. The United States also agreed to help. In addition to the $15 million it paid for the conquered territories, the U.S. government promised to provide an additional $200,000 for the repatriation of Mexicans. Towards this end, Mexico claimed it would pay out twenty-five pesos for each person over the age of fourteen (twelve pesos for minors).[48] But while both the Mexican and the U.S. governments proved willing to supply land and monies, neither could possibly know whether these resources would ensure a new and better life for uprooted New Mexicans.

In April 1849, Father Ramón Ortiz, the commissioner assigned by Mexico to oversee the recruitment and transportation of New Mexico families to Chihuahua, arrived in the territory. At Santa Fe, Governor John M. Washington and Secretary Donaciano Vigil greeted Father Ramón with open arms. Convinced that Ortiz would fail in his charge, Washington and Vigil attended to the father's needs with the most cooperative posture they could muster, even agreeing to supply the transportation needed to relocate New Mexico families. The governor's and secretary's disposition toward Father Ramón turned hostile, however, when they learned that Ortiz had acquired 900 solicitations at San Miguel del Vado alone. Vigil expressed a sense of dismay when he contemplated the numbers of discontented Hispanos in the territory. Still, it had become clear to him that the desire for repatriation was strong among his people, and that many were willing to lose their property in order to retain their Mexican citizenship. The patriotic sentiments of these Hispanos caused the secretary further anxiety when he discovered that some New Mexicans were even prepared to pay their own travel expenses to Chihuahua:

> Aunque sabían que no obstante las garantías del tratado de paz perderían todas sus propiedades, querían perderlo todo más bien que pertenecer a un gobierno en el cual tenían menos garantías y eran tratados con más desprecio que la raza de Africa.[49]

> [Although they knew they would lose all their property, notwithstanding the guarantees of the peace treaty, they preferred to lose all rather than to belong to a government in which they had fewer guarantees and were treated with more disregard than the African race.]

Secretary Vigil took it upon himself to thwart Father Ramón's recruitment efforts in New Mexico. He ordered Ortiz to abandon his mission until U.S. authorities could determine whether the petitions he had gathered were legitimate. Washington, D.C., expressed a special fear that Mexican emigrants might unite into a nationalist front bent on the reconquest of the ceded territories. In New Mexico, Governor Washington also tried to hinder the repatriation process. He discouraged Hispanos from emigrating, claiming that Mexico would make available for the indemnification of their lost lands only one-third of the $15 million the U.S. had paid for the conquered territories. The governor warned New Mexicans that they would be forced to live in northern Chihuahua, where defense against Indian raids could not be guaranteed, and he concluded that emigrants would be treated as "stepchildren in foreign lands."[50]

Try as they might, U.S. officials in New Mexico could not stop the repatriation process. Emigrant colonies soon emerged from the desert landscape along the Chihuahua–New Mexico frontier. Of these, La Mesilla, which is located near present-day El Paso, attracted the most attention from New Mexicans. Citizens from San Elizario, Isleta, Doña Ana, and Socorro, communities that had found themselves on the U.S. side of the border after the war, established this colony as an expression of their allegiance to Mexico. In April 1850, the Chihuahua state legislature officially recognized the La Mesilla colony as a settlement that would cater primarily to emigrants from New Mexico. The colony of San Ignacio was also established to accommodate re-patriated Hispanos.

Between 1850 and 1854, issues regarding the distribution of land and water in the emigrant colonies, the spread of disease, and poor treatment by local officials pitted New Mexicans against Chihuahuenses. These problems notwithstanding, the newly formed communities survived and prospered. By 1853, however, the settlers of La Mesilla faced a common enemy when Ameri-cans demanded that the colony be surrendered to them. As an excuse for this claim, the United States argued that La Mesilla had been created illegally since the Mexican government had not granted the colonists formal permission to do so. Mexico feared that its failure to succumb to U.S. demands might result in another invasion of its northern frontier, so the government agreed to turn over the colony and its inhabitants to the United States.[51]

CONCLUSION

The loss of La Mesilla signaled the end of hostilities between Mexico and the United States regarding New Mexico and its people. For Hispanos, however, the struggle to adapt to a new social and political order had just begun. Many New Mexicans believed that the actions of the Mexican government regard-ing the La Mesilla crisis mirrored the lack of support it had offered them dur-ing the U.S.-Mexican War. During the conflict, and after, New Mexicans fended for themselves in their efforts to sustain some semblance of power and to preserve their cultural heritage. While the majority of Hispanos opposed cultural annihilation through the process of withdrawal, some, like Donaciano Vigil, chose accommodation as a form of resistance. Finally, while it may be true that no centralized leadership administered New Mexico's armed revolts against U.S. occupation, this does not conclude that such resistance did not occur. The December Plot, the Taos and Mora rebellions, and the guerrilla war conducted by Manuel Cortez serve as testaments to the patriotism New Mexicans expressed in their struggle to maintain a sense of homeland during an era of U.S. imperialism.

Is there a place within the realm of historical scholarship where the Nuevomexicano view of the U.S.-Mexican War can be presented? To answer this question, perhaps it is best to turn to the words of Marc Simmons, one of New Mexico's most respected scholars. Simmons argued that to negate the New Mexican voice for events such as the U.S.-Mexican War is to for-get that "events that transpired in the old borderlands are as much a part of

American history as what happened in the thirteen colonies."[52] Not to heed Simmons's advice is to preserve the myths inherent in official histories of the U.S.-Mexican frontier. These slanted accounts not only are a disservice to New Mexicans and to the reading public in general, but they perpetuate the distortion of history.

NOTES

1. Martín González de la Vara, *México y Estados Unidos: orígenes de una relación, 1819–1981* (México: Secretaría de Educación Pública, 1987), 122.

2. Rudolfo Acuña, *Occupied America: A History of Chicanos*, 3d ed. (New York: Harper and Row, 1988), 55.

3. Col. Sterling Price to Secretary of War William L. Marcy, Feb. 26, 1847. As cited in Frank McNitt, "Navajo Campaigns and the Occupation of New Mexico, 1847–1848," *New Mexico Historical Review* 43 (1968): 173.

4. Genaro Padilla, *My History, Not Yours: The Formation of Mexican American Autobiography* (Madison: University of Wisconsin Press, 1993), 107. Vallejo wrote a 1,000-page history of California prior to Bancroft's request, but this work was lost in a fire. The amount of work involved in such a venture, and Vallejo's resentment toward the occupation of California by the Bear Flag rebels, influenced his resistance to writing a second history. He consented, however, when Bancroft assured him that California's story would be an impartial account of the territory's past.

5. This concept of history as entertainment is alluded to in Patricia Nelson Limerick, *The Legacy of Conquest: The Unbroken Past of the American West* (New York: W. W. Norton, 1987), 255–58.

6. Robert J. Rosenbaum, *Mexicano Resistance in the Southwest: "The Sacred Right of Self Preservation"* (Austin: University of Texas Press, 1981), ix. From this base theory of "nonresistance," other historical myths and fallacies about Mexicans evolved. For example, in the official histories of the west, the region began to be referred to as the "Southwest" even in reference to the Spanish colonial and Mexican periods. This historical untruth becomes clear when one remembers that, in fact, the region in question was part of Mexico's northern and northwestern territory. It would appear that U.S. writers hoped to justify the conquest of the territory by inventing the "idea" of the Southwest as a mode of analysis and presenting it not from an Indian, Spanish, or Mexican perspective, but as a part of United States history.

7. Ibid., 4.

8. Robert W. Johannsen, *To the Halls of the Montezumas: The Mexican War in the American Imagination* (New York: Oxford University Press, 1985). Johannsen's book rarely gives the Mexican perspective of the war. When it does, it usually involves anecdotes and quotes that portray the Mexican people as fearful, ignorant and, for the most part, passive in their resistance.

9. Padilla, 21.

10. Rosenbaum, 14–15.

11. Richard Griswold del Castillo, *The Treaty of Guadalupe Hidalgo: A Legacy of Conflict* (Norman: University of Oklahoma Press, 1990), 4–6.

12. Tobías Durán, "We Come as Friends: Violent Social Conflict in New Mexico, 1810–1910" (Ph.D. diss., University of New Mexico, 1985), 10.

13. González de la Vara, *México y Estados Unidos*, 27.

14. Ibid., 126–27.

15. Sister Mary Loyola, S.H.N, "The American Occupation of New Mexico," *New Mexico Historical Review* 14 (1939): 161, 167–68.

16. Durán, 10–21. See also Marc Simmons, *New Mexico: An Interpretive History* (Albuquerque: University of New Mexico Press, 1988), 113–16.

17. Hubert Howe Bancroft, *History of Arizona and New Mexico, 1530–1888* (Albuquerque: Horn and Wallace, 1962), 324, 327; as cited in Acuña, 57–58.

18. Donaciano Vigil, *Arms, Indians, and the Mismanagement of New Mexico: 1846*, trans. and ed. David J. Weber (El Paso: Texas Western Press, 1986). Aside from the Texan claim to the Upper Rio Grande, New Mexicans were also aware of John Slidell's efforts to buy their territory, as well as California, for the United States.

19. Stephen W. Kearny to the citizens of Santa Fe, Santa Fe, Aug. 18, 1846; as cited in Padilla, 46.

20. González de la Vara, *México y Estados Unidos*, 128.

21. Durán, 45–46.

22. Padilla, 47.

23. Bent had been instrumental in establishing economic ties between the United States and New Mexico. He settled at Taos, where he married a Mexican woman.

24. Weber, x–xi.

25. Ibid., xii–xvii.

26. Durán, 48.

27. González de la Vara, *México y Estados Unidos*, 129–30.

28. Sister Mary Loyola, 169.

29. Ibid., 168; and Durán, 49. The identification of the informant is open to speculation. Sister Mary Loyola argued that there were two possible suspects; the first, according to Colonel Sterling Price, was the mulatto wife of a conspirator, and the second was the famous female gambler from Taos, Doña Tules. Durán, however, suggests that one of the rebels, Agustín Durán, may have been the informant.

30. Durán, 52–53.

31. *Taos, 1847: The Revolt in Contemporary Accounts*, ed. Michael McNierney (Boulder: Johnson, 1980), 4.

32. Ibid., 8. This account of Bent's assassination was the official story issued by the U.S. government on Feb. 15, 1847.

33. Durán, 53. Montoya was a peasant whose record of sedition against the enemies of New Mexico stemmed from a revolt that took place in 1837. That year, Montoya participated in the assassination of a newly appointed governor from central Mexico who had been at odds with the New Mexicans over land issues.

34. Lawrence R. Murphy, "The U.S. Army in Taos, 1847–1852," *New Mexico Historical Review* 47 (1972): 34–35.

35. Charles Bent to Alexander W. Doniphan, Oct. 9, 1846, New Mexico Territorial Papers, National Archives, University of Northern Iowa, Cedar Falls, microfilm, reel 1; as cited in Alvin R. Sunseri, *Seeds of Discord: New Mexico in the Aftermath of the American Conquest, 1846–1861* (Chicago: Nelson Hall, 1979), 102.

36. González de la Vara, *México y Estados Unidos*, 133.

37. Ibid., 133.

38. Sister Mary Loyola, 171.

39. Sister Mary Loyola, 230–32. Vigil did express concern regarding his appointment as governor; he wrote to President Polk to ask that he be relieved of his office as soon as possible and recommended that Bent's business partner, Ceran St. Vrain, replace him.

40. James W. Goodrich, "Revolt at Mora, 1847," *New Mexico Historical Review* 47 (1972): 51–52.

41. Ibid., 52–57. The people of Mora did rebuild their homes. Ironically, months after the revolt Cortez and his guerillas returned to the settlement, where they discovered that the community had turned against them.

42. McNitt, 173.

43. González de la Vara, *México y Estados Unidos*, 138.

44. Ibid., 137–38.

45. Lee Myers, "Illinois Volunteers in New Mexico, 1847–1848," *New Mexico Historical Review* 47 (1972): 17–19.

46. Ibid., 21–23.

47. Luis González, comp., *Los presidentes de México ante la nación, 1821–1966*, 5 vols. (México: Cámara de Diputados, 1966), 1:347, and Agustín Cué Cánovas, *Los Estados Unidos y el México olvidado* (México: Costa Amic, 1970), 37; as cited in Martín González de la Vara, "El traslado de familias de Nuevo México al norte de Chihuahua y la conformación de una región fronteriza, 1848–1854," *Frontera norte* 6 (Jan.-June 1994): 3.

48. González de la Vara, "El traslado de familias de Nuevo México," 10.

49. Ramón Ortiz to the Minister of Internal and External Relations, Chihuahua, June 22, 1849, in Archivo de la Secretaría de Relaciones Exteriores de México, D.F., LE 1975, exp. XXV (1848), 120v; cited in González de la Vara, "El traslado de familias de Nuevo México," 12.

50. González de la Vara, "El traslado de familias de Nuevo México," 12–15.

51. Ibid., 16–20.

52. Marc Simmons, *The Last Conquistador: Juan de Oñate and the Settling of the Far Southwest* (Norman: University of Oklahoma Press, 1991), xiv.

Chapter Two

MARTÍN GONZÁLEZ DE LA VARA

The Return to Mexico

THE RELOCATION OF NEW MEXICAN FAMILIES
TO CHIHUAHUA AND THE CONFIRMATION OF A
FRONTIER REGION, 1848 – 1854

GUARANTEES OF THE TREATY OF GUADALUPE HIDALGO

Toward the end of 1847, and once Anglo-American troops had occupied Mexico City, the Mexican government seated in Querétaro was convinced that further struggle against the invader was impossible and peace talks were initiated between the United States and its southern neighbor. These negotiations resulted in the signing of the Treaty of Guadalupe Hidalgo on February 2, 1848. According to the treaty, Mexico accepted the loss of slightly more than half of its territory, in which approximately 115,000 people lived. The fate of these Mexicans was one of the main themes in the negotiations between the representatives of Mexico and the United States:

> I do not wish to conceal the truth in such solemn times, President de la Peña y Peña said after the signing of the treaty, nor much less the profound sentiment which the separation of Mexicans in Alta California and New Mexico from the national union has caused me; and I wish to leave in writing a testimony of my administration's perception of those citizens. I can assure you, sirs, that their future has been the gravest difficulty I have had in the negotiations; and that, had it been possible, the territorial cession would have been extended with the condition that these Mexican populations be set free.[1]

With this, the Treaty of Guadalupe Hidalgo stipulated certain basic rights for those Mexicans residing within the territories ceded to the United States. These rights included respect for their property, freedom of religion, the right to retain their Mexican citizenship or be readmitted into Mexico, where they would be given land, and an opportunity to start a new life. Article VI stated that

Mexicans established today in territories that once belonged to Mexico and who remain, in the future, within the limits of the United States, will be allowed to stay where they now live or move at any time to the Republic of Mexico as outlined by the present treaty.[2]

The national government had barely reestablished itself in Mexico City when it took the first legislative steps to design a policy intended to "diminish the disgrace" of their compatriots residing in the lost territories.[3] On June 14, 1848, a law made 200,000 pesos available that had originated from indemnification payments by the United States government in order to help those families that wished to relocate to Mexico.[4] Another law, dated August 19 of the same year, stipulated the manner in which such a transfer should occur. The Mexican federal government agreed to pay heads of households that emigrated to Mexico twenty-five pesos for every person over the age of fourteen and twelve pesos for each minor to cover the costs of relocation to Mexico. It agreed to endow these households with sufficient lands, to be donated by state governments. The federal government also agreed to appoint three commissioners, one for each province lost, to be in charge of registering and helping the families in the colonies assigned to them.[5] Shortly after, and "in light of the learned qualities, honesty, and patriotism which adorn him," the Secretary of Internal and External Relations, Mariano Otero, appointed Ramón Ortiz commissioner for the relocation of New Mexican families to the Chihuahua territory.[6]

In fact, Father Ramón Ortiz appeared to be the person best qualified for the job. He was born in Santa Fe, New Mexico's capital, in 1813 and studied for the clergy in Durango. He was appointed parish priest of El Paso in 1836. Several years later, he was characterized as a staunch opponent of North American intervention and was arrested twice by the invading military. This nationalistic attitude helped him get elected as federal deputy for Chihuahua. In the national congress, he fought to stop ratification of the peace treaty because of the territorial losses his state would suffer.[7] Relying on 25,000 pesos for initial costs, of which 2,000 constituted his salary, Father Ortiz left Mexico City in September 1848 to fulfill his mission in New Mexico.

RAMÓN ORTIZ'S MISSION IN NEW MEXICO

North American Forces took the territory of New Mexico in August 1846, placing it under the military jurisdiction of the United States. Although New Mexicans were initially unable to resist the invaders, they launched an important rebellion that took the occupation forces more than one year to suppress.

At the time of the signing of the Treaty of Guadalupe Hidalgo, New Mexico was the most populated of the provinces Mexico lost: it contained roughly 60,000 inhabitants, excluding Indians. Because of the demographics, it was thought that New Mexico could provide a large number of families willing to relocate to Mexico.

Commissioner Ortiz arrived at his El Paso parish at the end of November, 1848. Strong snowstorms kept him from continuing on to New Mexico. At any rate, he made the nature of his commission known among the Paseños so that a few days after his arrival in El Paso he had already accumulated twenty petitions for relocation to Mexico from some New Mexicans residing in that town. Due to this unexpected and premature success in his mission, Ortiz calculated that he could relocate between 2,000 and 4,000 families to Chihuahua.[8]

The harsh winter of 1848 did not allow Father Ortiz to continue his work in the north until March 1849. In the middle of April, accompanied by Manuel Armendáriz, he arrived in Santa Fe, where he held an interview with Governor John M. Washington and his secretary, Donaciano Vigil. Vigil was one of the few Mexicans who openly supported the North American invasion. The U.S. territorial authorities promised to help Ortiz in his commission and even offered to provide transportation should he need it. Even so, local authorities were alarmed when they discovered the nature of Ortiz's mission. They recognized the political problems he could cause them with the already resentful New Mexican population.

The Mexican commissioner initiated his work with many expectations. He began to register families from the small town of San Miguel del Vado, situated some 100 kilometers east of Santa Fe, who wished to settle in Mexico. Here, heads of households presented 900 petitions for relocation to Mexico from an approximate total of 1,000 families.

> I barely arrived to the outskirts of town, Father Ortiz informed, when enthusiastic inhabitants introduced themselves and requested that I enlist them and their families for relocation to Mexican territory. Although they knew they would lose all their property, notwithstanding the guarantees of the peace treaty, they preferred to lose all rather than belong to a government in which they had fewer guarantees and were treated with more disregard than the African race.[9]

Upon completing his work as registrar in San Miguel del Vado and other surrounding towns, Ortiz hoped to move on to Taos. However, fog forced him to retrace his steps to Santa Fe, whence he could redirect himself northward. Entering the Indian town of Pojoaque, the commissioner received a letter from Donaciano Vigil requesting that Ortiz abandon his mission due to disturbances he was causing among the population. Ortiz returned to Santa Fe, where he learned that local authorities had already prohibited him from personally registering families wishing to emigrate from New Mexico to Mexico. Ortiz discussed this issue with Vigil and convinced him to authorize the use of agents by which the father could continue his work. That same day, Ortiz appointed an agent who immediately went to work in Santa Fe. When Ortiz had registered about 200 families there, Vigil once again sent for the priest. At this meeting, Vigil informed the commissioner that he was prohibited from conducting any activities until the proper territorial authorities obtained signatures of possible emigrants who had explicitly declared their desire to maintain their Mexican citizenship.[10]

This issue of the signatures complicated Ortiz's task tremendously, for he had to surrender vast powers of decision into the hands of local authorities who did not want to allow the depopulation of their territory. Vigil's goal was to link the registration of families who wished to relocate in Mexico to their willingness to declare their desire to become Mexican citizens. The Treaty of Guadalupe Hidalgo stated that Mexicans residing in territories acquired by the United States could preserve their nationality as long as they expressed that desire publicly up to one year after the treaty was ratified by the congresses of both nations. The U.S. Senate ratified the treaty in June 1848. In New Mexico, however, a mechanism that allowed citizens who so chose to consider themselves Mexican was not created until the end of the following year. The reason for this delay was that territorial authorities blocked all such initiatives that were proposed. Toward the end of April, prior to Ortiz's arrival and before the local populace was confronted with this pressure, Washington, the new governor, issued a proclamation that stated that whoever wished to be Mexican had to register with county prefectures before May 30.[11] Nonetheless, these same authorities pressured the people so that they would not register on these lists. Despite this, Ortiz declared that he saw "hundreds of signatures."[12]

THE DIFFICULT ESTABLISHMENT OF THE CIVIL COLONIES

Frustrated by the obstacles he encountered, Ortiz decided to return to Chihuahua. He wanted to obtain the resources for the repatriations from federal and state governments. He calculated that he would be able to relocate approximately 80,000 persons to Mexican territory. For this $1,652,242, 145,360 bushels of corn and 38,963 bushels of beans would be needed to maintain the people before they could settle in Mexico and start cultivating land.[13] In light of Ortiz's inability to travel to the nation's capital to continue these efforts, Chihuahua's government appointed Manuel Armendáriz as special agent. Armendáriz traveled to Mexico City during the month of July.

When the commissioner's statement was received in Mexico City, an interchange of diplomatic notes took place between the Mexican and U.S. governments. Minister Luis de la Rosa demanded an explanation of the mistreatment of an official envoy from Mexico.[14] Authorities of the United States responded they had no way of recognizing Ortiz's official character, since the peace treaty did not anticipate the need to appoint a commissioner to relocate Mexican families to their nation of origin. To remove this obstacle the Mexican government decided to appoint Manuel Armendáriz General Consul to New Mexico.[15]

While Father Ortiz carried out his commission in New Mexico, the government of Chihuahua began to plan the establishment of the colonies that would receive emigrants from that territory. Governor Angel Trías favored immigration into the northern portion of his state, since a large population in the border region could hinder the influx of the *indios bárbaros*. He attempted various means to facilitate the work of Commissioner Ortiz and to find accommodations for the families he would relocate from New Mexico. In January 1849, he presented an initiative in the Chihuahua legislature that would approve the cession of land to New Mexican families wishing to emigrate. The plan was quickly ratified by the state assembly.[16] In April of the same year, the land surveyor, Genaro Artalejo, arrived in El Paso. He was charged by the local government with finding an adequate site on the south bank of the Rio Bravo, south of El Paso, where a civil colony would be established, to be called Guadalupe.[17] Toward the middle of 1849, when Father Ortiz reached Chihuahua from New Mexico, Governor Trías granted him the power to announce and give possession of the land needed to form new towns.[18]

When Ortiz made public the tremendous economic resources required for the relocation of families, Trías sought a way to aid the enterprise and presented certain initiatives in this regard to the state legislature. The latter, however, was unable to address the issue, since the incursions of the *indios bárbaros* consumed practically all of its first session in 1849. In response, the governor requested that sufficient resources be made available by the federal government to initiate the relocation program.

> Because this government has great interest, Trías wrote to the Minister of Internal and External Relations, in promoting the immigration of citizens wishing to preserve their nationality, and insuring that this will be

put into effect without delay, it is vital to make at least one-third the cost of importing seed to help farmers plant and harvest a crop sufficient enough for the families in their entrance to this state. In addition, it is crucial to determine the amount of resources needed to transport these New Mexican families to the state and to the diverse points they will colonize.[19]

Using Ortiz's estimations, and calculating that there would be only 900 New Mexican families willing to emigrate and who had already requested their relocation to Chihuahua, it was determined that the amount the federal government would have to spend to initiate the process of repatriation exceeded the 25,000 pesos initially assigned to the project by the national congress.[20]

For their part, local authorities in New Mexico stood firm in their efforts to stop the emigration to Chihuahua. Besides blocking efforts by New Mexicans to declare their desire to continue being Mexican citizens, they also tried to convince them that emigration was not worth their trouble. The official newspaper, the *Santa Fe Republican*, cautioned the prospective emigrants that

> fifteen million *pesos* is the indemnization that the American Congress has to pay Mexico for Texas, New Mexico, and California. If your government is truly paternal, you should expect that at least one-third of this total [will] be dedicated for the indemnization of the value of your properties and to alleviate the misery you will experience as a consequence of changing residence. You can see the enormity of the total costs you face for emigrating. As recompense for your properties, you shall receive others with the condition that you settle the frontiers of the State of Chihuahua. Here, you will make the sacrifice of living with and suffering the cruel invasions of the barbarous [Indians]. We recognize the demands of your government. Yet, in spite of this knowledge, we can only invite you to believe that we have tried to prove your devotion and suffering, and that they [the Mexican authorities] clearly do not wish you to return to the ranks of their family. . . . We expect you to act upon this issue of such importance with absolute liberty and that you will keep present those who council [*sic*] you in such [a] manner and the false prophets who preach and induce you to emigrate.[21]

In this way, from 1849 to 1850, New Mexico's local authorities attempted by all means to keep New Mexicans in their native land. They stated that in Chihuahua the New Mexicans would be treated as stepsons in a foreign land.[22] Although money flowed slowly from Chihuahua, many New Mexicans with economic resources began to relocate to Mexico at their own expense. From central New Mexico, people of status, such as Guadalupe Miranda and Juan Bautista Vigil, became dedicated promoters of emigration to the north of Chihuahua.

Later, during the second half of 1849, Father Ortiz initiated new efforts to found the town of Guadalupe. Nonetheless, an unexpected incident altered the plans. Toward the end of 1849, the course of the Rio Grande's main current shifted into a channel that ran to the south of San Elizario, Isleta, and Socorro. Since this river was the border between Mexico and the United States, these Chihuahuan towns ended up within U.S. territory. The U.S. armed forces almost immediately occupied these towns, and in spite of efforts by local authorities, they were never expelled for fear that this would cause a major incident. Months later, Mexican representatives of the border commission officially recognized the loss of these towns, since the Treaty of Guadalupe Hidalgo determined that the frontier line should follow the southernmost section of the Rio Bravo. The commission determined that the channel the river took was farther south than its ancient course.

The people of Socorro, Isleta, and San Elizario did not wait for the border commission's decision to act. Soon after the military occupation, some of the residents of these towns manifested their desire to move south of the river in order to continue living in Mexico. A similar situation presented itself in Doña Ana. Established by the Chihuahua government in 1833, this colony now found itself on the north bank of the Rio Bravo and therefore on U.S. territory. To complicate matters, some sixty colonists from Doña Ana, following Rafael Ruelas and pressured by Americans who had recently arrived in the area, relocated to the south bank of the Rio Bravo to settle in the Mesilla Valley in March 1850, before receiving any type of official authorization.[23] These new colonizers, who were not anticipated in the decree of June 14, 1848, asked the state government for aid in relocating to Mexican territory. An expert on such matters, Father Ramón Ortiz conveyed to Chihuahua's authorities the possibility that these people could consider themselves emigrants.[24]

Soon after, the local legislature responded in the affirmative. It issued a decree on April 4, 1850, that stated:

> To Chihuahuan residents of Doña Ana, Isleta, Socorro, and San Elizario, the government will provide lands, double in size those given to other Mexican immigrants of New Mexico or California, from uncultivated sections on the right bank of the Bravo River.[25]

An important obstacle in the establishment of civil colonies was the lack of resources in the state of Chihuahua. Between 1849 and 1850, the central government sent only the initial 25,000 pesos to cover the cost of relocating families to Chihuahua, plus a few more shipments not exceeding 15,000 pesos. It thus became necessary for the state government to make certain financial sacrifices in order to cover the needs of New Mexico's emigrants, and of those towns that used to belong to Chihuahua. Little by little, the state government supplied Ortiz and Armendáriz with resources, and in its eagerness to aid the immigrants, it went into debt with the merchant José Cordero for $5,000, at an elevated interest rate of 3 percent per month.[26]

Voluntary emigration, especially by people from towns that belonged to Chihuahua, grew in importance. In Guadalupe, immigration increased to such a degree that, by April of 1850, it was said there were already 600 families from New Mexico. In addition, Father Ortiz and the people of the old Chihuahua towns who settled in the colony began to seek land to the south. Here they hoped to establish a new site, to be called San Ignacio.[27] Although the emigrants from New Mexico were never as numerous as Father Ortiz initially expected, they managed to become an important demographic factor in the integration of the new frontier zone. The total number of emigrants from New Mexico was calculated as 1,552 people by the middle of 1850. Yet, emigration from zones once belonging to Chihuahua, and that went on to form a part of Texas and New Mexico, was also important. As of the middle of 1850, the El Paso region had received a minimum of around 2,000 new inhabitants.[28]

In the end, the results from one year of effort were not so negative, despite the difficulties. Toward the end of 1850, the Minister of Interior and Exterior Relations found a balance in the repatriation effort, remarking:

> The government has already given a great amount of money for this objective and it has the satisfaction to announce that new towns have been founded, composed for the most part by Mexicans who emigrated from the lands ceded to the United States . . . the government believes had it been able to dispose of larger sums, the number of those who relocated to Mexico would have been greater.[29]

For its part, the state government was also quite satisfied with progress made in the civil and military colonization of the El Paso area. This view was expressed in a contemporary account regarding advances made by the populace of Chihuahua:

> with the treaty [of Guadalupe Hidalgo], Chihuahua lost all the territory incorporated between the Bravo and Pecos [Rivers] along with the

colony of Doña Ana and the towns of Isleta, Socorro, and San Elizario. Even so, many of the residents of these sites reside today in El Paso and the new towns of La Mesilla, San Joaquín, San Ignacio, and Guadalupe. Surely, they were stimulated by their patriotism and by the V.H. [state legislature], who, on April 11 of last year, granted double plots on the right bank of the Bravo to those who wished to conserve their Mexican and Chihuahuan character.[30]

In 1850, the civil colony of La Mesilla was established spontaneously with people originally from Doña Ana. Nonetheless, other families from New Mexico slowly augmented the number of inhabitants in the colony. Toward the end of 1850, it was speculated that some 2,000 people lived in the La Mesilla Valley. This was an obvious exaggeration, for it had not been determined whether this population would end up in Mexican or U.S. territory, and an official colony had not been formed in the valley.[31]

Yet, it is undeniable that La Mesilla experienced extraordinary development throughout 1850 and 1851. It began to be populated more and more with immigrants from Doña Ana, to the point where that town was left almost completely abandoned. In March 1851, an American observer calculated the population of La Mesilla at between 600 and 700 inhabitants, and they had already organized a local government.[32] By the end of April 1851, La Mesilla was the most important immigration zone in northern Chihuahua. It was at this time that the border commission staked out the frontier line between Chihuahua and New Mexico. In addition, it determined that the colony's population was situated to the south of the border and thus within Mexican territory. This decision was very important for the colonizers, since many had decided to move even farther south should the settlement remain on North American lands. The delineation of the frontier was then celebrated in La Mesilla with dances, masses, and other festivities.

THE CONSOLIDATION OF THE FRONTIER REGION OF EL PASO

To acknowledge the official establishment of La Mesilla as a civil colony, Chihuahua's legislature implemented a regulation for state colonization issued in 1833.[33] In May 1851, Ramón Ortiz granted land to the citizens of the town.[34] Favorable land conditions attracted more immigrants from the interior of New Mexico. By October 1852, there were more than 1,900 people in La Mesilla; the colony was considered completely consolidated.[35]

The balance that, up to then, could be made between New Mexican and Chihuahuan immigration and the establishment of civil colonies in the El Paso del Norte area, was positive, despite ongoing problems. In the middle of 1851, Chihuahua's official government newspaper evaluated this colonization effort:

> [I]mportant towns have been, and are being founded which are known by the names of La Mesilla and Los Amoles. In addition, south of El Paso, Real, Seneco, Isleta, and Socorro, the military colony of San Joaquín [or El Paso] and the civil ones of Guadalupe and San Ignacio have also been founded. Because of this, a forty-league section of our frontier line can be considered to be moderately populated. . . . Colonization would be striking if the 200,000 pesos [earmarked for this] for the first time in article 22 of the general law of July 14, 1848, had been invested in its progress. But, as of today, only one-fifth of this total has been received, while impediments and damages have been incalculable.[36]

In fact, the civil colonies' first years were arduous ones for its inhabitants. From the start, Guadalupe and San Ignacio colonists experienced problems with those from San Joaquín de El Paso regarding the demarcation of their territories and individual plots within their territories. In addition, the slow work of topographers motivated certain speculations in the land, which, because of immigration, came to be coveted more and more. Likewise, the region had a water shortage, with Guadalupe and San Ignacio being affected the most since they were downriver of El Paso's agricultural region.[37]

A confrontation among the colonists of Guadalupe erupted, perhaps owing to a lack of sufficient natural resources. Immigrants from New Mexico began to feel alienated, for they thought that the people of Socorro, Isleta, and San Elizario were treated better and were given not only twice the amount, but also the best lands by the Chihuahua government. The New Mexicans, led by Juan Bautista Vigil, settled in this colony, but they were apprehensive and threatened to return to their native land. In the end, the commotion ceased when good harvests were obtained in 1851 and 1852, allowing the colony to survive the crisis.[38] A cholera epidemic, an increase in crime, and periodic attacks by the *indios bárbaros* also strongly affected the lower river colonies. Even so, by 1852 they were consolidated into towns of local importance. Guadalupe, for example, consisted of at least 500 inhabitants, originally from Albuquerque, Tomé, Belén, Socorro, or other towns from the south of New Mexico.[39]

In the northern zone of La Mesilla, rapid growth created grave disagreements within the colony. On the one hand, colonizers from Doña Ana and southern New Mexico began to complain of suffering a "true invasion" of El Paso as colonizers. They accused Father Ortiz of atoning for these problems by giving the best lands to his El Paso parishioners and of not paying em-igrants the transportation quotas still owed them.[40] A rumor also began to spread that many New Mexicans were determined to return home if their de-mands were not satisfied.

To make matters worse, political problems in the center of Mexico spread to the north of Chihuahua and increased the animosity between Father Ortiz, the colonizers, and the local authorities. At the start of 1853, Ortiz tried to pressure inhabitants of the three colonies into his charge in order to pre-vent their adherence to the Plan of Guadalajara, a feat already accomplished by Governor Angel Trías in Chihuahua. The commissioner's actions led Gov-ernor Trías to have Ortiz removed and to name Guadalupe Miranda the new commissioner.[41] The latter received his appointment toward the middle of 1853, but in practice, he accomplished little, owing to a lack of resources. Nevertheless, Chihuahua authorities intended to foster the flow of immigrants toward their state and recommended to Miranda that

> using his influence and sense of patriotism he should promote the im-migration from New Mexico; his talents would substitute [for] the lack of monetary resources which the government cannot provide.[42]

The colony at Mesilla kept on growing in such a way that the land for colonists became more and more scarce. Father Ortiz and Miranda had then to establish two new civil colonies around Mesilla. In February 1852, Ortiz al-lotted *parcelas* to eighty-three migrants from Mesilla. Eighteen months later, in August 1853, under Miranda, the new commissioner, the Mesilla colony was divided, and the Santo Tomás de Yturbide civil colony was founded in the southern part of Mesilla. These new colonies developed slowly because shortly after their establishment included in the territory they were acquired by the United States as part of the Gadsden Purchase, though they were rec-ognized as land grants during the late nineteenth century.[43]

In March 1853, a diplomatic conflict regarding the ownership of La Mesilla led to a crisis between Mexico and the United States. The governor of New Mexico had not accepted the line designated by the border commis-sion in 1851 and demanded that the frontier be relocated further south. In the colony, a majority of the inhabitants confirmed, by various means, their desire to remain a part of Mexico. Even so, due to their discontent with irregulari-ties in their relocation and the allocation of lots, some New Mexican immi-grants favored the United States' territorial demands.[44]

In the following months, the conflict over La Mesilla affected Miranda's efforts in his double role as commissioner and vice consul of El Paso. With neither proper funds nor the power to demand receipts from Ramón Ortiz, Miranda was unable to function.[45] By the middle of 1854, he realized that the immigrants of La Mesilla were still owed more than half of their pay and that thirty families settled in San Ignacio had never received aid from the government. This represented a potential problem for the region, since the colonists could unite with rebels from the center of the country or ally themselves with the Americans and their territorial ambitions.[46]

In the end, Mexico lost La Mesilla through diplomatic channels. Along with the colony, Mexico also lost much of its intent to create a strong and well-established frontier region. Nevertheless, the efforts of Ramón Ortiz, Manuel Armendáriz, Rafael Ruelas, Angel Trías, Guadalupe Miranda, and the emigrants were not in vain. Years later, Guillermo Prieto would say:

> [these efforts] have improved the condition of El Paso. They have in-
> creased its importance and made it worthy of the government's attention
> so that, from its example, a line of flourishing towns should be the best
> and most solid custodian of the Republic's independence.[47]

In effect, the civil colonies gave rise to permanent populations that were to help define the frontier character of the El Paso region. In addition, future migrations of Mexicans to their ancestral home would lead to the creation of new settlements in the area. In February 1859, Guadalupe and San Ignacio, today Guadalupe de Bravos and Praxedis Guerrero, received the status of chief municipality. In doing so, they achieved recognition of their importance on a regional level while, in the 1860s and 1870s, new emigrants from Texas and New Mexico would go on to establish the towns of Zaragoza and La Ascensión.[48]

NOTES

1. Luis González, comp., *Los presidentes de México ante la nación, 1821–1966*, 5 vols. (México: Cámara de Diputados, 1966), 1:347, and Agustín Cué Cánovas, *Los Estados Unidos y el México olvidado* (México: Costa Amic, 1970), 37.

2. Ángela Moyano, *México y los Estados Unidos: orígenes de una relación, 1819–1861* (México: Secretaría de Educación Pública, 1987), 179–80.

3. Luis Gonzaga Cuevas, *Memorias del Ministro de Relaciones Interiores y Exteriores* (México: Imprenta de Vicente García Torres, 1849), 14.

4. Manuel Dublán and José María Lozano, *Legislación mexicana o colección completa de las disposiciones legislativas expedidas desde la independencia de la República*, 50 vols. (México: Imprenta del Comercio, 1876–1880), 5:385–86.

5. Ibid., 5:439–41.

6. The appointment of Ortiz as commissioner appears in the Archivo de la Secretaría de Relaciones Exteriores de México, D.F. (hereafter cited as ASREM), LE 1975, exp. XXV, Sept. 6, 1848, 120v.

7. Biographical data on Ramón Ortiz can be found in Francisco R. Almada, *Diccionario de la historia geografía y biografía chihuahuense*, 2d ed. (Chihuahua: Universidad de Chihuahua, Departamento de Investigaciones Sociales, Sección de Historia, 1968), 385; Fidelia Miller Puckett, "Ramón Ortiz: Priest and Patriot," *New Mexico Historical Review* 25, no. 4 (Oct. 1950), 269–95; C. L. Sonnischsen, *Pass of the North: Four Centuries on the Río Grande*, 2 vols. (El Paso: Texas Western Press, 1968), 1:108–10, 118, 204; Marc Simmons, *Ranchers, Ramblers, and Renegades: True Tales of Territorial New Mexico* (Santa Fe: Ancient City Press, 1984), 3–7; and William E. Connelly, *Doniphan's Expedition and the Conquest of New Mexico and California* (Kansas City: Bryant and Douglas, 1907), 90–97, 397.

8. Ramón Ortiz to the Minister of Internal and External Relations, El Paso, Dec. 8, 1848, in ASREM, LE 1975, exp. XXV, 136.

9. Ramón Ortiz to the Minister of Internal and External Relations, Chihuahua, June 22, 1849, in ASREM, LE 1975, exp. XXV, 139. Other authors who have written on Ortiz's work in New Mexico include Moyano, *México y los Estados Unidos*, 179–84; José Agustín Escudero, ed., *Noticias históricas y estadísticas de la antigua provincia de la Nueva México*, by Pedro Bautista Pino (México: Imprenta de Lara, 1849), notes, 93–95; Frances Leon Swadesh, *Los primeros pobladores: antecesores de los Chicanos en Nuevo México* (México: Fondo de Cultura Económica, Sección de Obras de Antropología, 1977), 84–85; Ralph Emerson Twitchell, *The Leading Facts of New Mexican History*, 5 vols. (Cedar Rapids, Iowa: Torch Press, 1911–1917), 2:290–91; Angela Moyano, *El comercio de Santa Fe y la guerra del 47*, SepSetentas 283 (México: Secretaría de Educación Pública, 1976), 163–65; Ángela Moyano, *Protección consular a mexicanos en los Estados Unidos, 1849–1900*, Archivo Histórico Diplomático Mexicano (México: Secretaría de Relaciones Exteriores, 1989), 20–23; Luis G. Zorrilla, *Historia de las relaciones entre México y los Estados Unidos de América*, 2 vols., Biblioteca Porrúa, vol. 69, (México: Porrúa, 1965), 1:250–60; and Hubert Howe Bancroft, *History of Arizona and New Mexico, 1540–1888*, vol. 17 of *The Works of Hubert Howe Bancroft* (San Francisco: History Company, 1888), 472–73.

10. Copies of the correspondence between Ortiz and Vigil, in ASREM, LE 1975, exp. XXV, 142–4v. Also reproduced in Escudero, 93–95.

11. Proclamation by Gov. Washington, in New Mexico State Records Center and Archives, Santa Fe, N.M. (hereafter cited as NMSRCA), Governor's Papers (hereafter cited as GP), Washington Papers, reel 98, frame 204.

12. ASREM, LE 1975, exp. XXV, 139v. One of the ways in which New Mexicans were discouraged was to prohibit county officials from making lists of possible emigrants until they received precise instructions from the governor. At any rate, the list was already in the hands of Gov. Washington by Aug. 1848. Auditor Nangle to Washington, Santa Fe, Aug. 3, 1849. In NMSRCA, GP, Washington Papers 98, 202–3.

13. ASREM, LE 1975, exp. XXV, 140.

14. Luis de la Rosa to Clayton, México, D.F., Sept. 21, 1849, in ASREM, 2-13-2971,

17–18. This file contains two other diplomatic letters of protest regarding the same problem from Oct. 5 and Oct. 20, 1849.

15. The new town of Franklin, N.M., whose population would later form the beginnings of the city of El Paso, Tex., was assigned to Armendáriz as a consular see.

16. The transcript of this law has not been found, but other legislative depositions make constant reference to it. See *El Faro:* [official newspaper of the government of the free state of Chihuahua], May 16, 1850.

17. *El faro*, Apr. 24, 1849.

18. Angel Trías to the Minister of Internal and External Relations, Chihuahua, June 30, 1849, in ASREM, 2-13-2971, 3.

19. *El faro*, June 30, 1849.

20. Ibid., July 31, 1849.

21. This article appeared in the *Santa Fe Republican* on May 26, 1849, and was reprinted in *El faro* on Oct. 13, 1849.

22. NMSRCA, Donaciano Vigil Collection: s.f.

23. S. W. Cozzens, *Viaje a un país maravilloso: Arizona y Nuevo México* (Paris: Garnier Brothers), 22; Harvey Fergusson, *Rio Grande* (New York: Alfred A. Knopf, 1933), 54.

24. Archivo General de la Nación, Mexico, D.F. (hereafter cited as AGN), Historical Documents of Ciudad Juárez (Hereafter cited as DHCJ), reel 61.

25. *El faro*, Apr. 16, 1850.

26. *El correo de Chihuahua* [official newspaper of the state government, Chihuahua], Dec. 24, 1850. Complete estimates on expenses made by Chihuahua's government for the establishment of civil colonies do not exist. But it appears that the state contributed a sum totaling between 20,000 and 30,000 pesos during that year. See also *El correo de Chihuahua*, Jan. 21, 1851.

27. Emilio Langberg to the Minister of War and Navy, El Paso, Feb. 22, 1850. Printed in *El faro*, Apr. 4, 1850; also in AGN, DHCJ, 60.

28. These estimates are from Commissioner Ramón Ortiz, while a member of New Mexico's territorial government affirmed that emigrants did not surpass 1,500 in number. *El correo de Chihuahua*, Dec. 7, 1850, and George Archibald McCall, *New Mexico in 1850: A Military View* (Norman: University of Oklahoma Press, 1968), 80–82.

29. José María Lacunza, [Memorial read to the (Government) Chambers by the Secretary of Internal and External Relations] (México: Imprenta de García Torres, 1851), 29.

30. *El correo de Chihuahua*, Mar. 11, 1851.

31. Ibid.

32. John Russell Bartlett, *Personal Narrative of Explorations and Incidents in Texas, New Mexico, California, Sonora, and Chihuahua, 1851–1853*, 2 vols. (Chicago: Rio Grande Press, 1965), 1:212.

33. *El correo de Chihuahua*, May 24, 1851.

34. George Griggs, *History of Mesilla Valley or Gadsden Purchase, Known in Mexico as the Treaty of Mesilla* (Mesilla: s.n., 1930), 31–33.

35. Ibid., 214–15.

36. *El correo de Chihuahua,* May 10, 1851.

37. AGN, DHCJ, 60 passim.

38. Luis Zuloaga to the Minister of Internal and External Relations, Chihuahua, Oct. 3, 1853. In ASREM, 2-12-2902.

39. From an incomplete census of the town of Guadalupe, 1852, AGN, DHCJ, 61.

40. Testimony of Victor de la O., Chihuahua, Mar. 20, 1853, in ASREM, 2-12-2902.

41. Letters from Angel Trías to the Minister of Internal and External Relations, Chihuahua, Mar. 1 and 22, 1853, in ASREM, 2-12-2902.

42. José de Arellano to Guadalupe Miranda, Chihuahua, Nov. 23, 1853, NMSRCA, Guadalupe Miranda Family Papers.

43. J. J. Bowden, *Spanish and Mexican Land Grants in the Chihuahuan Acquisition* (El Paso: Texas Western Press, 1971), 27–28, 40–42.

44. See the letter of some seventy La Mesilla citizens to William Carr Lane, La Mesilla, Mar. 22, 1853, in NMSRCA, Ritch Collection, reel 1, exp. 578.

45. See ASREM, 2-12-2902, and the History and National Defense Archive, exp. XI/481.3/3504. In 1850, an ample region considered to be a part of New Mexico went to form a part of Texas, in which Franklin was located.

46. Guadalupe Miranda to the Minister of Internal and External Relations, El Paso, Aug. 6, 1854, in ASREM, 2-12-2902.

47. Guillermo Prieto, *Indicaciones sobre el origen, vicisitudes, y estado que guardan actualmente las rentas generales de la República Mexicana* (México: Imprenta de Ignacio Cumplido, 1850), 170.

48. See Almada, 236, 428, 574. See also Jesús Ramírez Caloca, *Nociones de geografía del estado de Chihuahua* (Chihuahua: Litografía El Cromo, 1955).

Chapter Three

ANSELMO ARELLANO

The People's Movement

LAS GORRAS BLANCAS

By 1890, San Miguel County was the largest and most populous county in the New Mexico Territory. The counties that bounded it were Mora on the north and Lincoln and Bernalillo on the south. Extending from the eastern flank of the Sangre de Cristo Mountains in the west to the Texas Panhandle in the east, San Miguel County boasted a population of 24,204 residents out of a total in New Mexico of 153,593. Las Vegas, the county seat, was the largest city in New Mexico, outnumbering Santa Fe and Albuquerque by a few hundred citizens.[1]

Native Hispanos comprised close to 80 percent of New Mexico's total population. For this reason, and because of its large commercial interests, San Miguel County continued to grow in influence. The power that the county held in territorial politics, as well as its enormous wealth in resources and people, helped it gain the reputation of being the "Imperial County." Within the county, the community of Las Vegas escalated to the forefront of territorial politics as it advocated and promoted issues that directly affected Hispanos. Many popular concerns that had long been submerged were now being addressed by Nuevomexicanos.[2]

The greater questions that concerned or directly affected the residents of San Miguel County in 1890 were land grants, property rights, tax laws, education, labor, and statehood. many felt that if the issues were to be confronted head on, a drastic change would have to be made in the political arena of the territory, because by now many were losing faith in their political parties— especially the Republicans. An organized effort addressing change, which directly attacked the county Republican Party, was initiated through a newspaper that had recently been transferred to Las Vegas: *La voz del pueblo.* This Spanish-language newspaper proved to be vital and especially effective in organizing the common people who resided on the Las Vegas land grant and in scattered settlements throughout the county.

La voz del pueblo had been established in Santa Fe during the early part of 1889 as a strong Democratic Party proponent for statehood. In the middle of 1890, however, E. H. Salazar, the owner of the newspaper, negotiated its transfer to Las Vegas. Salazar and his staff were convinced that the move was necessary in order for them—and the paper—to participate more actively and fully in New Mexico's diverse interests.[4] He continued as its administrator for about three years. Ownership eventually passed to Félix Martínez, a wealthy and prominent New Mexican who resided in Las Vegas. It is evident that the newspaper's transfer was planned as a political mechanism to publicize issues fermenting in San Miguel County and the rest of the territory. Salazar's parting words to his Santa Fe subscribers stressed that *La voz del pueblo* represented a people's army fighting for civil rights, and that due to an imminent major battle, they would be stationing their troops where they would have the most effect.[3]

The week after the newspaper was transferred to Las Vegas, Salazar greeted the people of San Miguel County with the first issue, informing them that the purpose of the newspaper would be to protect and defend New Mexico's interests in general and those of Las Vegas in particular. Salazar promised that the paper intended to do everything within its power to assist in the advancement and development of the native people. *La voz* also stated that it wanted to impress on the people's minds the need to awaken and break away, through energetic and legal means, from the oppressive situation they were in. The editor further stated that the newspaper did not move from Santa Fe because of a lack of support, but because of the business traffic and "political movement" that was becoming concentrated in San Miguel County. Many of the conflicts that were developing in San Miguel County were directly related to the vast land grants within its boundaries. The larger grants were the Las Vegas land grant, which was heavily populated, and the Beck, Ortiz, Antón Chico, Montoya, San Miguel del Bado, Pecos, Trigo, and Ojo del Apache land grants. There were also smaller grants within the county. Two of the larger grants had already been purchased by wealthy outsiders: the Beck grant was bought by Stoneroad Brothers and Dickinson, and the Montoya grant was purchased by a rich entrepreneur, Wilson Waddingham. The Montoya grant alone was thirty-six miles long and thirty miles wide and covered 800,000 acres.[5]

These Anglo outsiders and a few wealthy Hispanos who purchased many of the vast tracts of land established large cattle and sheep companies. San Miguel County surpassed all other sections of the territory in stock raising. The eastern section of the county, which extended to the Texas Panhandle, developed a large cattle industry soon after the Indian threat was quelled in 1882.[6] Hispanos and large cattle companies in San Miguel County consequently soon disagreed over fencing, boundaries, land titles, and water issues.

The main problem lay with the confusing status of the Las Vegas land grant, which contained 496,446 acres. The courts had not yet settled the title to it. Occupants of the grant were convinced that it was a "community grant" and that it should remain open to every *mercedario*, or legal heir, for grazing, wood, water, and other common needs.

Since about 1880, Anglo parties interested in ranching interests had been purchasing land from some of the heirs of the original colonists. Some of the Anglo purchases were small, but some were as large as 10,000 acres. These out-side settlers had their own concepts of land tenure, and they began to claim complete ownership. Furthermore, they fenced the land they claimed within the grant. A test case that challenged the claims of the original heirs was filed by a group of buyers and went to the courts in 1887. The Las Vegas Land and Cattle Company filed the lawsuit against José León Padilla and others, chal-lenging their claims of community inheritance. In October 1889, Chief Justice Long finally ruled in favor of Padilla and the other defendants. The ruling, which supported the rights of community land grantees and their descendants, inspired other occupants of the Las Vegas land grant to challenge outsiders who had purchased property within the grant.[7]

Land problems for New Mexicans had originated with the Ameri-can occupation and the Treaty of Guadalupe Hidalgo in 1848. During the ensuing years, Anglo-Americans—mostly lawyers and traders at the begin-ning—made major inroads into the territory. Lawyers, especially, were quick to note that under the Treaty of Guadalupe Hidalgo, they could gain vast wealth for themselves by securing the title to the land grants covering much of the territory.

By 1890 the Republican Party, which had dominated the politics of New Mexico for decades, was under attack from many Democrats and disillusioned party members. Land-grabbers in New Mexico were continuously under at-tack, and most of them were, in fact, Republicans. Some had already accu-mulated a large part of the 15 million acres of land within the land grants of the territory. The *Las Vegas Democrat* charged that some men had become ex-tremely influential, and that their greed and political ambition knew no bounds. It continued that those individuals controlled the territorial legisla-ture, the courts, and the political and economic affairs of many counties and municipalities.[8]

Many of the complaints of this period were directed at Republican leaders such as Thomas B. Catron and his friends, who allegedly formed the Santa Fe Ring, the epithet applied to Republican leaders who had organized the Republican Party in New Mexico in 1867. Catron, who received both notoriety and credit for leading the group, and his followers purchased or through other machinations assumed control of many of the land grants in New Mexico following the Civil War. They also controlled the politics of the territory.[9] During one protest in 1884, over two hundred Mexicanos and about twenty Anglos met in Santa Fe to denounce the alleged corrupt politics of the Santa Fe Ring. Eugenio Romero was among the prominent Las Vegans present at the meeting.[10]

That same year, one of the reporters from the *Las Vegas Daily Optic* asked Catron if there was such an organization as the Santa Fe Ring and whether he was associated with it. Catron, who complained that the *Optic* had brought him a lot of cheap notoriety during the past few years, allegedly told the reporter that "if there was such an organization as the Santa Fe Ring, he certainly belonged to it and was proud of it." The newspaper remarked that this was the closest the land "grabber" ever came to telling the truth.[11]

Miguel Antonio Otero, the San Miguel County District Court Clerk in 1890 and himself a Republican, corroborated many of the accusations directed at the party bosses. In later years, Otero recalled the politics of that period:

> At that, a justice of the peace could acknowledge deeds, mortgages, etc. and the "Ring" would elect their tools, picked and pliable men for such offices, in any precinct convenient and necessary for their nefarious practices. They also had a law passed, where, in case an original deed was lost, or had never been given, a certified copy might be used in proving title, with the same effect as would be the original. They would have deeds made out with forged signatures acknowledged by their justices of the peace, and recorded by the clerks, then destroyed and certified copies made.[12]

Whenever they secured titles to land grants, the alleged political thieves compounded their abuses by stretching the boundaries beyond those the Mexican government had intended. As a result, many community grants, such as that of Las Vegas, were invaded. The land-grabbers would then fence their own boundaries within these grants, thereby depriving the poor people who had lived on them for generations of the free use of grass, wood, and water on the public commons. These rights had been guaranteed by the Treaty of Guadalupe Hidalgo and confirmed by an act of Congress.[13]

In 1890, *La voz del pueblo* reported that the occupants of the Las Vegas Land Grant and other grants in the area could no longer tolerate the avarice of land speculators who continued to fence the countryside on common lands. It further stated that the "workingman, poor ranchers, and farmers" were diverting their concerns in the direction of continuing the organized social, political, and labor movement that had begun in 1889 with the emergence of the Gorras Blancas, or White Caps. The subsequent Moviemiento del Pueblo, or People's Movement, as it was called, emerged and blossomed as if it had been planned by a political mastermind.

As an organized group, the Gorras Blancas were probably the most secretive and closely knit association of men ever to exist in the territory of New Mexico. Their protest against the encroachment upon and theft of their lands began in 1889, and by the end of 1890, their notoriety had spread throughout the territory and reached the eastern states.

The majority of the families affected by land-grabbers were poor Hispanos with small landholdings whose limited economic means did not allow for litigation in the courts; consequently, they decided to employ the shortest and quickest means to alleviate their problems.[14] Las Gorras Blancas were organized early in April 1889 by Juan José Herrera and his younger brothers Pablo and Nicanor, with support from other poor people in the area of El Salitre, El Burro, Ojitos Fríos, and San Gerónimo. Eventually, all the settlements that fell within the boundaries of the Las Vegas land grant joined the organization.[15] Juan José was popularly referred to as "El Capitán" Herrera by the people of San Miguel County because he had been commissioned a captain with the Union forces during the Civil War. His father, Manuel, had been a soldier during the Mexican period and in the early 1850s during the territorial period.

Prior to the settling of Las Vegas and Tecolote, Manuel had patrolled the area with a small military squadron out of San Miguel del Bado. His assignment had been to protect livestock herders in the area and to escort Santa Fe Trail caravans as they approached San Miguel. After Las Vegas and Tecolote were settled, Manuel Herrera continued to maintain a small military outpost near Tecolote at a place called Plaza del Torreón. After the American occupation, Brigadier General Manuel Herrera headed seven companies of mounted militia and led organized campaigns against the Apache and Navajo Indians.[16]

"El Capitán" Juan José Herrera's military training served him well in organizing the Gorras Blancas in New Mexico. Sometime after the Civil War, Herrera left New Mexico to work as an Indian agent for the government in various states. At this time, he abandoned his first wife, Luisa Pinard, and spent time in Colorado, Wyoming, Kansas, Utah, and other states. By 1870, Juan José had returned and was living at Ojitos Fríos with his widowed mother and brothers. He was in the area in 1880 but apparently left New Mexico again, returning in 1888 to become actively involved in Las Vegas politics.[17]

During these intermittent jaunts away from New Mexico, Herrera learned English, French, and several Indian dialects very well. He also became familiar with political organizations, a labor organization called the Knights of Labor, and the struggles people faced in other parts of the United States. Herrera was aware not only of the militant activities of the White Caps in Illinois and the Midwest but also of a populist political movement and party that was gaining strength in the Midwest and eastern states—the People's Party. In 1888, Herrera became actively involved in helping F. A. Blake, editor of the *Las Vegas News,* and Anglo members of the Knights of Labor organize the People's Party in New Mexico.[18]

Soon after they established themselves in Las Vegas in 1886, the Knights of Labor drafted a resolution declaring that they wanted to align themselves with a few natives who knew English and Spanish equally well. Their intent was to establish lodges of the order for Spanish speakers as soon as the people were able to understand the principles and other workings of the organization.[19] A few weeks later, Mexicano laborers on the railroad vainly attempted to request better salaries from the Atchison, Topeka, and Santa Fe Railroad. They were told that their best recourse was to align themselves with the Knights of Labor so they could acquire bargaining power in seeking better working conditions and pay.[20]

Although the People's Party made a weak showing in the 1888 elections, Herrera retained a strong interest in a third political party that would address the needs of the poor people of San Miguel County. He also became one of the first Mexicanos to join the Knights of Labor, whose assemblies to this point had consisted mostly of Anglo members. On April 3, 1889, the *Las Vegas Daily Optic* carried an article on the destructive activities of the White Caps in Tuscola, Illinois. White Caps in that state had sent threatening letters to the members of a commission planning to construct an unpopular drainage canal in the area. Their warnings went unheeded, and soon afterward, a secret group of hooded night riders destroyed the barn and contents belonging to one of the commissioners, to the tune of $2,000 in losses. There were no clues "to the perpetrators of the dastardly work."[21] Twenty-three days later, the Gorras Blancas made their first appearance in San Miguel County. Masked riders destroyed four miles of new fenceline belonging to two Englishmen who were ranching near San Gerónimo. Fence posts were turned into kindling, and the barbed wire was cut into useless fragments.[22]

The Gorras Blancas did not discriminate in its attacks on those considered to be enemies. At the village of San Ignacio, riders attacked the farm and sawmill of José Ignacio Luján three different times during June and July of 1889, destroying his crops, fences, farm equipment, and sawmill.[23] Throughout 1889, these types of attacks continued on other fenced-in ranches of the land grant.

County Sheriff Lorenzo López had been serving warrants and indictments against members of the Gorras Blancas since early May 1889.[24] However, those individuals charged did not go to trial until much later, during the November term of the district court. On November 1, 1889, as the first trials approached, sixty-three Gorras Blancas rode into Las Vegas and surrounded the courthouse. Next they went to the home of District Attorney Miguel Salazar and finally to the county jail to show support for their fellow Gorras who were incarcerated.[25] When the Gorras Blancas threatened the jail, Sheriff López promptly sent a telegram to Governor L. Bradford Prince, requesting fifty rifles to defend the jail if the Gorras attempted to break their associates out.[26]

As soon as Governor Prince heard of the armed demonstration, fearing that the Gorras Blancas would carry out an assault on the jail he ordered Territorial Adjutant General E. W. Wyncoop to take fifty militia-type rifles and plenty of ammunition to Las Vegas.[27] An attack did not materialize, and on November 19, the first accused Gorra Blanca stood trial. Although it appeared that the evidence against him was very strong, the jury issued a verdict of not guilty. The prosecution subsequently dismissed the charges against the remaining twenty. The defendants had successfully argued in court that the charges were not related to Gorras Blancas activities; their problem had stemmed from a land dispute.[28]

During the last day of district court, twenty-six more indictments were handed down. They included forty-seven men who ranged in age from twenty to sixty-five years. Juan José Herrera and his brother Nicanor were among those indicted for fence cutting.[29] Judge E. V. Long probably averted an armed clash with the Gorras Blancas on that occasion when he lowered the bond from $500 to $250. Although the majority were poor individuals, they all somehow managed to post bond.[30] It is likely that wealthier individuals supporting the Gorras Blancas posted bond for them.

López himself became a victim of the Gorras Blancas. Following the destruction of A. N. Wright's fence near Fulton Station in early December 1889, the Gorras Blancas proceeded to López's ranch and destroyed eleven miles of fence line.[31] The attack on López may have been made because he had fenced in a large ranch and because he had been enforcing the warrants and indictments against the Gorras Blancas. Later, in 1890, López, who was a Republican Party boss in San Miguel County and was related to Juan José Herrera on his maternal Baca side, became a supporter of Herrera and the Knights of Labor.[32]

Throughout the winter of 1889 and 1890, the Gorras Blancas remained fairly active in their protests and actions. Immediate grievances and attacks had centered on the destruction of fences that restricted access to communal grazing and water on the land grant. Eventually their attacks spread to include haystacks, railroad bridges and ties, buildings, and crops. These highly secret, organized activities of the Gorras Blancas continued into 1891. They were carried out by several hundred armed and masked Mexicanos from Las Vegas and the many settlements and small ranches found throughout the land grant.[33]

Early in March 1890, about three hundred Gorras Blancas entered Old and New Town Las Vegas and posted copies in Spanish of anonymous leaflets announcing their "Platform and Principles." Although it was quite lengthy, the following major points were included in the manifesto:

- Our purpose will be to protect the rights of all people in general, and especially the rights of poor people.
- We want The Las Vegas Land Grant to be adjudicated in favor of all those it concerns, and we maintain that it belongs to all the people who reside within its boundaries.
- We want no more land thieves, or any obstructionists who might want to interfere. WE ARE WATCHING YOU.
- The people are now victims of partisan politics, and it would be best if politicians quietly maintain their peace; the people have been persecuted and mistreated in one thousand ways to satisfy the whims of politicians. They persist that their acts are customary. RETRIBUTION will be our reward.

Their platform was signed, "The White Caps, 1,500 Strong and Growing Daily." [34] It is likely that by this time the membership had in fact grown to over one thousand members.

The political adversaries of the Gorras Blancas retaliated against their platform by stating that the White Caps were attempting to intimidate the court system and peaceable citizens. One person complained that the Gorras Blancas did nothing more than scoff at and ridicule peace officers who already knew the White Caps were coming. The fearful officers, he stated, "ran and hid in their homes where they barricaded their windows with wool mattresses and other pieces of furniture to keep the White Caps from breaking in." The district attorney, Miguel Salazar, and the probate judge, Manuel C. de Baca, called them "revolutionaries," "anarchists," and "communists."[35]

In addition to their manifesto, the Gorras Blancas posted another notice throughout Las Vegas and in other strategic locations near the mountains. This one ordered the people not to cut lumber or railroad ties unless it was for a price approved by the White Caps. They also asked the people not to work for anyone unless the Gorras Blancas approved the work and the salaries they would be receiving. This notice was signed, "White Caps, Fence Cutters and Death."[36]

When district court convened for the spring term of 1890, all the accused fence cutters, including Juan José Herrera, presented themselves to honor their bonds. The three witnesses who had initiated the case against them, however, did not appear. The district attorney, Salazar, charged that the defendants had murdered the witnesses and wanted the trial postponed. The district judge, James O'Brien, finally ruled that the prosecution had no case without the witnesses, and charges against all forty-seven were dismissed. The Gorras Blancas and their families and friends then retreated to the plaza to speak about their victory, cheer, drink whiskey, and discharge their guns.[37]

Throughout the spring, the Gorras continued their nocturnal attacks on those they claimed as enemies. Eugenio Romero, a *jefe político*, wealthy merchant, and county assessor, soon became one of their targets. On one occasion, he claimed that they had destroyed 6,000 railroad ties he had contracted to the Santa Fe Railroad. In expressing their concern for the underpaid working man, the Gorras also destroyed and burned railroad bridges and tracks. Railroad workers were told to strike for higher wages, and timber cutters, who prepared railroad ties, were ordered to demand higher prices from the railroad.[38]

By July 1890, according to a letter submitted to the Secretary of the Interior, twenty-five acts of violence had been committed, hundreds of miles of fences cut, homes and haystacks sacked and burned, and agricultural implements broken and destroyed. Furthermore, railroad bridges and ties contracted for the railroad had been burned and destroyed. The letter also charged that people had been shot to death and many more had been wounded.[39] However, there is little evidence to support the statement that individuals had been killed by the White Caps.

During the early period of the Gorras Blancas' activities, public opinion both in favor of and against them grew. Eventually, however, public commentary increased in their favor. In June 1890, an article appeared in *La voz* commenting on the criminal charges that had been filed against the accused

Gorras Blancas and then dropped. The editors maintained the lack of a case proved that political enemies had accused those individuals of being Gorras Blancas, which they were not. But even if they were Gorras Blancas, they would not be society's enemies, *La voz* concluded.[40]

While the Gorras Blancas were gaining fame for their thunderous exploits across the countryside, Juan José Herrera and his brothers continued organizing the poor residents of the land grant and other communities in their struggle for survival. Their primary concerns centered on property rights and land titles. Others were concerned about their rights as members of the working class they had joined since the arrival of the railroad. Juan José, who had joined the Anglo-dominated Knights of Labor in 1888, was now seeking membership for the majority of those who had been labeled and accused of being Gorras Blancas. In Spanish, the Knights of Labor became the Caballeros del Trabajo, and as a labor party, it became a charter member of the national organization. The Knights were strong advocates of poor farmers, ranchers, and the working man, with most of their activities concentrated in the midwestern states.[41]

Their organizational efforts continued, and the Caballeros del Trabajo planned a large festive occasion for July 4, 1890, in Las Vegas. The members planned to announce their local organization and affiliation with the national labor group. As they prepared for their gala event, the Knights stated that for New Mexico's working population, the Fourth of July would also mark local independence from the social and political monopoly that had oppressed them. They would act as an independent body in addressing all public issues affecting the territory of New Mexico.[42]

La voz del pueblo supported the Knights of Labor in their efforts to expand their organization among the Mexicanos by expressing its opinion that the poor people of San Miguel County had the right to organize in order to protect their jobs and their families. The newspaper stated that for a long time the people had been oppressed by the despotic and extortive actions of their employers. Great pride was felt throughout the county as the Caballeros del Trabajo organized the masses of small ranchers and farmers, laborers, and farmworkers. The Caballeros were determined to challenge oppressive conditions and political dominance in San Miguel County and New Mexico.[43]

When the time of reckoning finally came for the San Miguel County working man, the events and celebration were regarded as the most colorful ever held in the territory, thanks to the enthusiasm demonstrated by the hundreds who attended. On the evening of July 3, the Caballeros del Trabajo celebrated vespers by parading through town on horseback, carrying torches to illuminate their resounding presence. The procession consisted of 1,000 proud men on horseback, two abreast, headed by a twenty-five-member string band playing Mexican music. The musicians were led by the public school teacher, organizer, and musician Jesús María Alarid.[44]

On the Fourth of July, the Caballeros del Trabajo again made their presence felt by holding a daytime procession through Las Vegas. One thousand men again paraded through town, led by County Sheriff Don Lorenzo López. This time, the men on horseback carried numerous banners and slogans in Spanish declaring their principles and objectives as an organization. Among them were "Free schools for our children"; "He who touches one of us answers to all"; "The villain who dares occupy a public position without being elected by the people shall be hanged"; "War against the public officials who don't account for their administration"; and "We seek protection for the worker against the monopolist." Throughout their procession the Caballeros' assuring cries were heard throughout Las Vegas: el pueblo es rey, y los oficiales públicos son Sus sirvientes humildes que deben obedecer Sus mandatos [the people are king, and public officials are her humble servants who must obey her mandates].[45]

Following the termination of the procession, everyone met at the Old Town Plaza, where Nestor Montoya, a Knight and one of La voz's editors, introduced the organization to the people. He was followed by Mayor Edward Henry from New Town, who welcomed the Caballeros del Trabajo and complimented them on their successful organizational efforts. Following a large barbecue given by the Caballeros, prominent citizens, including Governor Prince and members of the organization, delivered a series of speeches. Juan José, Pablo, and Nicanor Herrera were among the speakers who elucidated the purpose and goals of the Knights of Labor, their interests, and their desire to promote the order throughout the territory.[46]

After the celebration was over, the Knights of Labor worked assiduously day and night to perfect their territorial branch and pattern it after the model of the eastern and midwestern assemblies of the order. The grand master of the organization, T. V. Powderly, granted the San Miguel County organization a charter, which included rollbooks, by-laws, and all the accompanying paraphernalia.[47] Eventually, Juan José Herrera and his fellow Knights succeeded in establishing various assemblies throughout the territory and southern Colorado.[48]

As the ranks and assemblies of the Knights of Labor grew following the Fourth of July celebration, so did the activities and night rides of the Gorras Blancas. Due to these growing numbers of reported depredations and related complaints against the Gorras Blancas, Governor Prince was finally compelled to visit Las Vegas in August 1890 and personally inquire into the situation. Since the Caballeros del Trabajo were continuously accused of being associated with the Gorras Blancas, they sent a committee headed by Nestor Montoya of *La voz del pueblo* to speak with the governor and deny the accusations. They assured him of their good intentions and willingness to assist him in suppressing violence, fence cutting, and any other depredations by the Gorras Blancas.[49]

During his visit to Las Vegas, Governor Prince expressed the conviction that authorities and county residents should confront the issue and work to solve it together. He urged the Caballeros del Trabajo, for the preservation of their good name, to be the first in starting a movement for maintenance of law and order. He also issued a proclamation dated August 1, 1890, warning all the accused parties to discontinue their acts and called on the citizens to aid in the discovery of the criminals.[50] Governor Prince found many of the people in Las Vegas to be indifferent to the White Cap situation. He finally determined that half the people, including prominent citizens, were highly sympathetic to the fence-cutting activities that were taking place on the Las Vegas grant.[51]

Following Governor Prince's proclamation warning the people about "white capism," *La voz* reacted by saying that the proclamation should not have been limited to lawless fence-cutting elements in San Miguel County, but should also have applied to the lawless land-grabbers and speculators who were the primary cause of all the destruction and turmoil in the area. The editors of *La voz* also felt that many of the people's problems could be settled if a local court tribunal were established in New Mexico. Such a tribunal would do more to quell the disturbances and uprisings of the people than all the proclamations, rewards, and militia, which were not effective. The poor people did not want to be oppressed, and the grant owners wanted to secure titles to their lands.[52]

After Governor Prince left Las Vegas, the county commissioners called an open meeting, with the purpose of seeking ways and means to stop the state of agitation and lawlessness that existed in the county. Judge Booth explained why the meeting had been called and was then elected chairman. Nestor Montoya and Antonio Lucero, another *La voz* editor, acted as interpreters.[53]

Throughout the course of the meeting, the speakers urged the suppression and punishment of the perpetrators of lawless acts in the county. Others clamored for the "retrenchment and punishment of voracious, conscienceless land-grabbers and speculators, showing vividly that such class of cormorants were the main cause that led the people to defend their rights and withstand and punish their encroachments." The true sentiments of the people in the

meeting were plainly demonstrated by the enthusiasm they showed whenever the punishment of land-grabbers and speculators was mentioned by the
speakers.[54]

La voz del pueblo further reported that the people were not satisfied with
the one-sided measures that were being proposed to suppress the state of affairs in the county. The editors felt that the governor should also try, by
proclamations and other means within his power, to suppress the ruthless ap-
propriation of people's lands, whether grants or government property, and also
to guarantee their rights and privileges to wood, water, and grazing grounds.[55]

One of the speakers at the meeting declared forcefully that at the rate
fencing on the land grant was going on, the people had but one of two choices:
either cut the fences or sprout wings and fly over them. A motion was then
made that Judge Booth appoint a committee of seven citizens to devise some
plan to try to suppress the existing lawlessness and bring the guilty to justice.
Many of the people opposed the judge's committee and instead wanted the
members elected. The judge, however, commenced to appoint the committee
against the people's demands. This action resulted in a wild uproar, and the
people stormed from the building where the meeting was being held.[56]

During the same week, the Caballeros del Trabajo issued a long communiqué to Grand Master T. V. Powderly, referring to the insinuations that
they were encouraging lawless destruction of property. They mentioned that
all such charges were entirely false and without the slightest foundation in
fact. They did admit that they opposed Thomas Catron, Benjamin F. Butler,
and other political bosses who "entrench themselves behind technical forms
of law, in the possession of vast tracts of land, embraced in some of our community and colony grants, [and we have] taken a stand against clandestine and
violent resistance on the part of individuals, to the lawless and tyrannical ag-
gressions of these community land thieves and public corruptionists." [57]

Anglo members of the Knights of Labor who were visibly upset at Gorras Blancas attacks on Anglo and other properties also wrote to Powderly.
They protested the violence and destruction and stated that the ranks of the
Knights of Labor were now being increased tremendously by ignorant Mexicans.[58] The Las Vegas Daily Optic, although at times sympathetic with the complaints of the occupants of the Las Vegas land grant, also complained that the
Gorras Blancas had been recruited from the ignorant classes.[59]

Negative comments by the Optic and Anglo members of the Knights
about the "ignorant Mexicans" carried racial overtones and probably only exacerbated the hostility native Mexicanos held for those outsiders who were
taking over their lands. Although many of the natives had little or no formal

education, their values and historical experience had centered for generations on protecting their land from Indians and from outside encroachments after the arrival of the Santa Fe Trail. In these situations, the people knew that their property, survival, and livelihood were threatened should they yield. They were well aware that the long history of encroachments and threats against them were life-and-death situations. They had never been submissive, much less ignorant.

Within two months after the Caballeros del Trabajo had successfully organized and established their order, the impetus of the Movimiento was diverted to organize a new political party for San Miguel County, El Partido del Pueblo Unido, or the United People's Party. Patterned after the national People's Party, El Partido made a feeble showing in 1886 but finally began to gain some momentum in San Miguel County in 1888. El Partido del Pueblo Unido's philosophy and objectives in 1890 were in complete harmony with those of the Caballeros del Trabajo. However, as a populist party, El Partido included all concerned residents, regardless of party affiliation, who were seeking changes in county and territorial government.[60]

As the party's official mouthpiece, the editors of *La voz del pueblo* introduced it to the community by stating that it was forming due to the cry of discontent that had engulfed San Miguel County and the land grant, and because of the many abuses committed against the people. Hoping to address the wishes of the people, the organizing committee for the Partido called for one delegate from each of the county's sixty-three precincts to meet on September 8, 1890, to form a central committee. The committee would then officially form the Partido del Pueblo Unido, with each appointed precinct representative serving as a party delegate.[61]

The organizing committee that announced the coming of the new party was integrated by many influential residents and representatives from the settlements on the land grant. Prominent Anglos and merchants such as T. B. Mills, F. A. Blake, Lewis Lutz, and H. M. Loeb were also involved. The organizers mentioned that the new party would be composed of factions torn from the old, established Democratic and Republican parties. The new party would represent the working classes—laborers, farmers, mechanics, and ranchmen. These were people who had decided to bring about a determined and radical change in the management of public offices and county affairs. They called on all who were tired of the monopolistic regime of distributing public offices to challenge the county politicians who had existed for the benefit, gain, and ambition of a few privileged families.[62]

La voz stated that the people organized themselves to form the Partido del Pueblo Unido, steering their own political machine without the aid or counsel of any of the old parties. It continued that the Movimiento del Pueblo was assisted by many fair-minded and honorable citizens as an act of justice toward the masses of the people who were striving to overthrow peonage and servitude under political hacks and arrogant rich who believed that the people would be treated as simple tools to comply with their own wishes and demands.[63]

On September 4, the organizers of the Partido del Pueblo Unido and the sixty-three precinct representatives met at the courthouse to form the executive central committee. T. B. Mills was elected president, and Nestor Montoya, secretary. The other officers were Félix Martínez, a businessman and the owner of *La voz*; Juan Gallegos; Enrique H. Salazar, also from *La voz*; and Manuel Silva. The central committee then asked county residents to be present at the courthouse on the following Monday to attend the county convention and select their public servants for the ensuing two years. They stated that it would do a free man's heart good to witness, for the first time in the history of the county, the absence of political bosses and tools in the selection of a county ticket.[64]

When the day for the county convention finally arrived, weary travelers came from all parts of the county. Some had traveled on horseback or buggy from as far as 300 miles away, with one thing in mind: carrying out the defeat of the aristocrats. When the convention convened, there were over 1,500 people seated and standing in the great judicial hall of the courthouse, with many more surrounding the park, unable to gain entrance.[65]

Mills and Montoya delivered speeches that reinforced the purpose of the new party. They asked the people to remain objective and dispassionate while choosing their ticket. Félix Martínez was chosen chairman of the convention and was ably assisted by Juan José and his brothers in consolidating the purpose and harmony of the party and coordinating the selection of the new county ticket.[66]

The first county ticket, with candidates nominated as the free choice of the Partido del Pueblo Unido, was: probate judge, Dionicio Martínez; county commissioners, John Shank, José Montoya, and Antonio Montoya; probate clerk, Rox Hardy; assessor, Nepomuceno Segura; sheriff, José L. López (Lorenzo's son); superintendent of public schools, Charles F. Rudolph; treasurer, Jesús María Tafoya; territorial representatives, Félix García, Pablo Aragón, Pablo Herrera, and Nestor Montoya; and territorial councilmen, T. B. Mills, Hermerejildo Vigil, and Colonel José Valdez.[67]

The Partido del Pueblo Unido platform was also quickly developed during the three-day convention. The platform echoed many issues and concerns voiced by the White Caps and the Knights of Labor in their respective circulars and platforms. Among the stronger concerns expressed was their desire to demand that New Mexico's territorial delegate in Congress use all means possible to get a law passed that would secure the settlement of land titles in the territory in accordance with the Treaty of Guadalupe Hidalgo. They also demanded a uniform system of public schools that would require children to attend nine months out of the year. Additionally, they demanded a speedy settlement of the Las Vegas land grant issue and asked that it be resolved in accordance with the colonization laws of Mexico, under which law the grant was conceded.[68]

One last point in their platform was the condemnation of the legislature for refusing to enact legislation that would have secured an efficient public school system for the territory. They felt that the last legislature's defeat of a bill that would have established such a school system was a manifestation of hostility toward public education. The defeated bill was the Perkins Bill, which, to provide an educational school system for the children of the masses, required the taxation of large landowners.[69]

El Partido del Pueblo Unido needed to do little campaigning for November 7, 1890, since the People's Movement had been fomenting for months and everyone in the county was anxiously awaiting election day. The primary movers of the new party had been primarily Democrats, and their ranks had been augmented by many frustrated Republicans who were leaving their party. Many complained that they were unable to tolerate the party bosses any longer. Numerous letters from former Republicans who were openly voicing their total lack of confidence in the Republican Party appeared in La voz. Not surprisingly, they stated vigorously that they were willing and ready to support the new People's Party.[70]

El Partido emerged a resounding victor in the 1890 November elections, and the new party would figure as a strong representative for San Miguel County residents for years to come. Following the newly formed pattern of celebration and victory in county politics, the Partido gathered in another large public demonstration. Juan José Herrera and six marshals led 500 men on horseback through town in another nighttime procession. They wielded burning torches and flags and yelled as they rode through town, "¡Qué viva el Partido del Pueblo Unido en el Condado de San Miguel!" (long live the United People's Party in San Miguel County).[71]

Members of the victorious People's Party stressed that the people no longer had to worry about the devilish machinations of the bosses, or amos, of the Republican Party in San Miguel and other counties in the territory. Following the victory of the Partido del Pueblo Unido, newspapers throughout New Mexico associated them with the Gorras Blancas and the Caballeros del

Trabajo, usually stating that all three were one and the same. The *Santa Fe New Mexican* connected the Caballeros del Trabajo and the Gorras Blancas as one group controlled by Democratic Party scheming.[72]

Another Republican newspaper and political rival of the Gorras Blancas and Caballeros del Trabajo was also convinced the three organizations and their membership formed one social and political movement. Just prior to the November election, one of the newspaper's editors stated, "I have come to the conclusion that the only issue is whether the law-abiding citizen will vote for the maintenance of the law or whether they will endorse lawlessness; for no one can deny that the so-called White Caps—alias Knights of Labor, alias People's Party—[are responsible] for the depredations that have been committed in this county this past year."[73]

After the initial victory of El Partido del Pueblo Unido had passed, one newspaper reported that the ghost of the Republican Party was all that remained of the political battle. A political ally of *La voz*, the *Albuquerque Democrat*, lauded the success of the Partido del Pueblo Unido in a strong, scathing statement leveled against the Republicans:

> Out of all the surprises that were in store for the Republican Party, the County of San Miguel was a paralyzer. For many years that County has been controlled by the political parasites who make their headquarters of operation in the capital of the Territory. The Republican ticket of San Miguel County which met with just defeat was under absolute control of the Republican land ring of Santa Fe. They owned and controlled the Republican leaders of San Miguel County.[74]

The problems centering on the Las Vegas grant and other grants in New Mexico created such fierce agitation that the people of San Miguel County had no recourse but to organize themselves to protect their rights. The People's Movement had such a resounding impact that on March 3, 1891, Congress created a court known as the United States Court of Private Land Claims for the purpose of determining and adjusting land claims in the territories that were acquired from Mexico. The United States was bound to recognize and confirm those land claims within the territories of Colorado, New Mexico, Nevada, Utah, Arizona, and Wyoming under the stipulations of the Treaty of Guadalupe Hidalgo and the treaty of 1853 known as the Gadsden Purchase. Those claims that could not be settled in the Court of Private Land Claims could be appealed to the United States Supreme Court.[75]

Much credit is due the courage and determined efforts of the hundreds of San Miguel County citizens who joined ranks in a common cause while seeking justice. The different people's groups were all well organized and closely knit, and their large numbers presented such a menacing force that no one dared speak against them. Many of them were also affiliated with the secret religious order of the Penitentes, which also contributed greatly to the difficulty of convicting any of the Gorras Blancas. In one instance, Severino Trujillo of Guadalupita wrote to Governor Prince, directly blaming the Penitentes in his community for the damages and losses he suffered in attacks by the Gorras Blancas.[76] In many communities it was reported that the Penitentes were in political control, and owing to their strength, it was impossible to gain convictions against their members. One critic of the Penitentes complained that the order found it easy to gain control of both the petit and grand juries in San Miguel County.[77]

The mystery remains as to whether the Movimiento del Pueblo was part of a master plan of Juan José Herrera and other Democratic leaders to organize the people of San Miguel County, or whether it simply unfolded and grew as a result of the collective efforts of various individuals who addressed different societal concerns. Others, of course, participated in the movement for political reasons as they sought to gain power and influence.

Juan José Herrera was the prime mover and organizer of the various protest, social, and labor organizations that constituted the People's Movement, but other individuals, such as Félix Martínez and Sheriff Lorenzo López, also played major roles in the movement of 1890 and in San Miguel County politics throughout the 1890s. A wealthy realtor and businessman, Martínez acquired ownership of *La voz del pueblo* and effectively used the newspaper to organize the people and address the multiple concerns they faced at the time. Later, in the election of 1892, Martínez ran on the Partido del Pueblo ticket and was elected to serve on the territorial council.[78]

Lorenzo López, on the other hand, wielded so much power and influence over the people that he was called *el amo de los pobres*, the poor people's lord or overseer. He was known for his generosity to the poor people of San Miguel County. Politically, López was formidable and had been appointed and elected to various political posts since 1861, when he was named Inspector General of New Mexico's Second Militia by Governor Henry Connelly.[79] During the political and social upheaval of 1890, his son José was elected county sheriff, and in 1892, Lorenzo succeeded his son to serve as sheriff one more time. Early in 1907, one historian stated that

> Lorenzo López, one of the shrewdest native politicians did much to incite the ignorant classes to a show of rebellion against constituted au-

thority. To further his ends he joined the *Penitentes*, hoping thereby to gain their inalienable support. Many of these he persuaded to commit depredations to annoy and excite the Americans and peaceable Mexicans.[80]

The protest activities of Las Gorras Blancas as an organized movement subsided by the end of 1891. Politically, however, residents on the land grant continued to be very active through the end of the decade and into the early twentieth century. It is important to note that the occupants of the land grant rose in a collective effort to address multiple issues that threatened their survival on the community land grant on which they had settled many years before. The land grant issue in New Mexico is currently being rekindled by activists, on the eve of the 150th anniversary of ratification of the Treaty of Guadalupe Hidalgo. Many of these individuals participated in New Mexico's land grant struggle of the 1960s while they were but teenagers. It is their intent and hope that the United States Congress might once again review the blatant abuse and disregard of people's land rights that occurred during the late 1800s and early part of the twentieth century.

NOTES

1. T. B. Mills, "San Miguel County: A County Big Enough for a State," *Mill's Investor's Review* 1 (Oct. 1887): 1; *Revista católica* 8 (1882): 414–15; Anselmo F. Arellano and Julián Josué Vigil, *Las Vegas Grandes on the Gallinas* (Las Vegas, N.M.: Editorial Telaraña, 1985), 97. This census enumerates the number of inhabitants living in each of the voting precincts.
2. *La voz del pueblo*, Feb. 15, 1890.
3. Ibid., June 7, 1890.
4. Ibid., June 14, 1890.
5. T. B. Mills, *San Miguel County: Health, Wealth, Resources, and Advantages* (Las Vegas, N.M.: J. A. Carruth, Printer and Binder, 1885), 32. Some of the real estate brokers such as Mills also contributed to the problems of the county through their periodicals by encouraging outsiders to come in and settle. Besides the small book mentioned herein, Mills published a real estate periodical that had a circulation of 10,000. In it, Mills wrote that many of the farmlands along the streams were occupied by natives who were nonetheless willing to sell their small holdings for reasonable amounts. Consequently, outsiders were able to secure tracts of land already under ditch at cheap rates; see *Mill's Investor's Review*, Oct. 20, 1887.
6. Mills, *San Miguel County*, 25.
7. "Philip Millhiser et al. vs. José León Padilla et al.," E. V. Long Papers, New

Mexico State Records Center and Archives (NMSRCA), Santa Fe. The complete court transcript of this case can be found in this collection.

8. *Las Vegas Democrat*, Aug. 18, 1890. This issue of the newspaper contained a long article, "The Knights of Labor Send a Communication to Powderly," signed by José Valdez, Master Workman. The Knights became a major political force during this time, as will be related further on. Attacks on the Republican Party were especially pronounced in this article.

9. Victor Westphall, *Thomas Benton Catron and His Era* (Tucson: University of Arizona Press, 1973), 71, 97. Catron owned or had an interest in thirty-four land grants. At one time or another, he owned over 3 million acres of land in various New Mexico grants.

10. *Las Vegas Daily Gazette*, Mar. 8, 1884.

11. *Las Vegas Daily Optic*, Mar. 7, 1884.

12. Miguel A. Otero, *My Life on the Frontier, 1882–1897*, 2 vols. (Albuquerque: University of New Mexico Press, 1939), 2:229.

13. *Las Vegas Democrat*, Aug. 18, 1890.

14. *La voz del pueblo*, Aug. 9, 1890.

15. Rosa Herrera de McAdams, interview by author, Oct. 29, 1980. While the media and politicians of the period pointed an accusing finger at Juan José Herrera for being the organizer and leader of the White Caps, he always denied it publicly. In an interview with his daughter in 1980, the writer was assured that Juan José did indeed organize the Gorras Blancas. Rosa Herrera de McAdams, who was ninety-two years old at the time, stated that her father had been the organizer and leader of the White Caps about a year after she was born. When she was young, she said, people called her Rosita la Gorra Blanca. See transcript of the interview in Anselmo F. Arellano and Julián Josué Vigil, *Las Vegas Grandes on the Gallinas: 1835–1985* (Las Vegas: Editorial Telaraña, 1985), 103–9. Rosa Herrera De McAdams passed away on Aug. 15, 1981. See *Las Vegas Daily Optic*, Aug. 16, 1981.

16. The Territorial Archives of New Mexico (TANM), reel 87, frames 005–174, NMSRCA. This reel contains reports on the campaign activities of the military companies commanded by General Manuel Herrera; 1838 census, Plaza del Torreón, collected and transcribed from the Mexican Archives of New Mexico (MANM), NMSRCA, by Malcolm Ebright.

17. United States census, San Miguel County, 1870. Juan José appears in his mother's household in 1870, and his occupation is listed as "freighter." His father Manuel was still alive and fifty-eight years old in 1860. The family lived at El Salitre, about eight miles from Las Vegas. See U.S. census, San Miguel County, 1860. In 1866, Juan José left his wife, Luisa Pinard, who may have been the daughter of Juan Casimiro Pinard and María Touvere, who came from France and settled at La Cueva, Mora County, prior to 1860. See Mora County census, La Cueva precinct, 1860. See also the *Las Vegas Daily Optic*, Apr. 9, 1890. The Aug. 24, 1867, issue of the *Santa Fe Weekly Gazette* carried a short verse about Juan José that directly implies that he abandoned his

wife. "No te juntes con Herrera, / Que avandonó a la Francesa, / Porque es hombre muy cualquiera, / Esta es la pura certeza" (do not associate with Herrera, / because he abandoned the French lady, / because he is just an ordinary man, / this is pure certainty). Again, on Sept. 3, 1891, *El sol de mayo*, the newspaper established by Manuel C. de Baca and Eugenio Romero to rival *La voz del pueblo*, Herrera, and the Gorras Blancas, published a similar poem attacking him and alluding to his French wife. "¡¡¡Al gran Capitán Herrera!!! / No le aduléis con bajeza, / Porque es el mismo cualquiera, / Que abandonó a la Francesa" (to the Great Captain Herrera! / do not flatter him with such low regard, / because he is the same nobody, / who abandoned the French lady). Apparently, this verse and jocular criticism stayed with Herrera for a long time; Miguel Antonio Otero, *My Life on the Frontier, 1864–1882* (New York: Press of the Pioneers, 1935), 223. Otero and others visited Juan José Herrera in 1880 while they were speculating for gold and other minerals near Mineral Hill and San Gerónimo. Otero referred to him as "Juan José Herrera, a good friend."

18. In 1891, Manuel C. de Baca and his first cousin, Eugenio Romero, founded a newspaper, *El sol de mayo*, in Las Vegas. Manuel was an attorney and a highly literate writer, while Romero was a wealthy businessman, who probably provided the capital to initiate the newspaper. C. de Baca and Romero were also members of Los Caballeros de Protección Mutua, which was a counter-organization to the White Caps and other groups organized by Herrera. On Feb. 18, 1892, *El sol de mayo* commenced publishing a narrative on the Gorras Blancas in a series of articles. The narrative appears in prose, and the author is never mentioned. However, it is evident that Manuel C. de Baca, as the principal editor, was also the author. Juan José Herrera is referred to as "El Gran Capitán" in the narrative, and some of Herrera's history and related activities are taken from it. Manuel C. de Baca is known for his *Vicente Silva: sus cuarenta bandidos, sus crímenes y retribuciones* (Las Vegas: Spanish American Printing Co., 1896). In 1886, support for a People's Party in San Miguel County was being promoted ardently by Louis Hommell, a German who had immigrated to the United States in 1848. Hommell had established the *Las Vegas Gazette* in 1872 and was now editor of the *Las Vegas Chronicle*. A colorful and interesting figure, Hommell had joined many patriotic and popular causes; they included fighting the Seminole Indians in Florida in 1856, marching against the Mormons in 1858, joining the Union cause during the Civil War, and even fighting in Benito Juárez's independence movement against the French in Mexico. In 1886 he fought what he considered to be the abuses of the Santa Fe Ring and the Republican Party. See the *Las Vegas Chronicle*, May 20, 1886.

19. *Las Vegas Chronicle*, Mar. 18, 1886.

20. Ibid., June 17, 1886.

21. *Las Vegas Daily Optic*, Apr. 3, 1889.

22. District Attorney Miguel Salazar to Gov. L. Bradford Prince, Aug. 3, 1889, Governor L. Bradford Prince Papers, NMSRCA, Santa Fe (hereafter referred to as Prince Papers). Several articles, papers, studies, and a dissertation have covered the social and political movement that engulfed San Miguel County in 1889 and 1890. They

all focus on and highlight certain aspects of the White Caps, the Knights of Labor, and the United People's Party as they primarily involved and concerned the people of San Miguel County and, to a lesser extent, other citizens of New Mexico. Most of these studies appeared during the 1970s. The writer first became interested in the White Caps as a student in 1968. See Anselmo F. Arellano, "The White Caps of San Miguel County" (student paper, New Mexico Highlands University, 1968). The most comprehensive published work on the White Caps and protest movement appears in Robert J. Rosenbaum, *Mexicano Resistance in the Southwest: "The Sacred Right of Self-Preservation"* (Austin: University of Texas Press, 1981). A related book that concentrates on the populist party politics during that era of the territorial period is Robert W. Larson, *New Mexico Populism: A Study of Radical Protest in a Western Territory* (Boulder: Colorado Associated University Press, 1974). This chapter will discuss the social protest movement, which reached its apex among the residents of the land grant and county in 1890. It is presented from the primary sources of the time, as events and circumstances were expressed by the individuals who lived and forged that unique segment of New Mexico's colorful history.

23. José Luján to Gov. L. Bradford Prince, July 25, 1890, Prince Papers.

24. Miguel A. Otero, court clerk to Gov. L. Bradford Prince, Aug. 9, 1890, Prince Papers.

25. *Las Vegas Daily Optic*, Nov. 2, 1889.

26. Lorenzo López to Gov. L. Bradford Prince, Dec. 11, 1889, Prince Papers.

27. *La voz del pueblo*, Dec. 14, 1889.

28. *Las Vegas Daily Optic*, Nov. 25, 1889.

29. Ibid.

30. Miguel A. Otero, Clerk of the 4th Judicial District, to Gov. L. Bradford Prince, Aug. 9, 1890.

31. *La voz*, Dec. 14, 1889.

32. Herrera de McAdams, interview. In her oral interview, Herrera de McAdams revealed many of the familial affinities among the Herreras, Romeros, Delgados, Bacas, Ulibarrís, and C. de Bacas. In addition to bloodlines, many of the relationships involved *compadrazgo*, or godparenting. When Sheriff López's daughters and son married, Juan José Herrera and his wife were among the honored guests. Herrera was López's first cousin on his mother's side. See *La voz del pueblo*, Apr. 11 and 18, 1891. It is consequently easy to see the close relationship between López, Herrera, the Knights of Labor, and the subsequent Partido del Pueblo Unido.

33. *La voz del pueblo*, July 26, 1890.

34. *El sol de mayo*, Feb. 18–Mar. 17, 1892. The platform contained in this narrative is identical to the one they posted. See Prince Papers; see also *La voz del pueblo*, Mar. 22, 1890.

35. *El sol de mayo*, Feb. 18, 1892; District Attorney Miguel Salazar to Gov. L. Bradford Prince, July 23, 1890.

36. *La voz del pueblo*, Mar. 29, 1890.

37. *Las Vegas Daily Optic*, May 20, 1890; District Attorney Miguel Salazar to Gov. L. Bradford Prince, July 23, 1890, Prince Papers.

38. *Las Vegas Daily Optic*, Mar. 7, 1890; O. D. Barrett, "Report to General Butler," June 26, 1890, Prince Papers.

39. *La voz del pueblo*, July 26, 1890.

40. Ibid., June 14, 1890.

41. Ibid. For a discussion of the Knights of Labor, see the autobiography of their National Grand Master Workman: Terrance V. Powderly, *The Path I Trod*, ed. Harry J. Carman, Henry David, and Paul N. Gutherie (New York: Columbia University Press, 1940).

42. *La voz del pueblo*, June 21, 1890.

43. Ibid., July 5, 1890.

44. Ibid., July 12, 1890. Jesús María H. Alarid was a well-known teacher and musician who helped organize the Gorras Blancas and Knights of Labor in the Santa Fe area. From Galisteo, he taught in different New Mexico communities and was very active in the politics of Santa Fe and San Miguel Counties. Following the Civil War, he served as New Mexico Territorial Librarian under Gov. Henry Connelly. See the 1890 and 1891 issues of *El nuevo mexicano*, the *Santa Fe New Mexican's* Spanish counterpart.

45. *La voz del pueblo*, July 12, 1890.

46. Ibid.; *Las Vegas Daily Optic*, July 5, 1890.

47. *La voz del pueblo*, July 12, 1890.

48. Ibid., August 30, 1890. The Herreras, Jesús Alarid, Sheriff Lorenzo López, and his son, José L. López, who became county sheriff in 1891, were the most active organizers of the Knights of Labor through 1892. López and his son were especially active in the northern counties of Río Arriba and Taos as well as in southern Colorado. See *La voz del pueblo*, Jan. 23, Feb. 13, 1892.

49. Ibid., Aug. 9, 1890; *Las Vegas Daily Optic*, Aug. 12, 1890.

50. *Las Vegas Daily Optic*, Aug. 12, 1890.

51. Gov. L. Bradford Prince to Secretary of the Interior John W. Noble, Aug. 20, 1890, Prince Papers.

52. *La voz del pueblo*, Aug. 16 and Aug. 23, 1890.

53. Ibid.

54. Ibid.

55. Ibid.

56. Ibid.

57. *La voz del pueblo*, Aug. 8, 1890; *Las Vegas Democrat*, Aug. 18, 1890. This Las Vegas newspaper printed the complete text of Master Workman José Valdez's letter to Terrance V. Powderly, National Grand Master Workman.

58. Frank C. Ogden and John K. Martin and J. B. Allen to Terrence V. Powderly, National Grand Master Workman, Aug. 8, 1890, Prince Papers.

59. *Las Vegas Daily Optic*, Dec. 13, 1890.

60. *La voz del pueblo*, Aug. 30, 1890.

61. Ibid.
62. Ibid.
63. Ibid.
64. Ibid., Sept. 13, 1890.
65. Ibid.
66. Ibid.
67. Ibid.
68. Ibid.
69. Ibid.
70. Ibid.
71. Ibid.
72. Ibid.
73. *La cachiporrita del condado de San Miguel,* Oct. 18, 1890.
74. *Albuquerque Democrat,* as quoted in *La voz del pueblo,* Nov. 22, 1890.
75. George Anderson, *History of New Mexico,* 3 vols. (Los Angeles: Pacific States Publishing Co., 1907), 1:200; Also see Charles F. Coan, *A History of New Mexico,* 3 vols. (New York: American Historical Society, 1925), 1:476.
76. Severino Trujillo to Gov. L. Bradford Prince, Aug. 19, 1890. Penitente involvement in the People's Movement adds another dimension to the clandestine nature of the closely knit group of residents who rose in protest. For additional information on Penitente activity during the era of the People's Movement, see Marta Weigle, *Brothers of Light, Brothers of Blood: The Penitentes of the Southwest* (Albuquerque: University of New Mexico Press, 1976), 86–90.
77. Anderson, *History of New Mexico,* 1:521–22.
78. Anselmo F. Arellano, "Honorable Don Félix Martínez Made Highlands University Possible," *La Mecha* [New Mexico Highlands University student newspaper], Jan. 24, Jan. 31, 1977; Anselmo F. Arellano, "Father of the Normal University," *Southwest Wind: A Magazine of New Mexico Highlands University Arts* 1, no. 1 (Winter 1977), 30-48.
79. Anselmo F. Arellano, "Don Ezequiel C. de Baca and the Politics of San Miguel County" (master's thesis, New Mexico Highlands University, 1974), 135–36.
80. Anderson, *History of New Mexico,* 1:521–22.

Part II
The Twentieth Century: Overview

Nuevomexicanos entered the twentieth century with a strong sense of place and cultural identity. The Spanish-language newspaper industry continued to thrive and was instrumental in fostering the cultural scene by providing a space for the publication of creative literature. More important, newspapers provided a forum for projecting political agendas that promoted the interests of the Nuevomexicano community. Certain dominant themes, among them politics, class contradictions, labor conflict and organization, demographic changes, cultural perseverance, and the pursuit of civil rights stand out in the period immediately before and after statehood.[1] The specificity of these trends in their regional context makes up the essence of the Nuevomexicano modern experience.

Activities surrounding the struggle for statehood demonstrate that despite significant land loss, violence, and discrimination directed at Nuevomexicanos in the nineteenth century, the upper class remained powerful, affluent, and politically influential. Through alliances, arranged marriages, and smart political maneuvering, Nuevomexicanos remained entrenched. Economically, these Nuevomexicanos maintained their privileged role. They owned land and businesses, and they were professionals in critical positions. At the constitutional convention of 1910, for example, thirty-three of the 100 delegates were Nuevomexicanos, and their presence left its mark on the state constitution. This is particularly evident in the bill of rights, which alluded specifically to the Treaty of Guadalupe Hidalgo as the underlying justification for guaranteeing Nuevomexicanos their full measure of civil rights. Another significant article included in the constitution called for the printing of all official documents in both Spanish and English. This article was in effect until the 1950s, at which time it was eliminated through application of the sunset rule.

The election of Ezequiel C. de Baca as the second governor of the state and of Octaviano Larrazolo to the same office in 1918 further attests to the strong political position of Nuevomexicanos at that juncture. Though relegated to virtual erasure from communal memory, Larrazolo was a fascinating individual. A native of Mexico, he remained an outspoken and faithful defender of the Nuevomexicano population, frequently eliciting complaints from both Anglos and Nuevomexicanos for "fanning the race question." It was in this period that Nuevomexicanas also began to emerge as political leaders. Nina Otero Warren is an exemplary case, having been the first woman in the state to run for the United States Congress. Though her bid on the Republican ticket was unsuccessful, she was subsequently elected assistant superintendent of Santa Fe schools, a position to which she had previously been appointed. Other Nuevomexicanas eventually entered politics and were elected to positions on school boards, county treasuries, state offices, and the state legislature. In short, one cannot overemphasize the fact that the political position of Nuevomexicanos was unique, making their status and development different from those of Chicano communities in other regions of the United States.[2]

After statehood was granted in 1912, Nuevomexicanos and Nuevomexicanas were in a good position to enjoy the fruits of their new civil status and simultaneously to demand a legitimate, official space for preservation of their culture. However, numerous pressures intervened, forcing Nuevomexicanos to play down their struggle for cultural hegemony. Fears that the Mexican Revolution would destabilize the border, coupled with the exuberant Americanizing agenda linked to World War I, forced Nuevomexicanos to toe the line labeled "national loyalty." One decade after statehood, a decline in the Spanish-language press was readily apparent. The resolve, so prevalent at the close of the nineteenth century, to give Spanish official standing in public education turned to dust, and the arrival of eastern writers, who took it upon themselves to play the role of ventriloquists, speaking for and about native peoples, and the pressure they brought to bear on the demise of Spanish had an inexorable silencing effect on Nuevomexicano and Nuevomexicana writers. One such influential eastern writer was not timid about stating her position up front: "I regret very much," wrote Mary Austin in 1931, "that the Spanish language must go. There is no economic value in writing in Spanish and where talent exists it should be developed by writing in English, about things Spanish if possible . . . Spanish customs, life, language, history . . . anything."[3]

A few who had mastered the "master's" language dared to write, but they did so self-consciously, as is apparent in the following statement by Cleofas Jaramillo: "This quiet romance I will try to describe in the following pages of my autobiography, although I feel an appalling shortage of words, not being a writer, and writing in a language almost foreign to me."[4]

Jaramillo was joined by Fray Angélico Chávez, Nina Otero Warren, and Fabiola C. de Baca, whose writings, at least on the surface, seem to explain or translate local culture for the Americanos. But as Genaro Padilla and Diana Rebolledo have shown, their texts contain the encoded traces of cultural resistance that would form a backdrop for the more self-consciously contestatory Chicano and Chicana literature of the 1970s and 1980s.

Despite the disappearance of the written record of creative literature, the oral genres continued to thrive and to represent a robust medium for expression of self-determination and resistance to assimilation. It is in this oral tradition that communal expressive wealth and the native language would be stored and preserved.[5] Likewise, religious folk practices such as the cult related to *santo* worship never wavered, though the persecution of the Penitentes by the Catholic hierarchy was to force the brotherhood underground, as native peoples' religion had been forced underground under Spanish rule. And as was the case with native religions, persecution strengthened the people's desire to persevere.

Beginning in 1925, initiatives sponsored by the Spanish Colonial Arts Society, an organization committed to the preservation of traditional Spanish arts, played an important role in expanding the production of Hispanic arts and crafts. We must acknowledge the positive influence of Anglo-American artists such as Mary Austin and Frank Applegate in encouraging local crafts-men to revive the dwindling artistic traditions (the carving of religious icons, the construction of colonial furniture, weaving, embroidery of *colchas,* and dec-orative tinwork) of the region and in providing outlets for selling their art. However, we must also acknowledge that their intervention altered this art in-sofar as they pressed artisans to gear their work toward the taste of potential Anglo buyers and collectors. Signing a *santo,* for example, is an innovation prompted by these eastern entrepreneurs. There was a second revival of these traditions in 1950 when the Spanish Colonial Arts Society was reinstated and the Spanish Market reintroduced by E. Boyd.[6]

The Federal Arts Project of the Works Progress Administration (WPA) also contributed to the preservation and popularization of Spanish colonial art by supporting impoverished Anglo artists in the study and documentation of Nuevomexicano religious art. Another branch of the WPA, the Federal Writers Project, was instrumental in preserving the oral genres through a broadly cast documenting project carried out in 1940 and 1941. These efforts were important not only in preserving the rich Nuevomexicano artistic and folkloric traditions, but also in planting the seeds of public appreciation and a sense of communal pride that would flourish in the late twentieth century.

In the political and, to a certain degree, in the economic sectors, the nineteenth century elite and middle class steadily carved out their niche in af-fairs of the state. The folk, however, did not fare so well. One scholar wrote: "New Mexico had, by far the highest birth and death rates in the nation, with infant mortality amounting to 193.6 deaths for every thousand births. In the counties with a 50 percent Nuevomexicano population, infants died at the rate of 144.4 per thousand."[7]

Life for the majority of families, particularly in small communities, con-tinued to revolve around subsistence farming on small family-owned plots.

And while communal cohesion and strong kinship links formed the foundation for social structures and cultural practices in small towns and urban barrios, Nuevomexicanos also demonstrated great flexibility in adapting to economic and structural changes at the macro level. Males engaged in migratory
labor for brief or extended periods of time, while wives and families tended to
family plots.[8] Both men and women acted as *jornaleros,* or daily-wage earners,
as the need arose. Produce from the family *huerta* or homemade butter and
cheese were sold to neighbors or at the side of the road. Women were particularly visible public figures in the education arena, principally in rural schools
with large Spanish-speaking populations, where they served as links between
the communities they served and the world beyond—the world with which
they became familiar through their formal study at state normal schools and
summer institutes.

As Deutsch so perceptively notes, Nuevomexicanos did not become victims of their circumstances after Anglo-American incursion into New Mexico. They did, however, act as agents in the construction of bridges between
two modes of production, showing not only self-determination but also
tremendous adaptability in the process.[9]

In larger towns and cities, a small but viable middle class of business-
people, teachers, and public officials held their ground, and it was not long
before they would pave the road for the establishment of Nuevomexicano
political organizations, which would find fertile soil in the state. Organizations such as the League of United Latin American Citizens (LULAC) played
an important role in addressing racism when cases arose. Organized in Har-
lingen, Texas, by an incipient middle class in 1927, chapters were formed
shortly thereafter in New Mexico, Arizona, Colorado, and California. Although LULAC currently represents the middle and upper class in New Mexico, it has been neither homogeneous nor static in its evolution. Sources indicate an acute awareness by its members of their minority status:

> We solemnly declare once and for all to maintain a sincere and respect-
> ful reverence for our racial origin, for which we are proud . . . To erad-
> icate from our body politic all intents and tendencies to establish dis-
> criminations among our fellow citizens on account of race, religion
> or social position . . . We shall destroy any attempt to create racial prej-
> udices against our people, and any infamous stigma, which may be
> cast upon them. We shall demand for them the respect and preroga-
> tives which the Constitution grants to us all. . . . Secretly and openly,
> by all lawful means at our command, we shall assist the education and

guidance of Latin Americans . . . We shall oppose any tendency to separate our children in the schools of this country.[10]

The official documents of the League stated that "[t]his organization is not a political club." Nonetheless, rhetoric such as the following clearly points to the political intent of the organization:

> but as citizens we shall participate in all local, state and national politick [*sic*] contests. However, in doing so, we shall ever bear in mind the general welfare of our people, and we disregard and abjure once [and] for all any personal obligation which is not in harmony with these principles. With our vote and influence we shall endeavor to place in public office men who show by their deeds, respect and consideration for our people . . . In order that we may enjoy our rights more fully, we, as well as the members of our families, shall comply with the laws of the state in which we reside governing the right of franchise . . . We shall endeavor to secure equal representation for our people on juries and in the administration of Governmental affairs. . . . We shall resist and attack energetically all machinations tending to prevent our social and political unification.

In addition to seeking an end to socioeconomic discrimination, LULAC insisted on equality in political representation, particularly as this applied to the inclusion of Chicanos on all juries.[11]

Another political organization, the Asociación Nacional Mexicana-Americana (ANMA), was founded in May 1949 in Grant County, New Mexico. The ANMA was the direct outgrowth of a clash between Mexicano miners and Anglo law enforcement officers in the village of Fierro in May 1949, and by 1950 it had 1,500 members. Clashes led Nuevomexicanos to charge that "[t]he police force, on the whole, looks down upon the Mexican-Americans as an 'inferior' people. Instead of safeguarding the rights of the people, it uses intimidation and force to cow them."[12] With strong backing from the C.I.O., a local chapter of ANMA was launched in Grant County at a time when public opinion was inflamed and tensions ran high between the groups. According to the then national president, Alfredo Montoya, ANMA was a grassroots political movement. Its major interest lay in reaching all segments of the Nuevomexicano community and merging it into a unified force. Unlike the older organizations, it sought out the disadvantaged and offered them positions of leadership to make Mexican Americans as proud of their origins as possible.

The ANMA extended its protection to disadvantaged Nuevomexicanos and offered to intervene in cases where aged persons and dependent children were denied social security benefits, where veterans ran into difficulty with the Veterans Administration, or where tenants were threatened with eviction. ANMA also took an interest in cases of police brutality. Besides its civil rights program, the ANMA engaged in educational programs, stressing health issues, and in a drive for low-rent housing projects in Chicano sections of larger cities.

On February 1, 1950, the Association for the Advancement of Spanish Americans was organized. Its director was Daniel T. Valdes, the former head of LULAC and former chairman of the New Mexico Council on Human Relations. The organization was a nonprofit corporation established in order to promote political activity. It proposed to set up nonpartisan political action committees in every precinct in the state. According to Valdes, the action groups were "for the purpose of working for good government and governmental programs necessary to improve the economic, cultural, and social status of the Americans of Spanish ancestry in New Mexico." [13]

The Association for the Advancement of Spanish Americans did attempt to be nonpartisan. Its first chapter (Santa Fe County) had an executive board composed of twenty-four Republicans and twenty-four Democrats. Like the Asociación Nacional Mexicana-Americana, the Association for the Advancement of Spanish Americans made a bid for support from labor and from "liberal" Anglo-Americans. The organization advocated expansion of state and federal social security programs, health and educational facilities, and public housing for Nuevomexicanos. The conservation and development of natural resources was another of its objectives, along with comprehensive civil rights and labor legislation for the Nuevomexicano community.

In the electoral arena, the Democrats captured the United States Congress in 1930 and with one exception controlled successive elections. In 1932, the presidency fell into the hands of the Democrats, who managed to keep that office for twenty years. Even the Supreme Court assumed a Democratic complexion. Control of the national administration gave the Democratic Party in New Mexico great momentum. As national trends influenced local politics, large numbers of Nuevomexicanos switched from the Republican to the Democratic Party after 1930. Relief policies of the Roosevelt administration won the loyalty of the Nuevomexicano community. In addition, a rising tide of Democrats arrived from Texas and Oklahoma, and the influence of Bronson Cutting also strengthened the Democratic Party.

The strength of the Democratic Party boded well for New Mexico's new political rising star. Senator Dennis Chávez was to become influential in

Washington—certainly one of the most influential politicians from an American minority group. Through his active participation in fair-employment legislation, he was instrumental in placing Nuevomexicanos in the war industries, thereby enhancing their economic development. The central role played by the Los Alamos laboratories in the development of the atomic bomb was also a boon to Nuevomexicanos in northern New Mexico, as many were able to secure salaried government positions (albeit many of them low-paying labor and janitorial positions). Their dependence on government-supported jobs was to contribute in an interesting fashion to the political climate of the state. As one observer notes, "Although the Government may be the source of relief and public works, politics governs the machinery by which these are made available to them. This has led to a belief that a person's benefit from a government program will be in direct proportion to his participation in politics."[14]

The major case studies that have been made of Nuevomexicano communities underline an extraordinary preoccupation with politics at both the state and local levels. Political scientists have explained this interest in various ways. It may be ascribed to a realization that the government is the source of jobs, relief, and other aid, and that politics is the vehicle through which local and national government is influenced. Regardless of motive, it is clear that in politics, the "native" element competed favorably with the Anglo populace, whereas in education, business, and other activities, the Nuevomexicano population was at a disadvantage.

This disparity was due to prejudice and discriminatory practices toward Nuevomexicanos that would continue to be a point of contention and interethnic conflict throughout the first half of the twentieth century. The situation was particularly acute in eastern New Mexico, a region disparagingly called "Little Texas." Although Nuevomexicanos have not experienced the violent actions or extreme discriminatory measures, such as school segregation or the poll tax, that existed in Texas, racism and oppressive practices nonetheless constitute a difficult chapter in the Nuevomexicano experience.

In many towns in eastern New Mexico, Nuevomexicanos were barred from the "better" barbershops, restaurants, hotels, and places of amusement. Children of Mexican origin in that region of the state frequently attended schools that in practice, though not in theory, were segregated. Anglos and Nuevomexicanos attended separate churches, engaged in different forms of recreation, and very rarely met or interacted socially. There were examples of this in McKinley County, where not one Mexican American teacher had ever been hired, despite the fact that 50 percent of the population was Mexican-American. And Grant County had several segregated schools.

Analysis of educational expenditures indicates that a considerable disparity existed between Anglo-American and Mexican American counties. For example, a study in the 1920s showed that the average expenditure per pupil in Anglo counties was $74.26 higher than in Hispano counties. Although the constitution of New Mexico specifically forbids the segregation of Spanish-speaking children in the public schools of the state, Nuevomexicano leaders long contended that such discriminatory practices prevailed in various counties, particularly in the northern and southeast sections of the state.[15]

The Great Depression of 1929–39 checked immigration to New Mexico. The period between 1939 and 1949 reversed this trend and saw a record influx of people from other states. This prompted a Nuevomexicano political leader in Santa Fe to point out that the "native" population of New Mexico, though approximately 100 percent of the total population in 1830, had been reduced to less than half that percentage by 1940. Since that date, he argued, Anglos had greatly increased their numerical advantage over the Nuevomexicano community. These changes would be felt by certain sectors of society. A notable disparity is apparent in the professional class. In May 1949, for example, the following figures were recorded:[16]

TABLE 1. *Professionals in Albuquerque by Ethnicity*

Profession	Total Number	Anglo	Nuevomexicano
Physician	114	111	3
Dentist	50	48	2
Osteopathic physician	27	27	0
Certified public accountant	11	11	0

There was a serious problem in achieving adequate (relative to ethnicity) representation in organized labor. Nuevomexicanos have been consistent in their support of organized labor, and practically every local union in the state has members from their group as well as Anglo members. However, due to the low economic status of a great portion of the Nuevomexicano population, membership in the various craft unions was at times impossible. Furthermore, the only union within the state that admitted common labor was the Hod Carrier's Union, and the expense of belonging to it was prohibitive for most Nuevomexicano workers. In the thirteen-year period 1936–49, Nuevomexicanos showed increasing interest in labor unions. The official yearbook of the State Federation of Labor indicates, however, that Anglo-Americans still accounted for most of union leadership. The yearbook lists some 117 local officers, of whom only eighteen were Nuevomexicano.

Mexican American labor struggled also to achieve wage parity. There was considerable evidence to support the charge that highly discriminatory wage differentials had been established in New Mexico. Anglo and Nuevomexicano workers frequently were paid different wages for doing identical labor. Mexican Americans were also barred from certain types of employment that offered greater benefits. For example, in the two largest grocery stores in Santa Fe, there was one wage scale established for Nuevomexicanos and another for Anglo employees. In a Taos garage, G.I. apprentices of Anglo ancestry were paid twenty-five dollars per week, while their Nuevomexicano counterparts received a mere fifteen dollars per week.[17]

In the Grant County copper mines and the Carlsbad potash mines, jobs as mechanics, pump men, timekeepers, and hoist men were reserved for Anglos, while the low-wage-bracket jobs were consistently allocated to Nuevomexicanos. Reports from the Region Ten Fair Employment Practices Commission showed that 37 percent of all complaints received involved discrimination against "Mexicans" by employers or individuals.

These types of employment practices and sustained exploitative measures were bound to create labor conflict and subsequent organizing by Nuevomexicanos. Major strikes would occur in the 1930s and the 1950s. Two of the most dramatic labor conflicts were the mining strikes in Gallup in 1933 and the legendary strike at Silver City in 1954, popularized in the classic film *Salt of the Earth*. In each of these organizing efforts, key organizational roles and leadership activities were in the hands of Nuevomexicanos, as was the majority of the labor force.[18]

World War II was to draw many villagers in search of work to cities. This exodus from small towns led to increased contact with Anglo-Americans. In addition, scores of young men joined the service and left home to defend their country and "to see the world." As the veteran journalist Ernie Pyle wrote:

> A large percentage of the battalion spoke Spanish and occasionally I heard some of the officers talking Spanish among themselves. . . . That New Mexico bunch missed more than anything, I believe, the Spanish dishes they were accustomed to back home. Their folks occasionally sent them cans of chile and peppers, and then they had a minor feast. . . . They were part of the old New Mexico outfit, most of which were lost in Bataan. It was good to get back to these slow-talking, wise and easy

people of the desert, and good to speak of places like Las Cruces, Socorro, and Santa Rosa.[19]

This period marks an acceleration of the acculturation process and, at
the same time, an increased awareness of social discrimination. By the same
token, contact with Nuevomexicano troops had erased ideas of white superiority from the minds of some Anglo-American soldiers. The liberal American
Veterans Committee provided efforts to foster better intergroup relations.
And of great significance was the fact that the G.I. Bill of Rights provided
countless Nuevomexicano veterans with unprecedented educational and economic opportunities. Through the benefits allocated by the G.I. Bill, many
Nuevomexicanos were able to advance their educational and professional
skills. All these factors helped to create a new generation of leadership following the war.

Another significant step in the elimination of discrimination and the development of the Nuevomexicano community was passage of the Fair Employment Practices Act, an endeavor that attests to the active participation and
able leadership of U.S. Senator Dennis Chávez. The protection it afforded
merits consideration. The various sections of the act declared that the practice
or policy of discrimination against individuals by reason of their race, color,
religion, national origin, or ancestry is a matter of state concern, since such discrimination undermines the foundations of a free democratic state.

The Federal Employment Practices Commission (FEP) was also given
a major educational role. As it stated in section 9:

> In order to eliminate prejudice among the various racial, religious, and
> ethnic groups in this State and to further good-will among such groups,
> the Commission in cooperation with other departments of Government
> is directed to prepare a comprehensive educational program, designed
> for the students of the public schools of this State and for all other res-
> idents thereof, designed to emphasize the origin of prejudice against
> such minority groups, its harmful effects, and its incompatibility with
> American principles of equality and their fair play.[20]

In New Mexico, an employment practices bill passed the house of representatives by a twenty-five to twenty-four vote, and it was signed by the governor. Voting in the lower chamber on the bill strictly followed geographical
and cultural lines. All of the nineteen Nuevomexicano representatives voted
for the measure. All of the six Anglo-American representatives who voted for

the bill were from the western half of the state, where the Nuevomexicano influence is strong. Three of them represented districts where the Mexican American population constituted more than 20 percent of the total. Representatives from the eastern half of the state, an Anglo stronghold, unanimously voted against the measure. This act was to exert tremendous influence in controlling discriminatory practices in New Mexico.[21]

The 1950s marked a period of subdued civil rights struggles in New Mexico. The 1960s, however, saw an activism revival reminiscent of earlier grassroots movements and labor struggles carried out in the state. The Chicano movement significantly impacted the Nuevomexicano working class, politicians, students, and community activists and contributed to a robust cultural renaissance. Since that time, issues of ethnic identity as they relate to political processes have become more pronounced, and community activist groups have forced political elites to share the limelight on more than one occasion when issues concerning Chicano communities have arisen.[22]

Politically, Nuevomexicanos have continued to be influential at the local, state, and national levels. In recent years, two Nuevomexicanos, Jerry Apodaca and Tony Anaya, have been elected governor of the state—the only such occurrence in the nation. In the last decade, the state legislature has been led by Nuevomexicanos, and most recently, Congressman Bill Richardson (D-N.M.) was appointed U.S. Representative to the United Nations and later Secretary of Energy. Each election year, Nuevomexicanos gain more ground. Similarly, the Nuevomexicano presence and influence holds true for business, education, culture, labor, industry, and medicine. There is no profession, institution, or organization, be it in the private sector or federal, state, or local government, in which there is not strong representation from the Nuevomexicano community. In education, Nuevomexicanos show the lowest Chicano dropout rate in the nation.

In the creative arts, we find a new generation of Nuevomexicanos connecting with their cultural past and revitalizing the traditions of their ancestors. They add an element of hybridity characteristic of artistic tendencies in a globalized and borderless world. The works of both male and female artists have been exhibited in museums across the nation and the world. Each summer, the Spanish Market in Santa Fe draws 75,000 visitors, including national collectors and museum collectors. Among the contemporary crop of creative writers, Rudolfo Anaya, Sabine Ulibarrí, Denise Chávez, Jimmy Santiago Baca, and Demetria Martínez are included among the list of the most important Chicana and Chicano writers in the United States.

Yet the gains of the last three decades have not been universal. The benefits and privileges that certain Nuevomexicanos have achieved and maintained do not hold true for the entire Chicano population. There is an alarming percentage of Nuevomexicanos near or below the poverty level. The accommodationist model of interethnic relations has resulted, in many instances, in conditions in which Anglos still hold a large majority of decision-making appointments. The sharing of power across ethnic boundaries has created an interaction model that tends to abet the avoidance of ethnic confrontation and conflict. If Nuevomexicanos were to engage in a collective social movement geared toward uniting regions and social sectors, they would be a formidable, if not the dominant, community in the state. They certainly possess the education, experience, and strong sense of place and belonging necessary to transform the cultural and political complexion of the state. They, more than any other Chicano state population, hold in their own hands the potential for determining their. The Nuevo Sol will reveal the outcome.

NOTES

1. Doris L. Meyer, "Resistance Against Cultural Erosion," *The Bilingual Review/La Revista Bilingue* 2, no. 3 (1997): 99–106, offers a fine synthesis of this theme.

2. See Daniel Valdes y Tapia, *Hispanos and American Politics* (New York: Arno), 1976.

3. Margaret Abreu, "An Interview with Mary Austin." *New Mexico School Review* 11:2 (Oct. 1931): 22.

4. Cleofas Jaramillo, *Romance of a Village Girl* (San Antonio: Naylor, 1955; reprint, University of New Mexico Press, 2000), preface, unpaginated.

5. Two edited studies articulate this theme well: Erlinda Gonzales-Berry and Genaro M. Padilla, *Pasó por aquí: Critical Essays on the New Mexican Literary Tradition, 1952–1988* (Albuquerque: University of New Mexico Press, 1989), and Ramón Gutiérrez and Genaro Padilla, eds., *Recovering the U.S. Hispanic Literary Heritage* (Houston: Arte Público), 1993.

6. Susan A. Roberts and Calvin A. Roberts, *New Mexico* (Albuquerque: University of New Mexico Press), 1974–75.

7. Cited in Valdes, 87.

8. Nancie L. González, *The Spanish-American of New Mexico* (Albuquerque: University of New Mexico Press), 42–45.

9. See the recent solid study by Sarah Deutsch, *No Separate Refuge: Culture, Class, and Gender on an Anglo-Hispanic Frontier in the American Southwest, 1880–1940* (New York: Oxford University Press, 1987).

10. Benjamín Márquez, *LULAC: The Evolution of a Mexican American Political Organization* (Austin: University of Texas Press, 1993), 19.

11. Ibid., 69.

12. Cited in Juan Gómez-Quiñones, *Chicano Politics: Reality and Promise, 1940–1990* (Albuquerque: University of New Mexico Press, 1990), 50–51.

13. Ibid., 54.

14. Ernest B. Fincher, "Spanish-Americans as a Political Factor in New Mexico, 1912–1950" (Ph.D. diss., New York University, 1950), 271.

15. Fincher, 195–197.

16. Ibid., 57–67.

17. Carolyn Zeleny, "Relations between the Spanish Americans and Anglo-Americans in New Mexico: A Study of Conflict and Accommodation in a Dual-Ethnic Relationship" (Ph.D. diss., Yale University, 1944), 218–20.

18. See the excellent book chapter by Jack Cargill, "Empire and Opposition: The 'Salt of the Earth' Strike" in Robert Kern, ed., *Labor in New Mexico* (Albuquerque: University of New Mexico Press, 1983), 183–271.

19. Cited in Raul Marin, *Among the Valiant: Mexican Americans in World War II and Korea* (Alhambra: Borden Publishing Co., 1963) 187.

20. Fincher, 212.

21. Tobías Durán, "Politicas de reforma social en Nuevo México," in *El México olvidado: la historia del pueblo chicano*, ed. David R. Maciel, 2 vols. (Ciudad Juárez: Universidad Autónoma de Ciudad Juárez and University of Texas at El Paso, 1996), 2:212–39.

22. Flaviano Chris Garcia, "Manitos and Chicanos in New Mexico Politics" *Aztlán: Journal of the Social Sciences and the Arts* 5, nos. 1–2 (Spring–Fall, 1974): 177–89.

Chapter Four

JOHN NIETO-PHILLIPS

Spanish American Ethnic Identity and New Mexico's Statehood Struggle

*A great many of them have but a very small dash of white blood, others have a
pretty considerable dash of the African. No matter what their blood or race is; no
matter how or of what that population is made up, they are all our fellow-citizens
now—made so by the treaty; and it is too late now to regret the possibility that
some of them may be sitting along side of us here before a great while.*

   — REPRESENTATIVE JOSEPH M. ROOT OF OHIO, FEBRUARY 15, 1850

No quiso el Tío Samuel *[Uncle Sam did not want*
Admitirnos como estado *To admit us as a state*
Y al Nuevo México fiel *And loyal New Mexico*
El Congreso ha rechazado *Has been rejected by Congress]*

   — EL NUEVO MEXICANO, FEBRUARY 5, 1898

Standing before Congress in January 1848, Senator John C. Calhoun of South
Carolina implored his colleagues to exercise restraint. As officials thousands
of miles away negotiated the Treaty of Guadalupe Hidalgo, lawmakers in
Washington pondered the spoils of the United States' war with Mexico. Calhoun warned his colleagues that the United States should not annex all or
large parts of Mexican territory; to do so, he claimed, meant admitting Mexicans into the United States, something that would precipitate a collapse of
the racial order:

> [W]e have never dreamt of incorporating into our Union any but the
> Caucasian race—the free white race. To incorporate Mexico would be
> the first instance of the kind of incorporating an Indian race; for more
> than half the Mexicans are Indians, and the other is composed chiefly
> of mixed tribes. I protest against such a union as that! Ours, sirs, is the
> Government of a white race. The greatest misfortunes of Spanish Amer-
> ica are to be traced to the fatal error of placing these colored races on an

equality with the white race. That error destroyed the social arrangement which formed the basis of society.[1]

The United States' conquest of Mexico in 1848 did not destroy "the social arrangement" by which white Americans predominated over the "colored races." It did, however, add a new dimension to race relations in the western United States and prompted discussions in the halls of Congress about the Mexicans' racial character and their "fitness" for democracy. Lawmakers in Washington suddenly found themselves contemplating whether and how to "incorporate" more than 100,000 Mexican citizens into the nation's body politic, and asking: Were Mexicans "fit" for self-government or statehood?[2]

　　Some Anglo-Americans viewed Mexicans as political subversives or permanent rebels. "Never will the time come," Calhoun admonished, "that these Mexicans will be heartily reconciled to your authority. They have Castilian blood in their veins—the old Gothic, quite equal to the Anglo-Saxon in many respects." But, he continued, they remain too loyal to their Mexican nation to ever become U.S. citizens.[3] Calhoun posed important questions to his colleagues: If the United States was destined to reign over North America, was it capable of managing millions of mixed-blood Mexican subjects? Was it prepared to "incorporate" them into its citizenry? "Are Mexicans fit for self-government or for governing you?" he asked. "Are you, any of you, willing that your States be governed by . . . a population of about only one million of your blood, and two or three millions of mixed blood, better informed, all the rest pure Indians, a mixed blood equally ignorant and unfit for liberty, impure races, not as good as the Cherokees or Choctaws?"[4] With comments such as these, Calhoun sought to suggest that Mexicans were more "savage" than Indians and therefore were incapable of governing themselves or white Americans. Many Anglo-Americans shared this view. They perceived Mexicans in general, and New Mexicans in particular, to be persons of mixed (Spanish and Indian) blood, to have inherited the worst characteristics of both races, and to be "unfit" for U.S. citizenship or for self-government.[5] Not all congressmen, however, agreed. These perceptions—which lasted well into the twentieth century—elicited vocal resistance from many New Mexicans who, by the twentieth century, were beginning to insist that they were of pure (not "mixed") blood, and of the "Spanish" (not "Mexican") race, nationality, or culture.

　　During the last half of the nineteenth century, most of New Mexico's Spanish-speaking population variously referred to themselves as *vecinos*, Mexicanos, Neomexicanos, Nuevomexicanos, or Hispanoamericanos. By the twentieth century, however, they had begun to refer to themselves in English as "Spanish Americans." (For the sake of consistency, I will employ the term Nuevomexicano to refer to this population.) The transformation from Spanish to English nomenclature and from "Mexican" to "Spanish" racial referents reflects a broader transformation in the way Anglo-Americans viewed Nuevomexicanos and in the way "Spanish Americans" viewed themselves (or wished to be viewed). "Spanish Americans" began to invoke their European racial identity and long history of conquest and colonization to gain acceptance and recognition of their political rights through statehood. Both Anglo and Nuevomexicano statehood proponents made congressional approval of statehood possible by recasting New Mexico's "Mexicans" as Spanish in race, culture, and history, and American in citizenship and national loyalty.

Between 1848 and 1912, the struggle for statehood ebbed and flowed along with other political issues, such as land disputes, public education, and taxes, but it became particularly intense during three periods: 1848–50, 1872–76, and 1888–1912. At each of these junctures, the statehood debate illustrated how racial perceptions and relations played a major role in the formation of the Spanish American consciousness.

THE EARLY STATEHOOD STRUGGLE, 1848–1850

The United States' conquest of northern Mexico in 1848 reshaped ethnic relations and identities in New Mexico in two significant ways. First, federal and territorial officials reinstated the legal distinction between Indians and non-Indians that had formed the basis of Spanish colonial society, and that had been legally abolished in 1821 by the Plan de Iguala. The sociocultural division between *españoles* (or *vecinos*) and their Pueblo Indian neighbors persisted throughout the Mexican period. Under U.S. rule, federal and territorial laws formalized that ethnic division by treating Pueblo Indians and their lands as entities separate from non-Indians and their lands.[6] Though under article 9 of the Treaty of Guadalupe Hidalgo, Pueblo Indians were given the option of retaining their Mexican citizenship or acquiring U.S. citizenship by default after one year, the political and civic rights of Pueblo Indians were contested for a full century. According to the historian Joe Sando, "Not a single Pueblo Indian elected to retain Mexican citizenship."[7] This does not mean that they became full U.S. citizens with the same rights and privileges that Nuevomexicanos enjoyed. Rather, when New Mexico was organized into a territory in 1850, its enabling legislation gave only "free white male citizens" (which included Nuevomexicanos) the right to vote.

Three years later, New Mexico's largely Nuevomexicano legislature pointed to the Organic Act in deciding an electoral controversy. Having lost a bitterly contested election for a house seat to represent Santa Ana County, Miguel Montoya petitioned for a recount. A house committee determined that 139 Pueblo Indians from Zia and Jemez had "illegally" cast ballots that allowed Montoya's opponent, Jesús Sandoval, to win the election. Those votes were declared void. In ruling for Montoya, the committee referred to the territory's Organic Act of 1850, which stated that only "free white male citizens of the United States" were entitled to vote in territorial elections, and that Pueblo Indians were not white. Noted the committee report, "[W]ho will say that the Indians are white males?"[8] Sandoval's counsel countered that, according to both the Plan de Iguala and the Treaty of Guadalupe Hidalgo, Pueblo Indians were fellow "citizens of Mexico" who were later given all the "rights of citizens of the United States." Furthermore, he argued, "A free white male inhabitant has been repeatedly decided to be any person who is not the descendant of an African."[9] The committee's ruling reestablished the political and ethnic division between Indians and non-Indians.

The second way in which U.S. conquest reshaped ethnic relations and identities was by subverting Nuevomexicanos' traditional dominance over local resources and political offices. This subversion was carried out, in part, by denying New Mexicans statehood. Many congressmen initially opposed admitting New Mexico on the grounds that doing so would disrupt the balance of power between free and slave states, while others opposed granting statehood on racial grounds.

Just months after the Treaty of Guadalupe Hidalgo was signed, twelve prominent New Mexicans, led by Father José Antonio Martínez of Taos, convened in Santa Fe to discuss New Mexico's future within the Union.[10] The ten Nuevomexicanos and two Anglo-Americans petitioned Congress to replace the military government that had been imposed on them in 1846 with a temporary territorial form of government "until the time shall arrive for admission into the Union."[11] But their petition offended many Southerners. It boldly proclaimed that New Mexicans did not "desire to have domestic slavery within our borders. . . . We desire to be protected by Congress against the introduction of slaves into the Territory."[12] When read before the U.S. Senate on December 13, 1848, this passage reportedly caused "a storm of comment, especially from the pro-slavery senators, who were astounded at what they termed 'the insolence' of the language of the document."[13] Southern leaders had counted on New Mexico as a potential slave state to offset their pending loss of California. Thereafter, Southerners entrenched themselves against

statehood for New Mexico and impeded any action on the petition for a territorial government, leaving New Mexico's future unclear.

Frustrated by this response, political leaders reconvened in Santa Fe in
1850 and debated whether to adopt a state or a territorial constitution. The latter stood a better chance for passage in Congress, but the former promised
greater sovereignty. As they debated, the political climate at home was rapidly
changing. A rumor circulated that Texans were preparing to invade New Mexico, as they had done in 1841 and 1843. Fearful that New Mexico would be annexed or parceled out to Texas, convention delegates quickly agreed that statehood would better protect New Mexico's sovereignty. On drafting a state
constitution, they submitted it to a popular vote. Voters overwhelmingly approved it, 6,371 to 39. A state government was hastily formed and officials were
elected. Lieutenant Governor Manuel Alvarez, acting in Governor Henry
Connelly's absence, forwarded the constitution to Congress for approval. But
this bid for a state government proved fruitless. Fate interceded. While the
document was en route, President Zachary Taylor, a staunch supporter of
New Mexico's statehood, contracted cholera and died on July 9.[14]

Following President Taylor's death, New Mexico's principal statehood
advocate was Representative Joseph Root of Ohio. Despite overwhelming
opposition, Root lobbied steadfastly for New Mexico's statehood, insisting
that it was clearly mandated by the Treaty of Guadalupe Hidalgo. However,
in a gesture of compromise to statehood opponents, Root offered to grant
New Mexico territorial status and admit California as a free state. New Mexicans, he said, were now "a people belonging to the United States" who
needed "a clear law" and government. In response to opponents, Root argued
that Nuevomexicanos merited a territorial government until such time as they
could achieve statehood.[15] Their race or "blood mixture" was of little consequence to their ability to govern.

William H. Seward of New York was New Mexico's most vocal supporter in the Senate. In a contentious Senate exchange over the fate of the
western territories, Seward insisted that New Mexico merited statehood because it possessed more than the required minimum population of at least
60,000 residents to select a member of Congress.[16] Seward argued that "New
Mexico more than fulfills that condition. She has a population of over one-
hundred-thousand souls . . . , double that of Florida when she was admitted
as a state. Sixty-thousand inhabitants were deemed sufficient to entitle the
State of Ohio to admission. That same number was required of Michigan, Indiana, Illinois, and Iowa. And New Mexico exceeds it by more than two-
thirds." [17] Although New Mexico's actual population was later measured at

61,547 (not including Pueblo Indians) in the 1850 census, the territory did possess a population large enough to meet the requirement for admission to the Union.[18]

Seward further insisted that the population of New Mexico (presumably he was referring to the "Mexican" population) was eminently capable of self-government, despite declarations to the contrary on the part of people such as Calhoun. New Mexicans claimed a long and rich history of colonization that spoke of their fitness for self-government, said Seward.

> They are a mingled population, marked by characteristics which resulted from the extraordinary system of colonization and government maintained by Old Spain in her provinces. . . . The Anglo-Saxon colonization left the aborigines of this Continent out of its sympathy, and almost out of its care. It left them barbarous and savage; and they still remain so. . . . On the other hand, the peculiar civilization which the colonists of Spain carried into her provinces . . . operated successfully in winning the Indians to Christianity and partial civilization.[19]

That Spaniards were more successful in bringing "Christianity and partial civilization" to the Indians than their "Anglo Saxon" counterparts represented a challenge to the popular "black legend," which denounced all Spanish deeds in the Americas as "tyrannical" and "barbarous."[20] Seward implied that, to the contrary, Spain's colonization of the Pueblo Indians in New Mexico was both benevolent and peaceful.

Significantly, Seward's speech made no reference to the period of Mexico's administration of New Mexico (1821–1846), a time marked by political tumult and confusion. He completely refrained from invoking the term "Mexican," perhaps to avoid stirring up anti-Mexican prejudice. By praising the Spanish colonial past, Seward implied that New Mexico's Indians and Nuevomexicanos descended from a genteel, colonial society characterized by Christianity and racial order. His allusion to Pueblo Indians as peaceful and sedentary farmers, and to Nuevomexicanos as the descendants of Spanish settlers, suggested that New Mexico's "mingled population" was stable and racially "fit" to govern itself. Between 1850 and 1912, statehood advocates made numerous references to the Spanish colonial past. As we shall see, these allusions contributed to the arousal of a Spanish American ethnic and political consciousness.

Perhaps Seward overemphasized New Mexico's Spanish colonial past. Opponents in the Senate railed against New Mexico's admission on the grounds that her people were too fond of their imperial past, that they secretly aspired to a "kingly Government" founded on monarchical and Catholic principles—not democratic and secular ones. Opponents even found disturbing some fairly innocuous statements in the state constitution and read into them their worst fears. An example was the Nuevomexicanos' expression of belief in the supremacy of a higher spiritual power: "[We, the people of New Mexico,] Acknowledging with grateful hearts the goodness of the Sovereign Ruler of the Universe, and imploring His aid and direction in its accomplishment, do ordain and establish the following Constitution."[21] Many congressmen saw in this statement a plot by New Mexico's Catholic "Mexicans" to insinuate their religious beliefs into government, a scheme that made them patently incapable and unworthy of democratic self-government. To whom did New Mexicans pledge most allegiance, asked one senator, to an unnamed Catholic monarchy, or to the Constitution of the United States?[22]

Compounding New Mexico's woes in Congress was a long-standing boundary dispute between Texas and New Mexico. The former, since declaring its independence in 1836, had claimed half of New Mexico's present-day territory, including all land east of the Rio Grande—some 90,000 square miles. Seward proposed to grant New Mexico statehood but to refer the question of its boundaries to the U.S. Supreme Court. His proposal met with swift and fierce opposition from Texans, who, in solidarity with fellow Southerners, sought to expand the boundaries of slavery and feared New Mexico's admission as a free state. Seward's proposed solution proved fruitless and was rejected forty-two to one, with Seward casting the lone affirmative vote.[23]

Two thousand miles away, leaders in Santa Fe nervously awaited Congress's decision. Little did they know that New Mexico's fate had become enveloped by an issue much larger than the mere wording of their proposed constitution. The sectional controversy over slavery remained the nation's central concern.[24] In September, word finally arrived in Santa Fe from across the Great Plains about the Compromise of 1850: Congress admitted California as a free state and made New Mexico and Utah, and all lands acquired from Mexico in 1848, into territories, without reference to slavery. Texas abandoned its claim on New Mexico and in return received handsome compensation.[25] Congress had put the question of statehood to rest for a long spell. In the words of one historian, "[T]he people [of New Mexico] settled down to a new order of things, and nothing was heard of Statehood for several years."[26]

Not until the end of the Civil War was the issue resurrected in public debate. In December 1865, the territorial governor, Henry Connelly, revisited the issue in his annual address to the legislative assembly. In contrast to

Representative Root, who fifteen years earlier had praised the Spanish conquest as evidence of Nuevomexicanos' fitness for self-government, Governor
Connelly viewed the Spanish colonial past as a period of ineffectual administration. Noting the "retarded" condition of the territory, Connelly lamented
that two centuries of "paternal [Spanish] governments" had left New Mexico
without "all means of progress in the arts, industry, immigration, [and]
schools . . . by which our territorial neighbors have surpassed our condition."[27] While remaining ambiguous as to whether he supported statehood,
he simply remarked, "[T]his is a century of progress, and that race or community which decides to stand still amid a fervor of activity . . . will be run
over."[28] Within months of Connelly's address, statehood advocates reorgan-
ized, and the legislature passed an act calling for a constitutional convention
to meet in Santa Fe in 1866. "Apparently," observed one historian, "nothing of
a practical nature was accomplished under this act."[29] The same can be said
for a similar act of 1870, which produced no visible results. If New Mexicans
had reawakened to the issue of self-government following the Civil War, they
did not express sufficient resolve to fight for it.

THE SANTA FE RING AND THE STATEHOOD STRUGGLE, 1872–1876

The 1870s saw the revival of New Mexico's statehood campaign. The issue regained public attention, becoming the subject of sharp debate in newspapers,
in the territorial legislature, and in Congress. As before, the politics of race
permeated the struggle, though on this occasion the rhetoric and issues differed significantly from what prevailed during the antebellum period. Whereas
between 1848 and 1850 the issues of slavery and westward expansion were paramount, between 1872 and 1876 hostility focused on New Mexico's "Mexicans." Such anger, combined with the continued political marginalization of
these people, forced Nuevomexicanos and certain Anglos to reflect upon
Nuevomexicanos' racial and historical identity. This reflection sowed the
seeds of empowerment from which a "Spanish American" ethos later would
flourish.

The statehood struggle of the 1870s was not initiated by a groundswell
of popular sentiment, but rather by the political calculation and promotional
efforts of Anglo and Nuevomexicano politicians, lawyers, and *ricos*, the elite
class of landed Nuevomexicanos. Notwithstanding the 1850 and 1872 popular
elections for proposed state constitutions, it is difficult to assess what most
Nuevomexicanos—in particular, the *pobres* and nonliterate citizens—thought
about statehood. From what source did they derive their information and

opinions? What was the role of word of mouth or traditional political loyalties in forging popular opinion about statehood? These are questions that merit scrutiny, but they cannot be answered by the documents at hand. The *Congressional Record* and newspaper articles do not capture the voices of impoverished majority of Nuevomexicanos, but they do capture the voices of prominent political forces, such as the Santa Fe Ring.

During the mid 1870s and late 1880s, the Santa Fe Ring—a loose affiliation of Anglo and Nuevomexicano lawyers, politicos, and *ricos*—was an especially visible proponent of statehood. Its members propagated their views in newspapers throughout the territory, especially in those of the capital, the *Santa Fe New Mexican* and its weekly Spanish-language counterpart, *El nuevo mexicano*. What was the Ring's motivation for statehood? What did its members stand to gain from New Mexico's admission into the Union? Ostensibly, statehood was fought on behalf of Nuevomexicanos' right to full participation in national politics, but it was equally a campaign on the part of lawyers, politicos, and *ricos* to gain greater local control over land, resources, and political offices.

In considering the Ring's motivation for supporting the statehood campaign, it is important to recall that for the greater part of the nineteenth century, New Mexican society remained largely bifurcated. There were those who possessed education, wealth, land, and/or political power, and those who did not. The vast majority of Nuevomexicanos subsisted on small-scale farms and ranches and on communal land grants. Pueblo Indians likewise farmed and ranched. There were also the *ricos*, who, according to Ramón Gutiérrez, "enjoyed the life of comfortable regional gentry, engaged in mercantile activity, and lived by exploiting their retainers, their poorer kin, and their sharecroppers (*partidarios*)."[30] These *ricos*, along with Anglo merchants, land speculators, lawyers, and territorial officials, stood at the political and economic vanguard of society. Ultimately, the *ricos* and Anglo-Americans stood to reap the benefits of increased trade, industry, immigration, and statehood. Enormous stretches of disputed land as well as water rights hung in the balance. Statehood would mean greater local control over these, and it would create political capital by making possible thousands of political appointments and a great deal of patronage. But, as in the past, statehood hopes repeatedly would fall victim to the vicissitudes of national politics and the prevailing racial discourse in Congress and throughout the country.

During the first three decades of the territory's existence, Nuevomexicano and Anglo-American officials accumulated huge tracts of land through illicit claims and nefarious deals.[31] The Maxwell land grant, located in the northeastern portion of the territory, represents the most notorious example of such corruption. Confirmed by Congress in 1869, the grant encompassed 97,000 acres, or twenty-two leagues. The next year, a group of investors headed by the young Santa Fe lawyer Stephen B. Elkins and a wealthy Colorado mine owner, Jerome B. Chaffee, purchased the grant for $1.35 million. The pair then hired U.S. Deputy Surveyor for New Mexico W. W. Griffin to resurvey the grant. To no one's surprise, Griffin's survey estimated the grant to contain nearly 2 million acres—some twenty times the number confirmed by Congress. Griffin filed his report with the Department of the Interior, whence it was forwarded to Congress for confirmation.

Had Elkins and Chaffee awaited word from Washington on their claim, the story would have ended there. But they did not. They immediately sold their presumed 2-million-acre grant to a London-based company. The company then issued $5 million worth of stock to support their plans to mine, ranch, farm, and speculate in the land. Meanwhile, company officials appointed Elkins director and local attorney of the company. Elkins's associates—New Mexico Governor William A. Pile, Miguel Antonio Otero, and Judge John S. Watts—were all made vice presidents. These men, along with the territorial attorney and their business partner Thomas B. Catron, became the core members of the Santa Fe Ring, whose political interests were defended by a vast, mostly Republican, network of local politicos. By all appearances, Elkins's and Chaffee's investment had produced a tremendous profit, but in 1871, Secretary of the Interior Columbus Delano ruled Griffin's 2-million-acre survey invalid. To Elkins's disbelief, Delano declared the grant to contain only 97,000 acres as originally surveyed. The company was thrown into crisis and later went bankrupt. Eventually, much of the 2-million-acre claim was restored, but only after protracted litigation.[32]

The 1871 ruling exemplified the power that the federal government wielded in New Mexico during its territorial period. It was precisely this kind of intervention that Ring members and Nuevomexicanos throughout northern New Mexico despised about the federal government. Statehood promised to render more autonomy and local control over such issues. Had the grant been adjudicated by state authorities, it would no doubt have been confirmed at 2 million acres. But as citizens of a territory, Nuevomexicanos and Anglos alike were at the mercy of disinterested parties in Washington, D.C. It should come as no surprise, then, that Elkins himself set out for Congress to lobby for New Mexico's admission to the Union. The year following the ruling, Elkins ran for and won the office of Territorial Delegate to Congress. According to the historian Howard Lamar, Elkins "promised his constituents that he would settle all land claims and at the same time secure statehood for New Mexico. . . . Aided by promises, money, pressure, and fraud at the polls, he was elected by a majority of 4,000!" [33] During his four years in Washington, Elkins was New Mexico's most vocal advocate for admission.

If the Santa Fe Ring stood to profit by statehood, so, too, did other land agents. They initiated publicity campaigns to attract immigrants and garner their business. Publications that erroneously announced New Mexico's imminent admission began to reach East Coast residents. An 1873 publication authored by the Santa Fe land agent Elias Brevoort illustrates this point. Intended as a promotional brochure for East Coast immigrants and speculators, Brevoort's *New Mexico: Her Natural Resources and Attractions* urged land investors to act fast, because "[l]ike the sleeping giant, New Mexico has been reposing in the consciousness of her strength and power, to arouse when the time should come, and to assume among the political divisions and powers of the Union, and in the busy world, the position and rank [of state] which the laws of Nature and of Nature's God entitle her." [34] New Mexico, he said, was poised for statehood; and statehood promised further immigration and higher land values. According to Brevoort, of the territory's 77.5 million acres, only 11 million had been surveyed and settled. Between 9 and 10 million of these, Brevoort quoted New Mexico's surveyor general as saying, consisted of Spanish and Mexican land grants, grants that would be opened up for private purchase in the event of their legal dissolution.[35] Of the remaining unsurveyed lands, as much as one-tenth was arable and capable of sustaining "an extremely large agricultural, pastoral and mining population. . . . The table plains," Brevoort added, "are inexhaustible in pasturage and in the mountains are treasures of vast stores of mineral wealth." [36] Such claims bordered on the illusory, and clearly were based more on optimism than documentation. In 1874, New Mexico remained "very partially explored and scarcely prospected." Her material potential was unknown. Therefore, the mystery surrounding "her resources" raised expectations among speculators and miners, and heightened their sense of adventure and conquest.[37]

Like other land agents, Brevoort favored statehood because of his desire to profit from immigration and land speculation. Brevoort made no effort to hide his disdain for "the Spanish and Mexican race," which had "caused the country to progress scarcely a move in the march of material improvement and wealth beyond what it was in the days of the Spanish vice-royalty in Mexico to which it was once subject." [38] To many whites such as Brevoort, the "march of material improvement" embraced Protestant and decidedly capitalist ethics. The historian David Roediger has documented how notions of labor, commerce, and industry had become inextricably bound up in American "whiteness."[39] In a similar vein, Reginald Horsman points out that the United States' "Manifest Destiny" implied the domination of both the land and the people residing on it. "American Anglo-Saxon" racial ideology was shaped by the shifting demographic landscape of the nineteenth century, especially in the American West, where contact with "Mexicans" forced many "Americans" to reevaluate their own racial identity and competition over resources heightened ethnic boundaries.[40] The *Congressional Record*, journals, and newspapers nationwide documented Anglo-Americans' growing awareness of Mexicans' presence in the western lands.[41] In the debate over statehood, white "American" identity was articulated in juxtaposition to mixed-blood "Mexican" identity.

Although among some land agents, such as Brevoort, statehood was merely a tool for personal,financial gain, for other individuals—Nuevomexicanos and Anglos alike—statehood promised greater sovereignty over New Mexico's borders, which again were being violated. In 1872, Colorado had made clear its intention to annex six northern counties from New Mexico as part of its own statehood campaign. Those six counties promised to give the northern neighbor the additional population needed for statehood. This threat moved Nuevomexicanos to act quickly to defend their lands. In May, Colonel José Francisco Chaves presided over a hastily organized constitutional convention in Albuquerque, which many leading Nuevomexicanos attended. The legislature passed a resolution condemning Colorado's proposed annexation and affirming New Mexico's sovereignty. As long as New Mexico remained a territory, declared the resolution, it was subject to periodic raids on its land. At stake, however, was more than just land. Colorado's annexation in 1876 threatened the very livelihood of "native" New Mexicans. Statehood was seen as the only sure protection from such incursions. "We are impelled to [t]his course by our pride and our independence," the resolution stated, ". . . to prevent our people, our relations and our interests from becoming separated, divided and made tributary to a neighboring Territory; and we call on the people throughout the whole Territory, as they love their native soil, their homes, their wives and children . . . to vote for our admission into the Union."[42] The resolution's reference to "native soil" marked the beginning of a movement to politicize Nuevomexicanos' identity and their historical attachment to their land. Statehood offered protection for traditional Nuevomexicano land and lifeways and thus was a vehicle for what the historian Robert J. Rosenbaum has called "the sacred right of self-preservation."[43]

Two weeks later, Antonio Ortiz y Salazar presided over another convention in Santa Fe, which produced a similar resolution calling for statehood and promoting a state constitution.[44] The *New Mexican,* a Republican-owned newspaper and fervent statehood advocate, devoted a column and a half to "Reasons Why the People of New Mexico Should Adopt the State Constitution." Among other things, statehood promised New Mexicans the means

> [t]o avoid ruin, annexation to other territories, division of our people, our interests, and separation of our relatives; to sustain our pride, our independence, and our history, the oldest in the United States . . . , [and] to manage our own affairs and select our own officers.[45]

Whether most Nuevomexicanos agreed with or were convinced by arguments such as these is difficult to determine. The only known gauge of public opinion was the referendum conducted in June 1872 on the adoption of a state constitution. The results of that referendum suggest that citizens of Santa Fe and Albuquerque took a greater interest in the issue than did residents of outlying villages. This likely reflected the influence of the newspapers in shaping opinion in their respective areas of distribution. By contrast, writes one historian, "away from the centers of population the people were apathetic."[46] In several counties, certain precincts failed to participate in the referendum; in others, so few votes were cast that it raised the governor's suspicion that the referendum had been subverted. Voters in Santa Fe, who were most likely to have read the pro-statehood editorials of the *New Mexican,* overwhelmingly approved the proposed constitution, 424 to 77. Those living outside the city in the more remote parts of Santa Fe County voted against it, 269 to 130.[47] Due to the referendum's low turnout, Governor Giddings dismissed the results, saying the vote was not sufficiently large to represent the will of the people and would therefore be considered invalid by Congress.[48] The statehood movement ended before any petition reached Congress.

Ostensibly, the vote reflected the resolve of the people "to manage our own affairs and select our own officers . . . to make us a happy, intelligent, enterprising and prosperous people."[49] However, the referendum's returns showed that a substantial opposition to the constitution had arisen in the rural communities, though it is not known why.[50] It is unlikely that opponents objected to the principles of statehood, such as political equality, territorial sovereignty, and democratic representation. And since the constitution made no reference to such contentious issues as public education, taxes, or land-grant struggles, voters were not likely motivated by these issues either. Exactly what motivated the rural communities to oppose statehood cannot be deduced from the newspapers, whose pages seldom represented concerns of the countryside. It should be remembered, however, that partisan politics and traditional family loyalties remained very strong during this period, and these may have had a hand in shaping the referendum's results.

Given the nature of partisan politics in New Mexico, it is ironic that two years later Republicans and Democrats, Nuevomexicanos and Anglos, would come to an agreement on statehood. In 1874, New Mexico's legislature, also known as *la asamblea,* convened in Santa Fe and unanimously passed a memorial imploring Congress to grant statehood to New Mexico. The memorial argued that New Mexico was fast becoming a prosperous and populous territory and was deserving of equality with the states in the Union. The 600-word memorial rang in harmony with the words of Brevoort, the land agent. It boasted New Mexico's bright prospects for early investors and paid homage to the European and Anglo-American settlers who had brought with them industry and commerce.

The document's foremost concern seemed to be the portrayal of New Mexico as a territory being "civilized" through American and European immigration and the development of mines. It boldly, though erroneously, declared that New Mexico's population had grown more than 50 percent in just four years—from 91,000 in 1870 to over 140,000 in 1874.[51] Not counting "hostile Indians," New Mexico's residents were an industrious and civilized people, yeoman farmers, self-sufficient and democratic. The Pueblos (whose numbers were put at 10,000) were vividly portrayed in this light: "The Pueblos or Village Indians, who, from time immemorial, have been agriculturists . . . , [are] among the best citizens of our territory," and they remain "as truly loyal to the government under which they live as any people under the sun."[52]

By portraying the Pueblos as sedentary and peaceful, the memorial distinguished them from the less sedentary Apache and Navajo. In addition to alluding to such a distinction, the memorial portrayed New Mexico as a dynamic territory that was being culturally and demographically transformed by the influx of American and European migrants. It read, "We believe that, outside of the native Mexican population of this Territory, there are at least 40,000 people of American and European descent among us who are permanent residents."[53] Twenty thousand of these were recent migrants, "bringing with them capital and means. . . . This new population is dispersed very generally throughout the Territory, but will be found mostly in the mining-regions, which are fast becoming developed."[54] By associating white immigrants with increased mining activities, the memorial affirmed the idea, popular in Congress, that white Americans and Europeans were the progenitors of "civilization" and "industry." But the memorial must have left plenty of questions in the minds of Congress.

Exactly who comprised those "of American and European descent" and who comprised "the native Mexican population"? Where did the Nuevomexicano elite figure into the racial landscape they had painted? Did the wealthy Nuevomexicanos figure among the 40,000 permanent residents "of American and European descent"? One can only speculate how members of Congress racially classified the memorial's signatories—"Pedro Sanches [*sic*], *Presidente del Senado*," and "Grego. N. Otero, *Presidente de la Camara*"—or how these individuals classified themselves. Of what race did congressmen perceive "the native Mexican population"? Were they white? Spanish? "Mixed-blood?" "Fit" for democracy? In the coming decades, these were no small questions, and they would figure centrally in debates over New Mexico's statehood.

Much can be gleaned from the way the asamblea packaged and presented Nuevomexicano and Pueblo Indian identities in 1874—what the asamblea chose to include in or omit from the memorial. Nuevomexicanos presumably numbered 90,000, yet the memorial made no mention of their culture or lifeways, as it did for Pueblo Indians, Europeans, and "Americans." What prompted the Spanish-speaking asamblea to avoid any reference to *lo mexicano*—that which was Mexican—in their plea to Congress? Why did it label Nuevomexicanos "the native population" and not simply "Americans"? Did Nuevomexicanos not consider themselves "Americans"? The asamblea's decision not to elaborate on the racial, cultural, or demographic attributes of Nuevomexicanos suggests that it may have sought to avoid stirring up anti-Mexican prejudice among members of Congress. As later evidence suggests, Nuevomexicanos contributed to and sometimes undermined Anglo constructions of Nuevomexicano identity. In the decades to come, the statehood debate would center on the racial character of Nuevomexicanos and on their history, education, language, and religion.

When Elkins, the territorial delegate, introduced the memorial to Congress in 1874, he read a thirty-three-page speech that highlighted New Mexico's right to statehood based on the promise—made in the Treaty of Guadalupe Hidalgo—that former Mexican citizens would eventually be "incorporated into the Union of the United States and be admitted, at the proper time (to be judged by the Congress of the United States) to the enjoyment of all the rights of citizens of the United States according to the principles of the Constitution." [55] He also repeated the assertion, made in 1850, that New Mexico possessed the requisite population for statehood. [56] Like Brevoort's *New Mexico* publication, Elkins's testimony exaggerated the mineral and natural wealth of the land, but it also gave Congress a brief sketch of New Mexico's history, noting that Santa Fe was "the oldest town in the United States, except for San Augustine, Florida. . . . And her palace, old and unique, but dear to the people, furnishes a home for the present governor, as it has done for his long line of Mexican and Spanish predecessors reaching back nearly three hundred years."[57] Aside from proffering this brief history, Elkins's testimony, like the asamblea's memorial, refrained from discussing the "native Mexican" population and focused instead on the material progress that New Mexico had witnessed through immigration.

Following Elkins's speech, New Mexico's statehood effort gained broad support in Congress, winning the recommendation of the House Committee on the Territories. Statehood bills passed the House and Senate by a nearly three-to-one margin. The House Committee on the Territories produced a glowing four-page recommendation that highlighted the territory's vast terrain, its bountiful grazing lands, stands of timber, and "minerals of all kinds [which] exist in inexhaustible quantities, especially coal." It further pointed out that seventeen states previously had been awarded statehood while possessing fewer residents than New Mexico.[58] Although the recommendation made no direct reference to the region's "Mexican" population, it did conclude that admission into the Union would induce "Europeans" and "Americans" to migrate to the state, exploit its resources, and manage the affairs of the state. To substantiate this conclusion, the committee produced statistics showing how other territories, once admitted into the Union, had rapidly gained white population.[59] Versions of the statehood bill cleared the House and Senate, but lawmakers failed to reconcile them. The second session of the 43rd Congress adjourned without a compromise, leaving New Mexico a territory.

In 1876, under Elkins's command, a reinvigorated statehood campaign swept into Washington, D.C. New Mexico's asamblea issued a new memorial, this one more strident in tone. It chided congressmen for neglecting the territory's earlier plea and insisted that statehood had been promised under the terms of the Treaty of Guadalupe Hidalgo. It also voiced the asamblea's growing contempt for Congress, declaring that "[t]he citizens of New Mexico have noticed with the greatest mortification that their Territory and her claims, based on the high obligations of national treaty, have been disregarded and left without respectable attention or consideration."[60] The people of New Mexico, proclaimed the assembly, "should be admitted to the enjoyment of all the rights of citizens of the United States, according to the principles of the Constitution; they therefore . . . protest against any further discrimination and distinction against them and in favor of other Territories."[61]

The 1876 statehood bill did go on to win the support of the Committee on the Territories, but this time the bill met with openly racist opposition in Congress—possibly because of the contemptuous tone of New Mexico's latest plea. In a fifteen-page minority report, opponents argued that New Mexico possessed neither the "population, industry, intelligence, [nor the] wealth to entitle this Territory to admission in the Union as a sovereign state." [62] Not only had New Mexico's demographic and economic growth been misrepresented, the minority report argued, but hostile relations between "the native population" and Indians had also drawn a dark cloud over all traces of "American" civilization in the region. New Mexico remained a forsaken territory, savage and undemocratic. Its people's "peculiar character" made it unworthy of self-government. The report further disparaged Nuevomexicanos for their lack of formal education, their deficiency in English, their fervent Catholicism, and most important, their lack of European or Anglo-American ancestry or culture. It painted Nuevomexicanos as mixed-blood "Mexicans" of Spanish and Indian parentage, possessing only the worst of both races:

> Of the native population but few are pure-blood or Castilian, probably not more than fifty or one hundred families in all, the rest being a mixture of Spanish or Mexican and Indian in different degrees. With the decadence of early Spanish power and enterprise on this continent the inhabitants of this isolated region, with few exceptions, continued to sink, till now, for nigh two hundred years, into a condition of ignorance, superstition, and sloth that is unequaled by their Aztec neighbors, the Pueblo Indians. [63]

The minority report reveals the "scientific" racial ideology that had gained popularity in the latter half of the nineteenth century. [64] According to Reginald Horsman, this ideology viewed racial difference in either biological or environmental terms. Borrowing from the ideas of Charles Darwin and Herbert Spencer, American "Anglo Saxons," writes Horsman, believed that their racial superiority, their "manifest destiny," was rooted in racial purity— in not having mixed with the other, nonwhite races. "Miscegenation," they felt, would bring about the contamination of the races and lead to the decline of Anglo-Saxon supremacy. As an example, Horsman remarks that American visitors to the Southwest tended to "praise the [racially pure] Pueblo Indians in order to debase the 'mongrel' Mexicans." [65] Throughout the nineteenth century, as a multitude of ideas about race permeated the halls of Congress, each competed for legitimization through science. Phrenology, eugenics, biology, and anthropology served to reaffirm racist theories and inform political debates.

Horsman notes how American "Anglo-Saxon" ideology was the foundation for U.S. foreign policy from the Monroe Doctrine to Theodore Roosevelt's "big stick" diplomacy.[66] Yet domestic politics, too, were informed by scientific theories about "the races." Divergent approaches to the "assimilation" of Indians, the preservation or abolition of slavery, the segregation of blacks from whites, or the exclusion of Chinese immigrants turned on the principle that racial difference was broken down through racial mixture, and that the consequence of such mixture was the devolution of the "pure" races. For segregationists, interracial marriage and mixed-blood progeny threatened to break down the United States' Anglo-Saxon reign over society and invited unwanted scrutiny of the existing social order. White supremacy necessitated the social and sexual compartmentalization of the races.

By scientific standards, blood held the key to an individual's racial identity.[67] Thus, testimonials against statehood for New Mexico, such as this one from the minority report of 1876, often impugned Nuevomexicanos on the basis of their "mixed blood" and "inferior" racial stock, their religion, and their class:

> I am told, and I readily believe, that the mass of the people once constituted the peon class. These appear to have more Indian than Spanish blood in their veins. They are Roman Catholics, retaining yet some of their Indian superstitions. In secret the fires of Montezuma are kept burning as brightly and continuously as a century and a half ago.[68]

In the minds of many Anglo-Americans, Nuevomexicanos were an impure race, a "mixed-blood" and shifty people. Pueblo Indians, on the other hand, were deemed by some to be of purer blood, noble descendants of the Aztec empire. In appearance, Nuevomexicanos were too "swarthy" to be purely Castilian, yet too culturally Hispanicized to be pure-blood Indians. Unlike the Pueblo Indians, Nuevomexicanos were seen as a people without a clear racial identity or history. Although the U.S. census, beginning in 1850, deemed Nuevomexicanos to be "white" for the purposes of enumeration, members of Congress continued to refer to them as "Mexicans" and not "Americans," suggesting that the these terms carried racial connotations.

By the 1870s, Nuevomexicano legislators, as illustrated by their strength in the asamblea, had entrenched themselves in a regional variation of American democracy. At the same time, they were understandably enraged by the implication that as a "mongrel" race, they remained "unfit" for self-government. Although colonial caste distinctions had been abolished more than fifty years earlier, the "language of blood" had been resurrected by Anglo-American legislators.[69]

New Mexico's fate in 1876 also rested on the perception of economic stagnation. While a small sector of the population had begun to engage in wage labor—as miners, field hands, muleteers, and laundresses—few New Mexicans participated in large-scale industry. The railway had yet to arrive.[70] Other western territories, however, had boomed with precious-metal mining, nascent agribusiness, small manufacturing, and related industries, prompting statehood opponents to complain that "[t]here is none of the vitality that marks Colorado, Montana, and Territories purely of American immigration."[71] New Mexico, like its mixed-blood population, appeared stagnant and shiftless in the eyes of Congress. It lacked both the material wealth and a large white "American" population thought necessary for statehood.[72]

In the waning days of the 44th Congress, Colorado and New Mexico briefly joined forces in their statehood bid, but New Mexico's detractors ultimately managed to drive a wedge between them by introducing separate statehood bills for the territories. As Congress was preparing to adjourn, Colorado's Republican supporters managed to wrest crucial, last-minute crossovers among southern Democrats; its bill passed handily, making that territory the nation's "Centennial State." However, New Mexico's bill fell seven votes short of the required two-thirds majority.[73] The defeat was likely sealed by Elkins himself, who wandered into the House chamber in the middle of a "bloody shirt" speech, in which a northern Republican was deriding southern Democrats for their Civil War legacy. Without having heard a word of the oratory, Elkins joined others in congratulating the speechmaker by shaking his hand. Southerners looked on in horror. Historian Robert Larson believes that the famous "Elkins handshake" led statehood supporters from Alabama and Georgia to reverse their support.[74] With a simple gesture, New Mexico was swept into the politics of Reconstruction, just as it had been swept into the politics of slavery and westward expansion.[75]

By 1876, racial politics and perceptions—in addition to the territory's perceived material development or population size—dictated New Mexico's fate. Though the Bureau of the Census enumerated Nuevomexicanos as "white," both supporters and detractors of statehood operated on the assumption that Nuevomexicanos and Anglo-Americans personified two discrete races and cultures. This assumption shaped local, as well as national, politics. In Santa Fe, the capital's leading English-language newspaper, the *New*

Mexican, had since its founding in the 1850s employed the terms "Mexican" and "American" when referring to Nuevomexicanos and Anglo-Americans, respectively. Similarly, Spanish-language newspapers, such as *El nuevo mexicano* and *El independiente,* used the terms "mexicano" and "americano." The ethnic boundary between the two groups seems to have been mutually agreed upon, which is to say that each group recognized the other as ethnically "different." This does not mean, however, that the terms conjured up the same meanings for each group.

Although many Anglo-Americans viewed all "Mexicans" as a single "mixed-blood" race with loyalty to Mexico, others viewed them as fellow U.S. citizens. Many of Santa Fe's Anglo-American and European immigrants engaged Nuevomexicanos in trade, married into their families, and established common political agendas, especially within the Republican Party. Nuevomexicanos themselves, meanwhile, remained divided by class, education, language abilities, and family allegiances. From the 1880s to 1900, these divisions created internal obstacles to statehood, as some Nuevomexicanos defied their Republican leaders' call for public education, viewing it as a threat to their Catholic schools and beliefs. Nevertheless, Nuevomexicanos' continued marginalization from national politics—underscored by racist rhetoric—reinforced a common ethnic sensibility that centered on their "Spanish" history and identity and "American" citizenship and national loyalty. By the twentieth century, as internal dissension abated, the statehood struggle came to embody Nuevomexicanos' desire to become full members of the nation-state.

The minority report of 1876 invoked racial slanders to deny Nuevomexicanos full U.S. citizenship, establishing race as a central issue in the debate over New Mexico's statehood. Thereafter, Nuevomexicanos felt compelled to defend their racial "fitness" for self-government. Their most vocal leaders began proclaiming that as "pure-blood" descendants of the Spanish *conquistadores,* Nuevomexicanos were both racially and culturally fit to govern themselves. This counterargument became particularly pronounced during the third phase of New Mexico's statehood struggle, from 1888 to 1912.

BECOMING SPANISH AMERICAN, 1888–1912

For the better part of the 1880s, New Mexico's statehood effort was at a standstill. The asamblea's support for statehood had evaporated due to intense partisan politics. As a consequence, New Mexico's congressional delegates during this period—Trinidad Romero, Mariano Otero, Tranquilino Luna, and F. A. Manzanares—did not bother to lobby for New Mexico's admission into the Union.[76] Though the territory's population grew rapidly with the advent of

the railway in 1880, ethnic and political factions began to form over land disputes, taxation, and public education. There was a growing concern among
Nuevomexicanos that statehood could precipitate an "invasion" of Anglo-
American lawyers, corrupt officials, and land speculators who would attempt
to displace Nuevomexicanos from their lands. The territory's newspapers
made almost no reference to the statehood issue during this period, suggesting that public officials (the Santa Fe Ring, in particular) did not follow
through with their 1870s campaign to raise popular support for the issue. Nevertheless, Congress and newspapers nationwide did discuss New Mexico's
prospects as a future state.

In 1882, for example, Congress debated statehood but took no favorable
action. That same year, a Trinidad, Colorado, resident wrote to the *New York
Times* that New Mexico's admission would be "simply detestable" because
"about two-thirds of the population of the Territory is of the mongrel breed
known as Mexicans—a mixture of the Apache, negro, Navajo, white horse-
thief, Pueblo Indian, and old-time frontiersman with the original Mexican
stock." [77] According to this individual, Nuevomexicanos were racially mixed
and, therefore, unfit to govern themselves and Anglos. On reading this, New
Mexico's chief justice, Le Baron Bradford Prince, responded with indignation:

> His suggestion of a mixture of "Negro" blood in the general population
> is especially unfortunate, as the census of 1870 showed that even as late
> a date as that there were but 127 persons of African descent in the whole
> Territory. . . . While some of the Pueblo villages are quite near Spanish
> towns, yet no marriage or similar connections take place between the
> races; they are as separate in such respects as if a Chinese wall ran be-
> tween. [78]

Prince's response is significant for two reasons. First, it minimized the
extent of African "blood" in New Mexico, as if to eliminate the "darkest" and
most "inferior" racial element from the population. Second, it incorrectly argued that racial mixture between the "Spanish" and "Indian" races had never
occurred, and that the population was therefore of "pure" Spanish or "pure"
Indian blood. This biracial depiction of New Mexico's society would become
an essential referent in the making of a Spanish American consciousness—
one that would be premised on Nuevomexicanos' racial, cultural, and linguistic "purity." Since "the native people of New Mexico" possessed untainted
"Spanish" blood, wrote Prince, they necessarily descended from the first Spanish settlers and had inherited their traits: "A more courteous, hospitable, and
chivalric social element does not exist in the land. They are fit representatives

of the land of the Cid, and successors of the historic discoverers and conquerors of the soil." [79] In Prince's mind, the Nuevomexicanos' blood purity
and "Spanish" history distinguished them from what opponents called that
"mongrel breed" of "mixed-blood" Mexicans. In other words, by insisting
that Nuevomexicanos possessed "Spanish" origins and by denying racial mixture, Prince was showing them to be racially distinct from the mestizos and
"lower" classes of Mexico and New Mexico, possessing a "Spanish" colonial
heritage. It appears that, like many of his contemporaries, he operated on the
assumption that racial mixture was undesirable because it made a people unfit
for self-government.

Moreover, Prince felt that Hispanas (i.e., women), whom the Colorado
author of the *Times* article had derided as prostitutes, embodied authentic
"Spanish" traits. Defending the "virtue of our countrywomen" against the author's "vile" accusation, Prince declared that "[n]o more high-bred, noble, and
pure-minded women are to be seen on earth than among the Spaniards of New
Mexico. They are brought up with a care similar to that seen in Europe, and
which seems almost too strict to us who are accustomed to the freedom of girl
life in general in the United States." [80] Hispanas, according to Prince, embodied the purity of their race—purity of blood, culture, and character. On the
basis of these virtues, he argued, Nuevomexicanos were most capable of self-
government.

During the 1880s, Prince earned a reputation among Anglo-Americans
as New Mexico's most ardent statehood supporter and tourist booster. Later,
some would refer to him as "the Father of Statehood." [81] As an avid Republican, Prince was also associated with the Santa Fe Ring. In 1910, congressional
approval of New Mexico's enabling act was made possible, in part, due to
Prince's lobbying over the course of three decades. He served the statehood
cause in several capacities—as territorial chief justice (1879–82), territorial
governor (1889–893), president of the Historical Society of New Mexico
(1882–1922), and president of the Bureau of Immigration (1881–1912). From
1880 to 1924, Prince helped to reshape the way Anglo-Americans perceived
Nuevomexicanos (and the way Nuevomexicanos ultimately viewed themselves) by promoting an idealized, biracial (Spanish and Indian) image of New
Mexico's society and history. This Spanish colonial image served to attract
Anglo-American immigrants and tourists to the territory and rendered a new
and romantic understanding of Nuevomexicanos' "Spanish American" identity, history, and culture. But the impression of New Mexico that prevailed in
the 1880s was one of backwardness and racial mixture.

This impression was evident in 1888, when the House of Representatives revisited the statehood question. A minority report from the Committee

on the Territories opined that New Mexico should not be granted statehood because "the inhabitants, with the exception of a few Americans residing in the place, are ignorant and degraded. The place [Santa Fe] bears an evil reputation as one of the most reckless and miserable towns on the globe." [82] The minority report quoted numerous "authorities" on New Mexico, including one who had written: "[Santa Fe's] history is one long continued strife between the cruel and hated Spaniards and the native Pueblos." [83] The "black legend" was still indelibly imprinted upon the minority's historical imagination, leading opponents to ask, "Is it not apparent that the people of New Mexico are not yet prepared for intelligent, honest and capable management of State government?" [84] The minority report quoted William Hart Davis, a U.S. attorney in New Mexico during the 1850s, as saying: "The great mass of people are dark, a mixture, and only a few can legitimately claim to be pure-blood Spaniards. As long as there is intermarriage there is no hope of improving the color of the people." [85] Opponents once again proved successful in their efforts. New Mexico was eliminated from an omnibus bill that granted statehood to Montana, Washington, North Dakota, and South Dakota.

The following year, Prince was appointed territorial governor. From 1889 to 1893, Prince collaborated with Antonio Joseph, the territorial representative in Congress, in lobbying for three statehood bills, and in 1895, Joseph backed a fourth bill. Yet all four were defeated for essentially two reasons: first, there was a growing sense in Congress that residents were divided over statehood; and second, New Mexico's "Mexicans" were still viewed by some observers as incapable of self-government.

The first objection had merit. Congressional opponents argued that New Mexicans themselves were not in agreement on the issue, that there was insufficient popular resolve for self-government. And it was true; the territory was becoming deeply divided over statehood.[86] Democrats, overwhelmingly Anglo and oriented toward Southern ranchers' and small businesses' interests, feared statehood would bring about a demise in their political power unless accompanied by a provision requiring English to be used in the courts, schools, and polling booths. Moreover, merchants worried that the new state government would demand a sales tax, and ranchers feared the state would impose restrictions on grazing in the public domain. Without addressing these latter concerns, Republicans, who enjoyed overwhelming support among Nuevomexicanos, argued that an English-only provision was unnecessary because statehood would precipitate European and Anglo-American immigration and thus stimulate an inevitable and natural evolution from Spanish to English usage in all public spheres.

In place of a language provision, Republicans proposed improvements in secular education to teach Nuevomexicanos English, something that the Catholic church loudly opposed. Viewing secular education as a threat to their parochial schools and religious influence, church officials implored Nuevomexicano parishioners to oppose any state constitution that would mandate public education. And Nuevomexicanos complied. In 1890, many of them joined Democrats in voting down a state constitution, 16,180 to 7,493.[87] It should be noted that in Santa Fe County, the vote was much closer: 1,068 for and 1,549 against.[88] In areas of higher Democratic representation, such as San Miguel County, the vote was overwhelmingly against by a ratio of four to one. Over the next five years, the 1890 vote would serve to reaffirm the minority's impression that Nuevomexicanos simply were not ready for statehood.

The second argument against statehood was strictly a racial one. The opposition portrayed Nuevomexicanos as resistant to "progress" and education. In Washington, D.C., and nationwide, opponents continued to lash out against Nuevomexicanos, calling them "grossly illiterate, superstitious, and morally decadent." [89] In 1893, the *Chicago Tribune* editorialized that New Mexicans were "not American, but 'Greaser[s],' persons ignorant of our laws, manners, customs, language, and institutions." It noted that New Mexico would do well to seek joint unity with the Arizona territory, which boasted 60,000 white Americans and only 10,000 to 15,000 Indians, mestizos, or Mexicans.[90] The opposition repeatedly linked the issue of statehood to national and racial identity, education, language, and religion, a tactic that put advocates, especially Nuevomexicanos, on the defensive. One ally in Congress, the New Jersey Democrat William McAdoo, lamented that the issue had become enveloped in what he euphemistically called "misrepresentation." McAdoo responded that "[t]he Spanish Americans of New Mexico are Americans by birth, sympathy, and education." He pointed out that New Mexico had risked more soldiers for the Union cause than many existing states.[91]

Nuevomexicanos, for their part, were not silent in the face of racist attacks. In 1889, the Colorado lawmaker Casmiro Barela eloquently urged support for statehood and denounced its opponents:

> I know that the enemies of New Mexico's admission claim that its native population still are not qualified to assume the burden, rights, and obligations of citizenship. They charge that the Mexican population is ignorant and can be easily manipulated by talented but desperate American adventurers who have infested the Territory, and who seek to utilize the Mexican population as instruments in their corrupt plans. I reject that accusation with disdain. . . . Since 1848, the Mexican population

has advanced in education, in independence, in mental vigor, and in firm loyalty to the American Government.[92]

Barela's speech, later published in the Spanish-language newspaper *La voz del pueblo*, elaborated the material and intellectual developments that proved New Mexico was ready for statehood. He cited its 2,000 miles of railway; its mines, machinery, and agricultural lands; and, most important, its improvements in education: "I don't deny that the rate of illiteracy among the native population was high when New Mexico first became part of the American dominion, but this is changing rapidly. Official reports show that rate has been reduced by 20 percent over the last five years."[93] With regard to the charge that Nuevomexicanos were incapable of self-government because "four-fifths of the population are peon Aztec Indians," Barela responded: "When I speak of the character of the population, I find myself . . . resenting the many insults that have been leveled by its enemies. . . . The greater part of the native Mexicans are not as aggressive and volatile as their Anglo-Saxon brothers."[94]

Another prominent Nuevomexicano, José D. Sena, a Santa Fe delegate to the constitutional convention, wrote: "It is an insult to the descendants of Hidalgo, Morelos, and Iturbide when the opponents of statehood say, 'we' are not fit to govern ourselves."[95] Sena apparently referred to these Mexican heroes of the revolution to illustrate that Nuevomexicanos possessed republican, not monarchical, leanings. Antonio Joseph, who was of Nuevomexicano and Anglo parentage, concurred, saying, "It is not by blood or language that one measures the devotion of New Mexico's people to the United States and its institutions. For these are the descendants of the daring discoverers who abandoned the monarchical institutions of Spain and moved to the New World . . . to break away from foreign [Spanish] domination. The devotion to republican institutions on the part of the descendants of Spain and Mexico is no less than that of the heroes of the [Mexican] revolution."[96] According to Joseph, whether or not Nuevomexicanos possessed "mixed blood" or spoke only Spanish, they possessed a heritage of conquest, courage, and republican sentiment dating to the colonial period. By referring to them as "descendants of the daring discoverers," Joseph implied that Nuevomexicanos were ethnically, if not racially, "Spanish."

Some Anglo-American opponents of statehood feared that once New Mexico was in the Union, Nuevomexicanos would conspire against them and exclude them from political office. In 1893, *La voz del pueblo* responded to an accusation that New Mexico's Nuevomexicanos sought statehood as a means of placing their own people in positions of power. Calling these accusations "political strategies," an editorial countered, "Whatever their nationality, New Mexicans will vote for the most deserving candidate. The question of race never has come between New Mexicans, for they are too divided to unite on the question of race."[97] To be certain, Nuevomexicanos did not represent a monolithic political entity, despite the fact that they overwhelmingly supported the Republican Party in territorial elections. As noted, whatever ethnic solidarity they felt belied divisions based on family allegiances and local issues.

With the growth of Spanish-language periodicals in the 1890s, such divisions became less pronounced. In addition to the Las Vegas–based *La voz del pueblo*, such newspapers as Albuquerque's *El nuevo mundo* and Santa Fe's *El nuevo mexicano* increasingly advocated admission to the Union as a remedy for Nuevomexicanos' continued political marginalization. Perhaps due to their influence, a general consensus in favor of statehood emerged among Nuevomexicanos. Editorials regularly appeared that defended the patriotism of "those in whose veins runs the blood of Cortez, Pizarro, and Alvarado."[98] Like their ancestors and like other Americans, Nuevomexicanos valued patriotism and human dignity more than their own lives, stated the editorial. They would remain unquestionably loyal to the United States.

Ignoring Nuevomexicanos' growing consensus on admission to the Union, congressional opposition managed to squelch New Mexico's statehood efforts on five occasions between 1888 and 1895 by invoking overtly racist arguments. Ironically, during this period, a principal obstacle to statehood—the lack of public education—was overcome. In 1889, the territorial legislature—in spite of the Catholic church's opposition—established public education on primary, secondary, and postsecondary levels, including land grant universities and normal schools. By 1890, New Mexico boasted 342 public schools; 143 of them taught exclusively in the English language and 106 in the Spanish language, and 93 were bilingual. In addition, there were numerous private Catholic schools. Despite improvements in education, congressmen continued their opposition, thwarting every move toward admission between 1888 and 1895.[99]

The 1890s was a key decade in the making of Spanish American identity. Anglo immigration and tourism increased significantly. The use of the English language in public realms grew, as did the number of English- and Spanish-language newspapers.[100] A larger proportion of Nuevomexicanos was becoming bilingual and/or biliterate and, therefore, skilled in maneuvering between Anglo-American and Nuevomexicano political and cultural arenas. Literacy rates were improving. Nuevomexicanos now gained access to news from Spain, Mexico, and the rest of Latin America in newspapers such as the Democratic *La voz del pueblo*. In 1893, *El boletín popular* reported on a meeting of "la Prensa Asociada Hispano-Americana," which represented some "64 publicaciones hispano-americanas" published in the United States.[101] By that year, the five largest Spanish-language newspapers in northern New Mexico— *El nuevo mexicano, La voz del pueblo, El boletín popular, El independiente,* and *El nuevo mundo*—had begun to print stories favorable to statehood and critical of those who disparaged Nuevomexicanos.[102]

It is difficult to assess whether these newspapers promoted a sense of spiritual kinship with Latin America or Spain, but they clearly viewed statehood as a vehicle for ethnic solidarity. This solidarity expressed itself in pro-statehood articles advocating Nuevomexicano pride in their "Spanish" language, culture, and history, as well as in their "American" national loyalties. Changes in ethnic nomenclature evinced a growing "Spanish" consciousness. With increasing frequency, Spanish-language newspapers employed the term *hispano-americano*—which literally translates as "Hispanic-American," but was rendered loosely as "Spanish-American"—in place of *mexicano*. As historian Adrián Herminio Bustamante notes, "By the end of the 1890s the term *hispano-americano* becomes more prevalent" in newspapers. "*Hispano-americano* was a strategic term to use vis-à-vis the Anglo-Americans."[103] The term *hispano-americano* underscored a rise in Nuevomexicanos' "Spanish" ethnic sensibility and "American" national allegiance. At the same time, it relieved Nuevomexicanos of the "Mexican" label that Anglo-Americans had used to disparage them. Phillip B. Gonzales contends that "all ethnic identification is variable, in which case the meaning of Spanish identity is found to lie in the social and historical circumstances in which it is expressed."[104] In the context of their continued exclusion from national politics, and in light of the racist justifications for their exclusion, some Nuevomexicanos empowered themselves by redefining their identity in new ethnic, historical, and racial terms. This is not to suggest, however, that there was not a clearly commercial, tourist component to the "Spanish" ethos that began to flourish in the 1890s, for the Santa Fe Railway and the New Mexico Bureau of Immigration were keys to the promotion of a biracial ("Spanish colonial" and "Indian") image of New Mexico's native communities.[105]

The term *hispano-americano* might seem to possess transnational implications, broadly referring to "Spanish Americans" of any Latin American country, but in northern New Mexico it possessed a particular meaning and function in the context of New Mexico's struggle for statehood. That function was, in part, to resist social and political marginalization on both the national and the local level. Recall that statehood promised Nuevomexicanos national political participation and local control over resources and political offices. As employed in newspapers in northern New Mexico, the term *hispano* or "Spanish" expressed resistance to the "mixed-blood" scientific-racial characterizations that Nuevomexicanos had suffered in their statehood struggle. As *Spanish*-Americans, Nuevomexicanos possessed a clear racial identity and historical lineage that dated to the very "conquest" of New Mexico, beginning in the sixteenth century. This term restored their presumed "purity of blood" and, therefore, rendered them racially "fit" for self-government. The term *americano* or "American," on the other hand, expressed resistance to political marginalization and asserted a national (or nativist) political identity. As "American" citizens, Spanish Americans distinguished themselves from "Mexican" immigrants from Mexico. Simultaneously, the term implied a national loyalty to the United States.

As expressed both in newspapers and in the congressional hearings on New Mexico's statehood in the 1890s, the term "Spanish American" conveyed a distinctive pride in Nuevomexicanos' Spanish heritage. Gauging the popularity of the Spanish American consciousness is a precarious task, given the paucity of written expressions on the part of the Nuevomexicano masses. However, one can infer that newspapers shaped the worldview of those Nuevomexicanos who had access to them and could read Spanish. In 1893, Antonio Joseph issued yet another plea for statehood, noting that "[t]he result has always been the same. . . . They [members of Congress] have denied us statehood because . . . some of those individuals cannot see beyond the ends of the noses, and they have been and remain against the *hispano-americanos*, the legitimate owners of this land." [106] This statement draws a relationship among *hispano-americano* identity, resistance to racial discrimination, the denial of statehood, and ownership of the land. Whether or not a Nuevomexicano actually owned land, he or she often claimed a legacy of occupation dating to the Spanish conquest and, consequently, direct descent from the *conquistadores* who had conquered and settled the land. By the turn of the century, Nuevomexicanos began to employ a familiar racial rhetoric based on consanguinity, referring to their "blood," or lineage, as evidence of their European racial heritage.

On October 26, 1901, 600 protesters took to the streets of Las Vegas, New Mexico, to denounce an editorial published in the local newspaper, the *Review,* by a Protestant missionary, Nellie Snyder. Six days earlier, Snyder had attacked what she referred to as New Mexico's "Spanish Americans" as slovenly and semipagan, of mixed (Indian and Spanish) blood, and a people who lived in mud huts and slept on piles of rags for beds. Outraged citizens organized a protest rally at the old plaza, where a young lawyer, Eusebio Chacón, rose to address the crowd in Spanish:

[The] author [of the editorial] begins to amaze us by saying that the Spanish American or Mexican is part Spanish and part Indian; that he resembles his Spanish and Indian ancestors in language, customs, appearance and habits. How she has twisted the linguistic canons to combine the Spanish and Indian tongues is a mystery to us. . . . I am Spanish American as are those who hear me. No other blood circulates through my veins but that which was brought by Don Juan de Oñate and those illustrious ancestors bearing my name who later brought it. If in any part of Spanish America or in the former Spanish dominion the purity of physiognomic features of the conquering race has been preserved, it has been in New Mexico. Yes, some degree of mixture has occurred, but slightly and in only rare cases such that to say that we are, as a community, a mixed race is neither proven by historical facts nor withstands scientific analysis.[107]

Even if Nuevomexicanos were a mixed-blood people, Chacón continued, there would be no dishonor in that fact, for racial mixture was equally a feature of European peoples. Moreover, nothing, he stressed, "was superior to the temperament or intellectual abilities of the Native American race when our forebears conquered them."[108] Chacón's protest, embedded with popular assumptions about race and with divergent, even contradictory lines of reasoning, manifested an emerging ethnic consciousness among Nuevomexicanos.[109] As his speech indicates, the Spanish American ethos that evolved between the 1880s and 1920s centered on a heritage of conquest and colonization—of permanency on the land and struggle against social and political marginalization by Anglo-Americans—and on a European racial heritage that was juxtaposed to that of Native Americans.

Spanish Americans defined their link to the past in terms of consanguinity, or blood relations. Whether or not one could trace one's genealogy to the *conquistadores,* many self-labeled Spanish Americans laid claim to a history of conquest that, however inflated or constructed, represented the ideological underpinnings of ethnic consciousness. In 1901, to claim "Spanish" blood, as Eusebio Chacón did, was to declare one's identity relative to "Indian" and "Anglo" American neighbors, and to lay claim to a history of Spanish conquest and colonization of northern New Mexico. The language of blood was the language of identity. Chacón's protest against Nellie Snyder's racist editorial embodied a growing Spanish American consciousness, one bound up in notions of "Spanish" race, language, and culture, and American national loyalties. His statement clearly illustrates the "purity of blood" counterargument to statehood opponents and draws direct relationships among Spanish American identity, Spanish blood (both a medieval and a scientific metaphor for race), and historical lineage to the first "conqueror" of New Mexico, Juan de Oñate. "Since our forefathers came from Spain, we have lived on this soil, claiming it through our labors and populating it with our posterity."[110]

Chacón's oratory went on to discuss how Snyder's racist rhetoric was the same that Congress used to deny New Mexico statehood:

> The government, which boasts so much nowadays about educating Cubans, Puerto Ricans and Filipinos, has done nothing to spread education among us. The few educational institutions which there are among us are the fruits of our own labor. . . . We have patiently awaited the hour of our redemption; but that redemption is not borne, for sure, by those who insult our homes and our beliefs. We return today, with the zeal of those who know no other homeland or banner than the American, to petition, perhaps for the twentieth time, that overly desired admission to the sovereignty of Statehood.[111]

Chacón articulates a keen awareness of the broader national and international context within which Nuevomexicanos struggled for self-government. If many Americans felt it was the United States' "white man's burden" to liberate Spain's former colonies in the Caribbean and the Philippines, was it not also its obligation to liberate Nuevomexicanos from their colonial relationship to the federal government?

Many Americans apparently remained unconvinced of Nuevomexicanos' loyalty to the United States during the Spanish-American War. According to the historian Anselmo Arellano, "rumors began to circulate throughout New Mexico about their disloyalty and lack of patriotism. . . . Much of the criticism centered on the opinion that Hispanos did not want to fight against their mother country Spain."[112] A Silver City newspaper spoke of the "Spanish Americans' . . . link . . . with the language which has prompted an allegiance with their Spanish ancestors."[113] Such accusations moved one Nuevomexicano to publish the following poem in *El nuevo mexicano:*

Muchas son las opiniones	Many are the opinions
En contra del pueblo hispano,	Against the *pueblo hispano,*
Y le acusan de triador	And they accuse them of betraying
Al gobierno americano	The American government.
Haciendo un experimento,	Making an experiment,
Quedarán desengañados,	They will be disillusioned,

Que nuestros bravos nativos	Our brave native men
No rehusan ser soldados,	Do not refuse to be soldiers.
No importa lo que se diga	It matters not what is said
Y difame de su fama,	Or how they defame them
Pero pelearán gustosos	As they will gladly fight
Por el águilar americano,	For the American eagle.
A nuestro pueblo nativo	They accuse our *pueblo hispano*
Le acusan de ser canalla,	Of being rabble
Pero no ha demostrado serlo,	But they have not proven to be so
En el campo de batalla . . .	On the battlefield.
Como buenos compatriotas	Like good countrymen
Y fieles americanos,	And faithful Americans
Libraremos de ese yugo	We will free from that yoke
A los humildes cubanos . . .	The humble Cubans.[114]

Ironically, Nuevomexicanos' loyalty to the United States during the Spanish-American War would become a badge of honor for the generation that referred to itself as Spanish American.[115]

Although the authorship of this and other editorials in Spanish-language newspapers often went unrecorded, it is important to consider the class and education of Nuevomexicano authors. Chacón is representative of the Nuevomexicano literati. An articulate man, he had been educated at Notre Dame University in Indiana. As a lawyer, author, translator, and acknowledged intellectual, he can be counted among the "elite" Nuevomexicanos who possessed education and who claimed to speak on behalf of a constituency. But to what extent did literate Nuevomexicanos like Chacón vocalize a popular identity? Conversely, to what extent did they propagate their own particular notions of identity? Was Spanish American identity an elitist invention? These questions merit consideration, but they are difficult to answer with any precision.[116] Illiterate or semiliterate Nuevomexicanos left few records. Existing in somewhat greater numbers are the oral texts left behind in the form of unrecorded poems, songs, and folklore—subjects that attracted the attention of the linguist Aurelio Macedonio Espinosa at the turn of the century. His studies of New Mexico folklore emphasized similarities with the folklore of Spain and archaisms that date to the colonial era.[117] Though Espinosa's study of Nuevomexicano oral traditions has been widely contested, his assertion that Nuevomexicanos possessed a Spanish ethnic heritage seems to confirm the record left by literate and, especially, bilingual officials who occupied the middling ranks of society: court translators, postmen, merchants, and the like.

Evidence of Nuevomexicanos' burgeoning Spanish American consciousness—and of Anglo-Americans' growing perception of them as "Spanish"—can be found in the transcripts of congressional statehood hearings. In 1902, a delegation representing a subcommittee of the Committee on the Territories sought to ascertain whether Arizona, Oklahoma, the Indian Territory, and New Mexico merited statehood. The delegation visited various locations in New Mexico and conducted hearings involving Nuevomexicanos and Anglo-Americans. Although some of these hearings involved individuals who spoke only Spanish, several involved bilingual Nuevomexicanos who responded in English. To assess whether Nuevomexicanos were adequately prepared for or deserving of self-government, the delegation inquired into their ability to speak English and their racial identity. The following excerpts are revealing.

> Castaneda Hotel, East Las Vegas, N. Mex., Wednesday, November 12, 1902, 2 o'clock P.M. The committee began the hearing of testi-
> [sic] at the above-named place on the above date.

Nepomuceno Segura, first having been duly sworn, testified as follows:

Q. How long have you lived in the Territory?
A. I have lived all my life in the Territory.
Q. How old are you?
A. I was born in 1853, at Santa Fe, N. Mex.
Q. Are you the court interpreter here?
A. I am; yes, sir.
Q. The court interpreter is appointed by the judge of the court?
A. Yes, sir.
Q. Will you describe to the committees the duties—the nature of your duties in that office?
A. Yes, sir. The nature of my duties are to interpret from English into Spanish all evidence given before the court. There are very many Spanish-speaking people that come before the court as defendants and witnesses, and I have to interpret both ways—from the Spanish into the English and from the English into the Spanish; also the arguments of counsel, both into English and Spanish. That is the amount of the duties of a court interpreter.
Q. But in the majority of the cases in which your services are required—what is the nature of the majority of the cases in which your services are required?

A. Well, the majority of them are criminal cases, because I act as in-
    terpreter both for the United States court and for the Territorial
    courts; you understand they are both separate courts, of course.

Q. The majority of the cases under the Edmunds law has been due to
    the influx of the Mormon population?

A. No, I do not believe so. . . . Generally, it comes from the lower
    strata of our people (and when I say "our people" I mean the
    Mexican people) that are brought before the court under the
    law.

Q. Now, will you take up these counties in their turn and give your
    estimate as to the proportions of the population, native and for-
    eign, and the kind of cases that predominate in each county?

A. I will take San Miguel, which is the largest, I think, in New Mex-
    ico. We have that proportion of people here. Now, having that
    proportion of people here—of Mexican people here—foreign
    element you would call it—the Mexican element, so called,
    won't come up to half of the criminal proportion in the
    courts.[118]

This excerpt of Nepomuceno Segura's testimony is typical of the dozens of
Nuevomexicano testimonies during the 1902 hearings. All of the Nuevomexicanos who testified were fluent in English as well as Spanish, having occupied
positions as educators, court translators, or census takers. Most invoked the
term "Mexican" in referring to themselves and their "people." They established that "Mexicans" were the predominant component of the population
and that "Americans" comprised the minority, both demographically and
linguistically. Sometimes, the congressmen and Anglo-American witnesses
employed the terms "foreign" and "native" as euphemisms for "Mexican" and
"American," respectively; however, the opposite association was most common. Nuevomexicanos were regularly asked if they were "natives" of the
territory.[119]

   Similarly, although "Mexican" was the most common ethnic term employed, several Nuevomexicanos and some Anglo-Americans referred to
Nuevomexicanos as "Spanish" or "Spaniards." For example, there is the testimony of census taker Pablo Jaramillo of the Las Vegas precinct, who never ut-
tered the word "Mexican," even when directly questioned by the senators:

Q. What proportion [of your precinct] were Mexicans?

A. More than half of them.

Q. Do you speak Spanish?

A.   Yes, sir; I am a Spaniard.
Q.   And in taking the census you used both languages, did you?
A.   Yes, sir; where there were Spanish people I used Spanish, and
     where there were American people I used English.
Q.   Are you a native of the territory?
A.   Yes, sir.[120]

Jaramillo's refusal to use the term "Mexican" and his invocation of his "Spanish" identity reveal how some Nuevomexicanos had begun to distinguish
themselves from Mexican nationals, as if to vanquish Anglo impressions of
them as foreigners or of mixed blood. No Nuevomexicanos objected outright
to the use of the word "Mexican," but a number of witnesses did describe their
people as "Spanish," especially in association with language usage. The census
taker José Lino Rivera, for example, claimed to use the "Spanish [language]
with the Spanish people." [121]

Non-Nuevomexicanos, or so-called American witnesses, similarly described Nuevomexicanos as "Mexicans" or "natives." Justice of the Peace
H. S. Wooster, a New York native, summed up his impression of the racial
composition of New Mexico thusly:

Q.   The population over there [Las Vegas] is, as we all understand,
     principally Spanish?
A.   Chiefly Mexican. By that we distinguish the Spanish-speaking
     people from the others; there is some Spanish and some Indians,
     and a mixture of people.
Q.   Are most of these people who live out in the country away from
     the town Mexicans, as that term is used down here?
A.   Yes, sir.
Q.   And they speak what language?
A.   They speak the Spanish language, or try to; but I understand that
     it is not pure Castilian; it is a sort of a jargon of their own.[122]

The senator's phrasing—"Mexican . . . as that term is used down
here"—hints of his awareness of the complexity of ethnic nomenclature in
northern New Mexico. At the turn of the century, among both Nuevomexicanos and Anglo-Americans, "Mexican" and "Spanish" labels were often in-
terchanged to refer to Spanish-speaking, often bilingual, natives of New Mexico. Locally, the term "Mexican" did not have overt nationalist overtones or
refer to citizens of Mexico, as many congressmen apparently believed. By ei-

ther designation, Nuevomexicanos defined themselves in opposition to the objectified "Indian" and so-called "American." However, with increasing frequency, statehood proponents characterized Nuevomexicanos as "Spanish" and not "Mexican."

Appearing before the Committee on the Territories in 1903, L. Bradford Prince insisted that New Mexico's "Mexicans," as he referred to them, were "Americans of Spanish descent." The mayor of Santa Fe, appearing before that same body, concurred, stating, "Real Mexicans in our town are about as rare as they are in the city of Washington." [123] As the groundswell for statehood intensified, leaders of the movement tried to vanquish all "Mexican" impressions of these "Spanish" Americans. This was a formidable proposition, however. Congress refused to act on the statehood issue as long as Arizona representatives rejected jointure with New Mexico. As one Arizona resident put it, "Shall we join the Mexican greasers to Arizona and let them control it?" [124]

Popular support for statehood in New Mexico prompted intense lobbying efforts in Washington, D.C. On six occasions between 1901 and 1910, New Mexico leaders appeared before Congress pleading for statehood. Their receptions were mixed. But despite repeated setbacks, they maintained an appearance of optimism. Prince continued to boast of New Mexico's resources and vast improvements in public education while continually having to defend the use of Spanish in public documents, the courts' use of interpreters, and Nuevomexicanos' English competency and patriotism. As for patriotism, observed Prince during a 1903 congressional hearing, "no less than 1,089 volunteers" had enlisted for the Spanish-American War, and some 500 Rough Riders had valiantly marched up San Juan Hill with Roosevelt. These were no ordinary "Mexicans" from "Old Mexico," Prince explained. "I have used the term 'Mexican,' and 'American,' as they are commonly used there, the former to represent an American of Spanish descent and the latter of English descent." [125] When asked if statehood might "induce Mexicans to come in from old Mexico," Prince snapped, "Not one, probably. They never have come. Mexicans are as scarce in New Mexico as Alaskans; I have never seen over four or five in the twenty-four years I have lived there." [126]

Four days later, Ishmael Sparks, the mayor of Santa Fe, sat before the same body and reaffirmed the distinction between New Mexico's "Mexicans" and "Mexicans from Old Mexico."

MR. LLOYD   What is the relative population of the Americans and Mexicans in the city of Santa Fe?

MR. SPARKS   There is probably a small majority of Mexicans in the
   city of Santa Fe.
MR. LLOYD   What do you mean by "Mexicans?"
MR. SPARKS   The native-born people, of Spanish descent.
MR. LLOYD   Simply of Spanish descent? You do not mean by that,
   though, they were born in Mexico?
MR. SPARKS   Oh, no.
MR. LLOYD   What per cent of the population that you call "Mexican"
   were born in Mexico?
MR. SPARKS   I will put that very low.[127]

As the groundswell for statehood intensified, leaders of the movement tried to vanquish all "Mexican" traits from the population, underscoring the Hispanos' "Spanish" legacy. Notwithstanding such claims, many congressmen and Arizona residents remained unconvinced that Nuevomexicanos were as "Spanish" as they had claimed and were not willing to accept them as full "Americans." Moreover, Anglo-Americans worried that Nuevomexicanos, if elected to state positions, would collude to diminish Anglo political power and cultural importance. One immigration brochure tried to put this fear to rest, saying, "The Mexican population is not dominant, although it is sufficient to give a decided color to the prevalent impression. With the influx of immigrants from the eastern states, bringing with them the education and culture of their surroundings, the influence of the Mexican and his out-of-date customs will become less and less." [128]

Having been rebuffed in 1903, New Mexico's delegation believed that statehood could only be brought about if Arizona and New Mexico were admitted jointly. It called upon Arizona to support the effort. But, as before, Arizona leaders protested such an "amalgamation" because they feared "being dominated by people whom we do not believe should be mixed up with us at all." [129] New Mexico's delegation then worked to convince Congress that "jointure"—as many referred to the joint admission idea—was not only feasible, but desirable, since it would ensure a large English-speaking population and Anglo-American majority. The delegation even agreed to call the prospective state "Arizona," as opposed to some of the alternative names proposed, such as "Montezuma" or "New Mexico." In a 1905 address to Congress, President Theodore Roosevelt called for joint admission of Arizona and New Mexico, ostensibly to repay New Mexicans for their exemplary participation in the Spanish-American War.

The following year, against protests from both Arizona and some New Mexico officials, Congress complied with Roosevelt's request and passed a joint statehood bill, which Roosevelt readily signed. The measure, however, contained a major proviso: each territory had to hold an election to approve of joint statehood. On learning that the new state would be called Arizona, many New Mexicans expressed dismay at losing their territory's historic name and opposed the measure. Additional internal dissension came from prominent county bosses, such as Thomas Catron of Santa Fe, who warned that Arizona's growing population of Anglos would eventually dominate state politics and probably attempt to disenfranchise Nuevomexicanos with an English literacy requirement at the polls. Most New Mexicans desired separate statehood, observed Prince, but they nevertheless preferred "any kind of statehood to none at all." [130] Despite such opposition, voters approved joint statehood, 26,195 to 14,735. Most voters seemed to have agreed with L. Bradford Prince, a recent convert to joint admission.

Opposition outside New Mexico, however, proved insurmountable. Some newspapers, such as the *Boston Transcript* and the *Pittsburgh Times,* continued to emphasize the widespread use of Spanish as the territory's main liability and, according to historian Robert Larson, still referred to Nuevomexicanos as "a mongrel population too ignorant and lazy to assume the privileges of full citizenship." Not unexpectedly, Arizonans thoroughly rejected jointure, 16,265 to 3,141, thereby nullifying the enabling act. "New Mexico's predominantly Spanish-speaking population and Arizona's Anglo majority," surmises Larson, "seemed to many an incompatible combination." [131]

In 1909, Roosevelt made a last-ditch effort to bring about statehood. This time he abandoned the idea of joining the territories and sought separate statehood enabling acts. Unfortunately, those bills did not survive the Committee on the Territories, which was headed by a statehood foe, Senator Alfred Beveridge of Indiana, who unleashed damaging charges of scandal and corruption among New Mexico's territorial leaders. The following year, President William Howard Taft, eager to resolve the persistent issue, urged the 61st Congress to act swiftly. It passed bills authorizing separate statehood and referred them to the Committee on the Territories, where Beveridge, seeing the growing support for the bills, relinquished his opposition to them.

Sixty years after New Mexico's quest began, President Taft signed the enabling legislation admitting Arizona and New Mexico as separate states on June 20, 1910.[132] Their formal entry into the Union came two years later, despite numerous last-minute challenges on the part of some congressional Democrats who protested specific provisions of the constitution dealing with recall procedures. On January 6, 1912, after constitutions had been drafted and approved by both Congress and the president, New Mexico became the only state at that time to possess two official languages—English and Spanish. Its constitution mandated that all public documents be printed in both languages, that English proficiency not be a prerequisite for holding office or jury duty (translators would be provided), and that "children of Spanish descent" be guaranteed an education in their native language.[133]

Despite New Mexico's admission into the Union, some Anglo-Americans remained skeptical about Nuevomexicanos' capacity to govern themselves and continued to deride them as "a race speaking an alien language" and a people not possessing the "best blood on the American continent." [134] Such perceptions had earlier prodded Nuevomexicanos to redefine themselves as Spanish in ethnic origin and American in nationality, an effort that persisted and permeated many aspects of life following statehood.

NOTES

I wish to thank George Sánchez, Norris Hundley, Valerie Matsumoto, and Edward Telles for their patient reading of the initial draft of this article, which comprised a portion of my Ph.D. dissertation (University of California, Los Angeles, 1997). Their counsel was, and still is, invaluable to me, but they are not to be associated with any mistakes in judgment or factual errors contained in my work. I also wish to thank the Ford Foundation, the Smithsonian Institution, UCLA's Institute for American Cultures, and New Mexico State University for the wherewithal to carry out research for this article. It should be noted that since this article was first written, my understanding of New Mexico's statehood struggle has been transformed by my examination of Puerto Rico's political status and by recent monographs on U.S. citizenship as it has been historically defined and reshaped by imperialism, whiteness, and gender. Too numerous to mention all of them here, those works include Matthew Frye Jacobson, *Whiteness of a Different Color: European Immigrants and the Alchemy of Race* (Cambridge: Harvard University Press, 1998); Linda K. Kerber, *No Constitutional Right to Be Ladies: Women and the Obligations of Citizenship* (New York: Hill and Wang, 1998); Neil Foley, *The White Scourge: Mexicans, Black, and Poor Whites in Texas Cotton Culture* (Berkeley: University of California Press, 1997); Ian F. Haney López, *White by Law: The Legal Construction of Race* (New York: New York University Press, 1996).

1. *Congressional Globe*, 30th Cong., 1st. sess., 1848, 98.

2. Chicana and Chicano scholars have documented how U.S. conquest reshaped the lives and ethnic identities of Mexicans residing in the vanquished lands. Few have addressed how conquest reshaped the lives and racial perceptions of the conquerors. The body of literature on nineteenth-century Chicano and Chicana history is too vast to mention here, but major works include Rodolfo Acuña, *Occupied America: The Chicano's Struggle toward Liberation* (San Francisco: Harper and Row, Canfield Press, 1972); Mario Barrera, *Race and Class in the Southwest: A Theory of Racial Inequality* (Notre Dame, Ind.: University of Notre Dame Press, 1979); Albert Camarillo, *Chicanos in a Changing*

Society: From Mexican Pueblos to American Barrios (Cambridge: Harvard University Press, 1979); John R. Chávez, *The Lost Land: The Chicano Image of the Southwest* (Albuquerque: University of New Mexico Press, 1984); Sarah Deutsch, *No Separate Refuge: Culture, Class, and Gender on an Anglo-Hispanic Frontier in the American Southwest, 1880–1940* (New York: Oxford University Press, 1987); Deena J. González, *Refusing the Favor: Spanish-Mexican Women of Santa Fe, 1820–1880* (Oxford University Press, 1999); Richard Griswold del Castillo, *La familia: Chicano Families in the Urban Southwest, 1848 to the Present* (South Bend: University of Notre Dame Press, 1984); Lisbeth Haas, *Conquest and Historical Identities in California, 1769–1936* (Berkeley: University of California Press, 1995); David Montejano, *Anglos and Mexicans in the Making of Texas, 1836–1986* (Austin: University of Texas Press, 1987); Robert Rosenbaum, *Mexicano Resistance in the Southwest: "The Sacred Right of Self-Preservation"* (Austin: University of Texas Press, 1981); David J. Weber, ed., *Foreigners in Their Native Land: Historical Roots of Mexican Americans* (Albuquerque: University of New Mexico Press, 1973).

3. *Congressional Globe*, 30th Cong., 1st. sess., 1848, 99.

4. Ibid.

5. Calhoun was recorded as saying: "We make a great mistake, sirs, when we suppose that all people are capable of self-government. . . . None but people advanced to a very high state of moral and intellectual improvement are capable, in a civilized state, of maintaining free government." Ibid. For a discussion of white racial supremacy and Anglo-Saxonism, see Jacobson, *Whiteness of a Different Color*.

6. On July 22, 1854, Congress established the Office of the Surveyor General, whose job it was to survey all lands in New Mexico. The resulting report eventually led Congress to confirm and patent twenty Pueblo Indian land grants between 1858 and 1864. U.S. House, *An Act to Create a Land District in the Territory of New Mexico*, 35th Cong., 1st sess., 1858, H.R. 564; U.S. House, *An Act to Confirm the Land Claims of Certain Pueblos and Towns in the Territory of New Mexico*, 35th Cong., 1st sess., 1858, H.R. 565. New Mexico's land issues occupy books too numerous to mention here. For a general understanding, refer to Joe S. Sando, *The Pueblo Indians* (San Francisco: Indian Historian Press), 75–81; Roxanne Dunbar Ortiz, "Roots of Resistance: Land Tenure in New Mexico, 1680–1980" (Ph.D. diss., University of California, Los Angeles, 1980); and Charles L. Briggs and John R. Van Ness, eds., *Land, Water, and Culture: New Perspectives on Hispanic Land Grants* (Albuquerque: University of New Mexico Press, 1987).

7. Sando, 74.

8. New Mexico House, Dec. 6, 1853. Territorial Archives of New Mexico (TANM), reel 1, frame 260.

9. Ibid., frames 262–63.

10. Lamar writes: "New Mexican leaders saw in civil government and statehood the chance to escape military rule, achieve autonomy for their region, and gain local office for themselves." Lamar, *The Far Southwest* (New York: W. W. Norton, 1970), 71.

11. Petition of Oct. 14, 1848. Quoted in Le Baron Bradford Prince, *New Mexico's*

Struggle for Statehood: Sixty Years of Effort to Obtain Self Government (Santa Fe: New Mexican Printing Company, 1910), 10.

12. Ibid.

13. Ibid.

14. Ibid., 20; Lamar, 80–81.

15. U.S. House, *California and New Mexico: Speech of Hon. Joseph M. Root, of Ohio, February 15, 1850* [Washington, D.C., 1850], 2.; U.S. House, *California and New Mexico: Speech of Hon. James S. Green, of Missouri, February 15, 1850* [Washington, D.C., 1850], 4.

16. U.S. Senate, *Speech of William H. Seward on the Admission of New Mexico: Delivered in the Senate of the United States, July 26, 1850* (Washington: Buell and Blanchard, Printers, 1850), 4.

17. Ibid.

18. Lamar, 9–10.

19. *Speech of Seward*, 5.

20. David J. Weber, "'Scarce More than Apes': Historical Roots of Anglo-American Stereotypes of Mexicans," in *New Spain's Far Northern Frontier: Essays on Spain in the American West, 1540–1821*, ed. David J. Weber (Albuquerque: University of New Mexico Press, 1979), 293–307.

21. Senate, *Speech of Seward*, 9.

22. Ibid., 8.

23. Ibid., 14.

24. *Speech of Hon. A. W. Venable, of N. Carolina, on the Texas and New Mexico Question: Delivered in the House of Representatives, Thursday, August 15, 1850* (Washington: Congressional Globe Office, 1850), 8.

25. Lamar, 81; Prince, *New Mexico's Struggle*, 22–23.

26. Prince, *New Mexico's Struggle*, 23.

27. *Cuarto mensaje anual de S.E.D. Enrique Connelly a la Asamblea Legislativa de Nuevo Méjico, pronunciado diciembre, 1865* (Santa Fe: Manderfield y Tucker, Impresores, Oficina de El Nuevo Mejicano, [1865]), 18.

28. Ibid., 20.

29. Ibid., 24; U.S. House, *State Government for New Mexico: Memorial of the Assembly of New Mexico, in Regard to a State Government for That Territory*, 39th Cong., 1st sess., 1866, Misc. Doc. no. 57.

30. Ramón A. Gutiérrez, "Aztlán, Montezuma, and New Mexico: The Political Uses of American Indian Mythology," in *Aztlán: Essays on the Chicano Homeland* (Albuquerque: El Norte Publications, 1990), 175.

31. Malcolm Ebright, "New Mexico Land Grants: The Legal Background," in Charles L. Briggs and John R. Van Ness, eds., *Land, Water, and Culture: New Perspectives on Hispanic Land Grants* (Albuquerque: University of New Mexico Press, 1987), 40.

32. Lamar, 136–170.

33. Lamar, 144.

34. Elias Brevoort, *New Mexico: Her Natural Resources and Attractions, Being a Collection of*

Facts, Mainly Concerning Her Geography, Climate, Population, Schools, Mines and Mineral, Agricultural, and Pastoral Capacities, Prospective Railroads, Public Lands, and Spanish and Mexican Land Grants (Santa Fe: Elias Brevoort, 1874), ix.

35. Ibid., 119.

36. Ibid.

37. Ibid.

38. Brevoort, ix.

39. David R. Roediger, *The Wages of Whiteness: Race and the Making of the American Working Class* (London and New York: Verso, 1991).

40. Reginald Horsman, *Race and Manifest Destiny: The Origins of American Anglo-Saxonism* (Cambridge: Harvard University Press, 1981). On ethnic boundary formation and resource competition, see Edward Spicer, introduction and "Plural Society in the Southwest," in *Plural Society in the Southwest*, ed. Edward Spicer and R. Thompson (Albuquerque: University of New Mexico Press, 1972), 1–20, 21–76.

41. The historian Camille Guerin-Gonzales has documented how the term "American" came to refer to Anglo-Americans, while "Mexican" was applied to both Mexican Americans and Mexican immigrants in the workplace. She writes: "The language [white Americans] used to describe their [Mexican/Mexican American] workers became a justification for discriminating against those of particular ethnic and racial groups." Camille Guerin-Gonzales, *Mexican Workers and American Dreams: Immigration, Repatriation, and California Farm Labor, 1900–1939* (New Brunswick: Rutgers University Press, 1994), 51.

42. Quoted in Prince, *New Mexico's Struggle*, 30.

43. Robert J. Rosenbaum, *Mexicano Resistance in the Southwest: "The Sacred Right of Self-Preservation"* (Austin: University of Texas Press, 1984).

44. Prince, *New Mexico's Struggle*, 31.

45. "Reasons Why the People Should Adopt the State Constitution," *New Mexican*, May 29, 1872; reprinted in Prince, *New Mexico's Struggle*, 31.

46. Prince, *New Mexico's Struggle*, 30.

47. Ibid., 31.

48. Ibid., 32.

49. Ibid., 31.

50. *New Mexican*, Sept. 9, 1871. Quoted in Oliver LaFarge, *Santa Fe: The Autobiography of a Southwestern Town* (Norman: University of Oklahoma Press, 1959), 72–73.

51. Interestingly, legislators challenged the 1870 census data on the grounds that 10,000 miners living in the most remote regions of the territory had gone uncounted. In this case, the population would have grown just 40 percent, not the 50 percent the legislators had boasted. U.S. House Committee on the Territories, *Admission of New Mexico as a State: Report [to accompany H.R. 2418]*, 43d Cong., 1st sess., 1874, S. Rept. 561, 2.

52. Ibid.

53. Ibid.

54. Ibid.

55. Article 9, Treaty of Guadalupe Hidalgo, as it appears in Richard Griswold del Castillo, *The Treaty of Guadalupe Hidalgo: A Legacy of Conflict* (Norman: University of Oklahoma Press, 1990), 190.

56. *Admission of New Mexico as a State, Her Resources and Future: Speech of Hon. Stephen B. Elkins, Delegate from New Mexico, in the House of Representatives,* May 21, 1874 (Washington, D.C.: Government Printing Office, 1874), 5.

57. Ibid., 23.

58. U.S. House, *Admission of New Mexico as a State,* 43d Cong., 1st sess., 1874, H. Rept. 561.

59. Marion Dargan, "New Mexico's Fight For Statehood (1895–1912)," *New Mexico Historical Review* 14 (Jan. 1939): 6.

60. U.S. House, *Admission of New Mexico: Memorial of the Legislative Assembly of New Mexico, asking the Passage of an Enabling Act for Admission into the Union,* 44th Cong., 1st sess., 1876, Misc. Doc. no. 63, 1.

61. Ibid., 2.

62. U.S. Senate, *In the Senate of the United States: Report [to accompany S. 229],* 44th Cong., 1st sess., 1876, Rept. 69; U.S. House, *New Mexico: Minority Report [to accompany S. 229],* 44th Cong., 1st sess., 1876, Rept. 503, part 2, 15.

63. U.S. House, *Minority Report,* 1876, 12.

64. Weber, "'Scarce More than Apes,'" 293–307, 299; Reginald Horsman, "Racial Destiny and the Indians," in *Major Problems in the History of the American West: Documents and Essays,* ed. Clyde A. Milner II (Lexington, Mass.: D. C. Heath, 1989), 255. Reprinted from Horsman, *Race and Manifest Destiny,* 189–207.

65. Horsman, *Race and Manifest Destiny,* 211.

66. Horsman, "Racial Destiny and the Indians," 255.

67. Just as blood had become a signifier for race and culture in medieval Spain and Spanish America, so did it inform nineteenth-century scientific notions of race among Anglo-Americans and, later, Spanish Americans.

68. U.S. House, *Minority Report,* 1876, 12.

69. The importance of race or caste designations had declined since the early decades of the nineteenth century. Notwithstanding the deep division between so-called *indios* and the remaining Mexican citizenry, called *vecinos* (and sometimes *españoles*), New Mexico's social order had increasingly become defined in terms of landholdings, patronage, honor, and the regulation of marriage and sexuality. Ramón A. Gutiérrez, *When Jesus Came, the Corn Mothers Went Away: Marriage, Sexuality, and Power in New Mexico, 1500–1846* (Stanford: Stanford University Press, 1991).

70. Gutiérrez, "Aztlán, Montezuma, and New Mexico," 175.

71. U.S. House, *Minority Report,* 1876, 13.

72. Ibid., 15.

73. Prince, *New Mexico's Struggle,* 33, 58.

74. Robert W. Larson, *New Mexico's Quest for Statehood, 1846–1912* (Albuquerque: University of New Mexico Press, 1968), 132–33.

75. Ibid., 33–35.

76. Ibid., 37.

77. Le Baron Bradford Prince, "New Mexico, a Defense of the People and Country: A Reply of Chief Justice Prince to a Slanderous Letter in the *New York Times*" [from the *New York Times*, Feb. 28, 1882], 1, Prince Collection, New Mexico State Records Center and Archives.

78. Ibid.

79. Ibid. In this letter, Prince elaborated on the "better" classes of New Mexicans—those he deemed to possess Spanish blood—as if to imply that "lesser" classes possessed mixed (Spanish and Indian) blood.

80. Ibid.

81. Larson, 144.

82. Prince, *New Mexico's Struggle for Statehood*, 40.

83. Ibid., 40.

84. Ibid., 40–41.

85. William W. H. Davis, *El Gringo, or New Mexico and Her People* (Santa Fe: Rydal Press, 1938), 85–87; quoted in Tobías Durán, "We Come as Friends: Violent Social Conflict in New Mexico, 1810–1910" (Ph.D. diss. University of New Mexico, 1985), 192.

86. In the early months of 1888, the *New Mexican* surveyed 122 prominent citizens, such as bankers, merchants, ranchers, federal officials, and farmers. Ninety-one respondents favored statehood, according to the *New Mexican*, and twenty-one opposed it. An 1889 House Report cited the 1888 survey thus: "Of the 91 in favor there were 41 Republicans, 33 Democrats, and 17 of no particular party affiliations, or whose politics were not known. Of the 31 opposed there were 11 Democrats, 10 Republicans, 6 of no particular politics, and 4 who professed to be independent." *House Reports*, 50th Cong., 1st sess., vol. 4, Rept. 1025, 15–16; quoted in Marion Dargan, "New Mexico's Fight for Statehood (1895–1912), [Part] III: The Opposition within the Territory (1888–1890)," *New Mexico Historical Review* 15 (Apr. 1940): 142.

87. Archie M. McDowell, "The Opposition to Statehood within the Territory of New Mexico, 1888–1903" (Ph.D. diss., University of New Mexico, 1939), 66.

88. Ibid.

89. As quoted in Larson, 148.

90. Ibid., 154–55.

91. Herbert H. Lang, "The New Mexico Bureau of Immigration, 1880–1912," *New Mexico Historical Review* 51 (July 1976): 200, 205.

92. *La voz del pueblo*, Feb. 23, 1889.

93. Ibid.

94. Ibid.

95. *Santa Fe New Mexican*, Sept. 23, 1890.

96. *La voz del pueblo*, Apr. 5, 1890.

97. Ibid., Nov. 25, 1893.

98. Ibid., Jan. 30, 1892. Over a month later, another editorial protested that, on

occasion, *hispanos* participated in the denigration of themselves and "the character and dignity of their own—*Hispano-Americanos.*" Ibid., Feb. 13, 1892.

99. Ibid., Apr. 5, 1890.

100. On the growth of the Spanish-language press, see Doris Meyer, *Speaking for Themselves: Neomexicano Cultural Identity and the Spanish Language Press, 1880–1920* (Albuquerque: University of New Mexico Press, 1996), and A. Gabriel Meléndez, *So All Is Not Lost: The Poetics of Print in Neomexicano Communities, 1834–1958* (Albuquerque: University of New Mexico Press, 1997).

101. *El boletín popular*, Aug. 31, 1893.

102. The first edition of *Eco del siglo* appeared on Feb. 9, 1892, in Las Cruces, stating that a Spanish publication was necessary for various reasons, among them "to establish relations with our Colleagues, and take note of acts or amendments that might affect our interests." *El boletín popular* began circulating in Santa Fe in 1885 as a bilingual organ of the Democratic Party. Initially it opposed statehood efforts initiated by Republicans, saying that the Ring was merely seeking statehood as a means of enriching itself. See *El boletín popular*, Oct. 13, 1892. By 1893, however, the newspaper appeared to support the efforts of Antonio Joseph in combating the argument that New Mexico's "Mexican population" was still loyal to Mexico, some forty-odd years after becoming U.S. citizens. *El boletín popular*, Aug. 31, 1893. Similarly, *La voz del pueblo* appeared to reverse its earlier opposition to statehood, which had been based on Republican plans for public education. It printed reports of ongoing accusations against Hispanos. *La voz del pueblo*, Sept. 2, 1893.

103. Adrian Herminio Bustamante, "Los Hispanos: Ethnicity and Social Change in New Mexico" (Ph.D. diss., University of New Mexico, 1982), 125.

104. Phillip B. Gonzales, "The Protest Function of Spanish-American Identity in New Mexico," unpublished manuscript.

105. For a more elaborate discussion of the role of tourism and immigration in the making of Spanish American identity, see John Nieto-Phillips, "'No Other Blood': History, Language, and Spanish American Ethnic Identity in New Mexico, 1880s–1920s" (Ph.D. diss., University of California, Los Angeles, 1997).

106. *La voz del pueblo*, Oct. 7, 1893.

107. *La voz del pueblo*, Nov. 2, 1901; my translation. Also see Chacón's speech as translated in Anselmo F. Arrellano and Julián Josué Vigil, *Las Vegas Grandes on the Gallinas, 1835–1985* (Las Vegas, N.M.: Editorial Telaraña, 1985), 52.

108. Ibid.

109. At the turn of the century, many Pueblo Indians and non-Hispanic residents of New Mexico spoke Spanish in addition to their native languages. Here, however, I refer to a group of individuals who claimed to be of Spanish or Mexican descent and whose native language was Spanish.

110. Ibid., 54.

111. Ibid., 55.

112. Ibid., 57.

113. Ibid.

114. *La voz del pueblo*, May 28, 1898.

115. According to Howard Lamar, "The outbreak of the Spanish-American War meant that the United States was fighting the spiritual and cultural mother country of native New Mexicans. This proved no problem at all. In response to a call for volunteers, Spanish-Americans as well as Americans flocked to the colors with such enthusiasm that the New Mexican companies were oversubscribed." Lamar, 199.

116. For an interesting discussion of racial ideas in the latter half of the nineteenth century, see Robert E. Beider, *Science Encounters the Indian, 1820–1880: The Early Years of American Ethnology* (Norman: University of Oklahoma Press, 1986). The "science" of eugenics shaped government policy not only in the United States, but also in Latin America. For a stimulating discussion, see Eduardo A. Zimmerman, "Racial Ideas and Social Reform: Argentina, 1890–1916," *Hispanic American Historical Review* 71 (Feb. 1992): 21–46.

117. J. Manuel Espinosa, "Spanish Folklore in the Southwest: The Pioneer Studies of Aurelio M. Espinosa," *Americas* 35 (Oct. 1978): 24.

118. 57th Congress, 2d sess., H. Doc. 36 (4420), *New Statehood Bill: Hearings before the Subcommittee of the Committee on Territories on House Bill 12543, to Enable the People of Oklahoma, Arizona, and New Mexico to form Constitutions and State Governments and Be Admitted into the Union on an Equal Footing with the Original States, December 10, 1902, Submitted by Mr. Beveridge and Ordered to be Printed* (Washington: Government Printing Office, 1902).

119. Ibid.

120. Ibid.

121. Ibid., 16

122. Ibid.

123. Committee on the Territories, *Hearings on Statehood Bill*, Dec. 11, 1903, *U.S. Congressional Hearings Supplement: House Committee on the Territories*, 1904, 17. 124. Statement of Mr. Moon, "Statehood for Arizona and New Mexico," Jan. 16, 1906, *U.S. Congressional Hearings Supplement: House Committee on the Territories*, 1906, 22.

125. Committee on the Territories, *Hearings on Statehood Bill*, Dec. 11, 1903, *U.S. Congressional Hearings Supplement: House Committee on the Territories*, 1904, 13.

126. Ibid., 15.

127. Ibid., 17.

128. Rock Island System, *New Mexico, The Land of Sunshine: Agricultural and Mineral Resources, Irrigation and Horticulture, Gold, Copper, Iron, and Coal; A National Sanitarium; Playground of the Southwest* (Chicago: Passenger Dept., Rock Island System, 1904), 50.

129. Statement of R. E. Morrison, "Statehood for Arizona and New Mexico," Jan. 16, 1906, *U.S. Congressional Hearings Supplement: House Committee on the Territories*, 1906, 18–19.

130. Prince to Albert Beveridge, Feb. 1, 1905. Quoted in Larson, 245.

131. Larson, 244, 250.

132. The previous year, Arizona's legislature, by a two-thirds majority, had imposed

an English language requirement upon voters, effectively depriving 2,000 citizens of suffrage. Senate, *Statehood Hearing before the Committee on Territories,* Feb. 18, 19, 21, 1910, *U.S. Congressional Hearings Supplement: Senate Committee on the Territories,* 1910, 60–65.

133. New Mexico Constitution, articles 7 and 12; as quoted in "Education and the Spanish-Speaking: An Attorney General's Opinion on Article XII, Section 8 of the New Mexico Constitution," *New Mexico Law Review* 3 (May 1973): 268 n. 20, 372–73 nn. 66–67.

134. Quoted in Larson, 303.

1. The only known illustration of *Las Gorras Blancas*, published in *El Sol de Mayo*, a Spanish-language newspaper in Las Vegas, 1892. *(Reproduced courtesy of Anselmo Arrellano.)*

2. Felix Martínez was publisher of *La Voz del Pueblo* and a supporter of El Movimiento del Pueblo. A member of the New Mexico legislature in 1893, Martínez is regarded as the founder of New Mexico Highlands University. *(Reproduced courtesy of Anselmo Arrellano.)*

3. San Miguel County Sheriff Lorenzo López was a powerful political leader during El Movimiento del Pueblo. *(Reproduced courtesy of Anselmo Arrellano.)*

4. Ezequiel Cabeza de Baca, the first lieutenant governor and governor following statehood in 1912. *(Reproduced courtesy of Anselmo Arrellano.)*

De Seguro Nuevo Mexico será Estado.

5. Caricature of an anxious William "Bull" Andrews, New Mexico's delegate to Congress in 1908, adding New Mexico's star to the U.S. flag. (Note: The words in the bubble, "Pueblo de Nuevo México," are illegible on microfilm copy.) *El independiente*, Las Vegas, N.M., Dec. 10, 1908.

6. Octaviano A. Larrazolo, born in Mexico, educated in St. Michael's College in Santa Fe, was the first Nuevomexicano elected to the U.S. Senate. *(Museum of New Mexico Archives, 47799.)*

7. Nuevomexicano mailman, accompanied by child, delivering the mail to Peñasco, New Mexico. *(Russell Lee, Library of Congress, LC-USF33-12837-M4.)*

8. Finishing up a *matanza* in Chamisal, N.M. *(Russell Lee, Library of Congress, LC-USF33-12840-M4.)*

9. Spanish American woman putting loaf of bread into oven, Taos Co., N.M. *(Russell Lee, 1939, Library of Congress, LC-USF33-12420-M2.)*

10. English, Spanish, or both? Which was the language of instruction for this young Taoseño? *(Reproduced courtesy The Center for Southwest Research, University of New Mexico General Library.)*

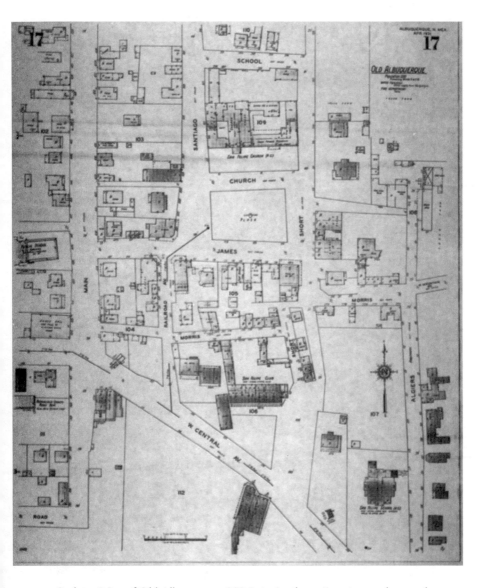

11. Sanborn Map of Old Albuquerque, N.M., in April 1931. It estimates the population at 1,200. *(Reproduced courtesy of the Sanborn Map Company, 1931. The Sanborn Library, LLC. All rights reserved.)*

12. Old Town Albuquerque fiesta procession, June 1951. Fiesta queen with escort carrying the statue of the patron saint of San Felipe de Neri church. *(Reproduced courtesy of The Albuquerque Museum, 1980. 186.537.)*

13. Alicia Valdez de Romero, secretary of state for New Mexico, 1946–1950. Romero, a Springer native, was born November 7, 1913. This photo was taken when she was acting governor. *(Reproduced courtesy of Anselmo Arrellano.)*

Las Vegas, N.M. has been the scene of Raza resistance to colonization since the days of Las Gorras Blancas in the 1800's. On April 30, 1973, a new phase of that struggle began when students from Robertson High and Middle School held a walkout in protest against Rowland King as superintendent of the East Las Vegas schools. These photos tell the story of that struggle from the marches, picket lines and arrests to the occupation of the Montezuma seminary, the birth of Escuela Antonio José Martínez (an independent Chicano school), and the battle for its survival. The story begins in the left-hand, upper corner of this exhibit. It is dedicated to Olivia Gallegos, 17-year old member of Chicanos Unidos para Justi-cia, who was killed on February 24, 1974.

14. Interpretive sign accompanying an exhibit on the history of Raza Resistance in Las Vegas, particularly in 1973. The following reproductions are from photographs in this exhibit. *(Reproduced courtesy of the Chicano Community Center, provided by David Montoya.)*

15. A protest in front of the police station against curfew and limits on freedom of assembly. *(Reproduced courtesy of the Chicano Community Center, provided by David Montoya.)*

16. Protest in front of a school board member's business in Las Vegas. *(Reproduced courtesy of the Chicano Community Center, provided by David Montoya.)*

17. Protest at the state capitol. *(Reproduced courtesy of Chicano Community Center, provided by David Montoya.)*

18. Robertson High School and Las Vegas Middle School students demonstrating against Roland King, appointed superintendent of the East Las Vegas public schools in April 1973. (*Reproduced courtesy of the Chicano Community Center, provided by David Montoya.*)

19. A march of 1,200 on Bridge Street in Las Vegas to protest the Roland King appointment. (*Reproduced courtesy of the Chicano Community Center, provided by David Montoya.*)

20. A rally following the march. Corky Gonzales is the speaker in the gazebo. *(Reproduced courtesy of the Chicano Community Center, provided by David Montoya.)*

21. A Chicanos Unidos para Justicia (CUPJ) protest at the school board meeting against the appointment of Ronald King as superintendent of the East Las Vegas public schools. Despite police presence, Gustavo Cordova, a CUPJ member, was stabbed during the meeting. *(Reproduced courtesy of the Chicano Community Center, provided by David Montoya.)*

22. Highlands University students protest efforts to eliminate Chicano Studies and instead seek the hiring of qualified Chicanos. (*Reproduced courtesy of the Chicano Community Center, provided by David Montoya.*)

23. NMHU requests meeting following arrest of 48 students. *Far Left:* Dr. Ralph Smith, academic dean; *Right Center:* looking toward Dr. Smith is Dr. Frank Angel, president of NMHU; *Far Right:* Robert Amai, president of the Faculty Policy Committee. (*Reproduced courtesy of the Chicano Community Center, provided by David Montoya.*)

24–25. Murals in the student union building at Highlands University were painted over in 1986, during president Gilbert Sanchez's administration. (*Reproduced courtesy of the Chicano Community Center, provided by David Montoya.*)

26. Chicanos Unidos para Justicia demonstrators rally to preserve the Antonio José Martínez private school in the mid-1970s. *(Reproduced courtesy of the Chicano Community Center, provided by David Montoya.)*

27. Reies Lopez Tijerina *(far left, standing)* presents land grant demands to Governor David Cargo *(far right, seated)* in the Capitol dining room in April 1967. *(Reproduced from Peter Nabokov, Tijerina and the Courthouse Raid [UNM Press, 1969]).*

Chapter Five

GABRIEL MELÉNDEZ

Nuevo México by Any Other Name

CREATING A STATE FROM AN ANCESTRAL HOMELAND

No es ni nuevo, ni México.
[It is neither "new," nor México.]
— FRANCISCO X. ALARCÓN, 1995

What exactly compelled the California poet Francisco X. Alarcón in 1995 to add a cryptic gloss[1] to the symbolic nameplate of New Mexico, the *manito* homeland, is anybody's guess. My experience leads me to think that it came as an attempt to decipher the perplexing image that Nuevo México and Nuevo-mexicanos conjure up in the political imagination of Chicanos and Chicanas from other parts of the country. I liken Alarcón's counterdefinition to a thin veneer added to the many layers of attribution and misattribution that have accumulated over the years and that shade the collective imagination regarding New Mexico and its *nativo* residents. Like coats of thick enamel applied one over the other for the periodic sprucing-up of old but still useful lawn furniture, these definitions both protect and hide the integrity of the face underneath. Then, too, Alarcón is absolutely correct in both his estimations. In purely historical terms—and here I refer to matters beyond the coinage of a name for a specific region in the Southwest—Nuevo México's past precludes the descriptor "new" in the dictionary sense of being "developed, made, produced, etc., for the first time." Nuevo México is so "old," in fact, that even before the ink was dry on the Treaty of Guadalupe Hidalgo in 1848, it was "old" by common standards (though some 150 years "younger" than it is today), but it was not, by that measure, México proper.

According to Robert Julyan, New Mexico's identity was solidly fixed over some 250 years, and it was only after the American arrival and in the years before New Mexico's final admission to the Union as a state that "objections were raised that the name would suggest that region still was a part of Mexico and not the U.S."[2] But the mere suggestion of changing the eponym set off a flurry of intense rebuffs from Nuevomexicanos, the power of which can still be observed by the contemporary researcher who, like me, comes upon them innocently enough in turn-of-the-century newspaper accounts.

My purpose here is to draw attention to the labeling hegemony[3] that surrounds New Mexico's struggle for statehood. I am most concerned with presenting the reactions of New Mexico's *nativos*, drawn from the heated polemic that resulted from moves to consolidate New Mexico with Arizona in the Congress of 1904–5. The consolidation or jointure movement was among the last of several dozen propositions, beginning in 1850 and ending in 1910, asking for the admission of New Mexico to the Union. Jointure produced strong opposition in both New Mexico and Arizona, much of which came as a result of "fundamental differences" between the peoples of the two territories and because two-thirds of the population in New Mexico was Mexican and Indian. The jointure proposition also called for the removal of New Mexico's historic name, a proposal that was disagreeable to Mexican Americans in New Mexico.

Not a simple issue on any level, moves to change New Mexico's name masked larger ethnic depurations tethered to suit the Anglo framers of New Mexico's bid for statehood. These moves, on the one hand, sought to disassociate the region from Mexico by employing an Americanizing eponym like Lincoln or Hamilton. On the other hand, certain capitalists and entrepreneurs among the pro-consolidation group had long sought to exoticize the New Mexico–Arizona region for tourist consumption and proposed that the two-for-one state be named Montezuma or Acoma.

In his insightful essay on the political uses of American Indian mythology, Ramón Gutiérrez would have us keep in mind that the pre-Columbian evocations of Montezuma (not Moctezuma), Acoma, and other substitutes for New Mexico's name at the turn of the century were not a concession to the cultural legacy of Indian people as we might think upon them today; rather, as Gutiérrez explains, these "must also be placed in the larger cultural movement begun in the 1880s to turn the harsh realities of New Mexico into a 'Land of Enchantment' for investors, tourists, health seekers, alienated literati and artists to explore in the west." Gutiérrez further asserts that cultural brokerage of this type had become as important to the Atchison, Topeka and Santa Fe Railroad in the 1880s as moving freight and passengers west. It was the railroad companies, in fact, who "tried to create a lost world and return to primitivism."[4]

The alterations required to primitivize New Mexico were unacceptable to most Spanish-speaking residents of New Mexico; attempts to do so totally disconcerted *nativo* self-inscription and *querencia* to an ancestral homeland. The prospect of a name change dominated the front pages of several Nuevomexi-

cano newspapers from 1903 until the time of New Mexico's final admission as
a state in January 1912.

UN OTRO, O NUEVO MÉXICO . . .
[ANOTHER, OR A NEW MEXICO . . .]

The use of the phrase *un otro, o Nuevo México* has been ascribed to several Span-
ish explorers and friars who from 1539 to 1598 traversed various routes across
Zacatecas and into upper Chihuahua and what is today west Texas and points
north. The best-known Spanish expedition was that of Francisco Vásquez de
Coronado in 1540, though we have no record of his referring to the region as
Nuevo México. Julyan, following T. M. Pearce, credits the Francisco Ibarra
expedition of 1569 with the invention of a name for New Mexico, but the
Nuevomexicano historian Benjamín M. Read raised questions in 1911 as to
whether Ibarra had actually visited or had merely skirted the present-day
boundaries of New Mexico as he journeyed north from Nueva Galicia, or Durango. Moreover, Read found that the descriptor Nuevo México was in common usage among Franciscan missionaries, as confirmed by earlier chronicles,
making it difficult to pin the attribution to any single individual or expedition.
After a detailed recounting of several Spanish-Mexican expeditions into New
Mexico, Read concludes:

> Queda, pues establecido que no fue Espejo quien dio a esta entonces
> provincia de España el nombre de Nuevo México, quedando igualmente
> comprobado que no se sabe en modo cierto quien fuera el autor y que
> bien se puede creer que lo fue Fray Agustín Rodríguez aunque hay es-
> critores muy antiguos que afirman lo contrario.[5]

> [It thus is established that it was not Espejo who gave this then prov-
> ince of Spain the name New Mexico, and it is equally proven that it is
> not for certain known who was the originator of the name and that it
> could well have been Fray Agustín Rodríguez [who visited New Mex-
> ico in 1581–82] who named it, although there are very ancient writers
> who affirm the contrary.]

What Nuevomexicanos generally understood on the eve of statehood
was that their forebears had played a decisive hand in shaping the history of a
region they considered their ancestral homeland. They vehemently and often
eloquently argued that their 300-year experience in the region should not be
dismissed and set about to challenge the view of the upstarts in the region—

Anglo-Americans only recently identified with the territory—who had begun to fashion revisionist histories of the area from which Nuevomexicanos were largely excluded. As I have documented elsewhere, a Nuevomexicano cultural movement designed to counter such dehistoricization had begun to produce historical writing and works of literature in the 1890s.[6]

It is not surprising that questions regarding the future of the Spanish-speaking people in New Mexico would surface in the jointure movement, which called for a radical reorganization in the political administration of the territory and promised to effect a no less radical reconceptualization of the politics of identity for *nativos*. In the two decades leading to statehood, the work of Nuevomexicano literates such as Benjamín Read was premised on two essential components that set historical precedent for Nuevomexicanos. The first was New Mexico's colonial past, a complex of myths, legends, and ethno-poetics filled with the particulars of history that forever fixed the region in the imagination of the Spanish and Mexican chroniclers as *un otro, o Nuevo México*. The second was the still fresh experience of becoming conquered citizens of the United States as a consequence of the Mexican-American War. Nuevo-mexicanos scrutinized the latter feature of their historical makeup not in search of answers to the question of their collective identity (since by this time they clearly knew who they were), but rather to interrogate the terms of their incorporation as citizens of the United States. It was not historic meaning that returned their interest time and again to the Treaty of Guadalupe Hidalgo, but the matter of the civil rights that had been systematically denied them in the six decades that New Mexico had been a territory of the United States.

THE BEVERIDGE REPORT

La cuestión del estado que ha sido tenida sobre el tapete largo tiempo, ha sido un tema inexhaustible que han explotado a su placer nuestros enemigos, quienes después de afirmar que la mayoría de nuestro pueblo se halla en condición semi-bárbaro y no está civilizada, pasan a declarar que el suelo de Nuevo México es en su mayor parte tan árido e infruc-tífero como el desierto de Sahara o como los terrenos en contorno del Mar Muerto.[7]

[The question of statehood has been kept on the table a long time; it has been an inexhaustible theme that our enemies have exploited with pleasure: after declaring that the majority of our people are in a semi-barbaric condition and are not civilized, they go on to affirm that the earth of New Mexico is mostly arid and barren like the Sahara Desert or the lands surrounding the Dead Sea.]

Before the Congress in April 1902 was an omnibus bill authored by William S. Knox of Massachusetts that sought to enable citizens in New Mexico, Arizona, and Oklahoma to form constitutions and state governments and to be admitted to the Union. The Knox Bill would find its strongest opposition in Albert J. Beveridge, a Republican from Indiana and the chair of the Senate Committee on Territories. Beveridge was unconvinced by the arguments in favor of statehood made by the territorial delegates of these western territories and by their supporters in Congress. He sought and obtained the approval of the Senate to carry out a fact-finding investigation to further examine the matter of statehood for New Mexico, Arizona, Oklahoma, and the Indian territories. After a thirteen-day tour of the Southwest, which some editors in New Mexico labeled a "flying trip," Beveridge delivered his committee's majority report to the Senate when Congress convened in December. He recommended admittance for Oklahoma, but argued against statehood for New Mexico and Arizona, further advising that such action be withheld indefinitely. The Beveridge report reserved its greatest remonstrance for New Mexico, listing as objections to statehood the territory's insufficient population, its high illiteracy, the aridity of its climate, the large number of Mexicans and Indians in the territory, and the fact that "a large percentage of the population could only speak in their native tongue".[8]

The Beveridge report fueled the generally anti-Mexican sentiment of the eastern press, and as the views of prominent eastern newspapers made their way back to New Mexico, they set off a chorus of protest by Nuevomexicanos that would last for years. The pages of the Las Vegas–based *El independiente* and the Albuquerque-based *La bandera americana* during these years provide some of the best commentary on the Beveridge report and on the complex of conflated issues—consolidation, name change, racialized politics, education, poverty, New Mexico's history, and its future—all dredged up along with the prospect of statehood for New Mexico. Nuevomexicanos, given their propensity for long memory, were never able to bring themselves to forgive Albert Beveridge for his disparagement of New Mexico's *nativos*. Even after years had gone by, local poets still indicted him for his part in the derision of Spanish-speaking citizens of the Southwest. One example, "Contra los difamadores de Nuevo México" [In protest against the defamers of New Mexico], appeared in *El independiente* in March 1909. Signed with the pseudonym "Neo Mex," the poem singles out Beveridge as the chief muckraker:

Beveridge, el cabecilla	[Beveridge, the leader,
Sin un pelo de estadista	without a modicum of the statesmen
Nuevos lauros se conquista	Wins new glory
Entre gente ruin y pilla	Among mean and crafty folk
Dando odios a su cuadrilla	By building hate among his band
Quiere anular la opinión	He wants to annul the opinion
Del Congreso de la Unión	Of the Congress of the Nation
Y tachando a nuestra gente	Besmirching our people
De inepta e incompetente	As inept and incompetent
Persuade a la comisión.[9]	He persuades the commission.]

Nuevomexicanos made clear distinctions between the obstructionist Beveridge and pro-statehood advocates such as Bernard S. Rodey, their delegate to Congress. When Rodey returned to New Mexico to seek reelection in 1905, one anonymous poet detailed the legislator's part in the statehood debate. The high praise of his verses seems quite in character, given Robert Larson's description of Rodey as "a human dynamo working in the cause for admission."[10] The newspaper poet tells us:

Quién con más ahinco y vigor	[Who with more vigor and earnest
Con más aserción y pausa	With more assertion and measures
Fue a defender nuestra causa	Went to defend our cause
¿Ante el Congreso de honor?	Before, an honorable Congress?
Rodey con amplio valor	Rodey with breath of valor
Y con todo, soberano,	And supreme throughout,
Defendió al Neo-Mexicano	Defended the Neomexicano
Cual, Beveridge en el Senado	That Beveridge had
Había injusto difamado	Unjustly defamed in the Senate
Ante el pueblo Americano.[11]	And before the American public.]

LA CONSOLIDACIÓN

En Arizona, Demócratas y Republicanos son del mismo parecer en cuanto a la cuestión del estado consolidado, y todos a una en sus juntas, convenciones y pláticas inventan la algarada de que en Nuevo México son demasiado numerosos los mexicanos, y que con eso basta para que no sea propia la unión del los dos territorios. Esa objeción la acompañan invariablemente con dicterios y difamaciones que no pueden menos de ser sensibles a nuestro pueblo que ni desea ni solicita tal unión. En esto se da a conocer que clase de gente es aquella que tan de buenas a primeras hinca el diente sobre los mexicanos como si ellos fueran responsables de la acción del congreso en pasar el proyecto de consolidacion.[12]

[In Arizona, Republicans and Democrats alike are of the same opinion in regard to a consolidated state, and, one and all in their meetings, conventions and talks raise the outcry that Mexicans in New Mexico are too numerous, and this suffices to make the union of the two territories improper. This objection is invariably accompanied by taunts and defamation that cannot but be unfeeling to our people, which neither desires, nor seeks such a union. This shows that at the drop of a hat, such people sink their teeth into the Mexicans as if they were responsible for action in Congress to pass the Consolidation Bill.]

As is obvious from the item above, debate over *la consolidación* or jointure with Arizona did not diminish with the defeat of the Knox Bill. To the contrary, it grew in intensity as similar measures were proposed in each new session of Congress. Senator Beveridge himself reversed his stand on the matter coincidentally with President Roosevelt's support of the jointure movement. But Nuevomexicanos remained skeptical of proposals to consolidate the territories. As Enrique H. Salazar (1858–1915), the editor of *El independiente*, saw it, there were any number of historic, racial, and political factors that made it difficult to find common cause in the movement:

Nuevo México, generalmente hablando, no quiere la unión con Arizona porque la contempla como un experimento peligroso en el cual nada ganaría y sólo llevaría la seguridad de perder hasta el nombre que ha llevado cerca de tres siglos. A más de esto, prefiere su atual [*sic*] condición territorial a todos los bienes que pudiera alcanzar con el estado consolidado. Arizona está radicalmente opuesta la unión con Nuevo México porque tiene presente aquello de que el pez grande se traga al chico, y porque abriga ambición de engrandecimiento propio bajo el estado separado para sí.[13]

[New Mexico, speaking in general terms, does not want to unite with Arizona because it sees this as a dangerous experiment from which it would gain nothing and would only bring the surety of losing the name it has carried for close to three centuries. Added to this, it prefers its present territorial status to all the benefits that it might obtain as a consolidated state. Arizona is radically opposed to a union with New Mexico because it is concerned with the matter of the big fish swallowing up the little fish, and because it shelters the ambition of its own aggrandizement as a separate state.]

Faced with the possible erasure of the historic name of their homeland, Nuevomexicanos appealed to history as they had at other times of impending crisis[14] to ward off disparagement and devaluation. Salazar, writing in December 1905, expressed his disdain for any proposal calling for the forfeiture of a Nuevomexicano legacy in the Southwest:

> Si algún pueblo tiene razones por enorgullecerse del nombre de Nuevo México es el pueblo cuya historia de tres siglos está llena de incidentes y hechos históricos que le dan mayor realce y lo colocan en puesto eminente entre las colonias primitivas de América. Unicamente los hombres extraños al sentimiento de patriotismo, cuyos corazones no sienten el apego a la patria de sus mayores y aquella en que nacieron y vivieron la primera luz, pueden prestarse a consentir el inicuo proyecto de que Nuevo México como comunidad distinta e independiente deje de existir y que su nombre sea borrado del mapa del continente americano.
>
> Esto indica cuando menos, un sentimiento de odio y menosprecio hacia la historia y hechos del pueblo que colonizó este Territorio, y que por siglos ha sido el actor principal en el mantenimiento y conservación del dominio adquerido y defendido a costa de tantos trabajos y sacrificios. No es extraño que un Beveridge, un Rodey y otros hombres de su laya tengan en poco el nombre y la historia de Nuevo México, y consideren su eliminación como la cosa más natural del mundo, por razón de que las ideas y principios de tales individuos se fundan en el antagonismo directo é irreconciliable contra las costumbres y origen del pueblo neo-mexicano.[15]

[If any people have reason to be proud of the name New Mexico, it is the people whose history of three centuries is filled with incidents and historical fact that lift it up and give it an eminent place among the primitive colonies of America. Only those men for whom the idea of patriotism is foreign, and who do not feel a closeness in their hearts to the homeland of their forebears—the place where they were born and first saw the light of day—can lend themselves to the ill-intentioned project to have New Mexico disappear as a distinct and independent community and to let its name be erased from the map of the American continent.

This action suggests something akin to hate and contempt toward the history and deeds of the people who colonized this territory and who for centuries have been the prime actor in the preservation and maintenance of a dominion obtained and defended at the cost of countless efforts and sacrifices. It is not surprising that a Beveridge or a Rodey or other men of their kind hold so insubstantial the name and history of New Mexico and consider its elimination the most natural thing in the world, evidence of which are the ideas and principles of these men founded on the direct and irreconcilable antagonism against the customs and origins of the people of New Mexico.]

Benigno Romero, a prominent merchant in upper Las Vegas, felt compelled to respond to the hostile views of a Philadelphia paper that suggested that New Mexico "suena mucho á mexicano y además . . . este nombre huele mucho a nombres monárquicos e Hispano-Americanos" [sounds too Mexican, and moreover . . . this name smells of a monarchical or Spanish-American title]. Moreover, Romero unmasked the hypocrisy of the eastern editor's position by countering that such names have precedent in the United States:

Parece que este Señor Editor estaba dormido y soñando o no ha notado que hay varios de nuestros estados que llevan los nombres de otros países extranjeros y que huelen á monárquicos como son "Carolina" "Georgia" "Louisiana" y otros con su adjetivo de "New" como son, "New Hampshire" y "New Jersey." [16]

[It seems that Mister Editor was asleep and dreaming, or has he not noticed that several of our states carry names from other foreign countries and which "smell monarchical," like "Carolina," Georgia," "Louisiana," and others that carry the adjective "New," like "New Hampshire" and "New Jersey."]

Romero alludes to precedent in arguing for the status quo, saying,

A mi humilde opinión el nombre de Nuevo México debe prevalecer por muchas y nobles razones. Primero, que por ser nombre fijado por nuestros antecesores a cuya raza pertenecemos, y al mismo tiempo dar un pequeño tributo que se le hace a la madre patria, y que se puede decir que casi no hay ningún hispano-americano que no esté en favor de que ese nombre prevalesca. [17]

[In my humble opinion the name New Mexico should prevail for many and noble reasons. First, since it is the name that was set by the ancestors of our race, and because it offers a small tribute to the mother country, and because it can be said that there is not a single Hispano who is not in favor of keeping this name.]

In closing, Romero suggests that should New Mexico become a state, the issue of recasting its name should be put to a referendum, as he is convinced that the people "seguro votarán por el nombre de Nuevo México" [will surely vote for the name New Mexico].

Nuevomexicanos well studied in the Treaty of Guadalupe Hidalgo refused to let themselves be treated differently from other Americans. They were aware that Anglo-Americans, and easterners in general, circulated very damaging views of them; thus, the name-change controversy was a harbinger of larger conflicts rooted in the ethnic and racial makeup of the state. Even those Nuevomexicanos who, after five decades of territorial rule, were the most desperate for statehood and the most willing to compromise on how to arrange it, countered the racial attacks leveled against Nuevomexicanos in the eastern press. *La bandera americana*, a generally pro-consolidation Republican paper, for example, took the *Philadelphia Record* to task for remarks the paper made regarding the character of New Mexico's populace. In a front-page commentary titled "Sin deberla ni temerla, insultos gratuitos arrojados sobre el pueblo del territorio de Nuevo México por un periódico del Oriente" [Without cause: unfounded insults tossed at the people of the New Mexico Territory by a paper in the East], the editor of *La bandera americana* called attention to the mischaracterization of his people:

> Debe saber *El Record* que el pueblo de Nuevo México, al cual trata con palabras bajas es tan honesto y delicado de todas maneras como el pueblo de cualesquiera [*sic*] otro estado y Territorio de la Unión Americana; debe saber que los insultos que nos dirije colectivamente son injustos y emanados de una mente preocupada y degradada, como ha habido en lo pasado muchas, aborrecedoras de nuestro pueblo, sin causa alguna. Este pueblo es tan americano, leal y sumiso a las leyes, como se puede encontrar en el estado de Pensilvania o en cualesquiera otra parte de nuestra nación.[18]

[The *Record* should know that the people of New Mexico, whom it treats with rude words, is as honest and refined in all ways as are the people of any other state and territory of the American Union; it should know that the insults it directs at us collectively are unjust and emanate from degraded and obsessed thinking, as has been [the case] in the past of many who hate our people without cause. This community is as American, loyal and respectful of the laws as any to be found in the state of Pennsylvania or any other part of our nation.]

La bandera's editor was quick to point out that by their record of service to the country, Nuevomexicanos had earned their place among other Americans: "han mostrado su lealtad a nuestras instituciones y gobierno, con su sangre en los campos de batalla, como lo han hecho cualesquiera otros hijos de la patria" [having shown its loyalty to our institutions and government, with their blood on the fields of battle just as other sons of the nation].[19]

But it was not only the eastern establishment that harbored hostility toward New Mexico and her people. Similar attitudes were common in Arizona, a territory where Anglos were a majority and dominated territorial politics. Jointure, according to Larson, heightened "[d]ifferences in the people of the two territories."[20] Anglo-Arizonans leveled a host of objections to consolidation. On the surface, they eschewed racial and ethnic antagonism by questioning how a state the size of Arizona and New Mexico combined would be administered, and how Arizonans would communicate with state government, located several hundred miles away in Santa Fe. But as Nuevomexicanos observed, the objections of Arizonans were constantly raised amid a barrage of racial and cultural animosities directed at their Mexicano neighbors. Most apparent in Arizona papers was xenophobia and an attitude of racial superiority on the part of the Arizonans.

On the front page and under the headline "Nuestros vecinos de Arizona y la antipatía que profesan a los Neo-Mexicanos" [Our neighbors in Arizona and the antipathy they profess toward the New Mexicans], El independiente summarized the prevailing attitudes in Arizona concerning jointure with New Mexico. First, it pointed out that Arizona had never lost its ambition to be a separate state. Second, Arizonans feared New Mexico's larger population, believing it would give New Mexican politicians dominance in the political arena. Third, Arizonans harbored intense racial hatred toward the native New Mexicans. In the view of El independiente's editor, the latter factor was at the root of all of Arizona's protests:

En tercer y último lugar, nadie niega que el recelo y antipatía que se abriga en Arizona contra Nuevo Mexico se dirijen principalmente en

contra de los neo-mexicanos que viene a ser un odio racial de las juntas
que se han tenido en Arizona sobre el asunto de la unificación, se ha
dado libre expresión a este sentimiento de repugnancia, declarado rápi-
damente y sin tapujos que los "hombres blancos" no consentirán jamás
ser gobernados por "mexicanos." Esta es la objección principal y la que
más influencia tiene en la actitud de los arizonenses, aunque nosotros
sabemos muy bien que está fundada sobre falsas premisas. A nosotros
los nativos de Nuevo México no nos causará sorpresa ni pesar saber
como nos trata el elemento dominante del vecino territorio, porque ya
estamos acostumbrados a la inquina malévola de individuos de semejante especie.[21]

[Third and last: no one can deny that the mistrust and antipathy sheltered in Arizona against New Mexico is primarily directed at the New
Mexicans and that it amounts to racial hatred as we have seen manifested in the meetings that have taken place in Arizona on the subject of
unification; these meetings have given free reign to this repugnant view
which is quickly and without qualms expressed in the sentiment that
"white men" will never consent to be governed by "Mexicans." This is
the fundamental and most influential objection that informs the attitude
of the Arizonans. Although we know that it is founded on false prem-
ises, it would neither surprise nor pain us native New Mexicans to learn
how we are treated by the dominant element of our neighboring territory, since we have become accustomed to the harmful spite of individuals of the same species.]

Judging from Spanish-language newspapers across New Mexico, few if
any citizens in the territory were against statehood, and none were immune to
the effect of a debate that spanned more than fifty years. One Las Vegas resident expressed exasperation over the quandary of statehood in the following
satirical verses:

Ha llamado mi atención	[My attention has been drawn
Lo que dicen del estado,	To what is said about statehood
Y entre tanta variación	With such variance in thought
Muy confuso me he quedado.	I am left very confused.
Se habla contra el Territorio	People speak against the Territory
Por su forma de gobierno,	And they say it's like Limbo

Y dicen que es purgatorio
Muy semejante al infierno.

In its form of government
Something very like a Hell.

De alabanzas al estado
Escucho incesante coro,
Y ya junto o separado
Lo ponderan gran tesoro.

I hear the incessant chorus
in praise of a new state
Separate or conjoined
It is thought to be a great treasure.

Entre tanta algarabía
Me callo como prudente
Y decida tal porfía
Quien fuera contribuyente.

Among such hullabaloo
I find it prudent not to speak,
Let him who takes part
Decide such a dispute.

Pues sea estado o territorio
Como me paro me pinto,
Y no importa si hay jolgorio
En tan recio laberinto

Well, be it state or territory
As I rise, I leave
Despite the revelry
of this forceful labyrinth.

Pero en fin que haya remuda
Para ver que cosa ofrece
Y si paga aquel que suda

But let's change the horses
To see what this might bring
And, if the one who sweats must pay

Lázaro es el que padece.
Si la tasación aumenta
Nada tenemos con eso,
Que afloje quien tenga renta
Y roa el que hallare hueso.[22]

Then Lazarus will be the one to suffer.
If taxes go up
We have nothing to fear
Let those with income pay
Let them that find a bone gnaw away.]

—NEUTRO

Hispanos in neighboring Colorado also registered much concern over the fate of the Hispano homeland. The deputy district attorney of Las Animas County, Eusebio Chacón, known to newspaper readers in New Mexico for his work in literature as the author of two novelettes and scores of poems, sent his observations on *la consolidación* in the form of a communiqué to *El independiente* on September 21, 1906. In his letter, Chacón calls attention to the struggle Nuevomexicanos have waged in seeking the full complement of their civil rights. A writer and private collector of historical documents, Chacón is quick to tie the present jointure movement to its historical antecedent in the

promises made by the United States to former Mexican citizens in the Southwest at the end of the Mexican-American War. Chacón observes:

> [E]n la dicha consolidación, dado el caso que se decretara, se negarán to-
> dos los derechos y privilegios del pueblo nativo de Nuevo México, un
> pueblo conquistado sí, pero acreedor a toda la ley del pueblo grande y
> vencedor que dictó las garantías del Tratado de Guadalupe-Hidalgo.[23]

> [With this consolidation, should it be decreed, all the rights and privi-
> leges of the native people of New Mexico will be negated—they are a
> conquered people, true, but one that is deserving of the full promise of
> the law of the larger nation, of the victor who dictated these guarantees
> in the Treaty of Guadalupe Hidalgo].

While Chacón alludes to the loss of the territory's name, he is more concerned with those amendments to jointure bills that add requisite qualifications for citizens in New Mexico to vote or serve as jurors. Chacón points out,
"En esta acta, además se le pone una condición como la 'sine qua non' del Estado, y es la de que para que un individuo ejerza en Nuevo México sus derechos de ciudadanía, tendrá que pasar ciertas calificaciones de educación" [Also,
in this bill a pre-condition is inserted as the *sine qua non* of statehood, and this
is that in order for an individual to exercise the right of citizenship in New
Mexico, he shall be expected to have certain educational qualifications].[24]
What Chacón calls educational qualifications are in fact language requirements stipulating that voters and jurors in New Mexico be able to write and
speak the English language with fluency. Not an inconsequential matter by any
means, such measures would resurface with the Enabling Act that finally
passed both houses of Congress in June 1910.[25]

Although Nuevomexicanos had long been in favor of bilingualism
and education in general, they strongly objected to language requirements,
since these threatened to limit rather than expand their rights as citizens,
something that Anglo proponents of such measures found particularly hard to
understand. They failed to see that in a region where upward of 90 percent of
Nuevomexicanos had Spanish as their first language and where the Spanish-
speaking had voted under territorial statutes for over five decades, restricting
their ability to exercise their citizenship was anathema to their support of
statehood which they believed was about making them fully participatory in
the American system.

Chacón saw such measures as particularly meanspirited, calling the latest effort to resurrect them in Congress, "un terrible guantón al pueblo de

Nuevo México" [a terrible slap in the face to the people of New Mexico]. In calling attention to the unfairness of these requirements, Chacón has before him a classic case of blaming the victim. He writes, "Fíjese bien Señor Redactor, para poder votar y ser jurados bajo el nuevo Estado tendrán los nativos, a quienes el gobierno jamás soñó ni por el mundo educar que ser ilustrados y capaces de saber ciertas cosas, que nunca han tenido la oportunidad de aprender" [Just think, Mister Editor, to vote and be a juror under the new state, *nativos,* who the government never in its wildest dreams thought to educate, will have to be lettered and have the capacity to know certain things which they have never had the opportunity to learn].[26] Here and in other writings, Chacón is highly critical of the poor record of the federal government with respect to New Mexico as a territory. He calls forth a record of egregious educational neglect of the Hispanos,

El argumento de más fuerza que presenta en favor de la consolidación algunos de mis buenos y queridos paisanos, es que el gobierno como un generoso y filantrópico papá les va a regalar, al adoptar el estado consolidado, cinco millones de pesos para la educación de la juventud. Es muy bonito saber que nuestro gobierno al fin de cincuenta años se ha acordado que tiene en Nuevo México un honorado y buen pueblo a quien educar. ¿Por qué no lo hizo antes? ¿Por qué no lo hizo cuando empezó a establecer escuelas en las Filipinas y en Puerto Rico? ¿Por qué no gasta esos millones ahora mismo, pues puede hacerlo y educar al pueblo sin necesidad que para ello tenga primero Estado?[27]

[The strongest argument that some of my good and dear countrymen present in favor of consolidation is that the government, like some generous and philanthropic father, upon the adoption of a consolidated state, is going to give them five million dollars for the education of the youth. It is good to know that after fifty years our government has finally remembered that it has just and honorable people in New Mexico to educate. Why did it not do this before? Why did it not do this when it began to build schools in Puerto Rico and the Philippines? Why doesn't it spend those five million dollars right now, since it could do so, and it could educate the people without first having a state?]

Chacón wrote his communiqué just as Congress approved a measure to put consolidation to a vote before the residents of New Mexico and Arizona. As it turned out, Chacón was correct in his prediction: "That Arizona will reject the measure without opposition is already known."[28] Robert Larson notes that two months later, "Arizonans killed the jointure proposal with a vote of 16,265 to 3,141."[29] In New Mexico, the overall count favored the measure but it is significant that in counties with the highest concentrations of Spanish-speaking *nativos*, majorities were recorded against it.[30]

Defeat in the November 1906 elections ended all talk of jointure for New Mexico and Arizona, but opened up another prolonged discussion of when and how each territory would be admitted into the Union. Defeat of jointure had not extinguished earlier moves to change the territory's names. Though never as intense as under the conditions of jointure with Arizona, suggestions to change New Mexico's name to Lincoln, Navajo, or Hamilton continued in the half dozen years prior to statehood. Adamant about the significance of the eponym Nuevo México and exasperated with the incessant moves to change it, Enrique H. Salazar at *El independiente* provided his readers with a list in an article he titled "Reasons Not to Change New Mexico's Name." Like Chacón, Salazar bases his opposition on the facts that use of the name goes back 300 years; that the change is being orchestrated by outsiders; that the name change puts Nuevomexicano autonomy in matters of self-government in jeopardy; and that it demeans New Mexico by treating it as a colony. Reproduced below are the last four of Salazar's eight points:

5. Porque ya que el Congreso se presta al fin a darnos el estado no es propio que atienda a los clamores de chismosos y entrometidos y nos ponga condiciones enojosas.

5. Because since Congress has finally consented to give us statehood it is not right that it heed the clamor of gossips and busybodies and place annoying conditions on us.

6. Porque este territorio fué originalmente bautisado con el nombre de Nuevo México, y no es permisible que á un individuo ó á una comunidad se le bautice dos veces.

6. Because this territory was originally baptized with the name New Mexico and it is not permissible to baptize a person or a community twice.

7. Porque los habitantes de un territorio tienen derechos que deben ser respetados, y uno de los principales es el de conservar el nombre que les señala y los distingue.

7. Because the inhabitants of a territory have rights that should be respected, a major one being the right to keep the name that identifies and distinguishes them.

8. Porque no somos colonia de Africa para que se no mude el

8. Because we are not a colony in Africa to have our name removed

nombre á antojo ó capricho de cualquiera, sino un territorio de los Estados Unidos.³¹ [at the whim or fancy of just anyone, but we are a territory of the United States.]

NEOMEXICANO REPRESENTATION BY PROXY

No ha vivido, ha vegetado	[It has not lived, it has vegetated
Por sesenta años y más	For sixty years and more,
Quedándose siempre atrás	Always lagging behind
En su camino cansado	Upon its labored road
Hoy que le ofrecen estado	Today, when they offered it statehood
Podrá hallar redención	Perhaps it will find its salvation
Si buscan con afición	If they seek in earnest
Libertad y soberanía	Liberty and sovereignty
Y podrá en cercano día	And perhaps in a not too distant day
Ser estado de la Unión.³²	It will be a state of the Union.]

Salazar's vitriolic call to oppose alterations that injured the collective identity of Nuevomexicanos had popular appeal among his readership. But the same issue produced more urgent and serious opposition, as can be seen, for example, in Nuevomexicano efforts to lobby Congress directly. Toward the end of the territorial period (1850–1912), Nuevomexicanos found themselves more excluded and less represented than ever in Washington. Issues that concerned them were increasingly mediated by their Anglo-American delegates to Congress, a situation that muted their demands before the institutions of government. Nuevomexicanos employed numerous strategies in their attempts to gain voice for their issues. One means of capturing the attention of Congress, cumbersome no doubt, was to capitalize on their friendship with the president pro tempore of the Colorado legislature, Casimiro Barela. Barela (1847–1920), the Senator from Las Animas County, was known as the "Perpetual Senator," having rendered forty years of service as a lawmaker in Colorado. He was a native son of New Mexico, and his sympathy for the land of his forebears had been established by a record of legislation authored in defense of Mexicano civil rights in Colorado.

As early as 1889, Barela managed to pass before both houses of the Colorado legislature a memorial bill urging Congress to grant New Mexico statehood. He authored a similar bill at the time of the name-change controversy. The resolutions in Barela's memorial urged Congress to respect the wishes of the New Mexicans, which stipulated, "que dicho territorio, cuando sea admitido a esta Unión, se le dé y se le permita retener el nombre de 'Estado de Nuevo México'" [that said territory, upon being admitted to this Union, will be given, and be permitted to keep the name "State of New Mexico"].[33]

In 1889 and 1909, Barela was able to gain the endorsement of a predominantly Anglo body of legislators to support the interests of the Spanish-speaking citizens of New Mexico. In drafting the memorials, Barela aimed to send a message, ratified by the Colorado legislature, to the president of the United States and members of both houses of Congress. Barela's biographer, José Emilio Fernández, records Barela's actions as effecting representation by proxy for his fellow Nuevomexicanos. He writes, "Y tan pronto como se oyó de que se contemplaba cambiarle el nombre, se levantó desde el Estado de Colorado é hizo oir sus razones en las aulas legislativas de Washington." [And as soon as it became known that a name change was being considered, he (Barela) rose up in the State of Colorado and made his reasons heard in the legislative chambers in Washington]. Fernández, seeking to place his subject in the best possible light, concludes that Barela's work was decisive in retaining New Mexico as a name: "El memorial surtió su efecto y cuando se pasó el acta de habilitación para Nuevo México no se cambió el nombre" [The memorial had effect and when the Enabling Act for New Mexico was passed, its name was not changed].[34]

PUJACANTE, LAND OF JAUJA, U.S.A.

The burning issue of statehood not only was cause for Nuevomexicanos to look back and reassert their history, but it also forced them to consider the impact that turning their ancestral homeland into a state would have on their future. What Eusebio Chacón clearly understood in this regard was that their condition as "un pueblo conquistado" [a conquered people] drove their fate and often sandbagged the resolve of their decisions at any given moment. Given this subaltern position, Chacón surmised, the future would be anything but secure:

[L]os habitantes de Nuevo México reducidos a la mansedumbre de corderos por cincuenta años de tutelaje, o cansados tal vez que en su Territorio predominan en asuntos públicos hombres incapaces y egoístas, han dicho "amén" a la medida y están para tragarse la píldora con toda vergüenza y deshonor. Huyen de un mal que conocen y buscan otro no conocido, y antes de que ejerzan su privilegio de votar será bueno que recuerden que el mal futuro puede ser más terrible que el presente.[35]

[The inhabitants of New Mexico, reduced to the meekness of sheep by fifty years of wardship or exhausted, perhaps, (by conditions), in their Territory (where) incompetent and egotistical men dominate public affairs, have said "so be it" to the measure and are about to swallow the bitter pill in shame and dishonor. They flee from the evil they know and seek another not known to them. Before they exercise their right to vote it would be wise for them to keep in mind that a future evil might be more disastrous than the present].

Refusing to be overwhelmed by insecurities, Nuevomexicanos tempered the rose-colored views of statehood that some among them held out as the panacea that would end all their social ills. Enrique H. Salazar had repeated the mantra of Nuevomexicano social decline since first issuing *El independiente* in 1894 and interrogated utopian views of Nuevo México, often employing wit and a caustic style to drive home his concern. In a short item in *El independiente* he sardonically titled "¿Cuándo estaremos en Jauja?" [When shall we arrive in Never-Never Land?], Salazar wheedled that Nuevomexicanos would know they had arrived in utopia when the following were features of life in New Mexico:

Cuando los órganos periodísticos no esgriman las armas de la difamación y de la calumnia.	[When the newspaper organs ceased to wield defamation and slander as their weapons.
Cuando el ex-delegado Rodey deje de meter baza en asuntos de Nuevo México y atienda más á los de Puerto Rico.	When ex-delegate Rodey stops butting into New Mexico's affairs and attends to those of Puerto Rico.[36]
Cuando Nuevo México sea estado sin tener que apodarse Acoma, Navajo, u, otro nombre que no le conviene.[37]	When New Mexico is a state and does not have to carry the nickname Acoma or Navajo or another name that does agree with it.]

For Salazar, Jauja would be a long time coming regardless of whether or not Nuevo México were allowed to retain its historic name. The trend Salazar consistently described in his editorials at *El independiente* was one of a continuing loss of political power, a steady erosion of cultural integrity, and an ever more pronounced absence of Nuevomexicanos in the economic life of the

Territory as Anglo-Americans gained dominance in various fields of public endeavor. Writing in May 1905, Salazar remarks, "Es indudable que en el renglón de la política el pueblo hispano-americano va teniendo de día en día menos prestigio y peso, nuestras demandas y peticiones no encuentran el aprecio que tenían antes, aun cuando está patente que nuestra superioridad númerica es siempre la misma" [It is undeniable that with respect to politics, Hispanos, day by day have less prestige and influence. Our demands and petitions are not received with the same appreciation as before, even when our clear numerical superiority is still the same].[38]

Salazar was convinced that cultural, political, and economic loss would not be arrested by statehood, much less that it would reverse direction. The stifling of Nuevomexicano life and society seems to have influenced Salazar's thinking as he sat down to pen "Nuevo México en el año 1950" [New Mexico in 1950], an item that appeared in *El independiente* on July 30, 1908. A fanciful and imaginative story, "New Mexico in 1950" presents Salazar's key concerns about the future of his community.

Employing humor and satire, Salazar confabulates the tale of a Nuevomexicano who dies at the beginning of the twentieth century and is able to return to life fifty years later. The subject of the story is never identified. Readers are told only that he was "a quite learned and experienced man who knew the land of his birth well from 1837 to 1900."[39] His request to return to his *antiguas querencias* is granted, as is common enough "according to the authors of imaginative works." Once returned to life, the former resident of Santa Fe wanders across New Mexico, informing himself of the changes that have come to his homeland. Like any good futurist, Salazar has the resurrected traveler inform his readers on the questions of politics, demographics, industry, agriculture, government, the military, and the fate of his people.

The soul from the other world enters the state from the north and finds that northern New Mexico is dotted by many new towns and has vast tracts of land under cultivation. The Taos Valley has a population of 200,000 residents living in several medium-sized cities. The Indians of Taos have disappeared for the most part, and the few who remained in the valley, he notes, "habían abandonado enteramente las costumbres de sus antepasados" [had entirely abandoned the customs of their ancestors]. Most people in the area, the traveler observes, are not of the same races that had inhabited the region in his own lifetime. The traveler reports seeing few Hispanos: only "en sitios apartados y poco productivos halló aldeas y poblaciones habitadas por los antiguos pobladores del país que poco á poco habían sido arrollados por la ola de inmigración de los nuevos colonos" [in remote sites, on unproductive land, did he find villages and settlements inhabited by the ancient settlers of the land who had been pushed there by a wave of immigration of new settlers].

Arriving in Santa Fe, his hometown, the visitor is astounded by the changes he sees. There, he finds,

> [T]odo estaba cambiado y transformado y sus moradores eran gente nueva que había venido de otras partes. Supo que los descendientes de los antiguos pobladores se habían dispersado, refugiándose en aldeas y poblaciones remotas del condado y una pequeña proporción residía en caseríos distantes algunas millas de la ciudad donde todavía conservaban algo de sus antiguas costumbres aunque enteramente desviados de la vida común de la demás gente.[40]

> [Everything was changed and transformed and its residents were new people that had come from other places. He learned that the descendants of its ancient settlers had been dispersed, and had taken refuge in remote villages and towns in the county and that a small portion of them lived in rural houses a few miles outside the city, where they still maintained their traditional customs, although they were completely outside the norm of life of the other people.]

He learns that New Mexico has finally become a state, but that Santa Fe is no longer its capital. New Mexico, he is informed, is now called "Pujacante," a name adopted at the behest of "several influential eastern senators, [who] detesting the name New Mexico and completely admiring every thing related to the Indian tribes, had fallen in love with the name Pujacante, since its meaning evoked the mysterious and frightful rites and ceremonies of the Indians."

News of other changes greets the traveler in Albuquerque, a town washed away long ago by the flooding of the Rio Grande. The former residents of Albuquerque have built a new town downriver near Americanópolis, the new capital of the state. Over half a million people now live between Americanópolis and the border. He is told that San Miguel County has been divided into four or five new counties, and that Las Vegas and the surrounding communities have a population of 100,000 residents. Pujacante, in fact, now has upward of sixty counties and a population of two and a half million.

He learns that Congress is comprised of two new political parties. The "Imperialista" party defends the interests of business, and the "Laborante" party defends the interests of labor. The United States has been involved in several wars in the twentieth century. It has a standing army of two million soldiers and the most powerful air force and war machine in the world. Canada has become a part of the United States, and three of Mexico's northern states have only recently been annexed to the United States. Dismayed by all he has seen and not wishing to know more, the beleaguered soul returns to "la tierra de las sombras" [the land of shadows].

The humor and satire of the story in many ways accentuate rather than mask the writer's uncertainty about the future. The subtext of Salazar's 1908 newspaper item evokes feelings of pain, loss, and unavoidable dispossession for Nuevomexicanos in their ancestral home. Sardonic and disturbing, the piece forecasts a future not entirely incongruent with the actual history of the state since statehood.

On some level, even the substitution of the name by "influential Senators" is a harbinger in New Mexico for what the anthropologist Sylvia Rodríguez has called the "tri-ethnic trap." Built on "the advocacy and emulation of Indian culture by *non-Indians*" (my emphasis),[41] one effect of the tri-ethnic trap has been to play Hispanos against Indians in New Mexico's contemporary tourist-dependent economy. For Rodríguez, the tri-ethnic trap—fabricated not by "influential Senators" but by artists, tourists, and writers—"constitutes the historical predicament in which Hispanos in Taos find themselves: conquered, dispossessed, dependent, ghettoized, and, above all, witness to the Indian's spiritual and moral elevation above themselves in Anglo eyes."[42] One need only look to present-day Santa Fe or Taos, where Nuevomexicano culture is ostracized from the essential fabric of public life, to appreciate Salazar's vision of the future. Although the particulars would have been indeterminable to Salazar, one cannot help but feel that, writing in 1908, he intuited the basic outline of Hispano social decline.

There is no doubt that the agonizing and bitter struggle for statehood marks the condition of Mexican Americans in New Mexico as distinct from that of other Latinos in the United States. If the politics of conquest ruptured Nuevomexicano social economy after 1848, the status of Nuevomexicanos as second-class citizens in the territorial period continued to destabilize it. In its initial years, the call for statehood was seen by a Mexicano majority in New Mexico as an avenue to self-rule and autonomy. As the decades passed and the balance of power shifted away from *nativos*, statehood as a mechanism for enfranchisement would place the onus of legitimacy back on the them. Made to feel suspect by nativists in Congress who considered Mexicans in the Southwest a foreign people, speaking an alien language, and undeserving of statehood, Nuevomexicanos were made to stand before the enabling institutions of their government and ask for rights owed and guaranteed them by the Treaty of Guadalupe Hidalgo. In a manner of speaking, Nuevomexicanos subjected themselves to a mass naturalization process—a second one—to safeguard their civil rights within the American body politic and, more important from a *nativo* point of view, to preserve them upon the ground of their ancestral homeland.

In the end, statehood reflected a political compromise for Hispanos. New Mexico's state constitution, drafted in 1910, made specific provisions to protect the voting, educational, and language rights of its Spanish-speaking citizens. Hispano delegates demanded and obtained a bill of rights safeguarding the language of their original compact with the United States. That bill of rights reads, in part: "The rights, privileges and immunities civil, political and religious, guaranteed to the people of New Mexico by the treaty of Guadalupe-Hidalgo shall be preserved inviolate." It was to be a compromise that avoided a rescripting of the Nuevomexicano part in the development of the Southwest. We might do well to ask ourselves today, would Nuevo México be recognizable to us now by any other name?

NOTES

1. The verse is attributed to Alarcón, a California-based poet, by Victor di Suvero in his introduction to *Saludos: Poems of New Mexico*, an anthology described as "the first attempt [to provide] in one volume both English and Spanish versions of the way poets in New Mexico speak and sing their poetry today." See Jeanie C. Williams and Victor di Suvero, eds., *Saludos: Poems of New Mexico* (Salt Lake City: Pennywhistle, 1995), 8.

2. Robert Julyan, *The Place Names of New Mexico* (Albuquerque: University of New Mexico Press, 1996), 241.

3. For a more complete discussion, see Phillip B. Gonzales, "The Political Construction of Latino Nomenclatures in Twentieth Century New Mexico," in *Journal of the Southwest* 35, no. 2 (Summer 1993): 158–85.

4. Ramón A. Gutiérrez, "Aztlán, Moctezuma, and New Mexico: The Political Uses of American Indian Mythology," in *Aztlán: Essays on the Chicano Homeland*, ed. Rudolfo Anaya and Francisco Lomelí (Albuquerque: El Norte/Academia Publications, 1989), 189.

5. Benjamín M. Read, *Historia ilustrada de Nuevo México* (Santa Fe: New Mexico Publishing Co., 1911), 117. In citing newspapers and other primary sources, I have elected to standardize the original Neomexicano Spanish only in terms of spelling and punctuation. I have provided my own translations into English of the originals.

6. For more on Benjamín M. Read and the Neomexicano cultural movement, see the chapters "News, Bio-texts, and Neo-Mexicano Historiography" and "The Poetics of Self-Representation in Neo-Mexicano Literary Discourse," in my *So All Is Not Lost: The Poetics of Print in Nuevomexicano Communities, 1834–1958* (Albuquerque: University of New Mexico Press, 1997).

7. "Opiniones prevalentes acerca de Nuevo México" [Prevalent opinions about New Mexico], *El independiente* [Las Vegas, N.M.], July 22, 1905.

8. Robert M. Larson, *New Mexico's Quest For Statehood* (Albuquerque: University of New Mexico Press, 1968), 215.

9. "Contra los diafamadores de Nuevo México" [In protest against the defamers of New Mexico], *El independiente*, Mar. 11, 1909.

10. Larson, 228.

11. "Rodey," *La bandera americana* [Albuquerque], Aug. 12, 1904.

12. "Demasiados Mexicanos" [Too many Mexicans], *El independiente*, Aug. 9, 1906.

13. "La consolidación" [Consolidation], *El independiente*, Sept. 7, 1905.

14. In *So All Is Not Lost* I have documented the origins and principal aspects of this cultural movement. It is a movement I summarize as "consigned to two major objectives. First, Mexican-American editors worked toward the development of an autonomous literary tradition among *nativos:* a corpus of writing self-styled as *una literatura nacional* (a national literature). A form of cultural regionalism, *una literatura nacional* became a way to voice the reality of Mexican Americans within the framework of the U.S. body politic. A naive position, perhaps, but one that challenged the miosis and ethnocentrism of monolithic Anglo hegemonic cultural perspectives in the nineteenth century. Second, this generation called for the publication of *nativo* history to correct misrepresentations propagated by writers from outside of that community" (Meléndez, 7).

15. "Nuevo México en la historia y los reclamos que tiene para mantener su integridad" [New Mexico in history and its claim to keep its integrity], *El independiente*, Dec. 28, 1905.

16. "Comunicado" [Communiqué], *El independiente*, Jan. 14, 1909.

17. Ibid.

18. "Sin deberla ni temerla, insultos gratuitos arrojados sobre el pueblo de Nuevo México por un periódico del Oriente," *La bandera americana*, Dec. 24, 1904.

19. Ibid.

20. Larson, 244.

21. "Nuestros vecinos de Arizona, y la antipatía que profesan á los Neo-Mexicanos," *El independiente*, Apr. 27, 1905.

22. "Una exposición neutral" [A neutral exposition], *El independiente*, May 22, 1905. This commentary in verse is styled in the form of a *décima* or *corrido*. In this case, it is used to produce satire that provides a humorous and comical release to the incessant talk of consolidation and statehood for New Mexico. As is typical of popular verse forms, the poet here opens with an extended apology in which he asks his readers or hearers to excuse his errors since he claims to be an untutored and unlettered member of the popular classes. The entire poem is reproduced below as it originally appeared in print:

> Una exposición neutral
> No blasono de elocuente,   [I don't boast of being eloquent
> Pertenezco al pueblo llano   I come from simple folk

Y me cuento entre la gente	And I count myself among people
Simplemente un ser humano	As simply a human being.
De talento distinguido	I am not, nor do I
No lo soy, no lo pretendo	pretend to be distinguished
Y si tengo algún sentido	And if I have any sense
En ello a ninguno ofendo.	I seek not to offend anyone.
Dedícome á cavilar	I dedicate myself to ponder
Sobre cuestiones del día	the question of the day
Como un burro á rebuznar	And I, like the braying donkey,
Cuando busca compañía.	Seek the company of others.
No entiendo de estadista	I lack the statesmen's understanding
Ningún pelo ni remiendo	Not a hair, not a patch,
Apenas algo la pista	Only something of the track
del run-run por el estruendo.	from the buzzing uproar.
Ha llamado mi atención	My attention has been drawn
Lo que dicen del estado,	To what is said about statehood
Y entre tanta variación	With such variance in thought
Muy confuso me he quedado.	I am left very confused.
Se habla contra el Territorio	People speak against the Territory
Por su forma de gobierno,	And they say it's like Limbo
Y dicen que es purgatorio	In its form of government
Muy semejante al infierno.	Something very like a Hell.
De alabanzas al estado	I hear the incessant chorus
Escucho insesante coro,	in praise of a new state
Y ya junto ó separado	Separate or conjoined
Lo ponderan gran tesoro.	It's thought to be a great treasure.
Entre tanta algarabía	Among such hullabaloo
Me callo como prudente	I find it prudent not to speak,
Y decida tal porfía	Let him who takes part
Quien fuera contribuyente.	Decide such a dispute.
Pues sea estado ó territorio	Well, be it state or territory
Como me paro me pinto,	As I rise, I leave
Y no importa si hay jolgorio	Despite the revelry
En tan recio laberinto	of this forceful labyrinth.
Pero en fin que haya remuda	But let's change the horses
Para ver que cosa ofrece	To see what this might bring
Y si paga aquel que suda	And if the one who sweats must pay
Lázaro es el que padece.	Then Lazarus will be the one to suffer.
Si la tasación aumenta	If taxes go up
Nada tenemos con eso,	We have nothing to fear
Que afloje quien tenga renta	Let those with income pay
Y roa el que hallare hueso.	Let him that finds a bone gnaw away.]
—NEUTRO	—NEUTRAL

23. "Eusebio Chacón habla sobre la consolidación del estado" [Eusebio Chacón speaks on the consolidation of the state], *El independiente*, September 27, 1906.

24. Ibid.

25. Larson, 270.

26. "Eusebio Chacón speaks. . . ."

27. Ibid.

28. Ibid.

29. Larson, 250.

30. Ibid.

31. "Razones para no cambiar de nombre a Nuevo México" [Reasons for not changing the name of New Mexico], *El independiente*, Dec. 17, 1908.

32. "Nuevo México," *El independiente*, Nov. 28, 1907.

33. José Emilio Fernández, *Cuarenta años de legislador, o la vida de Casimiro Barela* [Forty years as a legislator: the life of Casimiro Barela] (Trinidad, Colo.: Compañía Publicista de *El Progreso*, 1911), 338.

34. Ibid., 339.

35. The measure Chacón refers to is the jointure referundum which he believes will be defeated in New Mexico in the upcoming election. "The bitter pill" is the realization that New Mexico will remain a territory for an indefinite and unspecified time to come.

36. Larson reports that in 1905 Theodore Roosevelt appointed Rodey to be district judge of Puerto Rico, over Albert J. Beveridge's recommendation that Rodey be made governor of New Mexico. Larson also notes that Roosevelt already had George Curry, an old Rough Rider companion of his stationed in the Philippines, in mind for the job. The reference to Rodey here confirms the fact that Rodey's name reappeared in discussions of statehood for a time after his removal to Puerto Rico.

37. "¿Cuándo estaremos en Jauja?" *El independiente*, Apr. 16, 1908.

38. "La verdad sobre nuestras descalificaciones y atrasos" [The truth of our disqualification and drawbacks], *El independiente*, May 4, 1905.

39. "Nuevo México en el año 1950: lo que observó en el estado de Pujacante un alma del otro mundo que vino a visitar sus antiguas querencias" [New Mexico in the year 1950: what a spirit from another world saw upon visiting the places he once loved], *El independiente*, July 30, 1908.

40. Ibid.

41. Sylvia Rodríguez, "Art, Tourism, and Race Relations in Taos: Toward a Sociology of the Art Colony," *Journal of Anthropological Research* 45, no. 1 (1989): 91.

42. Ibid., 87.

Chapter Six

ERLINDA GONZALES-BERRY

Which Language Will Our Children Speak?

THE SPANISH LANGUAGE AND PUBLIC EDUCATION
POLICY IN NEW MEXICO, 1890 – 1930

I regret very much that the Spanish language must go. There is no economic value in writing in Spanish and where talent exists it should be developed by writing in English, about things Spanish if possible.
— MARY AUSTIN, NEW MEXICO SCHOOL REVIEW, 1931

New Mexico has long been a crossroads where peoples of distinct cultural and racial backgrounds have met, clashed, accommodated, and developed complex strategies to ensure cultural survival. The latter part of the nineteenth century was a period of especially intense conflict between Nuevomexicanos and Anglo settlers. Central to the struggle for cultural hegemony was the issue of the relationship of the Spanish language to the survival and maintenance of native Nuevomexicano culture, and particularly contested was the role it was to play in public education, first in the territory and, after 1912, in the newly created state. This essay examines the intricate web of maneuvers that pitted local educational needs and community desires against a broader national agenda that sought to use public education as the primary avenue for molding culturally homogeneous, English-speaking "American" citizens. This pressing agenda resulted, after a thirty-year struggle, in the expulsion—so to speak—of Spanish from the public schools of New Mexico.[1] In my efforts to reconstruct this piece of Nuevomexicano history, I have drawn from records and publications of the Territorial and State Boards of Education, the New Mexico Education Association, the territorial and state legislatures, and newspapers, particularly those issued by the Spanish-language press.

Progress in public education in territorial New Mexico moved slowly between 1848 and 1891. In one study devoted to this topic, George T. Gould states that what little progress did occur was owed to the enterprising Americanos: "Thus may the Americans be said to have entered upon the possession of this far western country with the banner of education flying in the front;

and yet for the next forty years but little was done more than a healthful agitation of the subject."[2] Gould further alleges that the lag in development of a public education system was the result of the isolation of New Mexico's villages and, in large measure, of the fact that the native Hispano population was not accustomed to being taxed to support public schools.[3] While these factors are certainly germane to the discussion, one important determinant that is rarely considered by investigators of this subject is that the Nuevomexicano population feared public education would spell cultural and native-language erosion.[4] As we shall see, their reservations were entirely justified.

With ratification of the Public Education Act in 1891, schooling became, as Jensen points out, "a question of politics—who was able to dominate the political process and how."[5] While politics more often than not meant party politics in New Mexico, ethnicity and the attendant language issue were also important in this power struggle.

That Nuevomexicanos, in fact, were able to wield some of that power accounts for the fact that Spanish maintained a somewhat privileged position in the early years of education development. In 1896, for example, a report issued by Territorial Superintendent of Public Education Amado Chaves defended the importance of Spanish to the educational mission of the territory and scoffed at the idea that speaking Spanish made Nuevomexicanos unfit citizens.

> In each and every one of my former reports I have called attention to the absolute necessity that teachers in school districts where the prevailing language is Spanish should have a fair knowledge of this highly important, interesting and sonorous language, and that our territorial institutions should require their graduates to attend a complete course of same. Spanish is, after English of paramount importance on the whole continent of America, of far greater practical value to our children than the rest of modern or dead languages. Spanish America offers a vast, unexplored field to the enterprise, energy and intelligence of the youth of the United States. It is a crime against nature and humanity to try and rob the children of New Mexico of this, their natural advantage, of the language which is theirs by birth-right, to deprive them unjustly of the advantages, great and numerous, which those have who command speech in two languages. English and Spanish are to go hand in hand in our schools, and only the height of bigotry and supine ignorance will or can ever affirm that the possessor of more than one language is unfit to be a good citizen.[6]

While Chaves explicitly defended native-language rights, he focused on two additional attributes to sustain his argument: the inherent beauty of the Spanish language and its utilitarian value. The aesthetic factor extolled by Chaves was frequently lauded in the Spanish-language press, and the language was repeatedly linked to Spain's illustrious tradition. This clearly constituted an attempt to prove the legitimacy of Spanish and the people who spoke it.

The Territorial Superintendent's Annual Report issued in 1899 similarly acknowledged the central role of Spanish in New Mexico, though it is clear that utilitarian argument was gaining ground over the more fundamental issue of native-language rights. In this report Manuel C. de Baca also disparaged claims that speaking Spanish disqualified Nuevomexicanos from citizenship:

> The situation and environment of New Mexico is peculiar. The wants and needs of her people differ in some respects from those of other sections of our country. This is particularly true concerning the necessary demands for knowledge of the Spanish language. The arguments and declamations of theorists concerning the patriotism manifested by an exclusive use of the English language have little weight when placed beside the fact that a busy world is making an urgent and increasing demand for more young men and young women competent to use fluently both English and Spanish.[7]

The ethnic configuration of the educational power base shifted in 1905 with the appointment of Hiram Hadley as Superintendent of Schools. Prior to Hadley's appointment, all superintendents of public instruction had been Hispanic males who—judging by the their annual reports—promoted local needs, particularly those related to the Spanish language. The shift from local control to an agenda that sought to align territorial education policy with progressive national trends was applauded by one professor of history at the Agricultural College in Las Cruces, who proclaimed: "This was the greatest triumph that the friends of education have ever reaped in this territory. Those of us who are familiar with education in New Mexico know very well that the present era of rapid progress in our school system dates from that time [Hadley's appointment]."[8] That there may well have been ethnically conscious undertones to Vaughn's characterization of the conflict as one between "school men" and "local politicians" is suggested when he further states, "It is a disgrace to any town or city in New Mexico to have an inefficient superintendent or body of teachers. It brands that town as a place where petty politics and kinfolks reign supreme."[9] These conditions, Vaughn assured his readers, were on the verge of being righted by men like him, who would free the masses from the yoke of nepotism represented by an old guard who saw the territory as a place to languish under the sun, in the proverbial Land of Sunshine. His messianic sense of duty could not be more explicitly stated: "Yet, my friends, we still have lying out before us a herculean task to perform before this great state is redeemed from the course of ignorance and transformed into the Land of Intellectual Sunshine." [10]

Whether there was a direct correlation between the fate of Spanish in public education and the change in the Superintendent's office from Hispanic politicos to Anglo "men of education" is hard to confirm. However, that a change of focus in the Territorial Department of Education from a local to a national agenda that would ultimately affect the status of Spanish was indeed taking place is gleaned from a statement issued in 1907 from Hadley's office:

> Until 1907, no general effort was made to secure the teaching of English in all of the public schools of our territory, but it seems that the time was ripe for the introduction of all English text-books and the enforcement of the uniform text-book law. Almost no opposition exists to the policy of having only English taught in the elementary schools where children attend for short terms and for only a few years. No greater advantage can be given by our public schools to the children of Spanish-American parents than a thorough training in English. [11]

Their loss of authority in the Territorial Department of Education notwithstanding, in the legislative branch Nuevomexicanos maintained a foothold and were able to influence the processes that led to the inclusion of some language protection measures, some of which carried over into educational policy in the state constitution of 1912. However, the events surrounding the admission of New Mexico to the Union in 1912 differed considerably from prior efforts. In 1902, for example, the Beveridge hearings, held at the behest of Congress in Santa Fe, Las Vegas, and Las Cruces, confirmed congressional insistence on the hegemony of English in the territory as a prerequisite for admission to the Union. In these hearings, Nuevomexicanos were called to testify regarding the extent to which Spanish was spoken in the territory in both the informal and formal domains. As a result of the hearings, the committee's recommendation to Congress was that statehood not be granted at the time because Spanish was too prevalent. [12]

Eight years later, in 1910, when Washington realized that the language issue could no longer be used as an excuse designed to forestall statehood for

New Mexico and Arizona, an Enabling Act, or model constitution, was presented to New Mexico. Two articles were of special concern to Nuevomexicanos. Article 21 of the Enabling Act read: "ability to read, write, speak, and
understand English sufficiently without the aid of an interpreter shall be a
necessary qualification for all State officers and members of the State legislature." [13] Reaction to this issue was initially a partisan one, with Republicans—
primarily Hispanos—opposing it and Democrats, including Hispanos, expressing support. Spanish-language newspapers linked to the Democratic
Party began by playing down the negative implications of this measure. They
alleged that Republicans had blown its importance out of proportion in order
to impede passage of the constitution and, consequently, admission to statehood in a year that did not bode well for the election of a Republican president.[14] A heated controversy erupted in the Spanish-language press, and eventually it became clear to Nuevomexicano Democrats that the clause indeed
spelled potential disenfranchisement for non-English-speaking Nuevomexicanos.[15] Op-ed pieces such as one written by Aurora Lucero, in which she argued eloquently against article 21, appeared in numerous newspapers and undoubtedly had a great deal to do with uniting Nuevomexicanos on this issue,
regardless of their party affiliation. Lucero affirms:

> In the act enabling New Mexico to become a state, passed by congress,
> it was provided that none except those who speak, read and write the
> English language with sufficient correctness shall be eligible to the leg-
> islature of the new state, or to any of the state public offices. It is claimed
> by some of those who passed this act that the Spanish-American will be-
> come a better citizen by depriving him of the use of his vernacular. In
> resorting to such a course, it would seem that the contrary effect might
> be produced in him by the unwarranted interference of congress with
> his natural rights, and instead of becoming a better, he might be made a
> worse citizen. Yet the Spanish-Americans of New Mexico have never
> been bad citizens. They have more than once proved their loyalty to the
> government and their love for the "Stars and Stripes," as their conduct
> in the Civil and Spanish-American wars, and in many of the Indian wars,
> abundantly testifies.[16]

In what was no less than a coup against the national mandate, the
framers of the New Mexico state constitution struck out the clause that would
have prohibited the use of Spanish in government transactions and inserted in
its stead an article that called for the publication of all legal notices in both

Spanish and English. This article was to be in effect for twenty years and to be voted upon as needed thereafter. This time limit suggests that Nuevomexicano legislators expected that the subsequent generation would be totally bilingual and that there might not be a need for printing laws in Spanish after 1931. In fact, the article was renewed in 1931 for ten years and again in 1943. However, sufficient funds to complete the project were never appropriated, and the article was eventually eliminated from the constitution. Ironically, this is the article that, even today, is frequently cited as proof of New Mexico's status as an officially designated bilingual state.

A second and crucial article stipulated that "[t]he right of any citizen of the state to vote, occupy office or be a member of a jury shall never be limited or forbidden for reasons related to religion, race, language or color, or the inability to read or write English or Spanish." [17] In addition, in their constitutional bid for first-class citizenship, Nuevomexicano legislators invoked the rights guaranteed to them by the Treaty of Guadalupe Hidalgo, as is borne out by article 2, section 5 of the constitution's bill of rights, which states: "The rights, privileges and immunities, civil, political and religious guaranteed to the people of New Mexico by the Treaty of Guadalupe Hidalgo shall be preserved inviolate." Apparently the blatant disregard of the treaty for over half a century, particularly as it pertained to land rights, had not diminished the faith of Nuevomexicanos in its legitimacy and potential for protecting their civil rights.

Despite these protective measures against language-based disenfranchisement, Nuevomexicano legislators had no choice but to capitulate on the actual issue of language of instruction to be used in the schools. Article 21, section 4 reads, "Provision shall be made for the establishment and maintenance of a system of public schools which shall be open to all the children of the State and free from sectarian control, and said schools *shall always be conducted in English*" (emphasis added). If taken literally, this article would have made the use of Spanish in the classroom illegal. However, in what can only be interpreted as a subversive maneuver, legislators included article 12, section 8, which implies that Spanish could in fact be used to teach Spanish-speaking students:

> The legislature shall provide for the training of teachers in the normal school or otherwise so that they may become proficient in both the English and Spanish languages, to qualify them to teach Spanish-speaking pupils and students in the public schools and educational institutions of the state; and shall provide proper means and methods to facilitate the teaching of the English language and other branches of learning to such pupils and students.

The language here is indeed vague. But was it, in fact, meant to create a space, albeit an ambiguous one, for the inclusion of Spanish in the classroom?[18] Nuevomexicanos were well aware that there was opposition to inclusion of native language rights in the constitution: "Pero entre ciertos delegados hay fuerte hostilidad en contra de la enseñanza del castellano y quieren a todo trance que se adopte el regimen absolutista que prevalece an la actualidad so-bre esa materia."[19] The truth of the matter is that for several decades the United States Congress had held a less than benign attitude toward the lin-guistic reality of New Mexico and had insisted on exclusive English-language public education as a prerequisite to statehood. In view of this hostility, how can we not recognize that Nuevomexicanos were in a very difficult posi-tion? On the one hand, they firmly believed the Treaty of Guadalupe Hidalgo guaranteed them the right to preserve their cultural legacy, including native-language rights. On the other, given that territorial status had denied them full material and civil benefits, they were eager to achieve statehood, and they un-derstood that the tenets of the national policy—English language proficiency and "Americanization"—were linked to admission and attendant privileges and benefits. If they spoke too forcefully for native-language rights, they would be accused of holding a retrograde position, thereby threatening ad-mission to the Union or, subsequently, of compromising New Mexico's posi-tion as the youngest member in a polyglot family bent on declaring English its only legitimate language. Caught between these two positions, subterfuge may have been the only strategy available to Hispanos in 1910.

We should not assume, however, that Nuevomexicano legislators did not fight a good battle. Just as they were pressured from Washington to com-ply with an explicit Americanizing agenda that directly influenced the lan-guage of public education, they also were urged by their local constituents to protect Hispanic interests. That they responded to this pressure is borne out by the following:

> Los delegados, Nestor Montoya, A. A. Sedillo, Isidoro Armijo y algu-nos otros están trabajando con empeño para que se introduzcan en la constitución cláusulas relativas a la educación para que no se prohiba del todo la enseñanza del idioma castellano en las escuelas públicas en con-dados hispano americanos. No intentan ni pretenden que se dé pre-ferencia a ese idioma sobre el inglés sino que ocupe segundo lugar si así lo desearen los vecinos de cualquier comunidad o distrito de habla es-pañola. Este reclamo es muy justo y debería ser atendido, y aun sería mejor si se diese campo para que los habitantes de cada distrito eligie-ran sus propios maestros entre aquellos que estuviesen calificados para

enseñar, pues de ese modo podrían escoger maestros que supiesen y pu-
diesen enseñar ambas [*sic*] idiomas.[20]

Given the fact that Nuevomexicanos made up only one-third of the constitutional convention, the vague nature of the language of article 12, section
8, and the lack of more explicit protective measures vis-à-vis the Spanish language as a language of instruction is understandable.[21] Speculation regarding
the reasons for the ambiguity of this article and section aside, what does become clear as we follow the extant record is that even though English was declared the only legitimate language of instruction, the issue of the role of Spanish in public education was left open for debate—a debate that would exact
the attention of educators, politicians, and citizens at large for a full decade
after statehood was achieved. However, the discussion was more often oblique
than direct, and, as we shall see, it tended to focus on issues of methodology
rather than on actual native-language maintenance or rights.

Three years after the admission of New Mexico to the Union, the Spanish language emerged at the forefront of national and regional concerns. With
the opening of the Panama Canal, the potential for more profitable trade with
Latin America loomed on the horizon, and the teaching of Spanish in the junior and senior high schools and the universities of the nation was promoted as
a sound national investment. Attention was given to the utilitarian value of
Spanish:

> Portuguese, as well as Spanish should be taught in the schools in the
> United States, in order to prepare for increased trade relations with
> Latin America after the opening of the Panama Canal. . . . With these
> two languages, says Mr. Reid, the young American business man will
> be in a position to transact business with twenty Republics of South
> America.[22]

The market-motivated privileging of Spanish-language instruction for
commercial use presented peculiar problems for New Mexico, where Spanish was not a foreign language. To enthusiastically promote the teaching of
Spanish might just give Nuevomexicanos the idea that they had free rein to
continue using it as a language of instruction in the classroom, impeding the
assimilation of "native" children. It was very important, then, to clarify that
while Spanish for utilitarian purposes was one thing, Spanish as a native language was another matter. The first had a place in the public schools; as for
the second, its status eventually was to become even more controversial.

The New Mexico legislature responded quickly to the national trade agenda and passed a measure introduced by A. A. Sena from San Miguel County mandating that "Spanish as *a separate subject* shall be taught in any public elementary or high school in the state when a majority vote of the board of school directors or board of education in charge of such school shall direct. Provided, that the time devoted to such subject shall be such as shall be provided for by the state board of education."[23] This law further stipulated that "except as herein provided, the books used and the instruction given in said schools shall be in the English language, provided, that Spanish may be used in explaining the meaning of English words to Spanish-speaking pupils who do not understand English."

This legislative act created a space for Spanish in the state's education policy, but there was no doubt that its status was that of a foreign language, always subordinate to English. That this status was officially sanctioned by educators is apparent in the numerous "how to" articles that appear in the *New Mexico Journal of Education*. They include a glossary series by Filadelfio Baca, Assistant State Superintendent of Public Instruction, a section called "The Spanish Department," and a scattering of articles and poems in Spanish. One such article is an announcement of the candidacy of Rupert F. Asplund for the office of State Superintendent of Public Instruction. Asplund, a former professor of Latin and Greek at the University of New Mexico, was at the time of his candidacy editor of the *New Mexico Journal of Education*. The journal also carried Spanish book lists and advertisements from Spanish-language publishers.

In 1914 a statewide controversy related to language and education erupted. One Professor Frank Roberts, from Highlands University, in an address to the State Association of Teachers, called for the exclusive use of Spanish and the teaching of Spanish literacy to monolingual Spanish-speaking children. He recommended that instruction be in Spanish for the first three to four years and that the teaching of English literacy skills be introduced only after children had learned to read in Spanish. Treading dangerous waters, Roberts also recommended segregated schools of two types: elementary schools for monolingual English speakers and elementary schools for monolingual Spanish speakers. Bilingual pupils would attend mixed schools.[24] Roberts's address, sections of which, if judged by today's pedagogical standards, were as visionary as they were perceptive, stirred up a heated controversy that was to last for the rest of the decade.

The Nuevomexicano community, anxious about heritage language and cultural preservation but also eager to get on with the process of Americanization so that its children could be fully integrated into the mainstream economic structure, was suspicious of Anglos who suggested that the learning of English could be postponed. They were particularly suspicious of Anglos who suggested school segregation, a practice prohibited by article 12, section 10, of the state constitution. Vehemently attacking Roberts's recommendation, Nuevomexicanos argued that if Americanization was to take place as rapidly as possible, their children needed to be exposed immediately to English. They disagreed on the role of Spanish in the classroom. Some saw the teaching of Spanish literacy as an impediment to the learning of English. Some openly argued that home language skills also should be developed. And a large number favored the "bilingual method," that is, the use of Spanish as a tool for teaching English.[25] Those who argued for the latter appear to have been concerned solely with the learning of English rather than the maintenance of Spanish.

However, given the national resistance to languages other than English and the pressures being brought to bear by hegemonic practices, it is very possible that Nuevomexicanos viewed the bilingual method as the only means of giving Spanish a modicum of legitimacy in the classroom. If insisting on equal footing for Spanish made them appear "un-American," arguments for the bilingual method as a step toward English acquisition could be methodologically justified. From the perspective of the struggle for cultural survival, this position may well have been an oblique strategy, an interpretation prompted by the fact that as the voices of agents of the Americanizing agenda increased in volume, Nuevomexicano demands for the "bilingual method" became equally clamorous.

World War I engendered a frenzied ideology of Americanization at the national level. A zealous patriotic rhetoric shored up a nationalist discourse that called for exclusive loyalty from American citizens to the English language. The rallying cry of the nation became "one flag, one country, one tongue," and the public schools were seen as the "first Americanization agent," and its teachers, the individuals responsible for teaching patriotism and for the inculcation of high ideals.[26] Theodore Roosevelt's proclamation that "[n]o language should be taught in the schools of common education in America but the English" and that "we intend to see that the crucible turns out our people as Americans and not as dwellers in a polyglot boarding house" greatly influenced this nationalist discourse.

Roosevelt's position, however, was not passively accepted. A professor of Spanish, D. B. Morrill, openly took him to task and became a major spokesman for native-language rights for Nuevomexicano children. In an article titled "The Need of Teaching Spanish," Morrill openly opposed laws inimical to the Spanish language and was especially critical of Theodore Roosevelt's "sensational statement." Calling the "inimitable Teddy" a "bully," Morrill stressed that the teaching of Spanish was critical if the United States was to compete favorably with Germany for the Latin American market. "[W]ho is so short sighted as not to see that these countries [Latin America] and the Colossus of the North must be politically bound together?"[27]

In response to a Texas statute that forbade the teaching of any foreign language in its public schools, Morrill had argued in an earlier article that Texas and New Mexico owed its Spanish-speaking children an education that would "make citizens of them." He blamed the failure of their education on rural teachers whose "attitude has been that of ignoring the teaching of English to them as a problem."[28] It is interesting that Morrill's arguments reflect the very position that Nuevomexicanos had held for years: mere exposure to English had not, in fact, yielded any practical results. In Morrill's words, teachers "supposed that learning English will come incidentally and as a matter of course to the Spanish-speaking child. . . . I have examined, line by line, an Institute manual and found that no reference was made in it to the subject of teaching English to Spanish-speaking children."[29] And while Morrill was certainly eager to promote the national Americanization agenda, his position veered away from the assimilationist ideology in that he saw Spanish as playing a crucial role in the general education of Hispanic children. He made a strong case for teaching them literacy in their native language:

> But this article has to deal with the second obligation to the Spanish-speaking child. This obligation is to teach him Spanish to the point that will enable him to write and to read it. . . . Little need be said on the score of the benefit to the child. The pupil, when he can read and write his language as well as he can talk it has a language added to his accomplishments. It is a distinction and a mark of culture to have command of an extra language. The native child having his illiteracy as to his native tongue removed can and will read his own literature in addition to his reading in the English. He is able to write letters to and to read letters from his mother and his people in the only language that he knows.[30]

In addition to advocating native-language rights, Morrill, like Filadelfio Baca and other prominent Nuevomexicanos, supported the use of the bilingual method for teaching English to Nuevomexicano children and frequently spoke out against the direct method: "The advocates and users of the direct method claim that the child, if taught in English, will pick up the language in-cidentally. His failure to do so is as complete as the theory is ridiculous."[31]

Joining Morrill and other prominent citizens in the methodological fracas was Governor Octaviano Larrazolo. Born in Mexico and highly literate in Spanish, Larrazolo defended the position of Spanish in the state, particu-larly when addressing Nuevomexicano audiences. In his official capacity, how-ever, he did not openly advocate native-language rights but rather pressed for the use of Spanish as an avenue for teaching English, thereby keeping in line with the seemingly more palatable strategy. In his first address to the 4th Leg-islature of the State of New Mexico, Larrazolo laid out his agenda for the session:

> It is difficult to see how the English language can successfully be taught to Spanish-speaking children who live in exclusively, or almost exclu-sively, Spanish-speaking communities, where they have no opportunity of speaking English with other children, unless the teacher in such schools is able to speak both the English and the Spanish languages fluently, so that he can explain to the children in their own language, that which they read in the English language, and unless that system be adopted, I confidently believe that the money spent in such schools is absolutely wasted to no purpose. I, therefore, recommend that a law be enacted requiring that all teachers in the public schools in such rural districts of our state as are inhabited principally by Spanish-speaking people, be able to speak, read and write both the English and Spanish languages, in so far as that may be practicable; that is, insofar as such teachers can be procured, and that said teachers be required to teach the children to translate their English reading into the Spanish language, to the end that they may understand that which they read.[32]

Under Larrazolo's strong ethnic leadership, a bill supporting bilingual education was proposed. That in addition to bilingual teachers the bill called for compulsory bilingual textbooks suggests that Larrazolo's position, while ostensibly about methodology, was also about native-language preservation. La bandera americana certainly saw his position as one that advocated for the preservation of Spanish. Appealing to the authority implicit in a rhetoric of both aesthetics and utilitarianism, this newspaper staunchly supported Larra-zolo and acknowledged what the governor himself could not openly admit: that the subtext of his plan for bilingual education was the preservation of Spanish.

El Governador Larrazolo . . . inició un paso que se ha necesitado en Nuevo México por muchos años. Hay razones para ello, la primera es que los niños y niñas aprenden dos idiomas perfectamente bien, á fondo, por principios elementales y puedan conservar el idioma de sus antepasados que es uno de los más hermosos, expresivos, históricos y necesario hoy día en este continente, para las relaciones sociales, comerciales y políticas de los Estados Unidos con una pléyade de Repúblicas al sur de nosotros que cuentan con más de 70 millones de habitantes de habla español; lo segundo y más importante aún es para que los hijos nativos de Nuevo México puedan aprender y entender propia y correctamente el idioma oficial y legítimo del país, el Inglés.[33]

In a letter to the *New York Times*, the powerful statesman Bronson Cutting also rose to Larrazolo's defense. His testimony, however, stood in sharp contrast to that of the editor of *La bandera americana* as he emphatically denied the native-language-preservation implications of the governor's agenda:

> The teaching of English must be compulsory and universal. On those matters there is, I believe, no difference of opinion in the State. The only question is as to the best means of improving the situation. As the employment of teachers who cannot speak Spanish has failed to give the results we hoped for, it would seem only just to give the Governor's program a fair trial and not condemn it beforehand as an attempt "to create a Spanish-speaking State on the border of Mexico."[34]

Judging from the response in the Spanish-language press to Larrazolo's plan, it is evident that this issue was a divisive one for the Nuevomexicano community. One anonymous contributor to the *New Mexico Journal of Education*, for example, called upon the authority of experience to argue against the bilingual method proposed by Larrazolo:

> The Governor himself says that at the age of 16 he could read English but did not understand it. That has been the case with many of us. And that is the case with all the children in the rural districts where they do not hear English spoken by anyone else besides the teacher—no matter how much translating is done in the school, no matter how competent the teacher may be, and whether the teacher can speak Spanish or not. The bi-lingual method has been tried by many teachers for many years and has been found wanting.[35]

La voz del pueblo carried numerous letters that argued forcefully against the Republican governor's support of the bilingual method. One such letter stated:

> El método que se pide en la medida, a mi modo de pensar, está malo en su principio. El objeto de las escuelas no es con el fin de habilitar a los niños a que se vuelvan pericos repitiendo en español lo que leen en inglés y viceversa, pero el desarrolar sus mentes por medio de darles realmente el trabajo el cual deberá ser ejecutado por medio de su propia iniciativa.[36]

The author of this letter proceeded to argue that to teach children bilingually—which was here understood as translation—would make learning too easy, and that in rural districts, where both children and teachers spoke Spanish, English was likely to be ignored in favor of Spanish. The author's concern that Hispanic children would forever lag behind if they failed to learn English is certainly justified. However, his characterization of their motives and those of their teachers reads as ideological overstatement at the service of party politics.

Clarifying its own position, *La voz del pueblo*, with its distinctively Democratic voice, stressed that it did not oppose the teaching of both Spanish and English in the public schools, so long as they were taught separately.[37] However, it emphatically opposed the bilingual method supported by Governor Larrazolo. Lamenting the fact that there were not enough well-trained teachers to teach Spanish "correctly," *La voz* conceded that "si no se puede enseñar correctamente, major es negligirlo del todo en lo presente."[38] *La voz*, perhaps blindsided by partisan loyalty, seemed to be moving in the direction of a nationalist discourse that was not willing to accommodate native-language rights.

The legislature's response to the various and contradictory pressures germane to the methodology issue is contained in Amended House Bill 155, passed in 1919. This bill stipulated that

> teachers in rural school districts inhabited principally by Spanish-speaking people, shall be proficient in reading, writing and speaking of the English and Spanish languages. All studies in such schools shall be taught in the English language, as in other public schools in the state. But it is made the duty of the teachers in such schools to teach Spanish reading to Spanish-speaking pupils and to such English-speaking pupils

as may desire to learn Spanish reading. Spanish-speaking pupils shall be taught to translate their English reading lessons into Spanish. The Spanish text books shall be those commonly used in Spanish schools.

Shortly after this law was passed, the State Board of Education, at a meeting presided over by Governor Larrazolo himself, adopted the following textbooks for the first through eighth grades: *Nueva castilla; Lectura infantil, libro primero; Lectura infantil, libro segundo; Lectura infantil, libro tercero; Lectura infantil, manual del maestro; Libro tercero de lectura; Libro cuarto de lectura; Elementary Spanish Grammar; Poco a poco;* and *Fábulas y cuentos.*[39] The record shows that at least one school district was pleased with the new law:

> There are 527 pupils enrolled [in the Socorro District], a large majority of them are Spanish-speaking. Owing to the large number of Spanish-speaking districts the law relating to teaching by the bilingual method is considered a godsend. By reason of this law the teachers are looking forward to a great advance along educational lines, as the method will solve the difficulties of each and give the Spanish-speaking child an equal chance with the English-speaking pupil.[40]

The State Board of Education, however, took a dim view of the new law and emphatically announced its continued commitment to the Americanizing mission of the public schools:

> *Must Teach in English.* The State Board of Education passed the following resolution at its recent session: The law of our state is mandatory in its provisions to the effect that all branches of learning taught in our schools be so taught in the English language, and in this regard it properly interprets the spirit and purpose of our institutions. This does not exclude the teaching of foreign languages, which indeed is quite commendable, but it certainly is opposed to the establishment and maintenance of primary schools where all branches of study are taught in a foreign language, and where the language of our country, which is the English language, is only incidentally taught.[41]

The board's resolution also rails against the existence of private schools taught in languages other than English and declares students attending such schools truants.

The official discourse of Americanization and its attendant agenda of

excluding languages other than English from the educational arena conquered
the heart of at least one influential Nuevomexicano:

> No hay más que un sólo modo de americanizar a una persona, no im-
> porta cual hayan sido sus antecesores, y esto es enseñando el idioma del
> Americano. Nadie puede negar ese hecho y entre más pronto lo realice-
> mos mucho mejor será para todos los concernientes. Yo hago objeción
> a la enseñanza de cualquier idioma que no sea in inglés como la base de
> americanización, y si el idioma español se enseña en los grados elemen-
> tales el único efecto que tendrá será causar a aquellos de padres his-
> panoamericanos, expecialmente en los distritos rurales, a adherirse a la
> madre lengua y aislarse a si mismos del resto de la población.[42]

The author of this letter, a declared admirer or Theodore Roosevelt's distinctive brand of Americanism, proceeded to accuse Nuevomexicanos who wanted
to conserve a space for Spanish in public education of using the language issue for political gains—that is, to get votes.[43] Whether or not he was correct
in his assessment, it is obvious that with these remarks, Dennis Chávez—then
a young clerk in Washington, D.C., who was to become the most powerful
Hispanic politician in the first half of the twentieth century—gave his bless-
ing to the demise of Spanish as a legitimate language of public instruction in
New Mexico.

Chávez's sentiments coincided with those of the members of the Educational Association of New Mexico, whose Declaration of Principles, drawn
up the same year, supports the position of the State Board of Education: "We
approve the sentiment as thus expressed: 'One flag and one language for America,' and oppose the teaching of any foreign language save as it may be presented in its proper place in the junior and senior high schools as a foreign language."[44] What Chávez, the New Mexico Educational Association, and the
State Board of Education failed to acknowledge was that Spanish in New
Mexico *was not a foreign language.* However, its treatment as such finally forced
Nuevomexicanos to give up the arduous struggle for native-language rights as
they pertained to the education of their children. After the appearance of Senator Chávez's letter, the public debate virtually ceased. Larrazolo's bilingual
law was repealed in 1923, and the issue of Spanish as a native language in the
public schools of New Mexico was laid to rest, not to be resuscitated until
1940 under the banner of Pan-Americanism, then again in 1967 in the wake of
national legislation on bilingual education.

Sifting through the discourse that sustained the thirty-year battle over
the role of Spanish in public education in New Mexico, I find a fascinating

collection of contradictions. But beneath them, I also find an unequivocal struggle for cultural hegemony. Depending on perspective, the subtext to this discourse was about whether teachers would be insiders or outsiders; it was about whether "Spanish American" children could really be Americanized so long as their native language remained an unwelcome guest in the classroom; and it was about the desire to claim native-language rights and to ensure literacy in the home language for Nuevomexicano children. On the surface, however, the discourse became enmeshed in the rhetoric of party politics, and politicians as well as community leaders lost sight of just how high the stakes were. Although immediately before and after statehood Nuevomexicanos stood as a united ethnic block in their attempts to protect the status of their heritage language in education, their embroilment in the methodology debate clearly points to a partisan fissure. Unfortunately, what may not have been clear to those involved in political jockeying was that this dispute would ultimately contribute to the eradication of Spanish-language literacy, and eventually of oral fluency, among future Nuevomexicano generations.[45]

By way of conclusion, I would ask that, lest we judge our forebears too harshly, we keep in mind that even as historical subjects are shaped as sites of consciousness and social agency, they are at the same time contained and constrained by "social networks, cultural codes, forces of necessity and contingency, that ultimately exceed their comprehension or control."[46] And I also remind myself that, as a reader of the texts that mediate between my present and the past of my forebears, I, too, am a historically situated subject—a professor of Spanish and of Chicana and Chicano literature, who daily laments the communal loss of native-language literacy among my people—involved in a process that "constructs and delimits [my] object of study."

NOTES

1. This is a point made in Lynne Marie Getz, *Schools of Their Own: The Education of Hispanos in New Mexico, 1850–1940* (Albuquerque: University of New Mexico Press, 1997). I am indebted to her for sharing her work with me prior to publication. Upon reading Getz's manuscript, I was surprised to discover that we were working with the same material and that we relied on many of the same sources, particularly the *New Mexico Journal of Education*. Her study is much broader and more complete. Mine brings to bear material from the Spanish-language press, and, as is to be expected, our disciplines and social positioning have yielded distinct interpretations.

2. George T. Gould, *Education in New Mexico from the Earliest Date to the Present Time*, East Las Vegas School Board, Mar. 27, 1893, 5.

3. Ibid., 6–7.

4. See Doris Meyer, "The Language Issue in New Mexico, 1880–1900: Mexican

American Resistance Against Cultural Erosion," *Bilingual Review/La Revista Bilingüe* 2, no. 3 (1977): 100.

5. Joan M. Jensen, "Women Teachers, Class, and Ethnicity: New Mexico, 1900–1950," *Southwest Economy and Society* (Winter 1978): 9.

6. Amado Chaves, *The Territorial Superintendent's Annual Report*, 1896, 9.

7. Manuel C. de Baca, *The Territorial Superintendent's Annual Report*, 1999, 71.

8. John J. Vaughn, *New Mexico Journal of Education* 7, no. 7 (Mar. 1911): 65. It is of interest to contrast Vaughn's, or, for that matter, Gould's assessment of the evolution of education in New Mexico to that of Benjamín Read, who also published a treatise on the topic. Positioning himself as a defender of Nuevomexicano culture, Read chose to view this history in a more positive light: "With this review I have made of the history of education in New Mexico, I believe we all have good reasons to be proud of our private and public schools and of the great sacrifices the people of New Mexico have made since the province was first settled by their worthy ancestors to keep alive the christian faith, and love of their intellectual enlightenment, though suffering and experiencing all sorts of handicaps, and that now we all understand that education includes all the agencies which enable a teacher to develop the human minds." *A History of Education in New Mexico* (Santa Fe: New Mexico Printing Co., 1911), 19.

9. Ibid., 69.

10. Ibid., 69. The progressive agenda of these "school men" was condescendingly reiterated time and again in the *New Mexico Journal of Education:* "The system of education which has been so recently established here, and which is now being so vigorously carried out, will result in a wonderful progress in a surprisingly short time. The mind of the native child resembles New Mexico's arid lands awaiting but proper cultivation to become fruitful and productive. After one or two generations have been under influence of the present system of education, there will be no native child to teach. He will be an American not because he will be living under the American flag, not because he will be speaking the English language, but because having received the same education, he will have the same aspiration and the same American spirit." Mrs. O'Connor Roberts, "Difficulties Met in the Education of the Native Child," *New Mexico Journal of Education* 3, no. 4 (Apr. 15, 1907): 10.

11. Hiram Hadley, *State Superintendent's Annual Report*, 1907, 17. The material examined in this paper indicates that Hadley was, if not mistaken, then perhaps Pollyannaish, regarding the lack of opposition to English-only schooling.

12. See 5th Cong., "New Statehood Bill," *Senate Documents*, vol. 5 (Washington, D.C.: Government Printing Office, 1902), 1–120. I am grateful to Phillip Gonzales for calling my attention to this information.

13. This article was part of an amendment introduced by Congressman Albert J. Beveridge, a declared foe of New Mexico's admission as a separate state. See Robert W. Larson, *New Mexico's Quest for Statehood, 1846–1912* (Albuquerque: University of New Mexico Press, 1968), 268.

14. "Los Republicanos en apuros," *La voz del pueblo*, February 12, 1910.

15. *La voz del pueblo* rescinded the position it had taken in the article cited above, writing on Mar. 5, 1910: "Se ve claramente que lo que quieren los republicanos en Washington es quitar siquiera una parte de sus derechos de ciudadanía a la mejor parte de nuestra populación hispano-americana. . . . Esto es igual a decir que esos ciudadanos están buenos para la carga, para pagar impuestos, pero no para tener derecho a disfrutar de los beneficios del gobierno a que pertenecen" [It is clear that the Republicans in Washington want to take away at least some of the rights of our Hispanic-American population. . . . This is like saying that those citizens are good for labor and for paying taxes, but not for exercising the right or enjoying the benefits of the government to which they belong].

16. Aurora Lucero, "Plea for the Spanish Tongue," *Santa Fe Daily New Mexican*, Jan. 31, 1911.

17. Article 7, section 3. This is the original language of the act. The wording has been changed over time, and the act currently reads: "The right of any citizen of the state to vote, hold office or sit upon juries, shall never be restricted, abridged or impaired on account of religion, race, language or color, or inability to speak, read or write the English or Spanish languages except as may be otherwise provided in this constitution." According to Robert Larson, "The stringent provisions regarding equality for the Spanish-speaking citizen were intended to overcome the fears and apprehensions of the native population that they might be discriminated against by the Anglo majority. One delegate described the inclusion of such clauses as being part of a compromise. In return for the Spanish-speaking delegates' agreement to permit women to vote in school elections—a provision contrary to the traditional role of women in their culture—these safeguards were enacted." Larson, 279.

18. Robert A. Moyers, writing on this issue in 1941, sees this as a distinct possibility: "The Enabling Act required instruction in public schools to always be given in English. The state constitution made the same requirement. But the state legislature tried to get around these requirements by providing for the employment of teachers who could speak Spanish in Spanish-speaking communities and by providing that Spanish might be used to explain to children the meaning of their English textbooks. When this attempt failed, teachers resorted to adding an extra year to the elementary school by establishing a pre–first grade." "A History of Education in New Mexico" (Ph.D. diss., University of Tennessee, 1941), 497.

19. *La revista de Taos*, Oct. 14, 1910. [But among certain delegates there is a strong hostility against the teaching of Spanish and they want at all cost to adopt the absolutist regiment regarding this matter that currently prevails.]

20. Ibid. [The delegates Nestor Montoya, A. A. Sedillo, Isidoro Armijo, and others are working hard to introduce in the constitution clauses relative to education so that the teaching of Spanish in public schools in the Hispanic American counties will not be prohibited. They do not intend nor desire that preference be given to that language over English, but that it occupy a second place if that is what citizens of Spanish-speaking communities desire. This reclamation is very just and should be

heeded, and it would be better if room were given so that citizens of each district could elect their own teachers from among those who are qualified to teach, for in this way they could choose teachers that know and could teach both languages.]

21. State attorneys general have been called upon to interpret this article on several occasions. For two diametrically opposed interpretations, one issued in 1968, the other in 1971, see Ray R. Montez, "Education and the Spanish Speaking: An Attorney General's Opinion on Article XII, Section 8 of the New Mexico Constitution," *New Mexico Law Review* (May 1973): 364–80.

22. "Portuguese and Spanish Schools in the United States," *New Mexico Journal of Education* 9, no. 6 (Feb. 1913): 16. That New Mexico responded to this national agenda is evident in an announcement in the journal: "A school of special training for service in Latin-American countries will soon be established at the New Mexico State University." "Training in Spanish," *New Mexico Journal of Education* 12, no. 2 (Oct. 1915): 30.

23. New Mexico Statutes, 1915, chap. 88; emphasis added.

24. See "Two Fundamental Errors in the Educational System of New Mexico," *New Mexico Normal University Bulletin* (Jan. 1915), and "Dos errores fundamentales en el sistema educacional de Nuevo México," *La revista de Taos*, Dec. 4, 1914.

25. See "Enseñanza del español en las escuelas," *La revista de Taos*, Jan. 8, 1915.

26. *New Mexico Journal of Education* 15, no. 8 (Nov. 1919): 23.

27. *New Mexico Journal of Education* 15, no. 4 (Dec. 1918): 7.

28. *New Mexico Journal of Education* 14, no. 9 (May 1918): 6.

29. Ibid., 4.

30. Ibid., 6.

31. *New Mexico Journal of Education* 13, no. 8 (Apr. 1917): 11.

32. *Message of O. A. Larrazolo, Governor of New Mexico, to the Fourth State Legislature* (Santa Fe: Santa Fe New Mexican Publishing Corporation, 1919).

33. *La bandera americana*, May 23, 1919. [Governor Larrazolo . . . initiated a step that has been needed in New Mexico for many years. There are reasons for this, the first being that children learn two languages perfectly well, in essence, through elementary steps and will be able to maintain the language of their ancestors, which is one of the most lovely, expressive, historical, and necessary today on this continent, for social, commercial, and political relations of the United States with the multitude of republics to the south of us that have more than seventy million Spanish-speaking citizens; second and more important is so that the children of native New Mexico can properly and correctly learn and understand the official and legitimate language of the country, English.]

34. "Language in New Mexico: English to Be Taught by Teachers Who Must Know Spanish Too," *New York Times*, Mar. 2, 1919.

35. *New Mexico Journal of Education* 15, no. 7 (Mar. 1919): 20.

36. "El Senador A. V. Lucero hace una declaración tocante a la enseñanza del español" [Senator A. V. Lucero makes a declaration regarding the teaching of Spanish]. *La voz del pueblo*, Feb. 1, 1919. The method called for in this measure, from my perspec-

tive, is based on a faulty premise. The goal of the schools is not to enable children to becomes parrots repeating in Spanish what they learn in English and vice versa, but to develop their minds by giving them the sort of work that can be executed through their own initiative.

37. This clarification may have been issued to reassure readers who may have reacted to an earlier article carried by *La voz*, in which the attorney E. V. Chávez declares: "Deberíamos de tener sólo un idioma como deberíamos tener sólo un país, porque | al extento que adoptamos otro idioma oficial diferente del idioma del país, a ese extento estorbamos y retrasamos el estandarte ideal de la perfecta ciudadanía" [We should have only one language as we should have only one country, because to the extent that we adopt another official language different from the country's language, to that extent will we be a bother and will we hinder the ideal standard of perfect citizenship]. *La voz del pueblo*, Feb. 22, 1919.

38. *La voz del pueblo*, May 10, 1919. [If it cannot be taught correctly, it is best to ignore it altogether at the present time.]

39. *New Mexico Journal of Education* 15, no. 10 (June 1919): 20.

40. Ibid., 26.

41. *New Mexico Journal of Education* 15, no. 9 (May 1919): 24.

42. *La voz del pueblo*, Feb. 8, 1919. [There is only one way to Americanize an individual, it matters not what his predecessor may have been, and that is by teaching him the language of the American. No one can deny this fact, and the sooner we realize it, the better it will be for all concerned. I object to the teaching of any language other than English as the basis for Americanization, and if the Spanish language is taught in the primary grades the only effect it will have will be to cause those Hispanic American parents, especially those in rural districts, to adhere to their mother tongue and to isolate themselves from the rest of the population.]

43. This statement is ironic if we consider that the newspaper that carried it was never reticent about its own party loyalty. The opposition to Governor Larrazolo's bilingual method came overwhelmingly from Democrats, and *La voz del pueblo* was the primary vehicle for their testimony.

44. *New Mexico Journal of Education* 16, no. 4 (Dec. 1919): 30.

45. There can be no doubt that the decline of the Spanish-language press, whose authority and influence had a tremendous impact on the Nuevomexicano community from the 1890s through the first two decades of the twentieth century, was linked to the defeat of the native-language-rights struggle in the education arena. For a moving history of the Spanish-language press in New Mexico, see A. Gabriel Meléndez, *So All Is Not Lost: The Poetics of Print in Nuevomexicano Communities, 1834–1958* (Albuquerque: University of New Mexico Press, 1997).

46. The language cited in this paragraph is from Louis Montrose, "New Historicisms," *Redrawing the Boundaries*, ed. Stephen Greenblatt and Giles Gunn (New York: Modern Language Association of America, 1992), 414–15.

Chapter Seven

MAURILIO VIGIL

The Political Development of New Mexico Hispanas

INTRODUCTION

The advent of the women's rights movement in the 1960s, climaxed by the valiant though failed effort to secure passage of the Equal Rights Amendment, has had profound implications for women in all facets of American life. Women are more active politically than they have ever been. More women are voting, running for and holding political office, serving in appointive positions, and participating in political parties and campaigns than ever before. In fact, most recent studies on the voting behavior of the American electorate reveal no significant difference in participation between men and women.[1] Less well known, but no less significant, has been the progress in the political process of women from ethnic minorities such as Hispanics, African Americans, and Native Americans. It is axiomatic that any effort to begin to document the transformation in levels of participation of minority women must begin at the local level.

This chapter will document changes in the political participation of Hispanic women in New Mexico from 1912, when New Mexico became a state, to the present. While the topic is significant in documenting changes in the political status of women, it is particularly interesting because Hispanic women, in addition to overcoming gender discrimination, also had to challenge Hispanic cultural norms, which relegated women to an apolitical, docile role.

As for contemporary views on Hispanic women and politics, a number of sources contain only short, isolated accounts, many of them biographical sketches of specific Hispanic women politicians. Joan Jensen and Darlis Miller's *New Mexico Women: Intercultural Perspectives*,[2] which provides the most comprehensive study of New Mexican women's political background, activities, and contributions, offers the first glimpses of Hispanic women in politics and the suffrage and equal rights movements. *Nuestras Mujeres: Hispanas of New Mexico*,[3] edited by Tey Diana Rebolledo, presents biographical profiles of Hispanic women that offer important insights into the personal backgrounds, struggles, and accomplishments of several notable Hispanic women of New Mexico. A recent article by Michele Jacquez-Ortiz, "Hispanic Women in Politics: Doing More than Treading Water,"[4] offers conversations with some of the more prominent Hispana politicians in New Mexico in the 1990s. Melissa Howard's "The First Woman to Govern New Mexico"[5] highlights the career of Soledad Chacón, the first woman secretary of state in New Mexico. And Martha Cotera's *Diosa y hembra: The History and Heritage of Chicanas in the U.S.*,[6] one of several works on Hispanas in the United States, is reflective of the general histories that attempt to trace the historical experience of Hispanas from the Spanish colonial period to the present.

While all of these works provide interesting and worthwhile anecdotal reference points on Hispanas, none attempts a systematic portrayal of the political development of Hispanic women in New Mexico. I will endeavor to do just that by describing the evolving political role of women in response to the emergence and resolution of women's political issues; the changes in the political rights of women; and the increased involvement of women in political parties, campaigns, and office holding.

HISTORICAL BACKGROUND: A PREFACE TO POLITICS

It is generally understood that in nineteenth-century New Mexico, women were quite limited in the political role they could play because they could not vote, sit on juries, or hold public office. Moreover, social norms relegated them to a primary domestic role as homemakers and family caregivers. It can also be said that there was no organized movement prior to 1900 to expand the political rights and status of women. Even here, however, it is possible to ascribe some significance to adaptations made by Hispanic women that enhanced their political role both at that time and later.

It is assumed that Hispanic women enjoyed few, if any, legal and political rights in New Mexico prior to the twentieth century. It is further assumed that they were even more bereft of such rights than were Anglo-American women at the same time. The stereotypical image of the Hispana, particularly in colonial rural New Mexico, is that of a submissive, cloistered, powerless woman. Victims of a highly patriarchal society and culture, Hispanic women had little control over their own lives, less over their small villages and none over the external world. But recent studies have refuted these assumptions.

Rosalind Rock, for example, using court records to explore women's rights in eighteenth-century New Mexico, reveals women's frequent court appearances in matters relating to property ownership, civil rights, domestic relations, and estate management. Her discovery of the broad extent of women's rights prompted Rock to conclude:

> When New Mexico women were observed by Anglos in the 1830s, it was said: "In contrast [to Anglo women] a New Mexican woman retained her property, legal rights, wages and maiden name after marriage." [7]

Not only were the legal rights of Hispanic women protected, but it was culturally and socially acceptable for a woman, if she were ambitious, assertive, and resourceful, to use the courts, political contacts, or government to enhance her economic and social position. Richard Ahlborn, in his review and analysis of the will of a prominent New Mexico Hispana, Juana Luján, shows how Luján secured property, distributed it, and otherwise managed her affairs as would any prominent Hispanic male of the period. According to Ahlborn:

> [t]he Luján documents define the role and status of a prosperous woman in colonial Hispanic society. Her family and social connections are reflected in legal statements, property listings, and distribution. As early as 1714, Juana Luján begins to acquire land, by 1721 she marries her daughter with a handsome dowry to a prominent citizen, and by 1762 she has created an estate of 6,000 pesos . . . Juana has the means to acquire silver and porcelain utensils . . . religious images . . . jewelry . . . Those trappings of upper-class consumer taste help to establish and maintain [her] social position . . . In short Juana fulfills the Hispanic model for women in her class, an elevated one in terms of the local society, through active participation in its social, legal and economic structures. [8]

In addition to inherent legal rights under the Spanish government, Hispanic women exercised considerable political power because of their work in and control over the home, family life, and the production of food. Hispanic women were responsible for the home in both a literal and a figurative sense. Women participated in the construction and maintenance of their homes through their roles in preparing the clay-mud mixture for adobe and plastering dwellings. They also produced the blankets, mattresses, and much of the clothing worn by family members. Women tended garden plots that produced a good portion of the vegetables and fruit required by the family and of course prepared the meals for the family. Because of the frequent absences of their husbands due to migratory or other seasonal employment, mothers became the primary caregivers for children, providing both moral and spiritual guidance. Rather than diminishing them, these familial roles enhanced a woman's status and power. As described by Sarah Deutsch:

> While the men dealt with external relations, it was the women who provided the main integrating force in the community. The lack of a rigid sexual division of labor allowed women to compensate for seasonal absences by men. But even their normal round of activities placed them at the community's center. Through their visiting, their sharing of food, plastering, childbearing, and most importantly their stability [and] production . . . women made up the "stable core" of the village and maintained its social as well as its physical structures . . . willing to act independently and even combatively in legal struggles over property, marriage and property owners and producers in their own right, Hispanic village women were hardly, after all, cloistered, powerless, or even, necessarily, submissive.[9]

The examples above reveal that while the formal political roles of women, such as voting or holding office, may have been nonexistent in colonial New Mexico, women were vested with substantial legal rights that could and did prove quite extensive when used skillfully by an individual woman. It is also important to consider that Spanish colonial society in New Mexico prior to the nineteenth century was quite hierarchical, stratified, and centralized. Governmental and political power was vested in a small aristocratic elite that had or could establish connections to the monarchy. In other words, political rights, even for men, were highly circumscribed due to the advantages given to the privileged classes.

The significance of these conditions in terms of the political development of Hispanic women is that they enabled women, especially those from the elite classes, to develop familiarity with and skills in utilizing available institutions to enhance their own economic and social status and that of their families. In doing so, they not only assured the preservation of their status and those rights but their subsequent expansion. This elite class of women would also serve as models for subsequent generations who would use those privileges and rights and their example as a springboard for the expansion of women's rights.

The annexation of the New Mexico Territory by the United States under the Treaty of Guadalupe Hidalgo at the end of the Mexican War in 1848 invested Hispanic males over twenty-one with all of the political rights and privileges of white American male citizens. Hispanic men in New Mexico would prove to be quite capable students of American politics and would become adept practitioners in voting, electioneering, office holding, and even emulating the seamier American political traditions such as machine politics and bosses (*patrones*).

Hispanic women, on the other hand, like their Anglo-American sisters, would have to wait until the twentieth century for social and political strictures to begin to relax. However, although frozen out of the formal political arena of voting and office holding, Hispanic women continued to wield political power in the more subtle ways to which they had become accustomed, as *patronas*, wives, and mothers, in the courts, and through their leadership of village communities.

INITIAL EFFORTS FOR WOMAN SUFFRAGE IN NEW MEXICO

Although western states are notable for having extended suffrage to women even before the adoption of the Nineteenth Amendment to the United States Constitution in 1920, New Mexico was not among them. The reasons for the delay as well as the role of Hispanic politicians and voters in the matter, has been a subject of debate among scholars. While some suggest a conspiracy of Hispanic politicians and Hispanic men in opposition to woman suffrage, the truth is that Hispanics, like Americans in general, were divided on the issue and appear as both advocates and opponents in the debate.

It is generally agreed that the earliest activity in support of woman suffrage in New Mexico was the product of women's clubs such as the Women's Improvement Association (WIA), which was affiliated with the National Federation of Women's Clubs in 1911. Another important organization was the Congressional Union. Because few Hispanic women were very active in women's organizations, the number who were in the suffrage movement was rather limited. Nina Otero-Warren, however, became a very prominent player in the struggle for the right to vote.[10]

The period between 1900 and 1920 witnessed a concerted effort on the part of women to expand their political rights in New Mexico. Led by the aforementioned women's clubs, women organized pressure groups, sponsored forums and rallies, prepared campaign literature (both to expand support and to educate the public), and actively lobbied elected officials.[11]

In 1909, nine women's clubs in New Mexico organized into one state women's organization, and the following year, its president presented a petition to the New Mexico State Constitutional Convention in support of partial woman suffrage. The proposal would allow women to vote in school district elections and to hold public office. The state convention also considered a blanket proposal that would give women the vote in *all* elections and a more conservative proposal that would postpone the issue until 1926, when all males and females aged twenty-one or over would decide by referendum if women would be allowed to vote.[12]

Recognizing that a push for the blanket vote in all elections was premature, the organized women's movement supported the partial suffrage proposal. A record of the roll call, showing how each of the 100 delegates voted on the woman suffrage issues in the 1910 convention, is not available. Consequently, it is necessary to rely on fragmentary information from newspaper accounts or memoirs to reconstruct the circumstances.

The assumption that Hispanic delegates were unanimously opposed is erroneous, since one newspaper account reports that only two of the thirty-five Hispanic delegates had protested against suffrage. On the other hand, Solomón Luna, one of the two leaders of the dominant Republican majority (along with Holm Bursum) and chair of the convention's steering committee, had declared his support of the partial suffrage proposal.[13] Luna was the uncle of Nina Otero-Warren, who in 1915 would become a prominent leader of the woman suffrage movement in New Mexico. However, it is not known whether she figured at all in her uncle's support in 1910 of partial woman suffrage.

The partial suffrage proposal was incorporated in the new constitution and took effect in 1912 when New Mexico became a state. However, a compromise provision was incorporated that allowed a majority of voters in a particular district to present petitions to the Board of County Commissioners requesting disfranchisement of women. If this occurred, women would lose their vote. Apparently, this curious form of a local-option reversal petition was necessary to mollify opponents of even partial woman suffrage in 1910.

The provision in the 1910 constitution that allowed women the right to vote in school elections and the right to hold school offices (such as superintendent, director, or member of the board of education) was a breakthrough for women in New Mexico, even if it did not grant universal suffrage. Interestingly, women had, in fact, held a few appointive positions even before the provision in the constitution. Women had served as superintendents of schools in Colfax and Roosevelt Counties. Lola Chávez de Armijo had been appointed to the position of Territorial Librarian by Governor George Curry in 1909. In 1912, the Democrat William C. McDonald was elected the first state governor, and he promptly submitted his nominations for various appointive offices. While the state senate responded favorably to most of his appointments, it rejected his nomination for the position of State Librarian. Consequently, Lola Armijo, as the incumbent, retained the position. Angered by the senate's rejection of his appointment, McDonald pressured Armijo to resign, which she refused to do. He then filed a motion in state district court that read in part:

> Lola Chávez de Armijo, being a woman and not qualified under the constitution and laws of New Mexico to hold office . . . assumes to discharge the office . . . without authority of law; contrary to the form of the statutes in such case made and provided against the peace and dignity of the State of New Mexico.[14]

Thus, in one ill-conceived move, Governor McDonald was attempting to secure legal reaffirmation of the age-old assumption that a woman's place was in the home and certainly not in the halls of government, in keeping with the "peace and dignity" of New Mexico. For Armijo, the recently adopted provision on partial suffrage in the 1910 constitution saved the day: District Judge Edmond Abot ruled in her favor. It is noteworthy that a Hispana, Lola Armijo, was at the center of this precedent-setting court decision affirming the new political status of women in New Mexico.

THE STRUGGLE FOR THE RATIFICATION
OF THE SUSAN B. ANTHONY AMENDMENT

Even as the 1910 constitution provided a breakthrough for women, it also slammed the door tightly against any further state-sponsored reforms regarding woman suffrage. The source was another provision in the constitution, article 7, section 1, which requires that a three-fourths majority in each house would be necessary in order to propose amendments to certain constitutional provisions pertaining to the elective franchise (voting). Moreover, ratification required a three-fourths majority statewide and a two-thirds majority in each county. These extraordinary amending requirements were designed to safeguard the very liberal provisions on voting and office holding for Hispanic males.[15] Since any amendment that extended suffrage to women would have to receive overwhelming approval, it would be virtually impossible to get it ratified.

This became abundantly clear to Ada Worley, a leading New Mexican advocate for woman suffrage, who wrote to Anne Martin of the Congressional

Union in 1916, "I have written you heretofore, the only hope for New Mexico is federal action."[16] In the same letter, Worley reported on the "campaign" to pressure New Mexico's congressional delegation to support passage of the Nineteenth Amendment (known as the Susan B. Anthony Amendment or the Woman Suffrage Amendment). In the previous month, Worley had written 100 "suffrage notes" to friends urging them to write U.S. Senator Thomas B. Catron in support of suffrage, but Catron remained steadfast in his opposition.[17]

In 1915, the Congressional Union (C.U.), a splinter group that had separated from the National American Woman Suffrage Association (NAWSA), sent Ella St. Clair Thompson to New Mexico to help organize the suffrage movement. Thompson located the most influential women in Santa Fe and then expanded her network throughout the state. She laid plans for a mass meeting, a parade, and a delegation to United States Senators Catron and Albert Fall. Since the network Thompson set up was coordinated through the women's clubs, only 7 of 107 members were Hispanic.

Among the Hispanas, however, two would play a very prominent role in the struggle for woman suffrage in New Mexico. The first Hispanic woman recruited was Aurora Lucero, the daughter of New Mexico's first secretary of state, the Democrat Antonio Lucero, who had formerly served as the editor of *La voz del pueblo*, the Spanish weekly newspaper. Thompson made a special effort to attract Hispanic women to her mass meeting, which was held on October 15, 1915. She printed leaflets in English and Spanish and scheduled Aurora Lucero to speak in Spanish at the rally. Lucero, who used a speech composed by Thompson, emphasized women's issues, but she also spoke on matters such as child welfare.[18] Lucero was a good choice for the speaker. Educated at New Mexico Normal School (later Highlands University), she would become a professor of Spanish at that institution. Lucero would later enter politics as San Miguel County School Superintendent.

A second and ultimately more active recruit was Adelina (Nina) Otero-Warren. A scion of two politically prominent New Mexico Hispanic families, the Oteros and the Lunas, Otero-Warren had entered active politics in 1917 when she was appointed School Superintendent of Santa Fe. A Republican, Otero-Warren was reelected in 1918 when she defeated a male Democratic opponent. Meanwhile, at the urging of Thompson and Alice Paul, head of the national C.U., Otero-Warren had accepted a position as vice president of the state advisory council of the C.U. In September 1917, she was made president of the New Mexico C.U. Speaking about Otero-Warren's political evolution and its impact on Hispanic women, her biographer says:

Having bilingual skills and Otero-Warren as a surname proved highly advantageous to her and to the C.U., giving her entreé to the highest Anglo circles and also generating confidence and trust among other Hispanic women, most of whom were socially marginal, unwilling to go against the grains of the entrenched patriarchal system, and unconcerned about their lack of voting rights. Although she was timid at first, when speaking before large groups and was severely criticized at times for leaving the "woman's sphere" to speak publicly, she soon overcame her shyness.[19]

Otero-Warren's tenure as president of the New Mexico C.U. fell during the time that the Nineteenth Amendment was being debated in Congress. Her primary role was to influence New Mexico's congressional delegation to support its passage.

The 1916 New Mexico election was propitious for the woman suffrage movement, because it resulted in the election of two new pro-suffrage members to New Mexico's congressional delegation. In the Senate, Catron had rebuffed all of the women's lobbying, and "[d]isgruntled women left his office feeling that all they were good for was 'to stay home, have children, have more children, cook and wash dishes.'"[20] Whatever role women opponents played in denying Catron renomination in his party's 1916 convention is lost to history, but it was probably felt indirectly and was well deserved, for he had been an uncompromising opponent. In a last parting shot as a lame-duck senator, he introduced an anti-suffrage resolution in February 1917.

Frank Hubbell, who was nominated over Catron by the Republicans, was himself defeated in the November 1916 general election by Andrieus A. Jones from Socorro. Jones, on entering the Senate, assumed the chairmanship of the Senate Committee on Woman Suffrage and from that pulpit proved his support by steering the Susan B. Anthony Amendment out of his committee and to the Senate floor, where it passed in June 1919. The other New Mexico Senator, the Republican Albert B. Fall, who had supported the women all along, also voted in favor of the amendment.

On the House side, William B. Walton, the Democrat who replaced Benigno "B.C." Hernández, began to falter in his support after initially promising to vote in favor of the amendment. This prompted a hurried message from headquarters urging Otero-Warren to "turn up the political heat [since] 'I think he is a little shaky and needs pressure from constituents.'"[21] Apparently Otero-Warren's lobbying efforts worked, because Walton voted in favor of the amendment, which passed the House in January 1919.

Thus, Nina Otero-Warren should have been well pleased by June 1919, when the Senate vote finally propelled the Susan B. Anthony Amendment out of Congress. Personally, she had evolved from the role of political bystander to an elected position as Santa Fe School Superintendent and on to leadership of the organization leading the drive for woman suffrage. However, even bigger challenges loomed on the horizon.

Since 1910, both major political parties, but especially the Republicans, had become aware of the increasing influence of women activists. Wary that the opposing party might capture the loyalty of the new women leaders and the larger constituency of women to which they appealed, the parties had begun to embrace some of the issues of concern to women. They had also begun to recruit some of them into the party. The logical choice would be offspring of some of the established male politicians. Thus, the Republicans had recruited Nina Otero-Warren and the Democrats sought out Aurora Lucero. Both women, it seemed, were being groomed, as men had been before them, for future leadership in their respective parties.

In 1919, Otero-Warren resigned the presidency of the C.U. in order to devote more time to her position as School Superintendent and to a position as chair of the Women's Division of the Republican State Committee for Women. This new position placed Otero-Warren near the very core of the Republican Party power structure in New Mexico. Otero-Warren would thus be in a key position within the dominant party to lobby for the impending struggle for ratification of the Susan B. Anthony Amendment in the New Mexico legislature. That same year, she was featured in an article in *Holland* magazine describing her as "having mastered the best attributes" of any American or Spanish woman. It praised her for emancipating herself from "what is useless in the old life, still retaining what is charming and worthwhile." It went on to say:

> No American woman could be more emancipated . . . businesslike . . .
> efficient . . . wide awake [yet possess] . . . that peculiar Spanish charm,
> graciousness, modesty . . . and the poise and consideration of others
> found so often in the convent bred woman.[22]

In February 1919, even before the Senate had acted on the Susan B. Anthony Amendment, the New Mexico legislature began consideration of a woman suffrage amendment to its own state constitution.

With Nina Otero-Warren lobbying the Republicans, the senate readily approved the state amendment on March 14, 1919, by a vote of eighteen to five, just enough to secure the three-quarters majority required. The five senators who voted against the measure were all Hispanos, indicating that there was some truth to the rumors of Hispanic males opposing suffrage. On March 15, however, the proposal was defeated by a majority of twenty-two to sixteen in the house of representatives. Six Hispanos in the house voted for passage, while ten voted in opposition. The defeat of the state constitutional amendment was a disappointment to state and national suffrage leaders because it forecast a possible rejection of ratification of the Susan B. Anthony Amendment by the New Mexico legislature. Thirty-six state legislatures would have to vote in favor in order to ratify. As it happened, a total of twenty-two states ratified in 1919, leaving the amendment just fourteen shy of the required total. National leaders were aware, from past experience, that the longer the ratification process took, the more difficult it would be to secure passage because the opposition could mobilize more effectively.

Women were not the only ones disappointed over the New Mexico house's defeat of the measure. The *Christian Science Monitor* noted that "equal suffrage resolved itself into something of a racial question in New Mexico this week . . . three fourths of those voting in the negative being Spanish speaking members," The *Portland Oregonian* joked, "Down *there* . . . they prefer to marry the women when they find them and keep them out of politics."[23]

The defeat in New Mexico, however, propelled a new and powerful ally to the forefront of the suffrage issue. Governor Octaviano A. Larrazolo had been an early supporter of woman suffrage. In his first "state of the state" message to a joint session of the 4th New Mexico Legislature on January 15, 1919, Larrazolo had said:

> The provisions of our state constitution seem to stand in the way of any legislative enactment on that subject [woman suffrage]. I therefore recommend that you propose an amendment to the state constitution, in the manner provided by law, to the effect that women may be admitted to the enjoyment of the right of suffrage on an equality with men. Slowly but steadily, the women of our country have been extending their sphere of usefulness. No longer confined exclusively to domestic duties, woman has been enlarging her field activity so that today we find her involved in many of the industrial pursuits of life . . . Therefore in this particular, they are entitled to the same protection that the law gives to the working man.[24]

Larrazolo was outraged when the house defeated the suffrage measure. He dispatched a scathing letter to both parties denouncing the legislators who voted against suffrage. He reminded his own Republican colleagues of his and the party's campaign promises in the 1918 election campaign and urged that they "discharge their duty [and] redeem these pledges and thus save the future of our party; or . . . betray them and doom our party to defeat."[25]

Larrazolo pledged to the women that he would call a special session of the legislature for the following year to consider the matter. On July 5, 1919, Mrs. (A. B.) Jessie Stroup, chair of the Resolutions Committee of the Women's Suffrage Committee of New Mexico, wrote to the governor:

> . . . We note with extreme pleasure your promise to call the extra session for ratification of the Nineteenth Amendment "whenever you can be assured of its passage!" Your administration has been conspicuous for the conscientious fulfillment of pre-election promises. We rely absolutely upon you to keep this one, so graciously reiterated upon your recent visit to Albuquerque.[26]

Equally vocal on the subject of woman suffrage was the opposition to it, as the governor soon discovered. One letter he received listed the evil of "what Woman Suffrage is, and does." Among the evils cited were that "[i]t [suffrage] makes bold women instead of gentlewomen . . . It develops female political bosses and rounders."[27]

Notwithstanding the opposition, Governor Larrazolo kept his word and called for a special session of the legislature, which convened on February 16, 1920. Arizona and Utah had ratified the amendment early in 1920, so if New Mexico ratified, it would become the thirty-second state to do so, the amendment then needing only four more for national ratification.

When the 1920 special session convened, the governor urged ratification, but it soon became evident that passage would be difficult and that some of the strongest opponents would be "old guard" and Hispanic Republicans from the governor's own party. As one biographer describes it, Larrazolo "saw the attitude of some of the legislators opposing ratification and immediately threw all of the power of the governor's office into the effort for ratification."[28] He called on Republican stalwarts such as Holm Bursum, the Republican National Committeeman, state Republican Party chairman George Craig, and Valencia County leader Ed Otero to lobby for the measure.[29]

Otero-Warren and other suffragists meanwhile stepped up their own lobbying efforts, countering the anti-suffrage propaganda now inundating the legislature. She took her cause directly to the Republicans, becoming the first woman to be given access to a Republican legislative caucus. On February 18, the senate voted for the amendment by a vote of seventeen to five. The next day, after a three-hour Republican caucus, Representative Dan Padilla withdrew his proposal for a state referendum on the matter. Representative R. L. Baca, an influential Republican, shifted from opposition to support, and the House then voted in favor of ratification by a vote of thirty to ten.[30] The same day, Otero-Warren received a telegram from Alice Paul in which she declared, "A Congratulations on New Mexico's victory. All women in the country are indebted to you on your splendid leadership. We have deepest admiration for your campaign."[31] Oklahoma, Washington, and West Virginia followed New Mexico, and then, on August 15, 1920, Tennessee ratified, making the Susan B. Anthony Amendment a part of the United States constitution and ending a century-long struggle for woman suffrage.

For Octaviano Larrazolo, the short seven-day special session was a triumph, as his diligent preparation resulted in approval of all measures he had placed before the legislature. However, in winning the battle, the governor antagonized old-guard Republicans, who would mobilize in 1920 to deny him the renomination of his party for the governorship.[32]

SECURING THE RIGHT TO HOLD ELECTIVE OFFICE

Even as they savored their long-sought victory, New Mexico's suffragists realized that the struggle was far from over. Getting the vote was one thing; getting women to exercise that cherished right would be another. They also realized that the right to vote would be incomplete until they secured the right to hold political office, which at the time was still limited to holding office as school officials.

For the political parties, the challenge was to try to attract the new women voters. The Republican Party, having already tapped leaders such as Otero-Warren, acted first. They appointed three women to the eleven-member executive committee and added fifty-seven women to the state central committee, eighteen of whom were Hispanic. The Democrats also named four women to their executive committee and fifty-six women to their county committees; only two were Hispanic. Both parties recognized that a big challenge would be to tap large populations of Hispanic women voters and accordingly made that a priority in their campaign and voter recruitment efforts. In the 1920 campaign, for example, Democratic and independent Republican women joined to formulate a bilingual appeal, "A las mujeres de Santa Fe." In the appeal, a circular reminded women that this was their first election and that they should not be timid but be prepared to strike a quick blow with their new-found power. It went on to point out that "it is to make our city a better place to live . . . 'we have been told that the men of the parties are equal and if Santa Fe is to be cleaned up, we the women must do it.'"[33]

The participation of women in the 1920 election was impressive. The overall participation of voters had increased from 40 percent in 1916 to 62 percent in 1920 despite the expansion of the electorate. Male participation in 1920 exceeded female participation only slightly. Women campaigned for school superintendent (the only office they could seek) in twenty-one of the twenty-nine counties and were elected in nineteen.[34] Of the nineteen women county school superintendents, two were Hispanic. Otero-Warren retained her position as Superintendent of Schools for Santa Fe County, a position she would hold until 1927. Additionally, Adela G. Gallegos was elected superintendent for Guadalupe County. Another barrier fell in a special election in 1921 when New Mexico voters approved a constitutional amendment that allowed women to hold any public office. The vote was 55 percent to 45 percent in favor of women's office holding.

HISPANAS IN PUBLIC OFFICE

The 1922 election would be the first milestone for Hispanic women in New Mexico as they showed they would be a new force in state-level politics. Less than two years after securing the vote and one year after securing the right to hold office, Hispanic women campaigned for the United States Congress and for the office of secretary of state.

In 1922, in a fitting climax to her efforts to secure the vote for women and reflecting her own political maturation, Nina Otero-Warren announced her candidacy for Congress. Her opponent for the Republican nomination was the incumbent, Nestor Montoya, who expressed his consternation at having a leading suffragist as his opponent after he had supported women's issues.[35] Otero-Warren had to endure the taunts of her opponent and newspapers, in particular the *Santa Fe New Mexican,* which doubted her ability and seriousness as a candidate. The *New Mexican* wrote, "[T]he diminutive 'woman politician' made the rounds of New Mexico towns and villages, smiling, shaking hands, making campaign speeches, and courting votes." If nominated, she promised to run on a platform of better education, solutions to labor problems, a protective tariff, reclamation, and enforcement of the prohibition amendment.

At the Republican nominating convention, Otero-Warren won overwhelmingly with 446½ votes to Montoya's 99½. She carried all but one of the predominantly Hispanic counties and became the first woman and first Hispanic from New Mexico to be nominated for a national office. In the general election, Otero-Warren faced Democrat John R. Morrow of Raton. Building on her appeal to Hispanic voters and women, Otero-Warren campaigned forcefully around the state but came up short, losing by 10,000 votes. Still, she was thankful that 49,000 New Mexicans had supported a Hispanic woman for Congress. Especially pleasing was the fact that she had carried all but one of the Hispanic counties, which only a year before had objected to a woman's right to hold office.[36]

The second Hispanic woman to make history in 1922 was a more obscure and unpretentious housewife and mother named Soledad Chávez-Chacón, who was baking a cake in her home in Albuquerque when five powerful Democratic politicians knocked at her door and, acting on behalf of the Democratic Convention, solicited her to run for the office of secretary of state. The politicians included the future United States Senator Dennis Chávez (her cousin) and the future governors John E. Miles and Thomas J. Mabry. They and others at the Democratic Convention were searching for ways to recapture control of state government from the Republicans. Someone suggested placing a woman's name on the ballot as a way to appeal to the newly enfranchised women of New Mexico. Immediately, others agreed that running a woman on the ticket would not only harness the women's vote but provide good balance to the ticket, which was headed by James F. Hinkle, the candidate for governor. It was agreed that the office of secretary of state would be the most appropriate position for a woman on the ballot. Lacking any woman with the name recognition of Nina Otero-Warren, the Democrats decided to look for a candidate from a politically prominent family.

Chacón was a high school graduate and had attended business school, but other than keeping active with church affairs and literary clubs such as the Minerva Club, she had not had any formal political experience. In addition to her cousin Dennis Chávez, an uncle (Felipe Chacón) advanced her name in the convention. She consulted her father, Melitón Chavéz and husband Ireneo, both prominent Democrats, and both consented, though her father was skeptical at first. At thirty-two, "gracious and pretty, Soledad Chacón made a good candidate." [37]

She received the nomination and was elected, along with Governor Hinkle and Isabel Eccles (as State Superintendent of Public Instruction) and most of the Democratic ticket in the November 1922 general election. Chacón was reelected in 1924. She served out two full terms and was regarded as a competent officeholder. In addition to carrying out her official duties, which included supervising elections and verifying returns, printing statutes, and publishing the official state register (*The New Mexico Blue Book*), she worked to improve record-keeping practices in the expanding state bureaucracy. Her occupancy of the office of secretary of state set a precedent, and thenceforth that state office would be regarded as a woman's domain.

Chacón, however, was better known for another distinction, which fell to her during the second year of her first term in office. In the spring of 1924, Lieutenant Governor José Baca died in office. Later in the summer, Governor Hinkle left the state to attend the Democratic National Convention in New York City. There being no lieutenant governor in office, the line of succession to the office went to the secretary of state. Thus, at the age of thirty-three, Soledad Chacón became the first woman to serve as governor (albeit acting governor) of the state of New Mexico. The *New Mexico State Tribune* declared on June 21, 1924:

> A new historical event has been recorded . . . and for the first time since the United States cut loose from the dominion across the seas, a woman has become the chief executive of one of the largest states in the union. She is a young woman, too, and a good looking one.[38]

Other newspapers trivialized the important occasion by reporting that the governor wore a "lavender summer dress" on her first day in office. Her only official actions as governor were the signing of a notary public's commission, endorsing funds for the National Guard, and issuing a conditional pardon to a felon. Chacón faced one of her biggest challenges toward the end of her term as secretary of state, when Democrats and Republicans in San Miguel County clashed over the election of the county sheriff. Republican Cleofas Romero was declared the winner in unofficial balloting, but the Democratic opponent, Lorenzo Delgado, charged that 100 votes were not legally documented. Secretary of State Chacón, escorted by armed guards, personally carried the precinct books to a meeting in the San Miguel County Courthouse, where she certified the vote total minus the 100 "phantom" votes and declared Delgado the winner by six votes.[35] Thus, less than five years after achieving the vote, a woman was playing the role of arbitrator in the battle between two of the most powerful political bosses in the state. Chacón served in the Electoral College in 1933, casting a vote as a Democrat for Franklin D. Roosevelt; she also served as a state representative from Bernalillo County in 1936.[40]

Following the 1922 election, when women were elected to the positions of Secretary of State and Superintendent of Public Instruction, these two offices would be reserved by both parties for women. Since nominations in those days were made by party conventions at both the state and the county level, the parties could set aside specific positions for women. Although men still controlled the party organizations, they were keenly aware of the increasing prominence of women politicians and the importance of women's votes, and made special efforts to cultivate both.

Following Chacon's pathbreaking effort, Hispanic women became regular occupants of the office of Secretary of State. They include Mrs. E. A. (Jesusita) Perrault (R), 1929–30; Marguerite P. Baca (R), 1931–34; Elizabeth Gonzales (D), 1935–39; Jessie M. Gonzales (D), 1939–42; Cecilia Tafoya Cleveland (D), 1943–46; Alicia Romero (D), 1947–50; Ernestine D. Evans (D), 1967–70 and 1975–78; Clara Jones (D), 1983–86; Stephanie Gonzales (D), 1990–98; and Rebecca Vigil-Giron (D), 1987–90 and 1999–present.

At the local level, the offices of County School Superintendent and County Clerk would be the ones most commonly set aside for women, but many were also elected County Treasurer and County Assessor. In 1926, women (including Nina Otero-Warren in Santa Fe and Aurora Lucero) held the offices of County School Superintendent. In 1928, women occupied ten county clerk positions and nine other county positions.[41] Thenceforth, Hispanic women were well represented in the traditional offices, particularly in the Hispanic counties.

The first Hispanic woman elected to the state legislature was María Cavanaugh, a Democrat from Lincoln County who served from 1929 to 1934. Others who served prior to 1960 were Fedelina Lucero Gallegos (1931–32), Porfiria Hidalgo Saiz (1931–32), Susie Chávez (1933–36), Soledad Chacón (1935–36), Concha Ortiz y Pino (1937–42), and Ernestine Evans (1941–42).

Reflective of these new women legislators was Concha Ortiz y Pino. Concha, the daughter of José Ortiz y Pino, was actually groomed for a political career to carry on the long political legacy of the Ortiz y Pino family, whose six generations of service in legislative bodies originated in the territorial period. She was twenty-three years old when she was elected to the House of Representatives in 1936, becoming the youngest legislator elected in New Mexico. She was reelected in 1938 and 1940, serving until 1942. In her last term of office she was the Democrat majority whip, the first woman in the United States to hold a legislative leadership position. As a representative, Ortiz y Pino was a supporter of the State Equalization Fund in Education, the merit system for state employees, and property tax reform.[42]

RETROSPECTIVE ANALYSIS: HISPANAS
AND THE PATH TO POLITICAL POWER

It has been suggested that even as middle-class Anglo and Hispanic women were finding their niche in New Mexico politics, "working-class women seldom had access to these political structures."[43] Though this is true, it should be remembered that the same was true for men. Historically, American politics has been the special domain of the upper classes of society, and part of the history of American political development has been the effort of the less privileged classes to enter the political power structure. Politics, in fact, has been an important agency for social mobility.

The history of American urban party politics, for example, is one where successive waves of minority groups rode the political escalator to personal power. It is therefore important to appreciate that the opening of channels to women, including Hispanic women, initially meant that middle- and upper-class women were the first beneficiaries. Later, women from the lower classes, inspired by the example of their predecessors, also entered the political arena. In northern New Mexico, for example, many women entered politics initially as political party workers, assisting in their husbands' campaigns as precinct workers, stuffing envelopes, escorting voters to the polls, conducting fundraising dinners, and performing other campaign-related chores. Eventually, as they established their credentials as loyal party workers, they would appeal to the local *patrón* or political boss for his endorsement in their own quests for political office.

Some working-class women began to enter the political arena as a result of their own or their husband's participation in labor union activities in the 1930s, 1940s, and 1950s. The film *Salt of the Earth*, which depicted the role of the Women's Auxiliary of Local 890 of the Mine, Mill and Smelter Worker's Union in the Empire Strike of 1950–1952, reflects the role of Hispanic women.[44]

By the 1970s, a new women's movement was sweeping the country. New, more militant organizations such as the National Organization for Women (NOW) were formed "to take action in bringing American women into full participation in the mainstream of American society *NOW*."[45] Women in New Mexico, among them many Hispanics, now formed their own organizations and joined the struggle to secure ratification of the new Equal Rights Amendment (ERA) proposed by Congress in 1972. In the same year, New Mexicans adopted a state equal rights amendment to the New Mexico constitution, and the state legislature became one of the first to ratify the national ERA (which ultimately failed when it did not secure approval from three-fourths of the state legislatures).

In 1973, Governor Bruce King established the New Mexico Commission on the Status of Women "to review women's situation statewide and act as an advocacy group before the legislature."[46] Notwithstanding the defeat of the ERA, the 1970s period of activism produced a new breed of Hispanic women politicians, tempered by the experience of their grandmothers and mothers, self-assured and confident as a result of unprecedented educational and employment opportunities, and driven by the assertive spirit spawned by the new feminism and activism.

Most often, the new Hispana politicians, such as Rebecca Vigil-Giron and Stephanie Gonzales, have sought traditional offices such as secretary of state. Vigil-Giron served two terms as secretary of state and later ran for the United States House but was defeated. In 1998, she was again elected secretary of state. Increasingly, however, others have broken new ground in pursuing nontraditional offices. The most noteworthy is Patricia Madrid, one of the first Hispanic women to graduate from the University of New Mexico law school, who went on to become a district judge (1983) in New Mexico. Madrid later ran for the U.S. House of Representatives (1988), New Mexico attorney general (1990), and lieutenant governor (1994), though she lost all three races. She was elected attorney general in 1998. The state's best-known Hispanic woman jurist is Petra Jiménez-Maez, another of the UNM law school's first Hispanic women graduates, who became district judge in 1981. In 1988, Jiménez-Maez ran for the state supreme court but was unsuccessful in her bid.[47] When she ran again ten years later, in 1998, Jiménez-Maez became the first Hispanic woman elected to the state supreme court.

Undoubtedly the most recognizable Hispanic woman politician in the state is Mayor Debbie Jaramillo of Santa Fe. The colorful, outspoken Jaramillo, known for her oversized square wide-rimmed glasses, began her political career when she led a fight against a development project in her west side Santa Fe neighborhood. Her activism led to her election to Santa Fe's city council where she served two terms. Then, when the incumbent mayor chose not to seek reelection in 1988, Jaramillo ran as an advocate for limited and controlled development and was elected.[48] She was defeated in a reelection bid in 1997.

A newcomer to the state political scene is Gloria Tristani, whose grandfather was the legendary New Mexico Senator Dennis Chávez. Tristani, in her first bid for state office, defeated a well-known and popular incumbent Democrat in the primary, then won a resounding victory against a male Republican opponent in the general election for the office of corporation commissioner.[49]

TRENDS IN THE POLITICAL DEVELOPMENT OF HISPANAS IN NEW MEXICO

The historical political evolution of Hispanic women in New Mexico having been traced, it is appropriate to draw a picture of the various events, circumstances, factors, forces, issues, causes, traditions, and movements that shaped

the political development of Hispanic women. What were the common de-
nominators and/or unique situations that shaped that development?

It is ironic that the initial stimulus to the political development of Hispanic women was derived from the decidedly nonpolitical role women played
as the center of the home and in village community life in rural New Mexico
during the territorial period. The role of women as mothers, caregivers, home-
builders, and food producers and preparers made them a vital part of family
and community life. That central role, combined with the legal rights and
equal status accorded women under Spanish and Mexican law, created women
who were strong, independent, and resourceful. These women operated on the
threshold of the male political world even if they could not enter it. Nevertheless, they wielded political power indirectly, through their influence on
their husbands and by using their economic or social position and contacts to
influence political leaders.

In the early years of the twentieth century, the increased activism of
American women in the suffrage movement also touched Hispanic women
such as Nina Otero-Warren and Aurora Lucero, who played a role in securing suffrage for women. These women used those experiences as springboards
for their own political careers. Having acquired the vote with the passage of
the Susan B. Anthony Amendment in 1920, Hispanic women were among the
first to pursue elective office. Some, as indicated, became active as an extension
of their suffrage activism. Others became active to fulfill a family tradition of
political involvement (albeit by men). Women such as Otero-Warren, Lucero,
Concha Ortiz y Pino, and Tristani were drawn to politics by the political lega-
cies left by father, grandfather, uncle, or other family members. In some cases,
the absence of male offspring propelled these women into politics; in others,
women were purposefully recruited by male political leaders as a way of bal-
ancing their ticket or for making a direct appeal for women's votes, as was
Soledad Chacón.

In more recent times, new circumstances have led Hispanic women into
the political arena. The activism of women in the 1970s in pursuit of the ERA
brought forth a new type of professional Hispanic woman who would challenge conventions by pursuing political offices not traditionally reserved for
women. Examples are Patricia Madrid and Petra Jiménez-Maez, as the first
Hispanic women district judges. Madrid also demonstrated this new attitude
in her quest for the offices of attorney general, congresswoman, and lieutenant
governor.

Other women pursued political careers as a natural extension of their careers in public life. Examples are Rebecca Vigil-Giron and Stephanie Gonza-

les. Vigil, like Ernestine Evans before her, also climbed the political ladder in pursuit of higher offices after serving in a lower office.

In recent times, Hispanic women have started their political base through activism and leadership on neighborhood issues. Debbie Jaramillo, for example, began her political ascension as a neighborhood leader opposed to development. This activism was parlayed into a seat in the city council and later into the position of mayor of Santa Fe.

In the 1994 New Mexico general election, a total of six women were major party candidates for the eight state elective offices available on the ballot. Five of the six women were Hispanas. Two of the Hispana Democrats included Gloria Tristani for corporation commissioner and Stephanie Gonzales for secretary of state. They were elected over their Republican opponents, also women. Patricia Madrid added to her list of firsts by being the first Hispanic woman to be nominated lieutenant governor, but she lost the race along with her running mate, Governor Bruce King.

The fact that five of the six women candidates were Hispanas is in itself a significant reflection of the progress Hispanas have made in New Mexico politics. Equally significant is the fact that two of those women (Madrid and Tristani) were pursuing offices never before held by Hispanic women. Also noteworthy is the fact that the campaigns in which these women were involved were devoid of issues that reflected on their gender. Nor did the media find it necessary to report on the significance of the number of Hispanas competing for such high-level state offices. Perhaps this best reflects the progress made in the political development of Hispanas in New Mexico.

NOTES

1. This phenomenon of women in politics is well documented in Nancy E. Mc-Glen and Karen O'Connor, *Women, Politics, and American Society* (Englewood Cliffs, N.J.: Prentice-Hall, 1995), Jane Mansbridge, *Why We Lost the ERA* (Chicago: University of Chicago Press, 1986), and Jo Freeman, *The Politics of Women's Liberation* (New York: Longman, 1975).

2. Joan Jensen and Darlis Miller, *New Mexico Women: Intercultural Perspectives* (Albuquerque: University of New Mexico Press, 1986).

3. Tey Diana Rebolledo, *Nuestras mujeres: Hispanas of New Mexico, Their Images and Their Lives, 1592–1992* (Albuquerque: El Norte Publications, 1992).

4. Michele Jacquez-Ortiz, "Hispanic Women in Politics: Doing More Than Treading Water," *La herencia del norte* 5 (Spring 1995): 30–31.

5. Melissa Howard, "The First Woman to Govern New Mexico," *Impact: Albuquerque Journal Magazine* (Nov. 2, 1982): 8–9.

6. Martha P. Cotera, *Diosa y hembra: The History and Heritage of Chicanas in the U.S.* (Austin, Tex.: Information Systems Development, 1976).

7. Rosalind Z. Rock "'Pido y suplico': Women and the Law in Spanish New Mexico, 1697–1763," *New Mexico Historical Review* 65, no. 2 (Apr. 1990): 159.

8. Richard E. Ahlborn, "The Will of a Woman in 1762," *New Mexico Historical Review* 65, no. 3 (July 1990): 338.

9. Sarah Jane Deutsch, "Culture, Class, and Gender: Chicanas and Chicanos in Colorado and New Mexico, 1900–1940" (Ph.D. diss., Yale University, 1985), 103–4.

10. Joan M. Jensen, "Pioneers in Politics," *El palacio* 92, no. 1 (Summer–Fall 1986): 14.

11. Ibid.

12. Joan M. Jensen, "'Disfranchisement Is a Disgrace': Women and Politics in New Mexico, 1900–1940," in Jensen and Miller, 302.

13. Ibid., 304–5.

14. Rosa Díaz, "Lola Chávez de Armijo, 1858–1929," in Rebolledo, 31.

15. See Maurilio E. Vigil et al., *New Mexico Government and Politics* (Lanham, Md.: University Press of America, 1990), 38–39.

16. Jensen, "'Disfranchisement,'" 301.

17. Ibid.

18. Ibid., 310.

19. Charlotte Whaley, *Nina Otero-Warren of Santa Fe* (Albuquerque: University of New Mexico Press, 1994), 83.

20. Ibid., 82.

21. Jensen, "'Disfranchisement,'" 314.

22. Ruth Loomis Skeen, "The Daughter of the Spanish Don," *Holland* (Aug. 1919).

23. Whaley, 92.

24. Paul A. Larrazolo, *Octaviano A. Larrazolo: A Moment in New Mexico History* (New York: Carlton Press, 1986), 109.

25. Whaley, 92–93.

26. Larrazolo, 139–140.

27. Ibid.

28. Ibid., 142–43.

29. Ibid.

30. Jensen, "'Disfranchisement,'" 316.

31. Whaley, 94.

32. Larrazolo, 143.

33. Jensen, "'Disfranchisement,'" 318.

34. Ibid., 320.

35. Whaley, 95.

36. Ibid., 98.

37. Howard, 8.

38. Ibid.

39. Ibid.

40. Ibid.

41. Jensen, "'Disfranchisement,'" 323.

42. "Concha Ortiz y Pino," in Rebolledo, 102–3.

43. Joan M. Jensen, "Pioneers in Politics," *El Palacio* 92, no. 1 (Summer–Fall 1986): 17.

44. Ibid.

45. Gary B. Nash et al., *The American People: Creating a Nation and a Society* (Philadelphia: Harper and Row, 1990), 1005.

46. Jensen, "Pioneers in Politics," 18.

47. Rebolledo, 104.

48. Jacquez-Ortiz, 31.

49. Ibid., 31.

Chapter Eight

MARÍA ROSA GARCÍA-ACEVEDO

The Forgotten Diaspora[†]

MEXICAN IMMIGRATION TO NEW MEXICO

INTRODUCTION

"Few of the [Mexican] wetbacks remain in New Mexico after the crops. The farmers keep them on the farms during the [cotton] picking season and then dump them. There is little reason for any of the wetbacks to stay on unless they can be given steady employment."[1] This assertion, made in the 1940s, became a common perception of Mexican immigrants to New Mexico. They were portrayed with disdain as undocumented sojourners who rarely settled permanently in the state. The relatively small economy of New Mexico (compared with that of other states) has led to the speculative conclusion that permanent labor from south of the border was not necessary.[2] Yet, through all phases of New Mexico economic development, Mexican workers have indeed played a critical role in certain of the state's economic activities, such as agriculture, mining, construction, and services.[3]

In addition, the high percentage of "native" Nuevomexicanos has veiled the contributions of the more recent waves of Mexican immigrants.[4] There has been a tradition in New Mexico that emphasizes its inhabitants' Spanish roots more than their Mexican influences. While there is some truth to this perspective in northern New Mexico, southern New Mexico is another matter. As Martín González de la Vara states in this volume, southern New Mexico has been linked to Mexico since 1848. Moreover, during the twentieth century, Mexican-born immigrants have immigrated to places all over New Mexico.

Finally, the effects of certain "simplistic myths" regarding the political participation of Mexican immigrants in general have been particularly pervasive.[5] Their status as "foreigners" and their alleged lack of insight into political efficacy have made them "invisible" in New Mexico's political arena and discouraged major scholarly interest in their contributions.

This chapter offers an initial step in the study and acknowledgment of the significance of Mexican diaspora to New Mexico. From the perspective of contextual historical analysis, the major purpose is to explore critical periods in the history of this immigration from the second half of the nineteenth century to the present.

It is the contention of this author that Mexican immigrants, attracted by the possibilities of employment and higher wages than those earned in their homeland, secured jobs available in cattle raising, agriculture, mining, construction, and the service industry in New Mexico. Many of these immigrants ended up settling permanently in the state. They have become part of the highest percentage statewide of Mexican-origin population in the United States.

The flow of people from Mexico has been controlled at the border. The boundary that separates the United States from Mexico has served as a "headgate," opening and closing to permit or limit the entrance of new immigrants. From 1848 to the 1920s, the border between the two countries was rather "soft." Mexican immigrants crossed, stayed in New Mexico, or returned to Mexico at will. Particularly in southern New Mexico, emigrants from Mexico—some of them blood relatives of previous settlers—crossed the border back and forth as if the political boundary were invisible. However, the flow of people was severely curtailed during the Great Depression. The current situation is puzzling. United States immigration policy is restrictive. There are initiatives by the Border Patrol to "seal" the border in the area close to San Diego–Tijuana and El Paso–Juárez. Yet, as an unintended consequence, thousands of Mexican immigrants are using the border between New Mexico and Mexico as a port of entry not only to New Mexico but also to other regions of the United States.

This study emphasizes how Mexican-born immigrants who settled in New Mexico organized and developed leadership roles, becoming proactive in the social and political arenas of the state. Furthermore, Mexican immigrants and native Nuevomexicanos have collaborated in community organizations. Their agenda has included the preservation of their common heritage and the promotion of civil and labor rights. Certain distinguished Mexican-born leaders, such as Octaviano Larrazolo, even managed to carve niches in the political history of the state.

This essay focuses on three critical stages of Mexican immigration to New Mexico: the early period (from 1848 to the end of the Mexican Revolution in 1920); a time of crisis (the years of the Great Depression and its aftermath); and the contemporary era (the 1990s). The lessons of the history of Mexican immigration to New Mexico suggest that the flow of population from Mexico to the "Land of Enchantment" has been constant, even when these immigrants encountered a less than welcoming border. Moreover, they have overcome their invisibility and made substantial contributions to the social and political landscape of the host country.

THE EARLY PERIOD: WHEN MEXICAN IMMIGRANTS BECAME ORGANIZERS

After the end of Mexican rule over New Mexico in 1848, emigration from Mexico to New Mexico was slow but constant. The possibilities of employment attracted pioneer groups of Mexican immigrants. The soft border between New Mexico and Mexico certainly helped foster this process. Many of these immigrants were in search of seasonal work, but as opportunities arose, they became permanent settlers.[6] As Mexican immigrants settled in New Mexico's society in the second half of the nineteenth century and the early twentieth century, many of them became involved in the social and political arenas of the state.

Cattle and sheep grazing, agriculture, and mining were the first magnets that brought Mexicans over the border.[7] These economic activities blossomed with the construction of large-scale irrigation and the railroad projects that began in the late nineteenth century. Labor-intensive agriculture, for example, created an abundance of employment opportunities for Mexican immigrants in New Mexico. In addition, by the turn of the century, the exploitation of coal, copper, iron, and silver mines also demanded cheap and readily available labor. Mexican-born workers fitted the bill perfectly, replacing central and southern Europeans as a major labor force.[8]

Besides searching for economic opportunities after 1910, Mexican immigrants came to New Mexico (as well as other areas of the United States) for political reasons. During this time, a social and political upheaval in Mexico broke out initially against the dictatorship of Porfirio Díaz. Later, the movement developed into a full-fledged civil war. As a consequence, intense domestic warfare wreaked havoc on an already fragile economy. Agricultural production fell drastically, as did other sectors of the Mexican economy, while unemployment and poverty skyrocketed. In addition, many Mexicans who had been on losing sides of the revolutionary factions left Mexico for fear of reprisals by the victors. This is evident in the case of the soldiers of the army of Francisco Villa. Many Villistas fled to American border states after defeats in 1914.[9]

Mexican immigrants to New Mexico in the early twentieth century faced precarious labor conditions. They usually resided in segregated headquarters. In the mines, for example, immigrants were "relegated to the hard and dangerous work of stripping and tunneling" and usually received the lowest payment—the "Mexican wages."[10] This practice was common throughout the state and lasted until the late 1950s. The wages for Mexican laborers also fluctuated according to the price of the metals they extracted. During shutdowns, unemployment in mining towns was rampant; Mexican workers were always the first to be fired. Even worse, the dominant society portrayed them negatively, and their contributions to the state's economy were rarely recognized.[11]

The need to secure a job in the United States, however, overwhelmed the harsh labor conditions, and the number of Mexican immigrants to New Mexico increased dramatically beginning at the turn of the century. According to the United States census of 1900, there were 6,649 individuals who identified themselves as foreign-born Mexicans.[12] In 1910, there were 11,918, and by 1920, the number of Mexican-born immigrants increased to 20,272 (see Table 8-1).

Mexicans settled in the southern New Mexican counties of Grant and Doña Ana; as job opportunities materialized, they moved to other areas of the state. At times, the immigrants from Mexico had to relocate to isolated mining areas (in 1920, 31 percent of all the miners in New Mexico were Mexican nationals). For example, they were recruited for the production of copper, coal, and other metals in Clifton, Dawson, Raton (Colfax County), and Gallup (McKinley County), and later in the San Juan Basin (Lincoln Country), Madrid (Santa Fe County), and Socorro (Socorro County). In Clifton, a group of Anglo entrepreneurs encouraged the immigration of miners from Sonora because of their expertise and knowledge of advanced techniques. In Dawson, the Mexican labor force contributed to the growth of the population of the town, which went from 100 in 1900 to 3,119 in 1910. In Gallup, the coal company attracted numerous Mexican workers in 1917. Because of their skills, they were hired permanently and settled in the suburb known as Chihuahuita.[13]

By the early 1920s, the population of Mexican-born immigrants had also increased to 2,000 in Albuquerque, the most populous city in the state. This figure was related to the fact that the city had also become a major port of entry (*centro de enganchadores*) for Mexican workers to New Mexico and other regions of the United States.[14]

The lax enforcement of the border at the dawn of the century permitted the flow of population from Mexico to New Mexico, and the distinction between documented and undocumented workers blurred. The United States

TABLE 8-1. *Mexican Immigration to New Mexico (1900–1990)*

	1900	1910	1920	1930	1940	1950	1960	1970	1980	1990
Total population of New Mexico	195,310	327,301	360,350	423,317	531,818	681,187	951,023	1,017,055	1,303,303	1,548,000
Mexican-born population in New Mexico	6,649	11,918	20,272	15,983	30,155	30,701	34,450	37,822	25,120	50,046
Percentage of Mexican-born population of New Mexico relative to total population of New Mexico	3.0%	3.6%	5.6%	3.7%	5.6%	4.5%	3.5%	3.7%	1.9%	3.2%

Sources: U.S. Department of Commerce, *Fourteenth Census of the United States: Population,* vol. 1, 1960; U.S. Department of Commerce, *1970 Census of Population Characteristics of the Population of New Mexico,* 1970; U.S. Department of Commerce, *1990 Census of Population: Social and Economic Characteristics, New Mexico,* 1990.

government implemented certain controls after 1917 that crystallized with the founding of the Border Patrol in 1924.[15] In reality, though, the border was not really enforced before 1929. Its porosity magnified the impact of the 1910 Mexican Revolution on New Mexico. Mexicans and Nuevomexicanos were engulfed in a dramatic incident at the vortex of the revolution. While the Southwest served as a refuge for Mexican political expatriates and its residents supplied arms to the various factions, New Mexico had the distinction of being the only American state to be invaded by a foreign army during the revolution's epic years.

The episode began when General Francisco Villa partially blamed the United States for his defeat at the battle of Celaya in central Mexico. He believed that Washington had deliberately sold him faulty ammunition while at the same time aiding the armies of his archenemy, Venustiano Carranza, by supplying ample arms and ammunition. A vengeful Villa planned an attack on American territory at Columbus, New Mexico, a small town that lay just two miles north of the United States–Mexico border.

Situated along the Southern Pacific Railroad line, Columbus housed 400 permanent residents along with elements of the Thirteenth United States Cavalry. General Villa believed that a raid on Columbus would embarrass Carranza's forces, so angering the United States that it would enter the fighting in Mexico. From Villa's perspective, American intervention would unite the country in support of his actions and turn the tide of battle in his favor.[16]

Villa's select army attacked Columbus on March 8, 1916, surprising civilians and soldiers alike. As the raid progressed, Villa's army occupied the town. The soldiers of the Thirteenth Cavalry responded quickly. The battle raged on until daylight, when the Mexicans retreated south. Ten civilians, eight U.S. cavalrymen, and ninety Villistas died. As news of the attack spread, angry American citizens expressed outrage, demanding action and intervention in Mexico.[17]

Responding quickly to such pressure, President Woodrow Wilson ordered General John J. Pershing to lead a force of 6,000 soldiers into Mexico with an order to capture or kill Villa. The force was known as the Punitive Expedition. Despite their large numbers, U.S. forces were never able to capture Villa. Instead, Pershing arrested several of General Villa's soldiers, who were later put on trial and sentenced to death. The fate of the prisoners would be part of the struggle for the civil rights of Mexicans in New Mexico, as discussed below.[18]

Even in the middle of the turmoil that characterized the arrival of Mexicans in New Mexico in the twentieth century, they managed to participate in the social and political life of the state through *sociedades mutualistas, comisiones honoríficas,* and labor unions. Their status as "foreigners" was not an obstacle to many Mexicans' becoming leaders. One such, Octaviano Larrazolo, deserves particular attention as the first high-ranking elected official in New Mexico who was born in Mexico after 1848.

In New Mexico, the Alianza Hispano Americana, founded at the turn of the century, was one of the numerous *sociedades mutualistas* (mutual aid societies) that sprang up all over the Southwest. The Alianza was a vehicle for meeting the economic, political, and social needs of both recent immigrants and native Nuevomexicanos. The literature on the subject has emphasized how the *sociedades mutualistas* (including the Alianza) exemplify Mexicans' reaction to a society that segregated them and diminished their contributions.[19]

The *comisiones honoríficas* have received less attention than *sociedades mutualistas,* even though they shared similar goals and agendas. These *comisiones* were established in various towns of New Mexico such as Albuquerque, Breece, Dawson, Gallup, Gibson, Grants, Madrid, Mentmore, and Raton. Both Mexican-born immigrants and native Nuevomexicanos participated in these community organizations. The *comisiones* were instrumental in providing assistance to recent immigrants from Mexico in civil rights matters, such as labor conditions, payment of salaries due, and legal counseling for the incarcerated. In addition, when a particularly acute problem related to the protection of the civil rights of Mexican nationals arose, the *comisiones honoríficas* studied it and then provided suggestions and took concrete action.[20]

In pursuing their objectives, the *comisiones honoríficas* worked in collaboration with the Mexican government through the consulate in New Mexico. In the early 1920s, the consulate was moved from Santa Fe to Albuquerque in order to better respond to the demands of the Mexican population and to strengthen its civil rights policies toward recent immigrants. The Mexican government considered the city of Albuquerque a prime location to better serve the needs of the increasing number of Mexican immigrants employed in the mines located in Colfax, Grant, and McKinley Counties.[21]

The *comisiones honoríficas,* as well as other community organizations (including the Alianza Hispano Americana), were interested in the enhancement of Mexican culture and the defense of the Spanish language. They frequently promoted cultural events such as the celebration of Mexican holidays, parades, and traditional Mexican civil festivities. The *comisiones* included the Círculo Cultural de Albuquerque, the Club Cultural Mexicano, the Comité Patriótico Mexicano, the Junta Patriótica Colonia Mexicana en Albuquerque, and the Sociedad Hidalgo y Morelos de Gallup.[22] Rafael Encino, the Mexican consul in Albuquerque, provided the impetus for these groups. He stated in the early 1920s that "the Mexican element [in New Mexico] has not been assimilated and maintains deep ethnic roots as well as the Spanish language."[23]

Mexican immigrants also participated in labor unions. Specifically, the second decade of the twentieth century brought to New Mexico a new crop of social leaders born in Mexico. Certain of them, such as Praxedis Guerrero and Jesús Pallares, left their mark on New Mexico's political landscape. They were more experienced as organizers than the local workers were because of their militancy in Mexico as well as in labor movements in the United States. Guerrero repeatedly attempted to unionize Mexican workers in the agricultural fields and mines. Eventually he was killed by American authorities on the border. Meanwhile, Pallares, along with other Mexican workers who resided in Chihuahuita, were active in the struggles of the miners, such as the Gamerco strike in 1922.[24]

The case of Octaviano A. Larrazolo is particularly significant. Born in Allende, Chihuahua, he crossed the U.S.-Mexico border at the age of eleven. At the peak of a meteoric career in politics, the charismatic statesman became governor of New Mexico in 1919. Aware of racism and a lack of economic opportunities for both native Nuevomexicanos and Mexican immigrants, Governor Larrazolo championed access to education for all Hispanos as a means of overcoming these social ills. He was a visionary in promoting bilingual education in elementary schools to guarantee the success of Spanish-speaking children. In addition, Larrazolo strongly advocated the preservation of the Spanish language. He argued that maintaining the language would help New Mexicans to contribute to a good relationship between the United States and Latin America.[25]

Larrazolo also defended the civil rights of Mexican immigrants, a struggle that had negative consequences for the governor. His enemies accused him constantly of "beating the drums of racial prejudice" and of "Mexicanizing" the state of New Mexico.[26] For example, he was highly criticized when he pardoned a group of Mexican soldiers from General Villa'a army, sentenced to death because of their participation in the Columbus raid. In this case, Larrazolo argued that his action symbolized the right to have a fair trial that all individuals in the United States had, regardless of their place of birth.[27]

Larrazolo was also a pioneer in consolidating links between the Nuevomexicano population and Mexico. He visualized certain common interests. For example, he stated: "I have attempted to defend my people [the Mexican-origin population of New Mexico] . . . they are my children, my brothers; they are Mexicans like me . . . they share the same aspirations that their great family of ancestors had; those who live on the other side of the Rio Grande."[28] As part of his outreach efforts toward Mexico, Governor Larrazolo collaborated closely with the Mexican consulate in New Mexico during the 1920s. Moreover, in December of 1920, he made a pioneering trip to Mexico City to attend the inauguration of President Alvaro Obregón. According to the chronicle of the consul, Carlos Palacios-Rojí, Larrazolo was well received in the capital, where he established permanent contacts with federal authorities.[29]

After Larrazolo left office, he maintained his interest in Mexican politics, such as the development of agrarian reform in Chihuahua and the negotiations between Mexico and the American oil companies over oil land. He also became a promoter of trade links with Mexico. Larrazolo maintained his ties with Mexico until his death in 1930, while he was serving as the first United States senator of Mexican ancestry.[30]

In summation, from 1848 to 1920, immigrants from Mexico were increasingly attracted to New Mexico. Their numbers grew in the early twentieth century for economic and political reasons. This flow of population took advantage of the porous border between the United States and Mexico. Once in New Mexico, the immigrants managed to participate in the social and political life of the state through labor unions and community organizations. The results of such efforts were mixed. Labor unions, especially those in isolated places, encountered major difficulties and achieved only minor success. Community organizations were more successful. In the end, however, the "foreignness" of Mexican-born immigrants (including distinguished ones, such as Larrazolo) was employed at times as a weapon against their plight.

A PERIOD OF CRISIS: THE GREAT DEPRESSION AND ITS AFTERMATH

The Great Depression profoundly affected the economy of New Mexico. Already a poor state (ranked forty-seventh out of forty-eight), New Mexico's personal income fell almost 54 percent during the years of the Great Depression and did not recuperate until the early 1940s. The decrease of jobs in agriculture, cattle raising, and mining was dramatic. Even some owners of medium-sized farms lost their land and became migrant workers.[31]

The crisis seriously curtailed the immigration of Mexicans to the United States, and the population of Mexican-born immigrants diminished dramatically. According to the United States census, in 1930 only 15,983 individuals declared that they were born in Mexico; the number in 1920 had been 20,272 (see Table 8-1). The lack of employment had a profound impact on the

number of Mexicans who traveled to New Mexico. In addition, border enforcement and repatriations to Mexico deterred emigration across the Rio
Grande. In the brief period from 1930 to 1932, more than 6,000 Mexican deportees returned to Mexico from New Mexico. Many were forced to leave,
while others returned "voluntarily" when they were unable to make a living in
the United States. United States authorities even deported American citizens
of Mexican descent who could not prove their citizenship.[32]

For the first time, the crossing of the U.S.-Mexico border was a chal-
lenging endeavor. The prerequisites for getting a United States visa tightened
up after 1929. Before entering the country, for example, Mexican applicants
had to present proof that they had a job offer. In addition, the 1929 immigration law made it unlawful for Mexicans to cross the border without proper
documentation; deportees were banned from readmission to the United
States. This legislation also established repatriation procedures. The times
when Mexicanos from both sides of the border did not recognize the political boundary between the United States and Mexico were gone.[33]

The enforcement of the border included a negative portrayal of Mexican immigrants. Conservative forces in the United States contributed actively
to a discourse that included constant references to "the uncontrollable wet-
back problem" in the United States. Mexican workers were used as public
scapegoats to diffuse frustration over the economic crisis. They were blamed
for the unemployment and poverty that prevailed in the states.[34]

Even in this difficult situation, the Mexican-origin population in the
early 1930s did not give up on its organizing efforts. Unions and community
organizations were still active in New Mexico. For example, the Liga Obrera
de Habla Española was established "to defend the rights of the workers in
mines and fields and to avoid discrimination."[35] The union's membership included both native Nuevomexicanos and Mexican-born immigrants. The Liga
organized a notable strike in 1934 against a coal company in Madrid. By 1935,
it had about 8,000 members.[36]

The Liga's membership declined with the deportation of many of its
Mexican-born leaders to Mexico and the destruction of Chihuahuita. In 1936,
Jesús Pallares (the president of the Liga), Julio Herrera, and other leaders were
sent back to Mexico, labeled undesirable "communist" aliens. This was a con-
venient way for American authorities to get rid of "foreigners" who participated in labor movements. The end of Chihuahuita, exemplified in the selling
of the land where it was founded, was a symbol of the hostility directed at
Mexican immigrants during the years of the Great Depression.[37]

While Mexicans' labor activism encountered serious obstacles, in other activities, certain Mexican community organizations were more successful. The *comisiones honoríficas*, for example, lessened the impact of repatriation of Mexicans during the years of the Great Depression. Members organized cultural events such as dances, *tertulias*, and theatrical and musical performances to raise money for the repatriated.[38] Their purpose was to help those repatriated Mexican workers who were stranded and unable to get either a job or the funds to return to Mexico. Particularly common was the celebration of the Mexican Independence Day (September 16) and of Mexico's defeat of the French army (Cinco de Mayo) in several New Mexico towns, such as Albuquerque, Gallup, Gamerco, and Gibson. The content of the festivities provides some evidence regarding the cultural background of the organizers and the audience. They included, for example, the singing of "Cielito Lindo," the dancing of "Jarabe Tapatío," the performance of plays in Spanish, and the recitation of patriotic poems.[39]

The *comisiones honoríficas* collaborated with the Mexican government through the consulate in Albuquerque. They worked together in critical repatriation cases in Allison, Dawson, Gallup, Grants, Hurley, La Ventana, Los Lunas, and Mentmore. In 1931, for example, distinguished members of the *colonia mexicana* (as the Mexican diaspora was known), along with the Mexican consul, Eduardo Soriano-Bravo, established a committee charged with channeling the resources for the relocation and other expenses of Mexicans workers in New Mexico and for the transit of deportees.[40] The consulate also served as a liaison to the Ministry of the Interior in Mexico in organizing the transportation of the deportees from Ciudad Juárez to their towns of origin in Mexico's interior.[41]

At times, Mexican immigrants in need organized themselves and asked for the help of the Mexican government. In the mining town of Dawson, a group of 118 Mexican miners wrote a letter to Mexico's president, Emilio Portes Gil, in 1929, complaining about the cruel treatment they received. They pointed out that they lived in an isolated area of New Mexico and, as mines had closed, could not get other work. These workers requested support to return to Mexico. Specifically, the workers said: "Mr. President, if we don't raise our concern to you . . . who else will care for your people?"[42]

Another dramatic episode took place in Gallup. A group of 100 Mexican families there also requested the Mexican government's help in returning to Mexico. They required about 1,200 pesos per family to pay for their transportation back to Mexico. Their problem was that the men of the family could work only one or two days a week, and they could not save enough money to afford the cost of the trip.[43]

In both cases, several bureaus of the Mexican government, including the Office of the President, the Ministry of Foreign Affairs, the General Consulate in El Paso, the consulate in Albuquerque, and the Ministry of the Interior (in charge of the transportation of the deportees from the border to the interior of Mexico) responded to the petitions. The consulates in Albuquerque and El Paso coordinated the support to the repatriated with the *comisiones honoríficas* of Dawson and Gallup. Such action was critical to successful repatriation.[44]

Immigration from Mexico was severely limited during the years of the Great Depression. For the first time, the doorway at the U.S.-Mexico border was almost closed while the number of jobs for Mexican immigrants already in the American labor market plummeted dramatically. This time of crisis, however, was also a time for actions of solidarity within the Mexican-origin community. The outcomes of their fortunes were mixed; many labor unions were severely weakened, while the community organizations managed to make substantive contributions.

THE CONTEMPORARY ERA: IMMIGRATION ON THE RISE

The number of Mexican-born immigrants to New Mexico increased from 50,043 in 1990 to 71,760 in 1998. Agriculture, construction, and the service industry are the greatest attractions for emigration from Mexico to New Mexico, while mining has declined. Some immigrants have even become entrepreneurs. The newcomers, especially those arriving as undocumented workers, have encountered a "hard" border. But these immigrants, once settled, have enhanced the social and political landscape of the *tierra del encanto*.

Agriculture in New Mexico, a labor-intensive activity, has continued to be highly dependent on Mexican workers, particularly in the southern part of the state (Deming, Hatch, Las Cruces, and Salem). For example, Mexican-born workers are critical in picking the state's famous multimillion-dollar chile crop. As an agribusiness employer said: "I cannot imagine what we would do without them [the Mexican immigrants]."[45]

In the state as a whole, the working conditions of Mexican agricultural laborers have not improved much. In 1994, the *Albuquerque Journal* interviewed a group of Mexican workers with more than twenty years of experience in picking chile in Hatch. The workers complained about the wages and harsh labor conditions to which they were subjected.[46] At times, the wages have been so low that the Mexican workers could not make a living for themselves and their families in the United States. Therefore, many of them, including legal residents, have to live in Mexico and commute every day to work. According to the Department of Labor of New Mexico, about 60 percent of the 14,000 Mexican workers who currently toil in the state's chile and onion fields reside in Ciudad Juárez.[47]

Construction is currently a key source of employment for immigrants from Mexico. Gary Lemons conducted one of the few studies on this subject, focusing on the roofing industry. He concluded that between 30 and 50 percent of the roofing labor force in Albuquerque is composed of Mexican-born undocumented immigrants. The most powerful factor in Mexicans' choosing to make New Mexico their home is the availability of jobs in the metropolitan areas of Albuquerque and Las Cruces. The specialization these workers have acquired in the roofing industry and the higher salaries in construction have contributed to their decision to stay in New Mexico.[48]

The presence of Mexican immigrants has been highly visible throughout New Mexico's service sector. They have been employed in restaurants, hotels, and other service enterprises, such as landscaping companies in the state's urban areas. Particularly important are those Mexicans who have become owners of service-oriented businesses. In the mid-1990s, the Small Business Development Center of New Mexico stated that immigrants from Mexico owned "up to 2% of all private business in Albuquerque," including restaurants, bakeries, clothing, music and auto stores, and shoe and boot repair shops.[49] As in other Latino communities in the United States, they are well represented at city swap meets—the places immigrants have traditionally used to recreate spaces that remind them of their homelands.[50] At first, these businesses were oriented to provide the immigrant community with goods or services they could not easily obtain otherwise. In Albuquerque, the South Valley, a traditional Nuevomexicano enclave, hosts most of these small- and medium-sized enterprises, which have contributed much to the revitalization of the neighborhood.[51]

More recently, certain Mexican-born entrepreneurs have expanded their horizons and ventured beyond the close social universe of the barrio into the mainstream market.[52] For example, Francisco and Pamela Roldán, the owners of a South Valley bakery called Panadería Azteca, stated recently that major retail stores in Albuquerque, such as Albertsons and Walgreens "have expressed interest in selling Mexican bakery products, such as *conchas*, a sweet egg bread pastry, fruit *empanaditas* and cookies" at some of their stores.[53]

Lured by employment and business opportunities, the number of Mexican-born immigrants to New Mexico has increased in the 1990s. According to the U.S. Bureau of the Census, in 1990, 50,046 New Mexicans indicated they had been born in Mexico. Eight years later (1998), the Current Population

Survey indicated a significant increase: 87,909 Mexican-born individuals residing in New Mexico. Of these, 23,016 had already applied for and obtained U.S. citizenship, while 48,744 are noncitizens; the remainder are minors. The figures for undocumented immigrants are sketchy. According to Immigration and Naturalization Services (INS), the estimated "illegal" immigrant population of New Mexico in late 1996 was 37,000, about 19,000 of whom were Mexicans.[54]

The profile of Mexican immigrants (documented and undocumented) has changed in the 1990s in terms of gender, place of birth in Mexico, socioeconomic background, and area of residence in New Mexico. In 1998, the number of Mexican men and women (older than sixteen) born in Mexico was 38,849 and 32,911, respectively. In addition, Mexican immigrants to New Mexico (both women and men) are no longer exclusively from Mexico's northern tier. Although many still come from the city of Chihuahua and the county of Cuauhtémoc in Chihuahua, an increasing number of people have immigrated from the city of Zacatecas and the county of Valparaiso in the state of Zacatecas. Others were born in central southern and western states of Mexico, such as Guanajuato, Jalisco, Michoacán, San Luis Potosí, Sinaloa, and the capital, Mexico City. INS reports about undocumented Mexican workers also confirm that immigrants are coming from different places in the interior of Mexico.[55]

The social and economic classes of Mexican immigrants are also changing. Border Patrol reports on deported undocumented Mexican workers state that there are more professionals and highly skilled workers trying to enter during the 1990s. An INS agent from Deming, New Mexico, Robert Velez, stated in 1996: "trained professionals [from Mexico] were seldom encountered [before], but now there are more and more."[56] Current immigrants from Mexico may be better educated than their predecessors.

As for place of residence, most current Mexican immigrants now settle in urban settings. According to the 1990 United States Census, 39,293 Mexican immigrants (out of a total of 50,046) lived in urbanized areas. The cities of Albuquerque, in Bernalillo County, and Las Cruces, in Doña Ana County, attract the majority of them (8,818 and 3,920 respectively). Both counties have the highest concentration of the Mexican-born population, as Table 8-2 indicates. Rural areas and towns of less than 10,000 inhabitants in New Mexico had a total Mexican-born population of 10,753.[57]

During the late 1980s and the 1990s, the permeability of the border helped shape the immigration flow to New Mexico. Changes in immigration law have imposed new conditions on Mexican immigrants. On the one hand,

TABLE 8-2. *Mexican-Born Residents of New Mexico, 1990 (by County of Residence)*

County	Number of Mexican immigrants
Bernalillo	11,254
Catron	12
Chaves	3,664
Cibola	209
Colfax	91
Curry	626
De Baca	76
Doña Ana	17,118
Eddy	1,542
Grant	811
Guadalupe	63
Harding	2
Hidalgo	287
Lea	3,449
Lincoln	362
Los Almos	49
Luna	2,178
McKinley	217
Mora	9
Otero	1,323
Quay	128
Rio Arriba	359
Roosevelt	669
Sandoval	599
San Juan	652
San Miguel	211
Santa Fe	1,725
Sierra	292
Socorro	247
Taos	117
Torrance	117
Union	110
Valencia	886

Sources: Bureau of the Census, *Current Population Survey*, Mar. 1998; Instituto Federal Electoral, *Informe final de la Comisión de Especialistas*, Nov. 1998.

the passage of the Immigration Reform and Control Act in 1986 opened new possibilities for undocumented Mexican residents to legalize their status. Its amnesty clause gave them the opportunity to remain in New Mexico. This legislation may explain the dramatic change in the number of Mexico's immigrants to New Mexico. There were 25,120 in 1980 and 50,046 ten years later (See Table 8-1).

On the other hand, the more restrictive 1996 immigration law has brought other consequences, especially for undocumented immigrants. In 1996, for example, the INS constructed a 1.3-mile-long fence in the border area of Sunland Park, New Mexico, and in 1997 it stationed about a hundred new agents in New Mexico. Moreover, the INS office in Deming began to coordinate with the highly sophisticated INS bureau in El Paso, Texas, in order to better seal the border.[58]

Using massive new enforcement resources, the INS has conducted frequent raids in the urban areas of Albuquerque and Santa Fe. Once, there were no more than two agents in charge of raids in work sites in these cities. The workplaces selected for the raids confirm the areas of the economy in which Mexican-born workers (legal or undocumented) can currently secure jobs: construction and services. From March to September of 1996, the number of Mexican deportees was 1,200. In just one week of August 1997, the INS announced that its agents arrested a record number of 300 "illegal immigrants" in Albuquerque and Santa Fe and sent them back to Mexico.[59]

The zeal to uncover undocumented workers took the INS agents in 1997 to a national security site, Sandia National Laboratories, located in Albuquerque. As a consequence of the raid, the INS imprisoned a team of twenty roofers. Sixteen of them happened to be undocumented workers from Mexico. The Goodrich Roofing Company had contracted these workers to repair the lab's roofs; the shortage of trained labor may explain the hiring.[60]

One may speculate that the draconian enforcement of the 1996 immigration law has caused the number of immigrants from Mexico to New Mexico, at least in terms of undocumented workers, to drop substantially. The data from the INS indicate that the number of deportees increased 147 percent during the fiscal year 1995–96. This figure, however, does not reflect the numbers of immigrants who managed to cross the border successfully, or those who reenter the United States after they were deported.[61]

Restrictive INS actions elsewhere have brought certain unintended consequences to New Mexico. Specifically, "Operation Gatekeeper," in San Diego, California, and "Operation Hold the Line," in El Paso, have pushed more undocumented immigrants into New Mexico. The area of Columbus and Deming in the southern part of the state has become an important port of entry for Mexicans. Certain newcomers are willing to pay more than $500 to smugglers for their transportation from Columbus to Albuquerque.[62]

The INS has joined efforts with those interested in portraying Mexican immigrants negatively. The immigrants, especially the "illegals," are considered undesirable people who can only bring problems to New Mexico. Thus, the 1990s has been characterized by a dual struggle between those whose priority is to restrict and deport immigrants (mainly Mexicans), and those, mainly Latinos and native Nuevomexicanos, who have employed different strategies to ensure the civil rights of Mexican immigrants. Among the New Mexican organizations currently committed to the defense of civil rights of Mexican immigrants (legal and undocumented) are the Albuquerque Border City Project and Latinos Unidos. These organizations have dealt with issues from the right to speak Spanish in the workplace to deportations.

At times, these civil rights actions have coincided with efforts promoted by the only Mexican consulate in New Mexico, located in Albuquerque. During the 1990s, the number of cases related to immigration issues and civil and labor rights has skyrocketed.[63] As a response, for example, the consulate co-sponsored, with Albuquerque Border City, Catholic Social Services of Albuquerque, Latinos Unidos, and other community organizations, a series of seminars in Albuquerque, Portales, and Santa Fe regarding the effects in New Mexico of the 1996 immigration law. Up to eight hundred people attended each of these meetings. Experts and members of the community participated in order to create awareness of the provisions of this legislation. In addition, officials of the consulate have been traveling periodically to other cities in New Mexico, such as Clovis, Farmington, Gallup, and Las Vegas, in order to provide assistance in legal and labor matters and other consular services to the Mexican nationals in New Mexico.[64]

The enhancement of Mexican culture, including the donation of books in Spanish to libraries, has been another priority of the consulate. Upon the request of the Mexican community, such library collections and series were allocated to those high schools and colleges in New Mexico at which the Mexican-origin population is particularly high. The consulate has also been committed to the organization of art and film exhibitions, performances of artistic groups, and other cultural activities.[65]

At times, certain spontaneous movements in favor of civil rights have flourished in New Mexico. For example, a group of tenants (including Mexican-born immigrants) on Coal Avenue in Albuquerque organized themselves with the help of advocacy groups to complain before the city government about their living conditions.[66] They met with an angry response from the landlord. In spite of such opposition, and with the help of these organizations, they managed to succeed. Moreover, a group of high school children and parents, all Mexican immigrants residing in Los Lunas, New Mexico, were the principals in a civil rights case. They organized walkouts and demonstrations against the low quality of education they received and the stereotypes of Mexicans that proliferated in their schools.[67]

The decade of the 1990s offers new trends in terms of Mexican immigration to New Mexico. So far, the enforcement of the border as a result of the 1996 federal legislation and other restrictive measures has not entirely deterred Mexicans from crossing. Those who have made it to New Mexico are part of a new crop of immigrants. Mainly employed in construction and services, these men and women from Mexico have brought to New Mexico the cultural traits of various regions of Mexico. They are more educated than previous immigrants, and their contributions to society have been greater. Their presence in the state's social and political arenas will increase and become more significant and long lasting.

CONCLUSIONS

"Here I have my people, my family. Here, I've worked, here I've made my sacrifices."[68] This statement from Refugio Estrada, a 67-year-old New Mexican legal resident from Mexico, vividly reflects the feelings of thousands of Mexican immigrants who live and work in New Mexico.

As in other areas of the United States, Mexican immigrants have come to New Mexico attracted by the possibility of securing employment. For most, immigrating was a matter of survival. During the 1910 revolution and immediately afterward, thousands of immigrants came to New Mexico, searching for refuge from political reprisal and in fear for their lives. The relatively small economy in New Mexico has not been an obstacle to thousands of Mexicans. Agriculture, mining, construction, and the service industry have been critical activities where Mexicans have contributed their labor. Their experience is an integral part of a comprehensive history of New Mexico, which is still to be written.

In a state where the Spanish roots of the native Nuevomexicanos have been stressed, the historical role of the Mexican immigrants has been deemphasized and all but forgotten. Ironically, at times they have been allies in labor and civil rights struggles. Moreover, in Albuquerque, Mexican immigrants have gathered in traditional Nuevomexicano barrios, such as the South Valley.

Meanwhile, in southern New Mexico, the interaction between native Nuevo-mexicanos and Mexican-born immigrants has been constant from 1848 to the present. In fact, *lo mexicano* (a sense of "Mexicanness") and a Mexican presence are quite noticeable in southern New Mexico.

Traditional avenues of political participation—such as voting—have been limited for Mexican immigrants. However, their status as "foreigners" has not precluded their participation in organizations such as *sociedades mutualistas, comisiones honoríficas,* and labor unions. On several occasions, groups of immigrants (for instance, the children of Los Lunas High School and their parents) have also expressed their concerns through ad hoc responses including demonstrations and walkouts. Furthermore, they have made transboundary alliances with the Mexican government, as in the case of miners during the Great Depression who wrote directly to the president of Mexico asking for his assistance.

Immigrants from Mexico have ventured to cross the border under a variety of conditions. The U.S.-Mexico border has been a headgate that regulates but does not ban the crossing between Mexico and New Mexico. In fact, it was not really enforced until the late 1920s. But the years of the Great Depression marked a profound change. The concept of the undocumented immigrant was created, and those labeled "illegals" have been portrayed negatively ever since. At present, the border is aggressively enforced. Yet so far the main areas of surveillance are beyond New Mexico. Thus, the state is becoming (as it was in the early 1920s) a port of entry for immigrants. Moreover, the enforcement of the border is also related to the permanency of undocumented workers, who stay in New Mexico to avoid the risks of crossing the border.

The immigrants in New Mexico have had different characteristics. In the early period, especially in the years of the Mexican Revolution, many social leaders and former soldiers of the revolutionary armies fled to the north. In the 1990s, when immigration from Mexico is once again flourishing, immigrants are very diverse in terms of place of birth, gender, education, and socioeconomic status. Moreover, immigrants who stay in New Mexico tend to come from all corners of Mexico, to include many women, and to be more educated and come from a more privileged socioeconomic background.

Currently, in New Mexico as elsewhere in the United States, Mexican labor has become institutionalized and is no longer invisible. Many sectors of the New Mexican economy are fully dependent on Mexican workers. As long as there is no real change in the availability of jobs and economic prospects in Mexico, Mexican immigration to New Mexico will continue and possibly increase.[69] And the long-term impact of such immigration is no longer just economic, but will increase the "Mexicanization" of the state in cultural, social, and linguistic dimensions.

Mexican immigrants are better equipped to participate in the domestic policy of their host state, New Mexico, and beyond. Alliances can certainly be built with native Nuevomexicanos and other segments of society sympathetic to their plight. These immigrants can also participate in the economic, political, and social changes taking place in their homeland. Many have already engaged in these transboundary actions. The Mexican diaspora in the United States will be able to construct and reconstruct its ties with the Mexican government through its consulates and other institutions. Its members, for example, could take advantage of the new legislation on dual nationality and dual citizenship recently passed in Mexico.[70]

NOTES

‡A brief description of the term *diaspora* is needed. The term is particularly appropriate when used to "describe a situation of a people who at one time were united in their own territory and then dispersed." It can be applied to those immigrants born in Mexico who settled in New Mexico after 1848. Robert Smith, "Reflections on Migration, the State, and the Construction, Durability, and Newness of Transnational Life" *Soziale Welt* 12 (1998). See also Gabriel Sheffer, ed., *Modern Diasporas in International Politics* (London: Croom and Helm Publishers, 1986).

1. "The New Mexico Pattern," *Common Ground* (Summer 1949): 2.

2. David R. Maciel and María Herrera-Sobek provide a review of different approaches on immigration. See "Introduction: Cultures across Borders," in *Cultures across Borders: Mexican Immigration and Popular Culture*, ed. David R. Maciel and María Herrera-Sobek (Tucson: University of Arizona Press, 1998), 3–36.

3. See, e.g., Robert Kern, ed., *Labor in New Mexico: Unions, Strikes and Social History since 1881* (Albuquerque: University of New Mexico Press, 1983).

4. When New Mexico became part of the United States, 90 percent of its population was of Mexican origin. Currently, in the 1990s, 38 percent of the population is Hispanic.

5. Juan Gómez-Quiñones and David R. Maciel, "'What Goes Around, Comes Around': Political Practice and Cultural Response in the Internationalization of Mexican Labor, 1890–1990," in *Culture across Borders: Mexican Immigration and Popular Culture*, ed. David R. Maciel and María Herrera-Sobek (Tucson: University of Arizona Press, 1998), 3.

6. Richard Griswold del Castillo and Arnoldo de León, *North to Aztlán* (New York: Twayne, 1996), 23–25.

7. See Carey McWilliams, *North from Mexico: The Spanish-Speaking People of the United States* (New York: Greenwood Press, 1968), and Juan Jose Peña, "New Mexico's Hispano Roots," unpublished manuscript, 1995, 29.

8. Carlos E. Cortés, *Mexican Labor in the United States* (New York: Arno, 1974), 477; Griswold and de León, 42, 61; Gerald D. Nash, "New Mexico since 1940: An Overview," in *Contemporary New Mexico, 1940–1990*, ed. Richard W. Etulain (Albuquerque: University of New Mexico Press), 4; and Harry R. Rubenstein, "Destruction of the National Miners' Union," in *Labor in New Mexico*, ed. Robert Kern (Albuquerque: University of New Mexico Press, 1983), 112.

9. Griswold and de León, 60.

10. Jack Cargill, "The Salt of the Earth Strike," in Kern, *Labor in New Mexico*, 194.

11. Ibid., 212–14.

12. Arthur F. Corwin, "Early Mexican Labor Migration: A Frontier," in Arthur F. Corwin, *Immigrants—and Immigrants: Perspectives on Mexican Labor Migration to the United States*, ed. Arthur F. Corwin (Westport, Conn.: Greenwood Press), 35; and Griswold and de León, 61.

13. Juan Gómez-Quiñones and David R. Maciel, *Al norte del Rio Bravo: pasado lejano, 1600–1930* (Mexico: Siglo XXI, 1991), 111; Robert Kern, "Century of Labor in New Mexico," in Kern, *Labor in New Mexico*, 11; and Rubinstein, 107.

14. See Secretaría de Relaciones Exteriores, Informe del Sr. Luis Sánchez, Inspector de Consulados, sobre el consulado en Santa Fe, N.M., al Sr. Cutberto Hidalgo, Secretario de Relaciones Exteriores, Mexico, D.F., Dec. 20, 1920; and Secretaría de Relaciones Exteriores, Acuerdo por orden del Sr. Secretario para que el consulado establecido en Santa Fe se traslade a Nuevo Mexico, Mexico, D.F., Mar. 2, 1921.

15. Griswold and de León, 60.

16. W. Dirk Raat, *Mexico and the United States: Ambivalent Vistas* (Athens: University of Georgia Press, 1992), 111–14.

17. Ibid.

18. Ibid.

19. Cynthia E. Orozco, "Beyond Machismo, *la familia*, and Ladies Auxiliaries: A Historiography of Mexican-Origin Women's Participation in Voluntary Associations and Politics in the United States, 1870–1990," in *Renato Rosaldo Lecture Series Monograph*, vol. 10 (Tucson: Mexican American Studies and Research Center, University of Arizona, 1994), 37–78.

20. Manuel Gamio, *Mexican Immigration to the United States* (New York: Arno, 1969), 132–33, 245.

21. Secretaría de Relaciones Exteriores, Dec. 20, 1920; Secretaría de Relaciones Exteriores, Mar. 2, 1921; and Secretaría de Relaciones Exteriores, Oficio del Subsecretario del Ramo al C. Rafael Múzquiz, Visitador de Consulados, relativo al consulado de Albuquerque, México, D.F., Nov. 17, 1922.

22. Gamio, 245.

23. Ibid.

24. Eugenio Martínez Nuñez, *La vida heroica de Praxedis G. Guerrero* (México: Biblioteca del Instituto Nacional de Estudios Históricos de la Revolución Mexicana, 1960), 39–54. See also Peña, 48, 58; and Rubenstein, 99, 115.

25. Juan Gómez-Quiñones, *Roots of Chicano Politics, 1600–1940*, 1st ed. (Albuquerque:

University of New Mexico Press, 1994), 329; and Paul F. Larrazolo, *Octaviano Larrazolo: A Moment in New Mexico History* (New York: Carlton, 1986), 102–7.

26. Larrazolo, 144; Peña, 33.

27. Ibid., 156–59.

28. Ibid., 160–61.

29. Consulado de Mexico, Oficio del Cónsul Palacios Rojí a la Secretaría de Relaciones Exteriores informando que el suscrito se hizo cargo nuevamente del consulado después de acompañar al Sr. Larrazolo en su viaje a esta capital, Albuquerque, N.M., July 16, 1920.

30. Larrazolo, 144–74.

31. Michael Welsh, "A Land of Extremes: The Economy of Modern New Mexico, 1940–1990," in *Contemporary New Mexico, 1940–1990*, ed. Richard W. Etulain (Albuquerque: University of New Mexico Press, 1994), 66–67; and Susan A. Roberts and Calvin A. Roberts, *New Mexico* (Albuquerque: University of New Mexico Press, 1988), 181–83.

32. Corwin, 116, 231; Gamio, 245–48.

33. Corwin, 145–48, and Peña, 48, 58.

34. Corwin, 145–48.

35. Peña, 58–60.

36. Rubenstein, 116.

37. Peña, 35–36; Rubenstein, 107–16.

38. Consulado de México, Organización de funciones de caridad para ayuda de los mexicanos, Albuquerque, N.M., Nov. 12, 1931.

39. Consulado de México, Memorandum del Cónsul de Mexico al Señor Secretario de Relaciones Exteriores, Albuquerque, N.M., May 14, 1931; Consulado de Mexico, Oficio del Cónsul de México al Secretario de Relaciones Exteriores sobre el programa de celebración de fiestas patrias en la ciudad de Albuquerque por la Colonia Mexicana, Albuquerque, N.M., Sept. 18, 1931; Consulado de Mexico, Programa de las fiestas patrias que celebró la Colonia Mexicana los dias 15 y 16 en Gibson, Gamero y Gallup, centros donde hay un buen número de obreros mexicanos, Albuquerque, N.M., Sept. 18, 1931; and Consulado de México, Nov. 12, 1931.

40. Consulado de México, May 14, 1931; Consulado de México, Oficio del Cónsul de Mexico, Sept. 18, 1931; Consulado de México, Programa de las fiestas patrias, Sept. 18, 1931; and Consulado de México, Nov. 12, 1931.

41. Secretaría de Relaciones Exteriores, Memorandum del Departamento Consular de la Secretaría de Relaciones Exteriores al C. Cónsul General de México en El Paso, May 12, 1932.

42. Carta de los trabajadores del campo de Dawson, N.M., al Sr. Presidente de la República Emilio Portes Gil, Dawson, N.M., Feb. 22, 1929.

43. Consulado de México, Oficio de Guillermo Robinson al C. Secretario de Relaciones Exteriores estableciendo Comision Honorífica en Dawson, N.M., El Paso, Tex., Jan. 12, 1931.

44. Ibid. Secretaría de Relaciones Exteriores, May 12, 1932.

45. Roberto González, "Migrants' Long, Hard Road," *Albuquerque Journal*, Nov. 20, 1994.

46. Ibid.

47. "Provoca sueldo que los braceros vivan en México," *Reforma* [Mexico City], Nov. 2, 1998.

48. Gary Lemons, *Roofing Careers in Albuquerque: An Analysis of Legal and Undocumented Labor*, Working Paper 109 (Albuquerque: Southwest Hispanic Research Institute, Fall 1984), 3, 6.

49. Patrick Armijo, "Dreams That Come True," *Albuquerque Journal* "Outlook," Dec. 2, 1996.

50. Richard C. Ainslie, "Cultural Mourning, Immigration and Engagement: Vignettes from the Mexican Experience," in *Crossing Borders*, ed. Marcelo M. Suárez-Orozco (Cambridge: Harvard University Press, 1998), 290–93.

51. Armijo, 8.

52. David G. Gutiérrez, "Ethnic Mexicans and the Transformation of American Social Space: Reflections on Recent History," in *Crossing Borders*, ed. Marcelo M. Suárez-Orozco (Cambridge: Harvard University Press, 1998), 311.

53. Armijo, 8.

54. U.S. Bureau of the Census, *1990 Census of Population: Social and Economic Characteristics of New Mexico* (Washington: Government Printing Office, 1991), 34; U.S. Department of Commerce, *Statistical Abstract of the United States* (Washington: U.S. Government and Printing Office, 1997), 13; U.S. Immigration and Naturalization Service, *Statistical Yearbook of the INS, 1995* (Washington: U.S. Government Printing Office, 1997), 184; and Bureau of the Census, *Current Population Survey*, Mar. 1998, cited in Rodolfo Corona and Rodolfo Tuirán, *Tamaño y características de la población mexicana en edad ciudadana residente en el país y en el extranjero*, anexo 1 (México: Instituto Federal Electoral, 1998), 6, 8.

55. U.S Immigration and Naturalization Service, 184, and Corona and Tuirán, 6. See also U.S. Department of Commerce, *1990 Census of Population: Social and Economic Characteristics of New Mexico* (Washington: Government Printing Office, 1993), 48; Roger Díaz de Cossío et al., *Los mexicanos en Estados Unidos* (México: Sistemas Técnicos de Edición, 1997), 310; and "Three Hundred Illegal Immigrants Sent Back to Mexico," *Albuquerque Tribune*, Aug. 19, 1997.

56. Rene Romo, "Immigrants Push at Deming," *Albuquerque Journal*, July 25, 1996.

57. Bureau of the Census, *1990 Census of Population*, 371; U.S. Dept. of Commerce, *1990 Census*, 48; Consulado de México, La Labor de Protección, la Imagen de México y el Programa para las Comunidades Mexicanas en el Extranjero, Albuquerque, N.M., Nov. 21, 1997, 1; "INS Finds Illegals at Sandia," *Albuquerque Journal*, Sept. 5, 1997; and Corona and Tuirán, 19.

58. Romo, "Immigrants Push at Deming"; and Rene Romo, "Illegal Immigration Has Many Faces," *Albuquerque Journal*, Aug. 12, 1997.

59. Consulado de México, La Labor de Protección, 1–4. "Three hundred," p. C-8.

60. "INS Finds Illegals"; Lemons, 3, 6.

61. Richard Parker, "Illegal Workers Flocking in New Mexico," *Albuquerque Journal,* Sept. 6, 1996.

62. Wayne Cornelius, "The Structural Embeddedness of Demand for Mexican Immigrant Labor: New Evidence from California," in *Crossing Borders,* ed. Marcelo M. Suárez-Orozco (Cambridge: Harvard University Press, 1998), 131; Romo, "New Americans Juggle Cultures," *Albuquerque Journal,* Aug. 4, 1996.

63. Consulado de México, La Labor de Protección, 1–2.

64. Ibid., 4–5.

65. Ibid., 4.

66. Christopher Machniak, "Tenants: Eviction Notices Issued after Complaints," *Albuquerque Journal,* June 17, 1977.

67. "Los Lunas Students Walk out," *Nuestro Aztlán* [Albuquerque] 1, no. 3 (Fall 1995): 3.

68. Refugio Estrada is a sixty-seven-year-old Mexican legal resident. He currently resides in Sunland Park in southern New Mexico. See Rene Romo, "New Americans Juggle Cultures," *Albuquerque Journal,* Aug. 4, 1996.

69. Coatsworth points out that the gap in wages between Mexico and the United States has been constant from the late nineteenth century to the present. Currently, it stands roughly "where it was 100 years ago." John H. Coatsworth, commentary, in *Crossing Borders,* ed. Marcelo M. Suárez-Orozco (Cambridge: Harvard University Press, 1998), 75–76.

70. A comprehensive study conducted by Mexico's Instituto Federal Electoral (Federal Electoral Institute) has calculated that 105 electoral booths in New Mexico would be needed in order to allow Mexicans to exercise their right to vote in Mexican presidential elections. Jorge Durand, "Distribución de los mexicanos mayores de edad (nacidos en México) en Estados Unidos a nivel nacional, estatal y por condado," in Instituto Federal Electoral, *Informe final de la Comisión de Especialistas,* anexo 3 (Nov. 1998), 7.

Chapter Nine

BENNY J. ANDRÉS JR.

La Plaza Vieja
(Old Town Alburquerque)

THE TRANSFORMATION OF A HISPANO VILLAGE,
1880S – 1950S

Tourism is the devil's bargain . . . Regions, communities, and locales welcome
tourism as an economic boon, only to find that it irrevocably changes them in
unanticipated and uncontrollable ways.

— HAL K. ROTHMAN, DEVIL'S BARGAINS

Strategically positioned at the crossroads of a trading network in northern
New Mexico, the villa of Alburquerque or La Plaza Vieja (Old Town) sat
in a broad valley on the east side of the Rio Grande, between the majestic
Sandia mountains to the east and sandhills to the west. Founded in 1706, Alburquerque changed little during the Spanish and Mexican eras. Even the
American conquest of New Mexico in 1846 had little impact on the villa. Thus
for 174 years, and under four flags (Spain, Mexico, the United States, and
the Confederate States of America), La Plaza Vieja managed to weather all
political storms. The beginning of radical change came in the wake of the
Atchison, Topeka, and Santa Fe Railroad's entry into the Middle Rio Grande
Valley in 1880. Crosscurrents buffeted La Plaza Vieja with the influx of Americans and European immigrants and the incorporation of Alburquerque into
American society via the railroad. Over the next six decades, Americanization,
the Great Depression, World War II, new economic and educational opportunities, and the commercialization of the Spanish and Indian past metamor-
phosed La Plaza Vieja into a tourist spot along Route 66.

Alburquerque's transformation had multiple causes and mixed outcomes. A useful way to understand these changes is through the lenses of ethnicity, economics, religion, politics, gender roles, and rituals. These themes
functioned as important arenas of social relationships. In addition to written
records and maps, the author interviewed six women and three men who grew
up in or often visited Old Town. All interviewees were Hispano except one
Italian American man, and all were born between 1903 and 1941.[1]

Prior to American conquest, Alburquerque served as an administrative center, trading post, and defense community along the Camino Real between Santa Fe, New Mexico, and Chihuahua, Mexico. According to Spanish town planning rules, Alburquerque was built around a rectangular plaza, with a Catholic church and homes and business surrounding the plaza to defend against Indian attack. *Acequias* (ditches) from the Rio Grande supplied water for the village. Ignoring authorities who implored villagers to live near the plaza for protection against Indian attack, most people lived in the outlying areas near their farms.[2]

In the Spanish and Mexican eras, Spaniards, Mexicans, Pueblos, Comanches, Navajos, and Apaches formed legal and extralegal sexual unions, creating an ethnically and culturally mixed population. A census taken in 1822 counted 2,302 people living in 416 homes widely dispersed along the river floodplain. Villagers in the nineteenth century forged a vibrant society of farmers, sheep and cattle ranchers, servants, craftsmen, manual laborers, textile makers, and merchants.[3] After the American conquest, the villa easily incorporated newcomers, and legal and extralegal sexual unions among Nuevomexicanos, Anglos, and Mexican and European immigrants continued to diversify the population and shape attitudes of ethnic and cultural inclusion.[4]

In 1880 a group of speculators representing railroad interests purchased land two miles southeast of Alburquerque, and the railroad built a depot in the new community. New Town, which grew as a separate community from La Plaza Vieja, was populated mostly by Anglos and European immigrants. The speculators christened their new town "Albuquerque" (dropping the first "r" from the original spelling) or "New Town" and referred to the villa as "Old Albuquerque" or "Old Town." Outsiders appropriated Alburquerque's name, anglicized it, and then symbolically relegated the village to the status of "old."[5] Thus, after 1880, Old and New Town were separated by space and ethnic and cultural heritage.

How was ethnic identity forged and manifested in Old Town's multiethnic environment? Evidence suggests that after 1880, La Plaza Vieja's majority identified themselves as either Spanish, Mexicano, or Hispano. Although "Hispano" was a term mostly used by writers and scholars until the late twentieth century, it is used in this essay because it has a geographical, cultural, and ethnic connotation indigenous to New Mexico.[6] "Mexicano" was discarded by most Spanish speakers during and after the Mexican Revolution because Anglos used the term to disparage Nuevomexicanos. As for the term "Spanish," its racial and cultural meanings originated in the Spanish era when descendants of conquistadors strengthened their cultural identity by claiming

"Spanish blood" as a racial privilege denoting a status distinct from that of Indians or mestizos. In order to retain their elevated position as Spanish—not tainted with Indian blood—they fabricated a fiction of pure Spanish biological lineage, which meant class as well as race.[7]

During the late Spanish colonial and Mexican eras, racial nomenclature tied the populace together by classifying individuals within a hierarchical social order. "Spanish" people presided over the masses, followed in descending order by Indians, mestizos, coyotes, mulattoes, and *genízaros*, an assortment of "inferior" people based predominantly on racial heritage, but heavily dependent upon wealth. Anglos mostly demolished this complex matrix of race and class identification when they supplanted the "Spanish" at the apex of New Mexico society and lumped all Nuevomexicanos into one group, rarely understanding the complicated social relationships among the people they now ruled.

In the decades after the Civil War, Anglos began categorizing "Spanish" people as an inferior race in order to gain superior status and greater rights and privileges. Anglos racialized Hispanos by superimposing stereotypical images upon them, categorizing them as filthy, superstitious, poor, lazy, immoral, stupid, mixed bloods, greasers, and Papists.[8] Hispanos during and after World War I countered that they were an ethnic, not a racial, cohort and thus equal to other European ethnic groups. Responding to racial degradation and in order to preserve their cultural identity, villagers took off the cloak of race and put on another one of ethnicity. Those who once thought of themselves in racial terms began proclaiming themselves Hispano or Spanish American, both ethnic designations. In other words, "Spanish" villagers joined mestizos, coyotes, and mulattoes (multicultural peoples who at one time could never claim the title "Spanish," for it was an exalted status) to form a new ethnic identity. Thus the complex racial categories of the Spanish colonial system collapsed into a more generalized Hispano ethnic identity. In constructing this ethnicity, Hispanos revealed the malleability of self-identity, for the term "Hispano" had both an ethnic and cultural definition, but not a racial connotation.[9]

Hispanos believed that they were a distinct people with a heritage separate from that of Tejanos, Californios, or Mexicans. Geographically isolated, holding land and livestock, constituting a stable population that included experienced merchants, able politicians, and an organized political base, Hispanos had many of the ingredients needed to maintain power in the face of American competition. The history of Hispanos in Old Town (and New Mexico in general) contrasts with what transpired in California, Arizona, and

Texas, where Americans took control, eliminated competition, and marginalized people of color. This makes New Mexico's history dramatically different from that of other parts of the Southwest, a fact mostly ignored by scholars, who have yet to develop a model to incorporate this chapter in the conquest narrative of the American West.[10]

To maintain their land and culture, La Plaza Vieja's Hispanos realized that they had to project political might and flex economic muscle. First, they fought successfully to keep their land (theoretically guaranteed by the Treaty of Guadalupe Hidalgo) and livestock. In New Mexico and elsewhere, Spanish speakers were often dispossessed of their property by illegal means. Many Nuevomexicanos lost land because of lack of titles, unscrupulous lawyers who used corrupt Hispano allies, and an inability to pay taxes. Many Hispanos, however, kept their property, enabling themselves to compete with Anglos for political and economic power.[11]

Second, knowledgeable from a long history of economic self-sufficiency and experience as merchants on the Camino Real and Santa Fe Trail, Hispanos used their experience to adjust to the demands of the market. La Plaza Vieja's economy boomed after 1846, when the U.S. army built a fort there. Times were rough after the military post closed in 1867, but merchants and ranchers like Salvador and Ambrosio Armijo made a comeback in the 1870s. *Ricos* had tremendous influence in the area, employing workers, helping the needy, and supporting schools.[12]

Third, Old Towners had a long history of political autonomy and experience with self-government. With a large population base that dwarfed the eastern immigrants, they used their numerical superiority for political advantage. By controlling the ballot, Nuevomexicanos ran politics in Old Town and Bernalillo County, using their numbers to elect ranchers, large farmers, and merchants like Salvador Armijo, Jesús Romero, Santiago Baca, and Manuel Springer to local, county, and state offices. *Ricos* insured that Alburquerque held the county courthouse, school, post office, and jail, providing the village with jobs and prestige. After the turn of the century, the Anglo influx began tilting the center of power away from La Plaza Vieja to Albuquerque. In 1891 New Albuquerque incorporated as a city, and Old Alburquerque continued to be governed by officials elected in countywide elections. New Town grew in size and influence, and in 1926 it wrested the courthouse away from the old villa, signaling a political power shift in Bernalillo County from Hispano to Anglo.[13]

Old Towners exploited the financial opportunities offered by the railroad and New Town. By 1900, La Plaza Vieja's 375 wage workers included nine professionals, twenty-three business owners, nine clerks, sixty-eight skilled and eleven semiskilled workers, three domestics, and 252 manual laborers. The next ten years saw an increase in economic mobility for people with skills or capital. The 581 wage earners included thirty professionals, ninety-seven business owners, thirty-eight clerks, sixty skilled and twenty-five semiskilled workers, two domestics, and 329 unskilled laborers.[14]

A 1902 Sanborn map of Old Town shows a rectangular community of about a hundred adobe and wooden residential and commercial buildings on eight short unpaved streets surrounding a dirt plaza. At the heart of the community, on the north side of the plaza, sat San Felipe de Neri Catholic Church. The church complex consisted of a church, a convent, a school, stables, and the rectory. Retail businesses and saloons were built next to each other. Around the plaza were a carpenter and cobbler shop, three boardinghouses, four saloons, a public school, two barbershops, a jewelry store, a post office, two grocery stores, a butcher shop, and a sausage factory. On the periphery of the village to the southwest were a dairy, the jail, and a hall for the Sociedad Nuevo Mexicana de la Mutua Protección (New Mexico Society for Mutual Protection), a local social welfare organization. The northeast corner had a large vegetable garden and packing shed. The courthouse stood on the southeast corner near two saloons.[15] Pastures, fields, and *acequias* ringed the village. By 1908 little had changed on the plaza except that a few businesses had closed and a drugstore, concrete company, and bowling alley were open for business. Five years later the population was estimated at 1,000 and a movie theater and "auto" business graced the plaza, but some boardinghouses had closed. A Sanborn map in 1919 noted a second auto business and estimated that 1,200 people lived in Old Town.[16]

In addition to the commercial opportunities offered by the railroad, New Mexico boosters in the late 1800s and early 1900s promoted Albuquerque as a medical haven for tuberculosis-infected "lungers." By one estimate, New Town in 1915 had 2,500 tuberculars out of a population of 11,020. With the coming of thousands of "pulmonary invalids," New Town's medical, construction, boardinghouse, hotel, railroad, real estate, home care, funeral home, and moving and storage industries prospered. Seeking additional ways to make money in the 1920s and 1930s, New Mexico boosters promoted tourism by pushing for a revival of Spanish and Indian weaving, handicrafts, and art. The railroad and the Fred Harvey Company fueled tourism by encouraging Indians to sell arts and crafts at the railroad station.[17] Adding to La Plaza Vieja's potential as a tourist center, Route 66 ran along Old Town's southern boundary.

As newcomers followed the railroad to Albuquerque, a contest over culture and social authority ensued between La Plaza Vieja residents and easterners. Among the newcomers were Protestant moral reformers determined to spread their gospel, which meant establishing schools, providing social services, and outlawing alcohol, prostitution, and gambling. Moralists waged a relentless campaign to shut down the red-light sectors in Old and New Town. After years of protest, most "houses of ill repute" were closed, and in November 1917, "progressives" successfully passed a prohibition amendment in New Mexico. These examples reveal Anglos' determination to impose their values on and wield cultural control over New Mexico's multicultural population. Old Towners, however, did not concede defeat. Mirroring what was occurring nationally, bootleggers, gamblers, and an alcohol industry flourished in the villa. Drinking and gambling were too valuable as cultural customs— ritually, recreationally, and financially—to be lost. As contentious as gambling and drinking were, education ranked alongside them as a major site of discord between Hispanos and eastern emigrants. Disagreements occurred over English or bilingual education and secular or religious schooling.[18]

Although battles raged over social issues, economic stability provided a basis upon which Old Town's cultural and social institutions flourished. Catholicism, for instance, dominated the cultural value and belief systems of the village, providing stability during a period of transition. Whether Hispanos (or other ethnic groups) were members of the Catholic church or not, their lives revolved around Catholicism's life-cycle rituals. This was illustrated through church attendance, baptisms, first communions, confirmations, marriages, holy days, celebrations, and funerals. Catholicism guided the lives of Old Town residents from birth to death.[19]

Even though Anglo as well as European and Mexican immigrants were embraced by Hispano society and culture, newcomers oftentimes maintained their values, beliefs, and language. With Spanish as the lingua franca, villagers from diverse ethnic groups met on the streets, transacted business, and attended festivals, dances, and Catholic ceremonies. Although Catholicism cast a wide shadow, Jews and Protestants resided in the village also. Tina Pérez, born and raised in La Plaza Vieja in the 1930s, recounted: "One of the interesting things about Old Town is that we always participated in San Felipe [de Neri church] even though our family was not Catholic. We went to the church functions, always." As a youngster, Tina said, "I used to come home with ashes on my forehead and I had been blessed." Non-Catholic children also learned Mexican dances and participated in Catholic festivities. Tina noted that festivals were "the highlight of the year." Everyone went to them. Aside from religious rituals, "they always had a carnival and it was just a really fun, fun time. Again, we were not Catholic, but we participated fully in the procession, in the dances, in the singing, and our school [Harwood Methodist], quite often, was part of the entertainment."[20]

People interviewed had no recollection of residential, educational, marital, or occupational segregation in Old Town in the early twentieth century. Interviewees articulated that assimilation and accommodation prevailed, even when cultural and religious differences surfaced. A tolerant atmosphere fostered an atmosphere of acculturation. Newcomers did not seek refuge in ethnic or religious enclaves, nor were they banished to separate neighborhoods. Even if allowance is made for some nostalgia, it is clear that all interviewees recalled La Plaza Vieja as a shared community.[21]

Entertainment, celebrations, and religious rituals reinforced identity and, like cultural ligaments, held the community together, regardless of religious or ethnic affiliations. San Felipe de Neri parish's annual fiestas on the plaza honored San Felipe, the church's patron saint. The fiestas contained booths, games, and dancing for locals and tourists, providing an opportunity for merriment and church fundraising. In addition, in the late 1800s, the Sociedad Nuevo Mexicana de la Mutua Protección held dances and community fundraisers, which supported church programs and brought in cash for community members suffering hard times, or paid for burial expenses for the poor.[22]

Entertainment during fiestas infused monies into the village and provided part-time jobs, but it also brought family and friends from the surrounding area. Religious celebrations honoring the patron saint drew people from small villages such as Barelas, the Atrisco, Corrales, Martíneztown, Los Duranes, neighboring pueblos, and residents from the mountains to the north and east. Catholics also came to La Plaza Vieja because San Felipe de Neri was the mother church in the Middle Rio Grande Valley, storing records for parishioners in the surrounding region. During fiestas, family members caught up with the latest news, romances bloomed, friends were made, and political ties were cemented. Fiestas also brought in tourists.[23]

Although celebrations, entertainment, and rituals offered possibilities for positive social relations, La Plaza Vieja was not paradise. Residents broke the law, feuded, gossiped, and at times ostracized individuals or families. As early as the 1880s, and especially during Prohibition, the gambling, liquor, and prostitution industries thrived. Cleto Durán recalled selling young rabbits to a madam of an Old Town brothel during Prohibition.[24] Bette Casteel moved to La Plaza Vieja in 1938 and noted in her memoirs that there were still "unsavory remnants of the Prohibition era scattered here and there" on the plaza.[25]

Evidence of feuds and social division emerged most clearly in the realm of politics. Political activism and debate in the village raised blood pressure like little else. Cleto Durán recounted seeing more fights over water distribution than any other issue. He contended that the most important elections were for *mayordomo de acequia* (supervisor of the irrigation canal). Most villagers farmed quarter-acre plots, and the mayordomo's job was to allot water fairly among the farmers. Therefore, electing a competent mayordomo was critical. Cleto emphasized "[t]hat water meant your survival."[26] If a farmer did not get enough water for his field, tempers flared and fights sometimes broke out.

Another topic interviewees vividly recalled was distinct gender roles. Residents lived within a social framework that idealized certain behaviors for men and women. Foremost in this social structure was the strongly held belief that women belonged in the home raising children, tending gardens, making clothing, and preparing food.[27] As Tina Pérez put it, "I was brought up [in the 1930s and 1940s] where they treated us [females] differently. My brothers could do just about anything they wanted to and I could not." She remembers being "very restricted." For example, "When I was a senior in high school I couldn't date and my brothers had already dated everybody in town that they could."[28] Reality, though, often refuted stereotypes. For instance, when interviewed in 1995, eighty-two-year-old Stella Martínez stated that she was a spinster. Stella's younger brother Abel (in his sixties) was a bachelor who lived with her. Catherine Espinosa, a single woman, had a "bachelor apartment" in Old Town in the early 1940s.[29] This gender-ordered world provided a guide for Old Town's residents. Ideally, men assumed positions as heads of household and worked for wages, and women labored to assist them in running the family. But this was the ideal, not always the reality.[30]

Knowing that power flowed from political office, Hispanos relished participating in campaigns and discussing issues. From the Civil War to the Great Depression, Republicans dominated New Mexico politics. Lucy Jaramillo, born in 1903 and nine years old when New Mexico became a state, declared that most Hispanos were Republican before the depression because they saw it as the party of Lincoln, which protected the downtrodden. She said, "my father was always telling us about slavery" and urged them to "[a]lways support the Republican party." Adding to the Republican allure, the Grand Old Party battled the solidly Democratic South and the hated Texans who had long coveted Nuevo Mexico.[31] The Great Depression dramatically altered the social, cultural, political, and economic structure of La Plaza Vieja.

With the economic and environmental disaster of the 1930s, the political pendulum in Old Town (and the rest of New Mexico) swung to support Democrats and President Franklin Roosevelt's New Deal. La Plaza Vieja remained a Democratic stronghold throughout the rest of the century.[32]

The economic calamity of the 1930s adversely impacted Old Town's economy. Prior to the Great Depression, generations of Hispanos had existed in a mixed economic system of part-time wages, barter, subsistence farming, and livestock ranching. According to the historian Joan Jensen, during the 1930s the high cost of seed devastated New Mexico's poultry and egg industry to the point where chickens and eggs had to be imported into the state. The economic downturn also curtailed seasonal labor opportunities. To make matters worse, the weather throughout the 1930s was scorching hot, drying up pastureland for livestock and crops. Other factors contributed to Old Town's suffering. The Middle Rio Grande Conservancy District Project, a reclamation effort in New Mexico, was directly responsible for thousands of Hispanos losing their land. It is estimated by one scholar that in 1937 alone, 8,000 people lost title to their property because they could not pay assessments and taxes to the Conservancy District. The loss was devastating to the subsistence economy and autonomous structure of Hispano communities.[33]

The depression dampened Alburquerque's truck farming and livestock industry, dried up railroad jobs, and hurt tourism. For many, subsistence living became a way of life. Times were tough but people survived. Tina Pérez recalls that during the depression her family was extremely poor but she did not realize it. She speculates that malnutrition may explain why she was constantly ill during her youth. Although her parents worked hard to feed and clothe their family, limited jobs made life difficult. Tina noted: "I loved my childhood. It was a happy, happy time. I didn't know we were poor because everybody was poor." Reflecting, Cleto Durán said, "[t]he Hispanic people were always very cooperative. They helped each other, always." Many Old Towners survived by planting small gardens and raising livestock on their land.[34]

Though there were few private-sector jobs, federally funded programs such as the Works Progress Administration (WPA) and the Civilian Conservation Corps (CCC) provided desperately needed employment. The federally supported labor force began an economic revolution in Alburquerque that carried on into World War II and the postwar era. Federal workers, including Old Town men, built more outhouses in Old Town (it did not have a sewage system), remodeled the plaza, built a library at the University of New Mexico, and worked on other projects. And the CCC, according to Cleto Durán, "forestalled migration to urban areas by infusing capital and cash into the stagnating economy."[35]

Even during hard times, some profited while others suffered. Cleto Durán remembers that during the 1930s Democratic leaders took advantage of the hardship by informing their constituents of government-supported meat giveaways, while punishing opponents by not telling them. He also recalls Democratic Party officials rewarding supporters with local and state jobs (such as teaching) and barring Republicans from those positions. Such actions sowed dissent in the community, but they also cemented La Plaza Vieja as a Democratic bastion. A combination of economic hardship, environmental disaster, and personal misfortune devastated many Hispano elites. Although it was now a Democratic precinct, few influential political figures from Old Town commanded respect in the region after the 1930s.[36]

The economic and political changes ushered in by the Great Depression challenged the village's social stability by eroding its economic self-sufficiency and reversing political allegiances. Old Towners, like other communities across the country, withstood the hard times by tightening their belts and accepting federal programs. World War II employment opportunities, paradoxically, also led to the fragmentation of Old Town's Hispano community. Joining mainstream American society shattered the community's structure, creating a more heterogeneous society, less coherent and stable, and economically dependent on the mass market.

Coming on the heels of the depression, World War II offered opportunities for many jobless men and women in Old Town. For many residents, an insatiable demand for paid labor ended subsistence living. With federal funds beckoning, those men not eligible for military service ventured to Colorado and California in search of industrial and military jobs in factories that sprang up almost overnight, often taking family members with them. Other Old Towners found steady and good paying jobs at Kirtland Air Force Base and the military laboratories in Albuquerque.[37] As funds from Washington, D.C., poured into Albuquerque, Hispanas joined the labor force, finding jobs cleaning houses, as clerks and typists, and in grocery and department stores. Reflecting the demand for workers, in May 1942 American Airlines advertised in Albuquerque looking for young Spanish-speaking women.[38] Because of the general lack of economic opportunities in a rural stock raising and agricultural community, Old Town Hispanas in increasing numbers worked in artisan shops around the plaza, restaurants, dry goods stores, bars, dry cleaning establishments, hotels, and grocery stores. The ideal role of women in the home existed, but economic necessity and a desire to work for pay prompted women to seek jobs outside the home, inaugurating a shift from home-based duties to a more complicated arrangement of household and wage labor.[39]

The war spurred other demographic changes. In droves, Old Town men heeded the call of a nation at arms. Peer pressure to join family and neighbors in the military and a desire to protect their country prompted them to enlist. Some joined the National Guard's 200th Field Artillery, already stationed in the Philippines. There they suffered on the Bataan Death March and endured three and a half years as prisoners of war. Half died, and many returned sick or injured.[40]

Recalling community solidarity, Tina Pérez said, "So many of our young men went [into the service] that it was a very frightening time." It was common for people "to gather to pray" for their safety. "We really listened for the news because we knew just about everyone that had gone. Many of them died and it was a very sorrowful time for us." During Easter we visited "all the different churches" and prayed. People "walked from one church to another" making promises to the Lord. Tina joined the Catholic marchers "because they were friends." Non-Catholics joined in and "were never discriminated against at all."[41]

The departure both to the military and outmigration for jobs had serious long-term consequences on the community's demographics. Many who left never returned. Some perished in the war, and others decided to live permanently in other states, often marrying non-Hispanos. Cleto Durán pointed out that "[m]any of our people that went to California to work in the defense plants never returned . . . to Albuquerque. They are returning now" after fifty years.[42]

In terms of social stability, this depopulation of the area had a devastating effect. For Hispanas, the permanent loss of potential marriage partners encouraged them to intermarry with non-Hispanos, many of whom they met in Albuquerque. Joining their husbands, clusters of these women moved out of Old Town into Albuquerque or to other states.[43] The absence of extended family members and friends had a detrimental impact on familial and cultural ties. In the short run, the families rallied around the flag and had a common goal: to win the war. In the long run, because Old Town was such a closely knit community, steady outmigration split families and neighbors.

After the war, newcomers, both Hispano and Anglos, moved to Old Town. With neighbors leaving and strangers moving in, the community's social structure continued changing. For instance, single and married women continued to find employment in local service industries. Before her husband died, Elizaria Castillo had never worked for pay. Her life changed after his premature death, and she began working full time. While some women worked full time, others, like Paula Padilla, worked part time to supplement the family's earnings. María Ortiz, according to her daughter, "was really a homebody." But periodically in the 1940s and 1950s, when her family needed money, María "went to work to help her children out."[44]

Although some Hispanas worked for wages, others mirrored the stereotype of married women, staying home while their husbands worked. It was also common for fathers, husbands, and brothers to demand that females in the family adhere to strict gender roles. Dionicia Jójola, for instance, followed the prescribed roles for women. In 1936 Dionicia married Gabino. For the first three decades of their marriage, before Gabino became blind in 1965, he forbade Dionicia to obtain employment, have friends, or even leave the house without his consent. Gabino expected Dionicia to expend her energy running the household. The author and Carmen Chávez interviewed Dionicia at the Barelas Community Center in Albuquerque in 1995. Carmen asked Dionicia a series of questions pertaining to her social life before her husband went blind:

> CARMEN CHÁVEZ ¿Quién eran sus amigas, y qué hacía durante el día? ¿Hacía alguna cosa, había sociedades, o . . . ?
>
> DIONICIA JÓJOLA Ni una, con mi marido, era muy estricto él, yo no salía.
>
> CARMEN CHÁVEZ En Old Town, la Plaza Vieja, ¿no tenía, no tenía amigas?
>
> DIONICIA JÓJOLA Pues, vecinas nomás una. A él no le gustaba, pero [yo] no tenía derecho de hablar con nadien. Carmen Chávez (to author): Oh, did you get that? He was very strict and she was not allowed to (have friends). She didn't have the right to talk to anybody else.
>
> AUTHOR (TO DIONICIA) So women couldn't come to your house to visit you?
>
> DIONICIA JÓJOLA Um hum.
>
> CARMEN CHÁVEZ (TO DIONICIA) And you couldn't go to their houses?
>
> AUTHOR Where did you, did you . . .
>
> DIONICIA JÓJOLA I sew, I make some wool quilts. Everything in the house has to be in the house, and [I would also] chop wood. Yo cuidaba lo de afuera y de adentro porque él pues trabajaba y todo los sábados iba a partir la leña. Iban a hacer eso, a partir leña. Y yo era la que tenía que hacer todo—meter el agua, partir leña.

Thinking back, Dionicia did not resent her limited social opportunities. On the contrary, she complied with her husband's rigid expectations. Although she recalls that her husband was "strict," she accepted his prerogative as a male to demand that his wife limit her social relationships. In her cultural outlook, Gabino's demands were within the boundaries of Hispano society and culture. Gabino, on the other hand, could and did come and go as he wished. Forced to support herself and Gabino when he became blind, Dionicia made handicrafts at home and sold them at the Greyhound bus station, in front of stores, and at the train station.[45] Unlike Hispanas, Hispanos had broader latitude in job choices. They could take jobs in Albuquerque, travel out of state for employment, or join the service. Many of these options were closed to Hispanas, especially after the war, when women lost industrial and military-related jobs to returning veterans.[46]

In the years immediately after 1945, while La Plaza Vieja's population fluctuated, Albuquerque's population exploded. The numbers illustrate the city's growth. In 1940 Albuquerque's population numbered 35,449. Ten years later it had grown to 96,815, almost tripling its size. Though this was partly due to inmigration, much of the population growth stemmed from annexed communities bordering the city. In 1940, Bernalillo County totaled 69,391 persons. In ten years the county's population had expanded to 145,673 and to 262,199 by 1960.[47] Thousands of people were drawn to the city because of job opportunities in defense-related careers and the tourism and service industries. Streets expanded in all directions and new suburbs sprouted like weeds.

As the expanding city of Albuquerque began surrounding the villa of Alburquerque, Old Towners moved to different neighborhoods of the state's largest city.[48] In 1930, La Plaza Vieja's population numbered 1,626, and it increased right before World War II to 2,593, or 1,284 men and 1,309 women. The census lumped Hispanos and Anglos together under "white." Only twenty-eight foreign-born males and twenty-three foreign-born female resided in the village. Ten African Americans and eight people listed as "other races" also lived there (Indians or Asians). By 1950, Old Town's population had reached 4,235.[49] Census statistics show Old Town growing in size from 1940 to 1950, but in their recollections, people noted the depopulation of the area around the plaza. Luigi Petrucci, whose family owned a grocery store, a bar, and later an arts and crafts business in La Plaza Vieja, commented that locals started moving out "little by little" during and after the war, while others, hoping to make a profit, converted part of their homes into businesses.[50]

After the war, Old Town's agricultural and livestock economy ended as land was sold to build houses and *acequias* were filled in. Mobile and part-time

workers had little choice but to enter full-time into the capitalist wage economy. In La Plaza Vieja, a full-blown national and international market system
replaced a barter and part-time wage agricultural and livestock economy.
What transpired in Old Town took place in many villages across the West
during and after the war, as federal capital and jobs altered or replaced local
economic structures.[51]

As the Cold War economy accelerated, tourism gained prominence
in the West. Visitors flocked to New Mexico as state boosters promoted
Route 66 and the "Land of Enchantment." Contributing to the tourist industry, a growing resident middle class spurred the commercialization of Hispanic and Indian art in Old Town and across New Mexico. Non-Hispano
shop owners, university professors, painters, and arts and crafts makers began
settling in the plaza area in the late 1930s, a trend that continued after World
War II.[52] Albuquerque and Old Town boosters and merchants promoted La
Plaza Vieja's Spanish and Indian past. Navajo and Pueblo artisans and rug
makers began selling their wares personally or to traders on the plaza. Com-
mercializing the Spanish and Indian past started during the Great Depression,
when federal programs spurred the making and selling of Indian arts and
crafts as a means to employ Indians. Getting the arts and crafts industry off
the ground in La Plaza Vieja took time and money. As late as 1949 local merchants helped buy the first neon sign on Central Avenue (bordering Old
Town), pointing out the plaza with an arrow. Shopkeepers also installed Mexican benches and lampposts on the recently remodeled plaza.[53]

When newcomers to Albuquerque realized the potential profits in
Spanish and Indian arts and crafts, they purchased homes in the plaza area,
buying out locals, and converted the homes into shops. Thus the commercialization of La Plaza Vieja began with the coming of non-Hispano business
owners, many of whom had no attachment to Old Town's past. Newcomers
had little understanding of the social and cultural world that had existed only
a decade before. Few assimilated into Hispano culture or intermarried. Cleto
Durán recalled that "Old Town became a tourist attraction."[54] Luigi Petrucci
remembers that "[l]ots of the people who lived in the Old Town area did not
like seeing all of this converting into business. They liked their little area the
way it was, but it divided the people. Even the church at one time . . . was
divided among the people for and against converting Old Town into a business area."[55]

Even as the village's demographics changed during and after World
War II, men and women continued to be politically involved. After 1920, when
women attained suffrage, Hispana votes were welcomed because they rein-

forced Hispano power in Bernalillo County. People interviewed for this study always recalled women voting, campaigning for candidates, working at polling booths, and openly discussing politics. In a reflection of the strength women had in Alburquerque politics, a Missouri transplant, Mary Selby Moya, an Anglo who married Luis Moya, became the village's first Democratic precinct chairperson.[56] Other women assisted the Democratic Party as well. Elizaria Castillo, now in her eighties and a widow with six children, began assisting Democrats in Old Town in mid-century. She said that she was "very involved in *la política*." She served coffee and refreshments at political functions, canvassed for politicians, and manned phones to encourage people to vote. In the 1990s, her son Anthony worked on Albuquerque mayor Martin Chávez's staff, and her daughter Flora worked for the city of Albuquerque. Following a family tradition, Paul Gonzales, Elizaria Castillo's nephew, recalls that his mother and father often discussed politics and voted. Similarly, Tina Pérez remembered that when she was a child in the 1950s her mother and father often debated political issues at home and sometimes even voted differently.[57]

As Old Towners struggled to cope with social, economic, and cultural changes caused by World War II, darker clouds of change appeared in the late 1940s. At this critical juncture in the community's history, people with diverse motives united in a campaign to annex Old Town into the city of Albuquerque. Pitted against them were a majority of villagers led by owners of non-tourist-related businesses and local leaders represented by Arthur Hannett, a former New Mexico governor, and his nephew as chief legal counsel. In the ensuing struggle, La Plaza Vieja and Albuquerque engaged in a political contest over the future of the community's status as an autonomous entity. The battle split the village, ripping further its tattered social fabric.

Five loosely allied pro-annexation camps, their individual members sometimes affiliated with several groups, united in a quest to bring the historic community into the city. The first group, Albuquerque boosters, provided the movement's impetus and energy. Concerned about competition from urban centers in neighboring states, city promoters searched for yardsticks to measure the city's economic strength and potential. Eyeing the upcoming 1950 census, boosters believed they would see dollar signs if only they could increase the city's population figures. Pro-growth proponents used the Albuquerque Chamber of Commerce and the *Albuquerque Journal* as their mouthpieces. Editors wrote jeremiads portending doom for the city if adjoining entities were not brought in. In June 1948 an editorial in the *Albuquerque Journal* stated, "The next official government census is not far off." Much of the city's future "depends on" the census numbers. Therefore, an "annexation program must be completed soon to have the proper effect on the city's future economy, welfare and prosperity."[58]

A second cohort—Old Town merchants—desired the greater publicity and infrastructure that would result if they were part of the city. As tourism and the arts and crafts industry gained prominence in the community's economy, traders from diverse ethnic backgrounds profited in Old Town, especially shopkeepers on the plaza. Business owners recognized tourists' infatuation with Spanish and Indian art, and they capitalized on Old Town's reputation as a trading center.[59] Employing locals both part time and full time, business owners gained support from some residents whose livelihood depended on tourist dollars. Merchants crossed ethnic and religious boundaries and united along class interests over ethnic or community associations.

A small number of Old Town residents who wanted water and sewer services made up the third base of support for annexation. James Bennett, for instance, who represented some village residents, argued that annexation was "a matter of life and death. We are running the danger of an epidemic any day" in a "highly congested area with its primitive sanitary facilities."[60] Bennett's position was shared by some Hispanos as well. Even the thought of outhouses evoked strong memories for Tina Pérez. She admitted that her home had "an outhouse in the back," and it was "awful."[61]

Next in line demanding annexation were three of the five City of Albuquerque commissioners, none of whom were Hispano. These commissioners wanted to bring Old Town and other suburbs into the city because they desperately needed sewer and water bonds, which were contingent on a larger tax base and therefore were being delayed by bankers. Under heavy pressure from residents because the quickly expanding city was not being serviced with sewer, water, and paved streets, City Commissioner Owen Marron made the motion to annex La Plaza Vieja. He revealed the city's desperation when asked what he thought if 80 percent of Old Towners opposed annexation. He replied, "It would be no evidence, to me at least, that there is rational basis for opposition. Rather it might mean that 80 per cent were misled by some who thought the proposal was harmful to them."[62]

Joining the fray, "progressives" or cultural supremacists formed the final pro-annexation front. Ridiculing Hispano culture, they aimed to anglicize La Plaza Vieja so that it more closely resembled the rest of the nation. Represented in the *Albuquerque Journal*'s editorial page, they desired to consolidate political entities as a means of control. The city "and its environs need to be welded into one unit where better sanitary, garbage, fire, water, street and police protection can be provided."[63] One editorial stated that annexing the suburbs and consolidating "municipal service is in line with what other progressive cities are doing."[64]

Cultural supremacists sought to control debate, stifle dissent, and grip the levers of legal and political power. Another *Albuquerque Journal* editorial acknowledged that county residents had succeeded in staying out of the city when it said that city leaders "must remove the soft gloves of persuasion and proceed with firmness and determination" in their annexation program. "If these outside areas persist in ignoring the value both to their own population and that of Albuquerque in coming into the city limits, then the solemn, even if painful, duty rests upon the Albuquerque City Commission to use whatever means is available to force annexation."[65] The *Albuquerque Journal* editor argued that the old village posed a health and safety threat to Albuquerque, and therefore the city needed to step in and alleviate the danger by bringing in the village. "Always there is the danger that polio and other epidemics will originate from improper sanitary methods. If the outside areas will not recognize this menace, then the city of Albuquerque must recognize it and act accordingly." Acting "accordingly" was a patronizing way of telling others that they dwelled in filth and needed be instructed in how to live properly.[66]

To city leaders, "progress" meant ending health and safety threats. "And efforts at extension of city limits now encounter opposition which can only be broken down by education in civic pride and progress."[67] By progress, they implied that Hispanos were culturally backward. Language was one of the most successful tools of cultural imperialism. Terms like "progress," "modern," and "forward" legitimized actions ranging from educational, economic, political, and marital segregation to neighborhood restoration. "Progress" ideology contended that peoples, societies, and cultures went through stages that could be judged inferior or superior, and that Old Town was clearly inferior to New Town.

Bette Casteel published an autobiography in 1996 reflecting on her years in Old Town in the late 1930s and 1940s. In several passages she perfectly articulates "progressive" ideology. For example, she writes, "After the trains divided Albuquerque, Old Town slumbered for years while adobes crumbled into dust and mud." Some urbanites "saw Old Town as rundown and useless, but others [like herself] were visionaries who saw something more, and set out to prove the area's worth." Casteel contends that Old Town had no intrinsic value before she and like-minded "progressives" moved there. She remarks that since 1938 "I have watched every stage of Old Town's development" in its "growth from a sleepy little village to an interesting center for tourists and locals."[68] Irene Fisher, Casteel's ideological partner in "progress," concurred. In a booster pamphlet published in 1962, Fisher proudly recounted that in the early 1930s "artists and writers and other hardy persons with vision" started "the development of Old Town" into an arts and crafts tourist center.[69]

Contentions of superiority merged neatly with the discourse of urban "progressives" who subscribed to the stale stereotype of the dirty Mexican or backward Hispano. "Progressives" symbolically linked Hispanos with filth and sewage. Metaphors and coded phrases such as "primitive," "filthy," "dirty," and "sleepy" made up the language of paternalistic ethnocentrism. Because of these stereotypes and prejudices, Hispanos often faced discrimination. "Progressives" joined hands and marched in step with business interests, city commissioners, and the city services crowd to annex the village.

Opposing the annexation forces, a majority of locals, while conceding that sanitation was an issue, argued that other factors were even more important. They foresaw a loss of political autonomy and destruction of their cultural way of life if the village were taken into the city. Mostly Hispanos, anti-annexationists cut across gender, economic, and ethnic lines. Voicing their opinions, they signed petitions and spoke out at city commission meetings and at other forums dealing with the issue. J. W. Hedges, Pablo Chávez, and Joe and Frank Del Frate led a group of over 300 Old Town property owners who felt "aggrieved" by the city's plan. They filed suit in district court stating "that residents in the area are not and will not be enabled to obtain the benefits of city government, police and fire protection or city water."[70]

At the proceedings over the dispute, Hedges savaged city officials. "The people loved the name and the city took it away and now wants to settle a mortgage on Old Town and then throw a lot of flowers around the funeral."[71] By "flowers," Hedges meant the services the city would provide. The anti-annexation forces' lawyer, Arthur Hannett, claimed that "[a]ll this talk about epidemics and unsanitary conditions existing in Old Town was, to put it in common parlance, pure baloney."[72] Recognizing duplicity when they saw it, residents and groups within and outside of the city rallied to oppose the commission.[73]

The debate over public services and public health was essentially a façade. What was labeled "filth" or deemed "clean" was often shaped by cultural standards, economic constraints, environmental surroundings, and class status. The struggle really boiled down to who would control La Plaza Vieja, for human waste and trash were not strangers in Old Town. Villagers had dealt with this for over 250 years. It is unclear whether Bernalillo County could ever have provided water and sewer services to La Plaza Vieja. All references to the county's financial status bemoaned its lack of funds. What is odd, however, is that county commissioners were conspicuously absent from the annexation debate.

Cleanliness was not an issue solely for the mid-twentieth century. When La Plaza Vieja was incorporated as a town in 1863, officials passed twenty-five ordinances, some of which dealt with health concerns such as human waste, trash, and clean water.[74] A century later, unrobing pro-annexationists' mendacity, a report to New Mexico governor Thomas Mabry in March 1948 listed fifty-four of sixty-two communities in eighteen counties that had a potentially unsafe water supply. Old Town was not on the list.[75] Even the city manager, Charles Wells, conceded that to his recollection an epidemic had never started in Old Town.[76] The issue of "progressive" health concerns dripped with irony. By their own logic, if the threat of epidemics were a valid issue, "progressives" would not have promoted Albuquerque as a medical haven for "lungers" and other disease-ridden easterners. If "progressives" were really sincere about the spread of vile ailments, they would have targeted the coughing and spitting easterners who were moving to Albuquerque.[77]

As the two sides argued, in 1948 Old Town's pro-annexation supporters circulated a petition to annex the village. The petition was the second attempt at annexation, for the city commission's first bid was tied up in court. Immediately complicating the situation, Pastor Libertini of San Felipe de Neri Catholic Church on the plaza signed the petition. Libertini's action caused an uproar among his congregation and dashed any opportunity for the church to take the moral high ground on an issue that fragmented the community.[78] Accepting the petition without verifying the validity of the signatures, the city commission began annexation proceedings.

Claiming that some names were forged, Arthur Hannett challenged the petition in court. Weeks and then months went by as both sides traded barbs at commission meetings and in the press. Hoping to entice Old Towners to accept annexation, Albuquerque officials began offering city services at city prices, even though Old Town was still a county entity. As Old Towners refused to buckle under the pressure, Wells, the city manager, furious with the annexation delay, threatened to double the water rates and cancel garbage pickup and police and fire protection if La Plaza Vieja did not stop resisting within one month.[79]

Village residents battling the city exploded with anger. One anti-annexation leader mocked the commission. "We believe that [at] some time" Old Town should be incorporated into the city, "but until the arrogant, incompetent and wasteful administration that is now in charge of Albuquerque's affairs has been retired we prefer to stay outside and let the people inside suffer from such incompetence."[80] Instead of negotiating in good faith or offering concessions, city commissioners used threats, insults, and undemocratic means to annex the village. As both sides fought it out, residents took to the streets. In one incident, Mary Selby Moya, an annexation supporter, had her house surrounded by "torch-toting vigilantes" threatening to burn it to the ground. An outsider, Mary Moya "knew what was good for the natives," and many resented her. She called their bluff, and they did not make good on their threat.[81]

Stumbling and frustrated by legal setbacks, commissioners switched tactics and used a new state law that allowed a seven-member annexation arbitration board to settle the dispute. The city could appoint three members, while three were elected by the area under consideration. A seventh person was to be appointed by the six selected members. Urging the commission on, the *Albuquerque Journal* editor urged city leaders to push their program to fruition.[82] After a fierce debate within the community and in the press—and a low election turnout—an anti-annexation slate won.[83] The vote suggests deep divisions within the village, as well as the city commission's success in dividing and demoralizing voters. Unable to agree on a seventh board member, a district court judge appointed Gilberto Espinosa, an Albuquerque attorney, local historian, and known "progressive," to join the commission. After months of meetings, the board finally voted on July 1, 1949, splitting three to three. Not surprisingly, Espinosa cast his ballot to annex Alburquerque. Undaunted, the opposition took their case to the district and then the state supreme court, but both quickly upheld the arbitration board's ruling.[84]

In the wake of the city's victory, the short- and long-term ramifications for the village came in many forms. The most obvious change was the loss of political power: prior to annexation, La Plaza Vieja was the center of Bernalillo County politics; afterward, however, Old Town became just another precinct in a growing city, its political relevance vastly diminished. The annexation of Alburquerque reveals that those who wielded power set the agenda, limited the parameters of debate, and made the ultimate decisions. This pattern continued as Old Towners now had to abide by city ordinances. One ordinance forbade public dances on Sunday. Historically, the Sociedad Nuevo Mexicana de la Mutua Protección hall had held dances every Sunday to raise money for the Catholic church and for a burial fund for poor people. It also served as a site for entertainment, music, and dancing. Elizaria Castillo remembers that as a sixteen-year-old, at the height of the Great Depression, she "used to like to go dancing" at the hall every week.[85] After annexation, Old Towners had to petition the city commission for a waiver to conduct Sunday dances. Although the city granted the request, asking permission to conduct such a time-honored event symbolized La Plaza Vieja's loss of autonomy.[86]

Adding to the loss of political influence, the community suffered economically. Old Town's rural lifestyle ended because livestock were not permitted in city limits and streets were paved, and many residents lost an important economic supplement. The enduring sights and smells of livestock,
such a vital part of Alburquerque for centuries, ended with the stroke of a pen.
And, as many had anticipated, taxes increased significantly. City Manager
Charles Wells estimated that Old Towners would have to swallow a whopping
33 percent tax increase. Bernalillo County landowners already paid five times
the average of other New Mexico counties, and residential rates increased to
pay for water and sewer bonds and trash service.[87]

With the multiple blows of demographic upheaval, economic change,
the loss of political authority, and gentrification, the mechanisms of social
control weakened. Reciprocal relationships and duties, forged in geographic
isolation and dependence on a barter economy, evaporated. Cultural sinews
that had once held the village together stretched and tore. Further compounding these problems, the moral authority upholding the old social order
lost stature when it split into competing factions over the community's political status. Respected local leaders not only dwindled in number, their authority weakened. Old Town's experience resembled what was occurring in
other Hispano neighborhoods.[88]

The loss of an articulate, respected moral voice was evident in the 1950s,
when crime skyrocketed. Old Town, like all communities, suffered from petty
crime and endured residents who deviated from acceptable behavior. Engulfed
within a growing city and increasingly surrounded by strangers masquerading
as neighbors, crimes mushroomed. Luigi Petrucci recalled that crime started
"in the late fifties." He remembers that his father's store and later his own business in La Plaza Vieja were never robbed between 1935 and 1958. But between
1958 to 1970 he was robbed eight times.[89]

With the commercialization of the Spanish and Indian past gaining
steam in the 1950s, additional outsiders purchased land in Old Town, mirroring what was transpiring in urban areas across the American West. Newcomers often bought property for a fraction of its market value and built shops
and expensive homes. This increased the value of the land, which in turn
caused property taxes to rise. Higher taxes combined with willing buyers convinced many residents to sell their property and move out.[90] This pattern of
working-class outmigration and gentrification continued the transformation
of Old Town into a tourist center.

The selling of Old Town picked up steam after annexation. Conflicts
did not end with annexation: people feuded endlessly over La Plaza Vieja's
meaning and identity. Local bickering made the news in 1956 when a group of

merchants, hoping to attract more publicity, hauled the old jail to the plaza directly across from the church. Outraged at the lack of decorum, a delegation supported by about "500 petition signers" pleaded with city fathers to remove it. But Bill Mollenkopf, the president of the Old Town Business Administration, defended the jail as a tourist attraction. He told the press that tourists were "inquiring about it and taking pictures." Mollenkopf added, "The Plaza and Albuquerque" could "get some nationwide publicity through those pictures."[91] Under pressure, city officials finally removed it.

Two years later, La Plaza Vieja obtained a historic zoning ordinance. This protected historic buildings and laid out strict guidelines for land use and architectural style. When the city learned that it owned the coveted portal of La Placita restaurant, it decided to allow non-Indians to join Native Americans selling their wares there. This infuriated the Indian vendors, who claimed they alone had a historic right to trade there. Many shopkeepers and arts and crafts makers supported Native Americans on this issue. City leaders initially ignored the pleas to ban non-Indian vendors under the portal until verbal insults and physical assaults forced them to enact an ordinance mandating and restricting licenses to sell there.[92]

Capitalizing on the tourist market, city officials encouraged merchants to make the plaza more tourist friendly. By the early 1950s the mixed architectural buildings were being remodeled into a "Spanish" town. Workers covered the fronts of Victorian buildings such as the Romero house and the church rectory with adobe. By 1961, nightly "Indian dance exhibitions" were being performed for those who wished to "acquaint themselves with" Indian culture. In the 1960s, local boosters hosted the New Mexico Arts and Crafts Fair. The four-day street fair allowed artists using a variety of media, such as "oils, watercolors, graphics, and sculpture, and craftsmen in textiles, ceramics, metals, woods, leather, glass and kindred media," to display their goods for sale. Prizes also went out to the best cultural exhibit. The festival also included "Indian dances and songs, Spanish dancing and singing, and folk songs and square dances."[93] Although the fair was locally planned, not all the decisions were made by Old Towners. Merchants and artists felt the city's power over decisions that affected the plaza.

Land use changed dramatically from the 1940s to the 1950s. In 1940, the area around the plaza consisted of a few taverns, barbershops, restaurants, grocery stores, and curio shops. By 1951, there were four restaurants and thirty shops. Commercial enterprises continued to open, and by 1964 six restaurants and sixty-five shops were open for business. In 1972 the number had increased to eight eating establishments and eighty-five shops. La Plaza Vieja boosters were even able to get the city to build a first-class museum adjacent to the plaza in 1979. By 1980 an incredible 104 shops (selling toys, kitchenware, crafts, and upscale clothes), eighteen galleries, and ten restaurants vied for customers. Even more dramatic than the increase in businesses was neighborhood depopulation. As outsiders offered what many Old Towners considered high prices for homes, more and more locals sold and moved out. In 1960, 116 people resided on the plaza. By 1980, the number had dwindled to about two dozen. Old Town's streets to the east and west of the plaza also declined in number, from 4,891 in 1960 to 4,289 in 1970.[94]

For many Hispano residents, La Plaza Vieja was a symbol of an old, cherished past, not something to profit from. Nostalgia for the Hispano community of the past runs deep with elderly Old Towners, who resent that the old village has become a commodity to be sold to tourists. Every few years after annexation another issue over neighborhood self-determination cropped up, and latent disgruntlement became public. Continued anger stemmed, according to Art De La O, from "the old residents who chose to stay, come hell or high water, [and who] resented the fact that their neighbors moved out [and] gave away" their property or "sold out for bucks or whatever" to outsiders. In addition, "oldtime residents" just outside the plaza area "hated to see these people give up their properties and allow further commercialization."[95] Without recognizing the irony, in 1996 Bette Casteel, the pro-annexation "progressive" and a longtime shopkeeper on the plaza, lamented that "[t]he dream to preserve Old Town as a beautiful place, without a flea market atmosphere, prevails with many of us. The problems involved are over-development and lack of sensitivity to the essence of the little village founded in 1706."[96]

This study is not an analysis of the rise and decline of a Hispano village. La Plaza Vieja still exists, but it is no longer an autonomous Hispano-led community. The interconnected social cords that once tied the community together frayed over the years, slowly cut by economic opportunities and social mobility. Since Old Town's incorporation into the city, a gradual pattern has emerged whereby neighbors often have only superficial contact with each other. Farming and ranching have disappeared, replaced by wage labor. Pockets of expensive homes contrast with clusters of housing needing repair. Still a Democratic stronghold, Old Town is a coveted precinct in political elections. The fiestas, celebrations, and rituals that once served as guideposts throughout the year are a pale reflection of years past, if they exist at all. The prohibition against parking anywhere on the plaza hinders access to San Felipe de Neri, angering many churchgoers. They blame the shopkeepers, who

262 LA PLAZA VIEJA (OLD TOWN ALBURQUERQUE)

support limited parking to accommodate tourist pedestrians. In addition, since the war "ideal" gender roles that at one time seemed clear have become blurred or obliterated. Incorporation even affected how community members assisted each other in need. According to Cleto Durán, the Sociedad Nuevo Mexicana de la Mutua Protección dissolved in 1965 for lack of interest.[97]

The evidence presented here suggests that by 1960 La Plaza Vieja was no longer a stable community tied together by vibrant social customs and reciprocal relationships and responsibilities. Together, the Great Depression, World War II, postwar opportunities, and tourism shattered the village's social and cultural structure. Alburquerque had been transformed from a Hispano village into a heterogeneous, fragmented community, its long history mostly forgotten. The irony is that this once model community, mostly crime-free and functioning in relative social and cultural unity—the dream many Americans have yearned for—was destroyed by its incorporation into a nation characterized by conflict and disunity. Old Town, like communities across the American West during and after World War II, grappled with cultural, social, political, and economic changes as it adjusted to consolidation into America society. By the 1950s, La Plaza Vieja was a neighborhood of working-class homes surrounding a gentrified plaza packed with shops and restaurants selling a distorted Spanish and Indian past to tourists.

NOTES

The author thanks David Maciel, Erlinda Gonzales-Berry, Elizabeth Jameson, Denise Pan, and John Martin for commenting on this essay. I also thank Howard Rabinowitz, for this essay originated in his seminar on the urban West. Although our interpretations rarely agreed, Howard's criticisms improved this work.

1. All interviews listed here are located at the Center for Southwest Research, Zimmerman Library, University of New Mexico, under Benny Andrés, Jr., transcripts for "Old Town, Alburquerque."

2. Marc Simmons, *Albuquerque: A Narrative History* (Albuquerque: University of New Mexico Press, 1982), 81–137.

3. Ibid., 129–30. Virginia L. Olmsted compiled New Mexico censuses of the late Spanish and Mexican eras. Her contribution sheds light on the complex familial households, occupational statuses, and ethnic diversity in Alburquerque. Virginia L. Olmsted, *New Mexico Spanish and Mexican Colonial Censuses, 1790, 1823, 1845* (New Mexico Genealogical Society, 1975), and *Spanish and Mexican Censuses of New Mexico: 1750–1830* (New Mexico Genealogical Society, 1981).

4. Simmons, *Albuquerque: A Narrative History*, 161, 202; see also Darlis A. Miller, "Cross-Cultural Marriages in the Southwest: The New Mexico Experience, 1846–1900," *New Mexico Historical Review* (hereafter *NMHR*) 57, no. 4 (Oct. 1982): 335–59.

5. Simmons, *Albuquerque: A Narrative History*, 229–30; Cathy Robbins, "A Community At Odds," *Impact /Albuquerque Journal Magazine*, Dec. 30, 1980, 5. The source of this article was a 1980 dispute in Old Town over granting a liquor license to La Placita restaurant, which was sixty-five feet from San Felipe School and across the street from the church. The theft of the name Albuquerque still irritated residents a century later.

6. The term "Hispano" had been used in the nineteenth century to denote individuals in the Americas influenced by Spanish culture. "Hispano" is still used in the late twentieth century for the same purpose. The label was also used in response to Anglos' derogatory use of the word "Mexicans" in reference to Nuevomexicanos. For instance, in the 1890s a newspaper named *El hispano-americano* circulated out of Socorro, N.M., and another out of Las Vegas, N.M. *Hispano-americano* was published in Socorro, N.M., in that same decade. *Alianza* (1907–1961), issued by the Alianza Hispano-Americana, a Mexican American fraternal insurance society in Tucson, Ariz., continued the tradition of representing people of Spanish cultural roots as "Hispanos." In Roy, N.M., about 1904, a newspaper titled *Spanish American* or sometimes *El hispano americano* began publishing and ceased around 1926. In Belen, N.M., a Spanish-language newspaper called *Hispano-americano* began publication circa 1913.

There are several books with "Hispano" in the title. See Salvador Novo, *Antología de cuentos mexicanos e hispano americanos* (Mexico, 1923); Sylvestor Baxtor and Manuel Toussaint, *La Arquitectura hispano colonial en México* (Mexico, 1934); Julio Silvio, *Estudos Hispano-Americanos* (Rio de Janeiro, 1924); and Sturgis E. Leavitt, *Hispano-American Literature in the United States: A Bibliography of Translations and Criticism, 1932–1934, with Additional Items from Earlier Years* (Chapel Hill: University of North Carolina Press, 1935).

"Hispano" has been used throughout the twentieth century. In 1965 the Albuquerque Hispano Chamber of Commerce was organized. At least two newspapers named *El hispano* have been published since World War II, one in Sacramento, Calif., in 1969, and the other in Bernalillo County, N.M., from 1966 to 1986. Richard Norstrand, *The Hispano Homeland* (Norman: University of Oklahoma Press, 1992), continues the popularity of the word. After World War I, "Spanish American" gained popularity. See Nancie L. González, *The Spanish-Americans of New Mexico* (Albuquerque: University of New Mexico Press, 1967), 80–81. By the early 1970s Hispanic New Mexicans were extremely divided on how to identify themselves. See Joseph V. Metzgar, "The Ethnic Sensitivity of Spanish New Mexicans: A Survey and Analysis," *NMHR* 49, no. 1 (Jan. 1974): 49–73.

7. Physical markings often had less to do with racial status than with class position. "Spanish" carried connotations of a culture thought to be superior to that of the Indians. See Ramón Gutiérrez's brilliant *When Jesus Came, the Corn Mothers Went Away: Marriage, Sexuality, and Power in New Mexico, 1500–1846* (Stanford: Stanford University Press, 1991).

8. Susan R. Kenneson, "Through the Looking-Glass: A History of Anglo-American Attitudes towards the Spanish-Americans and Indians of New Mexico" (Ph.D. diss., Yale University, 1978), 261–84.

9. Doris L. Meyer explores this topic using evidence from the late 1800s in north-

ern New Mexico: "Early Mexican-American Responses to Negative Stereotyping," *NMHR* 53, no. 1 (Jan. 1978): 75–91; see also Metzgar, "The Ethnic Sensitivity of Spanish New Mexicans," 52–54.

10. Two books on internal colonialism are Rodolfo Acuña, *Occupied America: A History of Chicanos*, 3d ed. (New York: Harper Collins, 1988), and Patricia Nelson Limerick, *Legacy of Conquest: The Unbroken Past of the American West* (New York: W. W. Norton, 1987).

11. Anglo theft of Hispano property was common in the late 1800s in northern New Mexico, but stolen land was often part of huge land grants deeded during the Mexican era to citizens as well as immigrants. Complicating the issue of land theft was the duplicity of elite Hispanos who brazenly profited by taking advantage of fellow Nuevomexicanos. See William DuBuys, *Enchantment and Exploitation: The Life and Hard Times of a New Mexico Mountain Range* (Albuquerque: University of New Mexico Press, 1985).

12. Byron A. Johnson, *Old Town, Albuquerque, New Mexico: A Guide to Its History and Architecture* (Albuquerque, 1980), 24, 26, 31. See also John O. Baxter, "Salvador Armijo: Citizen of Albuquerque, 1823–1879," *NMHR* 53, no. 3 (July 1978): 219–37; Howard Bryan, "Off the Beaten Path," *Albuquerque Tribune*, June 27, 1974; Simmons, *Albuquerque: A Narrative History*, 152–53.

13. Simmons, *Albuquerque: A Narrative History*, 230–31, 406 n. 29; Johnson, 83–84, 90, 98, 101.

14. Judith B. DeMark, "The Immigrant Experience in Albuquerque, 1880–1920" (Ph.D. diss., University of New Mexico, 1984), 130, 133.

15. "Old Albuquerque, N.M.," [Sanborn Map Co.,] July 1902.

16. "Old Albuquerque, N.M.," [Sanborn Map Co.,] July 1908; Old Albuquerque, N.M.," [Sanborn Map Co.,] May 1913; "Old Albuquerque," [Sanborn Map Co.,] Aug. 1919.

17. Joan M. Jensen, "'I've Worked, I'm Not Afraid of Work': Farm Women in New Mexico, 1920–1940," *NMHR* 61, no. 1 (Jan. 1986): 38–39; Jake W. Spidle, Jr., "'An Army of Tubercular Invalids': New Mexico and the Birth of a Tuberculosis Industry," *NMHR* 61, no. 3 (July 1986): 190.

18. Margaret Connell-Szasz, "Albuquerque Congregationalists and Southwestern Social Reform: 1900–1917," *NMHR* 55, no. 3 (July 1980): 238–43; Charles D. Biebel, "Cultural Change on the Southwest Frontier: Albuquerque's Schooling, 1870–1895," *NMHR* 55, no. 3 (July 1980): 209–30; Joan M. Jensen, "Canning Comes to New Mexico: Women and the Agricultural Extension Service, 1914–1919," *NMHR* 57, no. 4 (Oct. 1982): 361–86; Félix D. Almaráz, Jr., "Bilingual Education in New Mexico: Historical Perspective and Current Debate," *NMHR* 53, no. 4 (Oct. 1978): 347–60. Both the secular and the Catholic schools of Old Town had rejected bilingual education by the mid-twentieth century. At school students experienced physical punishment for speaking Spanish. See Tina Pérez [pseud.], interview by author, Mar. 3, 1995. English-only education infuriated the bilingual education advocate George Sánchez. See

Michael Welsh, "A Prophet without Honor: George I. Sánchez and Bilingualism in New Mexico," *NMHR* 69, no. 1 (Jan. 1994): 19–34.

19. Cleto Durán, interview by author, Feb. 28, 1995.

20. Pérez, interview.

21. Cleto Durán, interview by author, Mar. 7, 1995; Luigi Petrucci [pseud.], interview by author, Apr. 10, 1995; Pérez, interview.

22. Durán, interview, Mar. 7, 1995.

23. Paul Gonzales, interview by author, Mar. 16, 1995; Pérez, interview; Durán, interview, Mar. 7, 1995.

24. Johnson, 97, 108. For saloons, gambling houses, and prostitution, see Howard Bryan, "Sunnyside Was Popular Spot in Old Town in the Gay '90s," *Albuquerque Tribune*, June 25, 1964; Howard Bryan, "Off the Beaten Path," ibid., July 31, 1980; Durán, interview, Feb. 28, 1995.

25. Bette D. Casteel, *Old Town, Albuquerque and Vicinity in the Nineteen Forties and a Little Beyond* (Corrales, N.M., 1996).

26. Durán, interview, Feb. 28, 1995.

27. Dionicia Jójola, interview by author and Carmen Chávez, Apr. 7, 1995.

28. Pérez, interview.

29. Stella Martínez [pseud.], telephone interview by author, Mar. 16, 1995; Casteel, 37.

30. Not all Nuevamexicanas were the stereotypical passive, subservient women of lore. See Janet Lecompte, "The Independent Women of Hispanic New Mexico, 1821–1846," *Western Historical Quarterly* (hereafter *WHQ*) 12, no. 1 (Jan. 1981): 17–35.

31. Lucy Jaramillo, interview by author, Mar. 8, 1995. Nuevomexicanos were fiercely anti-Texas (and thus anti-Democrat) because Texas had tried several times in the nineteenth century to annex New Mexico. See Jack E. Holmes, *Politics in New Mexico* (Albuquerque: University of New Mexico Press, 1967), 155.

32. Holmes, 153–74.

33. Jensen, "'I've Worked, I'm Not Afraid of Work,'" 36–34; González, 52.

34. Pérez, interview; Durán, interview, Feb. 28, 1995.

35. Durán, interview, Feb. 28, 1995; see also Charles D. Biebel, *Making the Most of It: Public Works in Albuquerque during the Great Depression, 1929–1942* (Albuquerque: Albuquerque Museum, 1986); María E. Montoya, "The Roots of Economic and Ethnic Divisions in Northern New Mexico: The Case of the Civilian Conservation Corps," *WHQ* 26, no. 1 (Spring 1995): 15–34.

36. Durán, interviews, Feb. 28 and Mar. 7, 1995. The Albuquerque novelist Harvey Fergusson forged a career arguing that the Hispano *ricos*, or the "Great Houses," evaporated because they did not posses the same talent, energy, and destiny that Anglos brought to New Mexico; see Arthur G. Pettit, "The Decline and Fall of the New Mexican Great House in the Novels of Harvey Fergusson: A Classic Example of Anglo-American Ethnocentricity," *NMHR* 51, no. 3 (July 1976): 173–91.

37. Pérez, interview; Durán, interview, Feb. 28, 1995.

38. Although Carmen Chávez grew up in the Hispano neighborhood of Barelas, across town from La Plaza Vieja, her experience mirrors what is argued here. See her biographical essay, "Coming of Age during the War: Reminiscences of an Albuquerque Hispana," *NMHR* 70, no. 4 (Oct. 1995): 383–97; *Bernalillo County Beacon*, May 22, 1942.

39. Nearly all the people interviewed noted the social and gender role changes wrought by the war. See Durán, interview, Feb. 28, 1995, Pérez, interview; Elizaria Castillo, interview by author, Mar. 9, 1995; Gonzales, interview; and Paula Padilla, interview by author, Apr. 11, 1995. For an overview, see Gerald D. Nash, *The American West Transformed: The Impact of the Second World War* (Lincoln: University of Nebraska Press, 1985).

40. Chávez, "Coming of Age During the War," 385–86; Petrucci, interview, Apr. 10, 1995.

41. Pérez, interview; Petrucci, interview, Apr. 10, 1995.

42. Durán, interview, Feb. 28, 1995; Petrucci, interview, Apr. 10, 1995.

43. Pérez, interview; Durán, interview, Feb. 28, 1995. For a discussion of Hispano marriage patterns in Bernalillo County and the gradual rise of intermarriage rates, see González, 165–72.

44. Castillo, interview; Padilla, interview; Pérez, interview (María Ortiz is a pseudonym).

45. Dionicia Jójola, interview by author and Carmen Chávez, Apr. 4, 1995, and June 2, 1995.

46. Chávez, "Coming of Age During the War" 396–97. Although people of color are mostly ignored, see Elaine May, *Homeward Bound: American Families in the Cold War Era* (New York: Basic Books, 1988).

47. 1950 Census, Population of Cities of 10,000 or more from Earliest Census to 1950; 1960 Census, Area and Population of Counties, Urban and Rural: 1960 and 1950 (U.S. Department of Commerce, Bureau of the Census, n.d.).

48. Joseph V. Metzgar, "Guns and Butter: Albuquerque Hispanics, 1940–1975," *NMHR* 56, no. 2 (Apr. 1982): 117–39; Dorothy I. Cline and T. Phillip Wolf, "Albuquerque: The End of a Reform Era," in *Urban Politics in the Southwest*, ed. Leonard E. Goodall (Tempe: Arizona State University, 1967), 7–22.

49. Sixteenth Census of the U.S.: Population, 1940, Characteristics of the Population, New Mexico; 1950 Census of Population, vol. 2, Characteristics of the Population, part 31, New Mexico (U.S. Department of Commerce, Bureau of the Census, n.d.). Unfortunately, the 1960 census of Albuquerque is not available by precinct as in past censuses, so a statistical comparison is not available for Old Town.

50. Petrucci, interview, Apr. 10, 1995.

51. Only a trickle of books explore the impact of World War II on the South and West. Most have been written by urban historians focusing more on politics and economics than on social and cultural patterns. See Richard M. Bernard and Bradley R. Rice, *Sunbelt Cities: Politics and Growth since World War II* (Austin: University of Texas Press, 1983).

52. *New Mexico Magazine* exemplifies booster literature. Note Fremont Kutnewsky, "Albuquerque—Seven Years Wonder," *New Mexico Magazine* (May 1953), 13–17, 51; William E. Tydeman, "A New Deal for Tourists: Route 66 and the Promotion of New Mexico," *NMHR* 66, no. 2 (Apr. 1991): 203–15; Casteel, *Old Town.*

53. For New Deal programs that promoted the arts and crafts industry in New Mexico, see Suzanne Forrest, *Preservation of the Village* (Albuquerque: University of New Mexico Press, 1989); for the sign, see Casteel, 22.

54. Durán, interview, Feb. 28, 1995.

55. Petrucci, interview, Apr. 10, 1995.

56. Castillo, interview; Gonzales, interview; Pérez, interview; Robbins, 6. See also Joan M. Jensen, "'Disfranchisement is a Disgrace,'" 5–35.

57. Castillo, interview; Gonzales, interview; Pérez, interview.

58. *Albuquerque Journal,* June 25, 1948.

59. See the sociological study by Tómas Atencio, "Social Change and Community Conflict in Old Albuquerque, New Mexico" (Ph.D. diss., University of New Mexico, 1985).

60. *Albuquerque Journal,* Jan. 20, 1949. See the reference to a petition by two Old Town residents in ibid., July 14, 1949.

61. Pérez, interview.

62. *Albuquerque Journal,* June 30, 1948.

63. Ibid., June 14, 1948.

64. Ibid., June 29, 1948.

65. Ibid., July 6, 1948.

66. Ibid.

67. Ibid., Dec. 2, 1948.

68. Casteel, 6, 47.

69. Irene Fisher, *Old Albuquerque: Past, Present* (Albuquerque: Old Town Books, 1962), 6, 9.

70. *Albuquerque Journal,* Aug. 19, 1948.

71. Robbins, 5. According to the Albuquerque Museum's staff the transcripts from the board's proceedings could not be located in its archive.

72. Ibid.

73. *Albuquerque Journal,* July 21, 1948.

74. Johnson, 27.

75. *Albuquerque Journal,* Mar. 17, 1948.

76. Robbins, 5.

77. Simmons, *Albuquerque: A Narrative History,* 343–45; Jake W. Spidle Jr., "An Army of Tubercular Invalids," 179–201. See also Marc Simmons, "Hygiene, Sanitation, and Public Health in Hispanic New Mexico," *NMHR* 67, no. 3 (July 1992): 205–25.

78. *Albuquerque Journal,* Jan. 5, 1949.

79. Ibid., Feb. 2, 1949.

80. Ibid., Feb. 3, 1949.

81. Robbins, 6.

82. *Albuquerque Journal,* Jan. 1, 1949.

83. Ibid., Apr. 12, 1949.

84. Ibid., July 1, 1949.

85. Castillo, interview; *Albuquerque Journal,* Aug. 25, 1948.

86. Robbins, 6.

87. Ibid. For the rise in tax rates, see *Albuquerque Journal,* Sept. 1, 1948; ibid., Sept. 18, 1948; ibid., Oct. 17, 1948; ibid., Aug. 11, 1949.

88. Metzgar, "Guns and Butter," 123; Chávez, "Coming of Age during the War," 395.

89. Luigi Petrucci, interview by author, Apr. 24, 1995. For the rise of crime rates in Bernalillo County, note González, 136–39.

90. Durán, interview, Feb. 28, 1995.

91. *Albuquerque Journal,* June 3, 1956.

92. Casteel, 46.

93. Robbins, 6; *New York Times,* Jan. 8, 1961; Fisher, 7, 15.

94. Robbins, 6, 12.

95. Ibid., 6, 8.

96. Casteel, 46.

97. Durán, interview, Mar. 7, 1995.

Chapter Ten

DAVID R. MACIEL AND JUAN JOSÉ PEÑA

La Reconquista

THE CHICANO MOVEMENT IN NEW MEXICO

INTRODUCTION

In the 1960s, the Chicano community undertook a unique, dramatic, and multifaceted social struggle of affirmation. This historic phase of activism became more and more varied and complex than previous struggles, reflecting all hues of the political, labor, educational, and social spectrums. This activist process and affirmative discourse would be known as the Chicano movement, *El Movimiento*, or La Reconquista.[1] El Movimiento is a Spanish term for the Chicano movement, which most scholars agree arose around 1965 and was active through the late 1970s in various regions of the country. It differed from previous civil rights struggles because of its broad appeal and collective mobilization and, more importantly, because of the material conditions and ideological climate of the 1960s in the United States.

The Movimiento had overriding priorities, a sense of motive, and a goal of raising the status of the Chicano community in an Anglo-dominated world. The initial underlying current was disenchantment over Chicanos' current political, economic, and social status within the United States. By all standards, the Chicano community ranked alarmingly low in the overall measuring scale of American society.[2] Major change was called for.

Activists and participants from all states and regions and of all social strata and generations sought a more critical awareness of the forces of economic, political, and class exploitation and how they affected the Chicano community. A related question dealt with the negative and lasting impact of racism on the community. An acute sensitivity emerged that focused on questions of alienation, ethnicity, class, culture, and gender. Paramount in the struggle was the need to develop a sound historical understanding of the Chicano experience.[3] Out of these emerging perspectives, the Chicano movement carried out a new political agenda throughout the Southwest and other regions where Chicanas and Chicanos resided.

Chicanismo, the ideological construct of the movement, was at times a set of general and nebulous notions, but the core of these did translate as a radicalization of political, labor, and educational struggles. Chicano activism became a major challenge to the assumptions, ideology, and traditional principles of the established dominant order and the assigned societal place of Chicanos.

The Chicano struggle from its inception expressed various tendencies that at times appeared contradictory. Political and labor organizing strategies and agendas in the 1960s were overwhelmingly liberal and reformist, but the Chicano movement also included radical tendencies. The extreme radical currents of the Movimiento encompassed separatist and anticapitalist tendencies. Regardless of the particular ideological orientation of the participants, confrontation politics, intense conflict, and heightened ethnic consciousness characterized the Chicano movement through the late 1960s to the 1970s.[4]

The emphasis of Chicanismo upon dignity, self-worth, pride, uniqueness, and a feeling of cultural rebirth made the ideology attractive and inclusive for the majority of the Chicano community, cutting across gender, class, regional, and generational lines. Class and racial oppression were at the very root of the Chicano struggle. Since most Chicanos had directly or indirectly experienced economic and social discrimination and racism, they could relate to the struggle. These collective negative experiences increased the appeal of Chicanismo, which emphasized Mexican cultural consciousness and heritage, pride in the Spanish language, and the quest for economic opportunity and political representation.[5]

The Chicano movement had its own multifaceted dynamics and processes. Its leaders and militants for the most part shared fundamental goals, but they carried out their own priorities and agendas. Inspired by the catalyst forces generated by the movement, Chicanos in New Mexico engaged in many of the most significant struggles of the early years of the Reconquista. Moreover, as the oldest area of settlement north of Mexico, it had special historical significance. In actuality, New Mexico was one of the principal areas of contention for the forces of the struggle. The Chicano movement in New Mexico addressed issues of the land struggle, political empowerment, community activism, antiwar sentiment, education, and cultural rights.[6]

Moreover, the Reconquista in New Mexico shattered two long-standing myths of the Nuevomexicano experience: first, the so-called Spanish myth: the affirmation of the legacy of Spanish culture and simultaneous negation of

Nuevomexicanos' cultural roots and connections to Mexico; and second, the imaginary interethnic harmony of the state. This myth refers to the official interpretation that because of the particular history of New Mexico, Nuevomexicanos had not been subjected to the same discriminatory patterns or violent acts of other states, such as Texas. In other words, the myth prevailed that New Mexico was a model of tricultural accommodation, and therefore Chicanos had better overall conditions than in other states.[7] The Movimiento seriously called into question this long-accepted truism. Furthermore, the Reconquista brought to the surface the deep class contradictions of Nuevomexicano society and its impact on the contemporary civil rights struggle. These contradictions repeatedly impacted the dense political history of New Mexico from the nineteenth century to the present.

What follows in this chapter is an overview and interpretation of the Chicano movement in *la tierra del encanto*. As such, it does not pretend to be exhaustive or to encompass each and every phase or manifestation of the Movimiento. Rather, it offers highlights, trends, and a critical assessment of the Chicano movement in New Mexico. More than all else, this chapter is an acknowledgment and a tribute to all those Nuevomexicanos who struggled so courageously and with such deep commitment for a better life for their people. In New Mexico, that courage and commitment have been expressed in various forms of resistance and affirmation, particularly in relation to land rights and land tenure relations.

REIES LÓPEZ TIJERINA AND THE LAND STRUGGLE

In New Mexico, land ownership became a paramount issue of the Chicano movement. After the signing of the Treaty of Guadalupe Hidalgo in 1848, many Nuevomexicanos claimed that much of their land had been illegally usurped though deception, fraud, and violence. They were victims of greedy landowners and corrupt state officials. In addition, the federal government through the U.S. Forest Service arbitrarily took millions of acres, some of them in the traditional Nuevomexicano grazing lands of northern New Mexico. For years, the heirs of those who had received land from the Spanish Crown or the Mexican government had sought judicial and legislative action to regain the lands given to them. But for the most part, their plight and struggle received no justice or resolution through either U.S. federal or state courts.[8]

In this long-standing and bitter Nuevomexicano struggle, a figure from the neighboring state of Texas would provide leadership in the land issue.

He was Reies López Tijerina, known as El Tigre. Through his actions and charisma, he would propel the land struggle of New Mexico into the national and international conscience during the 1960s. Born in Falls City, near San Antonio, in 1923, Tijerina came from a Mexican-origin working-class family. Spanish was his native language, and Mexican traditions provided his upbringing; he did not learn English formally until he was almost twelve. Five years later, he was offered the opportunity to attend a three-year Assembly of God school on the outskirts of El Paso, Texas. After graduation, Tijerina carried out evangelistic missions on both sides of the border.[9] In Arizona, along with other families, he founded a cooperative village named "Valley of Peace." In 1957, however, powerful agricultural owners drove the families out of the state. They did not want Tijerina influencing agricultural workers in any manner.

Upon leaving Arizona, Tijerina accepted an invitation in 1959 to continue his ministry in northern New Mexico. He had first visited Rio Arriba County in the 1940s. Afterward, he had been in contact with former members of La Mano Negra, a secret organization that fought for lost lands. When Tijerina settled in New Mexico, he quickly became fascinated with the region and soon thereafter became committed to the land issues of Nuevomexicanos. He perceived that "New Mexico was the only spot in the Southwest where there was a spark of hope for Spanish-Americans—where they could make their rights felt in the eyes of the government."[10] He based this assertion on the numerical strength of Nuevomexicanos, their history and traditions, and the class structure of New Mexico.

El Tigre quickly began to make the land issue a personal priority. He brought a religious zeal to the struggle and articulated the issue in terms of social justice and civil rights. For the next three years, Tijerina and his family worked in various jobs to finance his fact-finding trips to the archives in Mexico City, and later to Spain. He carried out extensive research into primary and secondary sources that dealt with land claims and issues and in time became an expert on the subject.[11]

Tijerina gave new impetus and a sense of priority to the land-grant movement of Nuevomexicanos. In 1963, he founded the Alianza Federal de Mercedes Libres. The Alianza endeavored "to organize and acquaint the heirs of all Spanish land-grants covered by the Guadalupe Hidalgo Treaty" with their rights. Tijerina repeatedly stated that more than 100 years had gone by since the Treaty of Guadalupe Hidalgo was enacted, "yet the question of the land grants, far from being resolved, has sunk into a morass of fraud, forgery and perjury." He addressed not only individual private holdings, but also what he considered illegal federal occupation of Nuevomexicano lands. Tijerina pointed out that "none of these grant lands and waters which the United States asserts it acquired from Mexico under the Treaty . . . ever formed any part of public domain. These lands and waters therefore cannot be taken for that purpose."[12]

Cultural symbolism became a rallying force for collective action. The creation of the Alianza was supported by people still on the land and also by student activists. Individual donations and fundraisers financed the Alianza. Among the followers were men and women of all ages, but especially conspicuous was the presence of elders, whose motivating force was the desire for the land and the preservation of their traditional way of life. They sought to foster pride in their heritage and force Anglos to respect them. For example, members of the Alianza spoke Spanish, seldom using English.[13] As one former Aliancista recalled:

> Reies and the Alianza gave us a new hope. They rekindled the fire of resistance that had never died. They helped us to realize that we did not have to accept defeat and injustice. We could do something, we could fight back. This was the message that the Alianza spread, from the city to the smallest village at the end of a dirt road. Alianza members talked to small farmers, families living on welfare, construction workers, old people and the young. They would talk in the kitchens of poor homes and in big auditoriums.[14]

By 1964, membership in the Alianza had increased dramatically. The organization had over 6,000 members and had gained wide support from diverse sectors. A year later, its membership had increased to 14,000, and at its 1966 convention the number stood at 20,000.[15] Tijerina had worked around the state bringing grantees into the Alianza and students into the Alianza Youth Organization—the Caballeros de las Indias. In their recruitment efforts, the Alianza stated:

> You have been robbed of your lands by Anglo-Americans with some Spanish American accomplices. No one is willing to help you recover your lands, protect your water rights, or secure your grazing permits. The federal and state governments are not interested in you. Join the Alianza. Together we will get your lands back or adequate compensation for them, and protect your grazing and water rights. This will be done preferably through court action. If the courts do not respond, then we will have to resort to other methods.[16]

The Alianza's actions focused on the Tierra Amarilla and San Joaquín de Chama land grants. Tijerina and the Alianza's arguments for the reclamation of lost lands rested upon two key historical documents: the "Recopilación de Leyes de las Indias," a seventeenth-century document that had been the legal framework for the Spanish land grants, and the 1848 Treaty of Guadalupe Hidalgo, which legalized the transfer of more than 50 percent of Mexican territory to the United States and guaranteed that Mexican land grants would be respected. The Alianza contended that the United States government had violated in spirit and practice articles 8 and 9 of the Treaty. According to the Alianza, these were the articles that guaranteed property and citizenship rights to Mexicans who remained in the Southwest.[17] Thus, Mexico and the Mexican state, historically, had parts to play in the evolving Alianza scheme.

In an attempt to expand its base, the Alianza cultivated ties with Mexico as well as with other minority groups in the United States. Tijerina made several trips to Mexico to meet with high-ranking officials, including President Luis Echeverría, in quest of support and further legitimacy for the Alianza and the land struggle. Tijerina went to great lengths to convince Mexican politicians to pressure the United States to act in favor of his land struggle.[18] In addition, more than most other leaders of the Chicano movement, Tijerina sought out alliances with Native American and African American leaders, including mainstream black leaders and eventually black-power advocates. The leader of the Alianza perceived these partnerships as a way to radicalize Nuevomexicanos into direct action. He stated:

> we have been forced by destiny to adopt two languages; we will be the future ambassadors and envoys to Latin America. At home, I believe that the Southwest is breeding a special kind of people that will bridge the color-gap between black and white. It will be the brown that fills the gap. . . . We are the people the Indians call their "lost brothers."[19]

Reies López Tijerina represented the radical wing of the Chicano movement, not in ideological terms, but in practice, because he raised the issue of property rights. He was a leader who advocated action when words failed. Rather than allowing the land-grant struggle to appear as an issue between communities, landowners, and the federal government, Tijerina framed the conflict as one between Nuevomexicano and Anglo-American societies. In his discussion of land grants, Tijerina constantly emphasized to Nuevomexicanos that they had been on the land hundreds of years before Anglo-Americans and had established institutions that predated the American conquest of the Southwest.[20] Tijerina eloquently articulated his points:

> They took our land away and gave you powdered milk! They took your trees and grazing away from you and gave you Smokey the Bear! They took your language away and gave you lies in theirs. They took your manhood away and asked you to lie down and be a Good Mexican. They told you we are lazy and cowardly and backward, and you believe them.[21]

Feeling that a successful resolution of the land-grant issue might not be possible, his movement at times even advocated separatism. In order to exemplify the claims of the heirs to these lands, the Alianza set up and proclaimed the Republic of San Joaquín del Río de Chama in the Kit Carson National Forest. In October 1966, a confrontation occurred between forest rangers and members of the Alianza. Three rangers were taken prisoner by the Alianza, tried, convicted of trespassing, given suspended sentences, and released along with their trucks. As a consequence, Tijerina, his brother Cristóbal, and three other Alianza members were arrested by FBI agents and charged with assault on two forest rangers and converting government property to personal use.

The state and national prominence of the Alianza caused great anxiety and concern and brought out the deep class contradictions in New Mexico. An influential and powerful sector of the Nuevomexicano conservative elite seldom, if at all, lent support to the goals of the Alianza, and even less so to Tijerina. They saw him as a troublemaker and an outsider who had come to upset the status quo. In fact, certain Hispanos even conspired in or actively sought his downfall. For example, the highest-ranking Chicano politician, U.S. Senator Joseph Montoya, lashed out against Tijerina, stating that "the last thing the Spanish-speaking need is agitation, rabble-rousing, or creation of false hopes." He also labeled Tijerina an "outsider who sparked violence and set back racial relations and an enemy of the United States."[22]

Because of the pressure and harassment against the Alianza, the organization changed its name to Alianza Federal de Pueblos Libres. The new organization called a meeting in June 1967 in the village of Coyote. The first order of business focused on the San Joaquín land grant. Alfonso Sánchez, the district attorney of Rio Arriba County, sought to stop the Coyote meeting and issued arrest warrants for Tijerina and the leaders of the Alianza. Sánchez alleged that the Alianza was inspired by communists and outside agitators. He had the state police set up roadblocks to arrest Alianza members. During the meeting, eleven Aliancistas were taken into custody. Tijerina and many members of the Alianza, though, slipped through the roadblock and met near the town of Canjilón. The Alianza condemned the arrests as illegal acts designed to derail the organization.

Up to this point, Alianza statements, though radical, had been only rhetorical rejections of the liberal agenda and symbolic acts to affirm historical rights. The clear split from traditional politics occurred with the Tierra Amarilla raid on June 5, 1967. On this date, Tijerina, along with young radical members of his movement, attempted to make a citizen's arrest of the district attorney Sánchez at Tierra Amarilla. Armed Aliancistas entered the Tierra Amarilla courthouse and wounded a state police officer, Nick Saiz, in the chest when he drew his weapon after being warned to drop it. When the Aliancistas failed to find Sánchez, they headed for the mountains near Canjilón with two prisoners, a deputy sheriff and a newspaper reporter.

E. Lee Francis, the lieutenant governor of New Mexico, serving as acting governor (Governor Cargo was out of the state), ordered the National Guard out as well as an array of law enforcement agencies under General John Pershing Jolly to arrest all members of the Alianza involved in the incident. As one scholar states:

> National Guard convoys, state police from all northern counties, local sheriffs and unofficial posses, Jicarilla Apache police and cattle inspectors, all joined the search, equipped with two ammunition tanks, clattering helicopters, droning spotter planes, a hospital van and patrolling jeeps, these forces combed every hamlet, gully and pasture for the insurrectionist who had staged the "bold daylight raid."[23]

About fifty Nuevomexicanos—including old men, women, and children—were held in dire circumstances by the National Guard for hours without shelter, food, or water as bait in an attempt to lure Tijerina and the other Aliancistas out so they could be captured and arrested, or killed if they resisted.

Tijerina was apprehended a short time later and charged with fifty-four criminal counts, including kidnapping and armed assault. At the trial, he defended himself with the help of two court-appointed lawyers, stating, "[Y]es, we are guilty of claiming our lands, guilty of believing in the Treaty of Guadalupe Hidalgo." After a spirited defense, he was acquitted of all charges stemming from the Tierra Amarilla courthouse raid. Upon his release, Tijerina loomed even larger as a hero of the Movimiento, especially to young Chicanos, who saw in him the revolutionary to be emulated. He was seen as the man of action, who not only spoke of ideas, but carried them out, even going so far as to take the law in his own hands.[24]

In 1968, Tijerina ventured into the electoral arena as another way to bring visibility to the Alianza's agenda. He founded the Partido Constitucional del Pueblo and ran under its banner for governor. In his campaign speeches, Tijerina stated that if he were elected, he would represent the poor and the working class. He also promised to establish citizens' police review boards, eliminate property taxes for native Nuevomexicano veterans, investigate all corporations and organizations that had speculated on and profited from the lands of the people, and also address other grassroots issues. In addition, the Partido ran candidates for president and vice president of the United States, for Congress, and for district attorneys and other political offices. However, the campaigns were never to be, since all Alianza candidates were ruled ineligible by the state attorney general and denied ballot status by the New Mexico Secretary of State and the New Mexico Supreme Court.[25]

U.S. government agencies persisted in their attempt to jail Tijerina. It resurrected old charges and added new ones. Tijerina's bail from his 1967 conviction was revoked, and he was sentenced to serve in the Federal Correctional Institution at La Tuna in Anthony, New Mexico-Texas. In early 1970, Tijerina was sentenced to prison for charges related to the 1967 Tierra Amarilla courthouse raid. The presiding judge, Garnett Burkes, denied defense claims of double jeopardy. The leader of the Alianza, who was already serving his federal sentence from 1969 for aiding in the burning of two Forest Service signs, was sentenced for false imprisonment and other charges. He served a little over two years (from June 1969 to July 1971) in a federal prison.[26]

The persecution of other Aliancistas continued. The New Mexico state government filed fifty-four charges against ten other members of the Alianza. Among them were Gerónimo Borunda, Tobías Leyba, Moisés Morales, Jerry Noll, Reies Hugh Tijerina Jr., Juan Valdez, and Salomón Velázquez. After court trials and appeals, they were freed, although for years they lived "under the shadow of prison."[27]

While Tijerina was in prison, the Alianza declined. No one could effectively replace him, and in the absence of his initiative and passion, leadership and membership structure weakened because of unresolved internal ideological and organizational issues. A major shortcoming was its failure to develop ideas beyond those with which it had begun. Other problems stemmed from the fact that the Alianza was never able to develop a foundation of organizational discipline or structure. Another limitation was the fact that the organization could not raise critical funds beyond those collected at rallies; its financial base became precarious, further debilitating the organization.[28]

In 1971, Tijerina was placed on five years' probation on the condition, among others, that he not be an official in the Alianza for a period of time. He was freed from the federal penitentiary at Leavenworth, Kansas, and returned to Albuquerque in July 1971. The experience in prison had greatly changed El Tigre. He was an entirely different person when he was released. Tijerina declared that he had "outgrown militancy."[29]. He no longer preached ethnic pride and confrontation. Specifically, he stated that the bilingual Indohispano should promote "brotherhood awareness" and bridge the gap between the Spanish American countries and the United States, and between blacks and whites. The change was much more than political or ideological; he simply was not the Tijerina of before. What remained were his tendencies toward biocultural constructs.

There were many rumors and much speculation that the leader of the Alianza had been subjected to physical and/or psychological torture while in jail. In addition, his family was constantly harassed and harmed by police officers. (Tijerina's wife and son levied charges of assault and rape against certain law officers.) Continued death threats as well as incidents against his home, such as bombings and shootings, had taken their toll on the leader.

After his release, Tijerina found profound changes in the Alianza and in New Mexico. The land-grant issues no longer dominated the political program of the activists within the state. They were now part of a larger agenda similar to that being raised across the Southwest: political parity, economic equality, educational equity, and full and equal participation in all sectors of the state at every level from top to bottom. In addition, Santiago Tapia y Anaya, one of the former Alianza vice presidents, split from Tijerina and took half of the Alianza members with him because of serious disagreements over the use of the organization's funds for Tijerina's individual activities. Tapia y Anaya also argued that the Alianza did not provide much assistance to many of the land grants outside of Rio Arriba County.

In 1972, Tijerina attempted to reformulate his program and engaged in certain political activities. He organized the Congreso de Tierra y Cultura under the banner of brotherhood awareness. There was tension during the meeting, at which he showcased mainstream Chicano businessmen and politicians. A letter from Rodolfo "Corky" Gonzáles was read that criticized the Alianza and specifically Reies López Tijerina for hobnobbing with and mixing with those he and others termed *vendidos,* or sell-outs. In addition, during the Congreso, many Raza Unida activists insisted that a resolution be passed that recognized the Partido de la Raza Unida as the political representative of the Chicano movement. Tijerina refused to accept it or even allow it to be considered. José Angel Gutiérrez came on stage to speak on the question. In fact, Gutiérrez supported Tijerina's right to set the ground rules for his own Congreso, but most of the rest of the Partido members disagreed. They argued that as conference participants and delegates, they should have a say in the Congreso's outcome. On the second day of the congress, Tijerina walked out. Juan José Peña was then elected permanent chairman and continued with the discussion of the Congreso priorities. In the end, attendees approved the resolution.[30]

The Congreso marked the last major event Tijerina and the Alianza sponsored. It was a failed effort to set a new temper and horizon for the movement. Although the Alianza continued to hold meetings, it began to lose membership and to decline in importance statewide and nationally. After 1972, Tijerina continued his research on land grants in libraries of Mexico and Spain, seeking assistance for his cause from the Organization of American States and the United Nations. He also published his autobiography, *Mi lucha por la tierra*, in Mexico.[31] Clearly this was an effort at political self-promotion, though without organizational context.

In the mid-1970s, a Mexican state-owned production company— CONACINE—produced *Chicano*, a narrative film loosely based on Tijerina's life and political activities. The stated intentions of the producers "were to disseminate information about Alianza's struggle in New Mexico,"[32] yet the film was disappointing and confusing in its depiction of the land struggle and of Tijerina himself. Ultimately, *Chicano* responded more to subject and filmmaking opportunism than to any kind of art or politics. It could have been an important narrative statement on one of the critical segments of the Chicano movement, but it turned out instead to be an incongruent work that focused mainly on sensationalism and stereotypical characters and situations. Tijerina was also the subject of a documentary on commercial television called *The Most Hated Man in New Mexico*. This was a truly negative and misleading documentary that falsified the role and significance of Tijerina and the Alianza.

By then, Reies López Tijerina's influence in the Chicano movement had seriously declined. The establishment had accomplished its task of undermining and ultimately delegitimizing Tijerina, the Alianza, and their program. It has been well documented how the U.S. government systematically and ruthlessly sought to destroy radical movements like the Black and Brown Berets and the Black Panthers. Such was the case with Tijerina. The dominant order could ill tolerate having El Tigre continue to challenge the status quo, inspire generations to bring about social change, and carry forth justice on the issue of land grants. That alone would involve millions of dollars and trample upon some of the most powerful individuals and institutions in New Mexico. As with other leaders of the turbulent 1960s, Tijerina's fate was sealed the minute he joined defiance and passion to action in his struggle. He ultimately relocated his headquarters to a ranch at Coyote, New Mexico. Years later, the leader moved to Albuquerque to be closer to his children. Ever since a mysterious fire destroyed his Albuquerque home, he has alternated between Albuquerque and El Paso, Texas.[33]

Still, Tijerina and the Alianza's legacy endures. In spite of his decline and the lack of resolution of the land claims, the land struggle changed New Mexico and Nuevomexicanos. The Alianza brought hope to many and showed that Chicano resistance to injustice was alive and could surface and struggle even against overwhelming odds. Tijerina's contributions as well as those of the other members of the Alianza forged an inspirational legacy for the Chicano movement and for Nuevomexicano history.

THE RAZA UNIDA PARTY IN NEW MEXICO

Within the Chicano movement, one of the most important initiatives and new perspectives for social change was the creation of the Raza Unida Party in Texas. This party was founded upon a radical alternative to the dominant parties (Democratic and Republican) for greater Chicano representation and the articulation of a Chicano political agenda. Many Chicanos had become dissatisfied with the exclusion and indifference of the dominant political parties regarding critical issues facing the Chicano community. The Democratic and Republican Parties were not responding to or including Chicano issues as part of their political agendas. The Democratic Party did not seek the empowerment of Chicanos—only individual votes at election time. Once the electoral process was over, Chicanos became low to nonexistent in party priorities. The Republican Party was practically indifferent toward the Chicano community. Thus, the creation of a political alternative seemed like one viable experiment in a quest for greater political representation and influence.

The Raza Unida Party had its greatest impact in South Texas, where it was founded. However, it did attract members and followers in other regions and states, including New Mexico. The chapter of La Raza Unida (El Partido de la Raza Unida) in New Mexico would play a substantial role in the development of the Chicano movement. Outside Texas, the Raza Unida Party was not successful in getting its candidates elected to public office. The issues and agendas the candidates presented and ran on, however, clearly encompassed the ideology and concerns of Chicanismo. Particularly important for this party were issues of labor, education, land, police brutality, cultural nationalism, and electoral empowerment.

The Raza Unida Party in New Mexico was formed in late 1971. It established early chapters in Bernalillo, Santa Fe, and San Miguel Counties, then added ones in Rio Arriba, Taos, Union, Lea, Doña Ana, and Grant Counties.

Ideologically, La Raza Unida of Nuevo Mexico had various influences. An obvious one was their own immediate radical heritage of past militant struggles. The New Mexico chapter, moreover, followed ideas that combined Rodolfo "Corky" Gonzales's militant nationalism with José Angel Gutiérrez's political and electoral pragmatism, these men being the two principal ideologues of the national party. Nuevomexicano party members studied and were also influenced by the texts of Pablo Freire on education and Saul Alinsky on community empowerment.

Various Marxist ideologies also became influential in the chapters of La Raza Unida of New Mexico (especially in San Miguel County). For example, the crossover militancy of certain members of La Raza Unida and the Trotskyite Socialist Workers Party facilitated working on a number of issues. The political agenda of La Raza Unida of New Mexico received national coverage in the Socialist Workers Party's newspaper, *The Militant.* This association, however, also brought the New Mexico chapter of La Raza Unida into a major dispute with the national leadership, especially with Gonzales, who emphatically disagreed with the alliance.

La Raza Unida sought to develop a political philosophy that would be compatible with the history of the political struggles of the Chicano people in New Mexico. Thus, they pressed issues of concern to Nuevomexicanos at both the state and local levels. The agenda of the Partido in New Mexico included a variety of critical local issues. For example, in Union and Rio Arriba Counties, the main issue was police brutality; in Taos County, the Partido took up labor issues. The Bernalillo County chapter worked largely on labor and land-grant issues along with matters of police brutality and student organizing with MECHA (Movimiento Estudiantil Chicano de Aztlán) on the University of New Mexico campus. The party in San Miguel County went most strongly into politics and ran candidates at the county and city level as well as for the East Las Vegas School Board.

Even though the New Mexico Raza Unida (like other state chapters) worked its agenda pretty much independently from the national party, certain ties existed. In 1972, the New Mexico chapter was present and active at the

National Convention of La Raza Unida. The following year, New Mexico Raza Unida members attended the national congresses in Denver and Chicago. There, the New Mexico delegation became immersed in the dispute between Gutiérrez and Gonzales. Although various efforts were made to unify the party, they ultimately were unsuccessful. The Raza Unida Party remained bitterly divided at the national level between the followers of the two leaders. This struggle further weakened the party in its overall efforts.

Back home, the candidates of La Raza Unida in New Mexico had to run as write-ins because they encountered many bureaucratic obstacles to being formally included in the ballots. Both the Democratic and the Republican Parties—especially the former—perceived La Raza Unida as a direct threat to votes in their electoral base. Among the first New Mexico Raza Unida candidates were Juan José Peña (who would later become president of the New Mexico chapter), Pedro Rodríguez, and Manuel Archuleta.

In addition to the political aspect, the Partido also developed a strong cultural component made up of supporting artists such as Jesús Aragón and Francisco LeFebre. They made silkscreen posters of Chicano movement themes, especially of "La Familia" (which was the symbol of the party), woodcuts and plaster casts of the Aztec calendar, and flags and banners for marches and demonstrations. In addition, Roberto Archuleta founded El Teatro Norteño, which presented productions of the *actos* of Luis Valdez and related them to issues relevant in New Mexico. The actors were almost all Partido members. The Teatro Norteño was very popular and much in demand all over New Mexico. The Partido also produced its own newspaper and magazine, *La voz del pueblo*, which circulated throughout the state, keeping readers informed on party activities and candidates.

The year 1975 marked the high point of El Partido de la Raza Unida in New Mexico. It had almost 5,000 registered members statewide, with chapters in the counties of Bernalillo, Colfax, Doña Ana, Grant, Lea, Otero, Rio Arriba, Santa Fe, Sandoval, San Miguel, and Taos. La Raza Unida put an electoral strategy into practice in many of the counties where the party had a substantial membership. In other counties, where the membership was small, candidates served as a pressure group, forcing the two traditional parties to include Chicano issues in their platforms.

That year, the Partido ran a full slate of candidates for state and local offices in New Mexico: Juan José Peña for U.S. Senate, Ernesto Borunda for U.S. House of Representatives, Isabel Blea for governor, and Larry Hill for state attorney general. The Partido made a respectable showing in these elections, despite the fact that Nuevomexicanos had faithfully supported candidates from the Democratic and Republican Parties. None of La Raza Unida's candidates were successful in gaining elected office.

In 1976, after the resignation of Gutiérrez, the remaining state presidents of Arizona, California, New Mexico, and Texas elected Peña as national president of the Raza Unida Party. Gutiérrez felt that the time of the Partido had passed and that community organizations would carry on future challenges. Conversely, Peña believed that the Partido should continue to work in the vanguard of the Chicano movement.

As part of a new agenda, the New Mexico Raza Unida Party became interested in Mexican immigration issues. In 1977, the party took a large delegation to the National Conference on Immigration and Social Impact, attended by organizations such as the Socialist Workers Party, the Centro de Acción Social Autónomo (CASA), and the August 29th Movement (ATM). There the delegates agreed on various resolutions that supported the civil rights of undocumented immigrants, principally from Mexico.[34]

By the late 1970s, Raza Unida had suffered a slow but progressive decline. Eventually, its activities were reduced to Rio Arriba, San Miguel, and Otero Counties. Several factors account for this decline. For one thing, the national social climate had changed, and activism in general was declining. In New Mexico, remaining activists were economically strapped, though they initiated various unsuccessful fundraising programs. Others left the party when it broke its ties to the Socialist Workers Party to create community organizations such as Chicanos Unidos para Justicia in Las Vegas, or they joined the Democratic Party to push for Chicano issues in a more traditional manner. Moreover, many core members of La Raza Unida were blacklisted and could not obtain employment in New Mexico. Gradually, they went in different directions, some leaving the state and politics entirely.[35]

During the 1980s, only the chapters of La Raza Unida of San Miguel and Rio Arriba Counties remained active. Also in the 1980s, Enrique Cardiel started a student group in Bernalillo County that advocated for the Raza Unida Party at the University of New Mexico. The chapter was called Raza Unida Estudiantil. Through his efforts, Raza Unida was finally re-registered in New Mexico. However, the party has never regained the importance it once had.

The Nuevomexicano candidates of La Raza Unida were not successful in statewide elections; they were not elected to office in any of the races they entered. However, their role and significance transcended such losses. In essence, the Partido played a positive role in the political arena of New Mexico. Through political campaigns, Raza Unida candidates gained valuable experience in the art and management of politics. They would use their experience in later endeavors. More importantly, La Raza Unida brought certain Chicano issues into the political debate that the traditional parties consistently omitted. Clearly, it was the Democratic Party that La Raza Unida threatened in the polls and ultimately forced to alter its agenda. As a consequence, Democratic candidates from then on generally included and addressed Chicano issues, and more important, fulfilled their election promises.

STATEWIDE SOCIAL ACTIVISM

The Chicano movement in New Mexico involved many individuals and organizations that singly and collectively labored to bring about significant social change. In fact, various manifestations were at the grassroots level and focused on specific issues that were of major concern for the Chicano community. Particularly outstanding was the community organizing work conducted by María Varela and the communication work of Elizabeth "Betita" Martínez. Both women have been widely recognized for their seminal activities. Grassroots initiatives took different forms of action and may have appeared to be independent of each other, yet they all had the common goal of achieving a greater degree of empowerment for the community. Out of the multitude of such initiatives, a sample of the most important are discussed below.

The Movimiento in Santa Fe was of particularly importance. Ricardo Maes, one of Santa Fe's leading Chicano activists, was instrumental in setting up the Escuela Tonantzin in Santa Fe, supported by the Comité Central de Barrios. Named after an Aztec goddess to pay homage to the Chicano's indigeneous Mexican heritage, the Escuela Tonantzin was established in the old Our Lady of Victory convent. This was the first Chicano movement school to open in New Mexico. According to Maes, the courses at the Escuela Tonantzin consisted of "basic requirements, such as reading, spelling and math, but will be taught with Chicano methods and content rather than the traditional educational philosophy."[36] The school was well received and supported. Despite its fine beginning, however, it soon ended.

Shortly after it was founded, police chased some youths from downtown Santa Fe to the school, and a barrage of gunfire and tear gas ensued that lasted until the next morning. Accounts varied regarding who had started the shooting and whether the first shots had come from inside the school or from the police. A number of residents of the school were wounded in the fusillade, but no one was killed. The school was closed after the incident. The sponsoring church felt that they were running too high a risk of liability if the school were to be kept open and another incident occurred. With limited success, similar efforts at providing alternative education to Chicano youth continued in Santa Fe throughout the 1970s.

Labor organizing and conflict was an ongoing aspect of the Movimiento. Chicano workers undertook a period of intense labor struggles all over New Mexico during the 1970s. Chris Eichwald Cebada of La Raza Unida Labor Committee worked with Santiago Maestas and other activists to organize and mobilize state workers, especially those involved in delivering social services and in corrections. Sanitation workers in Artesia went on strike and almost immediately gained support from Chicano movement organizations around New Mexico. The Bobby García Memorial Clinic sent its medical van to Artesia to assist the workers. The Chicano Youth Association and the organization AHORA at Eastern New Mexico University joined the efforts of the workers for better working conditions and better pay. César Chávez came to New Mexico several times in support of the Artesia strikers, who made important gains in the settlement of the strike.

Other labor movements organized by Chicano workers flourished throughout New Mexico during the 1970s. The strikes continued a long tradition of labor conflict and organizing movements carried out by Nuevomexicano workers throughout the twentieth century. For example, there were strikes by molybdenum miners in Questa, sanitation workers in Albuquerque and Santa Fe, supermarket workers in Taos, lumber mill workers in Española, hospital workers in Silver City, garment workers and janitors in Albuquerque, meat cutters in Clovis and Albuquerque, and Southern Union Gas Company employees in Albuquerque. Ultimately, Nuevomexicano workers managed to improve their job conditions and lives. The workers were inspired by the greater Chicano civil rights struggle in New Mexico and elsewhere.

Chicanos against the Vietnam War carried out specific mobilizations. The student movement in New Mexico against the war was intense and sizable, and demonstrations within the state were influential and a matter of grave concern for state and national authorities. Chicano students were an integral part of these movements. They had a good reason besides those of conscience and principle to oppose American involvement in the war: many Nuevomexicanos fought in Vietnam. As it turned out, 77 percent of New Mexico's draftees for the war effort were Chicanos, and the vast majority wound up in combat units, where they and other Latinos accounted for about 20 percent of the total U.S. casualties. The student organization United Mexican American Students (UMAS) organized and led protests against the war.

On October 15, 1969, the day of the Vietnam Moratorium and the peak of the antiwar mobilizations, over 3,000 people participated in a huge demonstration in Albuquerque. In addition, about 300 protested in Santa Fe, and other demonstrations took place in Taos and other New Mexico cities.

Chicano students were an integral part of antiwar demonstrations in the early 1970s. On May 8, 1970, there were massive protests by UNM students against the Kent State University killings by the National Guard. Chicano workers at the UNM physical plant also walked out on strike. Student protesters gathered at the Student Union building, and shortly thereafter, the New Mexico National Guard charged the crowd, wounding several and sending the others fleeing in panic. Meanwhile, the Chicano physical plant workers were detained in the medical building. Other student protests against the Vietnam War were also disbanded through repression.[37] These demonstrations and protests by Chicanos continued in the last years of the war and were instrumental in pressuring for a settlement of the armed conflict.

One person who made significant and multifaceted contributions in organizational efforts was María Varela. Born of Mexican immigrants who labored as farmworkers in the northeastern United States, she moved to New Mexico during the mid 1960s. She quickly became an active supporter and member of the Alianza Federal de Mercedes and the Crusade for Justice.

In the late 1970s, Varela collaborated with Reies López Tijerina's brothers in establishing La Clínica del Norte, where she served as overall coordinator. In addition to her services with the Clínica, she was instrumental in establishing a ranch and farm cooperative, called La Cooperativa. Her skills in getting people to come together for a goal or issue were remarkable. Through these efforts, essential and much-needed services were brought to the Chicano community.

In 1979, Varela, together with two of her neighbors and friends, formed another cooperative, Ganados del Valle, whose purpose was to establish an organized market for cattle ranchers; to set up and market weaving and livestock products and thus help create jobs; to protect ancestral land and water cultures; and to create business structures to better develop product and marketing strategies. The cooperative was most successful in aiding over 200 artisans and farmers to refinance, package, price, and market their products successfully. In addition, Ganados del Valle provided crucial individual loans to members. The cooperative also defended the lands and water rights from outside developers and fringe environmentalists. An innovative college program was funded to help staff and community members continue their education.

Varela subsequently formed her own company, the Rural Resources

Group, which stressed economic development, policy studies, and recommendations to lawmakers. In this organization as in previous ones, Varela promoted and galvanized extensive and intense participation by Chicanas.

EDUCATIONAL AND CULTURAL RENAISSANCE

The Chicano movement inspired and served as a catalyst in generating a cultural renaissance that encompassed all the arts and educational endeavors. New Mexico was an integral contributor to this flowering and produced critical student movements and several of the most gifted Chicano artists and writers. Their works derived from the years of struggle and its aftermath. This artistic dynamism continued, concurrently with efforts to revitalize higher education for Chicanos, even after overt political activity had declined or transformed. Efforts in education are of special note and had lasting consequences.

CHICANO STUDIES: AN EDUCATIONAL ALTERNATIVE

As on many other university campuses, Chicano movement inspired students were clearly the principal driving force for the creation of Chicano studies at the University of New Mexico in the early 1970s. In addition, select faculty and the community lent their support. The initial effort toward the creation of Chicano studies came about with the rise of the Chicano student movement. The political and social climate of the 1960s significantly influenced this student generation, as did early Movimiento activists. Students reacted strongly to the lack of interest in incorporating themes or issues dealing with the Chicano experience into the existing university curriculum and established fields of study. Not only was there an absence of coursework and materials on the Chicano community, but also Chicano faculty were scarce in the academic departments at UNM.

The Chicano student organization, UMAS, exerted intense pressure on the central UNM administration, calling for the creation of Chicano studies. Its members were part of the first student generation that had been aided by such programs as the College Enrichment Program. This provided financial aid and made possible the means for a university education for substantial numbers of Chicano and Chicana students. By the late 1960s, Nuevomexicano students had increased their numbers at UNM, but they only made up about 10 percent of the entire student body. In a state where the total Chicano population was around 40 percent, the situation was in dire need of attention and resolution.[38]

Chicano faculty were almost invisible at the University of New Mexico in the mid 1960s. Only five full-time Chicano faculty members were on tenure-track appointments: three in the School of Education, one in the Department of Spanish and Portuguese, and one in the Department of Mathematics. For the most part, the existing faculty did not endorse the goals or strategies of the Chicano movement; they were indifferent and at times even hostile to the creation of Chicano studies. Faculty members, almost without exception, were from a patriotic and conservative earlier generation. They supported gradual social change, managed through the rules of the system. The majority of the Chicano faculty emphatically opposed confrontational politics and what they perceived to be the radicalism of the Chicano movement generation.

After sustained student pressure, the initial response of the UNM administration was to reluctantly broaden the concept of Chicano studies to include other minority groups. Originally, the central administration proposed the creation of a program of ethnic studies, lumping all ethnic group studies into one program. Students rejected this model quickly and soundly. UMAS demanded the creation of a separate Chicano studies program.

Finally, in the early 1970s, the UNM central administration named the first full-time director of Chicano Studies: Richard Griego, of the Department of Mathematics. The conceptual ideas and structure of the Program of Chicano Studies were not entirely worked out at first. The creation of a major in Chicano studies was the most salient goal. Students remained the single most influential force in the first phase of the program, as was clearly reflected in its emphasis on student services and needs. After its first year, Antonio Mondragón assumed the directorship of the Chicano studies program.

By the mid 1970s an important change had occurred. Chicano studies was divided into two separate programs—one that continued its student and service orientation, and another that focused upon a teaching and research agenda. Mondragón continued to serve as director of the student services program. The first specialist in the field of Chicano Studies, Tobías Durán, was hired as director of the academic program. He held this position until the mid 1990s. From the outset, Chicano studies served as a coordinating unit for the teaching of the Chicano experience at UNM. The academic program also offered a modest teaching program through the Department of American Studies; its director consistently taught various courses and hired part-time faculty to offer others. Thus, for a long time, Chicano studies exposed students, however imperfectly, to the training and research of the Chicano experience.

Women, while not visible in leadership roles, were certainly active in campus events and sought to expand the curriculum in Chicano studies by offering courses on the Chicana. Beverly Sánchez, a master's student in sociology, and Erlinda Gonzales-Berry, a doctoral student in Spanish, taught the first such course. After offering the course for two semesters through women's studies, a group of female students called a meeting with the director of Chicano studies and invited all interested students to attend. They proposed that the course be made part of the Chicano studies curriculum. After intense discussion of the role of feminism in the Chicano movement, the group voted to move the course to the Chicano studies program. "La Chicana" was offered for several semesters as part of the curriculum. Eventually it reverted to women's studies, where it is still taught today.

Erlinda Gonzales-Berry recalls:

Those were heady days. The atmosphere at the meeting was filled with tension, but the *mujeres* were prepared to battle the male front like true *soldaderas*. As I recall, the *vatos* were very civil and we left the meeting feeling elated because we had moved the cause of Chicanas an inch forward within our sheltered university environment. I don't know how the course ended up back in women's studies, since that happened after I left UNM. Perhaps the director couldn't handle all those pushy *viejas*. A less jaundiced explanation is that it may have been part of a financial strategy for expanding our curriculum. In other words, get someone else to pay for the course.[39]

In the 1980s, two important phenomena changed and dramatically improved Chicano studies at UNM. First, traditional academic departments, among them anthropology, economics, education, English, history, political science, sociology, and Spanish and Portuguese, began hiring Chicano and Chicana professors whose main field of specialization was in Chicano studies. Eventually, a critical mass of academicians was offering a wide range of coursework and research initiatives on the Chicano experience.

The second major development was the founding of the Southwest Hispanic Research Institute (SHRI). The Chicano core faculty believed that although UNM had a prestigious teaching and research program on Latin America, it was lacking one on the Chicano experience. The UNM Latin American program did not include coursework or carry out research on Chicanos or Latinos in the United States. The program followed tradition by restricting its study to themes and subjects south of the U.S.-Mexican border. The central administration agreed to examine the request of the Chicano faculty concerning initiatives that would stress a Chicano agenda. A committee was appointed to examine alternatives and present suggestions applicable to the needs and purposes of UNM. After reviewing programs and centers nationwide, the Chicano faculty presented a report with concrete suggestions. It called for the creation of an academic unit, an institute, that would serve as a catalyst and promoter of a substantial research agenda on the Chicano experience. The goal was for the new institute to foster and develop a knowledge base upon which the Chicano faculty could design and carry out a new and comprehensive curriculum on the Chicano experience.

The creation of SHRI meant that Chicano studies at UNM was now expanded through the research aspects and initiatives of the new institute. The teaching responsibilities were to be principally held by the existing Program of Chicano Studies. David R. Maciel, of the Department of History, was appointed the first director of the SHRI. He was succeeded by Mary Lucy Jaramillo, of the School of Education, José Rivera, of Urban Planning and Public Administration, and Felipe Gonzales, of the Department of Sociology.

From their inception to the present, Chicano studies and the SHRI have been distinct. Chicano studies remained for the most part on the fringes of the greater university agenda. Its founding base was restricted to the support of the program director and minimal part-time faculty. To a large degree, the program remained static. Chicano studies did not receive full support from such critical actors as the central administration, faculty from the rest of the university, and the community. Nonetheless, Chicano studies played a paramount role in advancing critical goals and purpose. Its main contribution was in effectively pressuring existing departments into hiring Chicano and Chicana faculty. In addition, Chicano studies offered coursework on Chicano issues until the gap began to be filled by traditional academic departments. And most important of all, it exposed and provided training in the Chicano experience to generations of students who otherwise would never have discovered certain aspects of their history, culture, and society.

It is a paradox that in a state such as New Mexico, where the population base of the Chicano community, compared with that of the dominant society, is the largest in the United States, and where Chicanos occupy positions of importance in all facets of the state, Chicano studies did not develop into one of the premier programs in the nation. Its potential is great, but it remains to be seen whether faculty, students, leaders, and community support can make it so in the future. Perhaps the program's future will be more glorious than its past.

The Southwest Hispanic Research Institute, on the other hand, has substantially increased its founding base and its role within the university. SHRI has successfully engaged in fundraising activities, created joint appointments (thus increasing Chicano and Chicana faculty), organized research, and at times been a critical lobby in university affairs.

The most recent development in Chicano studies programs at UNM was the creation of the Center for Regional Studies in the early 1990s through an initiative introduced by Tobías Durán. He secured a line-item allocation of the state budget from the New Mexico legislature, which generously funded the creation of the center. Its main purpose and priorities were to sponsor research and outreach programs, principally on the Nuevomexicano experience. Over the years, the center has supported research, artistic programs, publications, and outreach programs and has granted numerous undergraduate, master's, and postdoctoral fellowships.[40]

The Movimiento at New Mexico Highlands University (NMHU) had a different experience from that at UNM. Situated in the middle of a predominantly Chicano population center (east Las Vegas was 75 percent Chicano, west Las Vegas 95 percent), NMHU had not developed any academic programs related to the Chicano experience by the late 1960s. Out of 106 full-time Highlands faculty members in 1969, only 5 were minorities. The reason, according to then-president Thomas Donnelly, was the lack of qualified individuals.[41] In reality, Highlands was a reflection and a symbol of the deprivileged status of Nuevomexicanos in their own land.

By that time, however, echoes of the Chicano movement and other civil rights organizations had reached Las Vegas and student mobilizations started. At Highlands, veterans of Vietnam (who enrolled at NMHU on the G.I. Bill of Rights) and returning students were the ones who initially participated in this emerging student movement. The influence of the Alianza's youth organization, Los Caballeros de las Indias, was critical, as were Tijerina's actions and personal charisma. In 1969, the Spanish American Student Organization (SASO) was founded. Its title would seem disruptive to the Chicano movement, given its stress on a particular definition of identity politics. Yet, in spite of using the traditional term "Spanish Americans," SASO's agenda included the empowerment of Chicanos at NMHU. Specifically, the organization sought a stronger voice for its student membership, the hiring of Hispano faculty, the preservation of Nuevomexicano culture and the Spanish language, and the naming of buildings on behalf of illustrious Nuevomexicanos. Furthermore, SASO supported the causes of the Movimiento. For example, the organization began its activities by picketing the Columbia Market in Las Vegas for selling grapes and lettuce, which were boycotted by the United Farm Workers and its leader, César Chávez. In order to fulfill its goals, SASO took over the *Highlands Candle* (NMHU's student newspaper) and also published the underground newspaper, *El machete*.

SASO struggled successfully for control of the Highlands Student Senate in 1969. Certain faculty members such as Willie Sánchez from the Department of Mathematics guided the organization through the shoals of university politics. Black students and Anglo liberals were SASO's allies. One of the student leaders, Francisco "Comanche" Gonzáles, stated: "[W]e saw how we had to take over the whole institution. We did it legally; we started by first taking over the Student Senate. We started by doing and changing things that were fun for students, showing them that there was success in unity, and then went for the big fish."[42] Once SASO took over the senate, its members called for an investigation of racial discrimination at Highlands. They voiced complaints regarding the lack of Chicano professors and inadequate counseling for minority students.

Particularly important were the ties that SASO managed to create with the community, and specifically with certain local politicians who were openly critical of the entrenched Anglo administration at Highlands. One of the most vocal critics was a Highlands alumnus: San Miguel's district attorney, Donaldo "Tiny" Martínez. He was a key founder of the Chicano Action Committee, which supported changes in the university. Martínez allegedly was also the publisher of an underground magazine, *La revista norteña*, which disseminated information about the student movement. Martín Suazo, the commander of the Las Vegas capter of the American G.I. Forum, was another critical ally in this effort. He called for an investigation into possible racial discrimination at NMHU. In addition, the leader of the San Miguel Republican Party, Junio López, headed a special legislative committee to investigate allegations of racial discrimination at Highlands.[43]

SASO and its allies pressured the NMHU central administration. As a consequence, President Donnelli announced his retirement in late 1969 and a search for a new President started. Students and the community alike perceived a window of opportunity for the nomination of a Chicano president. They favored John Aragón. However, when the selection procedure was completed in 1970, the university committee selected Charles Graham from Wisconsin. Joe Otero, the only Chicano member of the Board of Regents, resigned because of the blatant discrimination the committee displayed regarding Aragón's candidacy.

Student and community mobilizations against the president-elect sprang up. When students peacefully occupied the Highlands administration building, a large rally was held at the Plaza in west Las Vegas to show support for the students. The central administration tried to resolve the case using force. Roberto Mondragón, the lieutenant governor, supported the students and opposed policy action against them. Moreover, the American G.I. Forum of New Mexico and the League of United Latin American Citizens (LULAC) took strong positions against the selection of Graham. Martínez filed charges of discrimination against three members of the Board of Regents as well as a temporary restraining order that prevented Graham from securing his position as president. Seeing the pronounced opposition against him, Graham turned the offer down.

In the early 1970s, while Ralph Carlisle Smith was interim president (September 1970–August 1971), conditions were propitious for the implementation of various points of SASO's agenda. Governor Bruce King, inaugurated in 1971, designated new regents (two Nuevomexicanos and another three who supported the Chicano agenda to some extent). One was Father James T. Burke, the pastor of Our Lady of Sorrows Catholic Church in Las Vegas; he was instrumental in helping SASO disseminate information about its movement.

A Chicano agenda had a brief period of flowering at NMHU in the early 1970s. Highlands's mission statement was altered to promote policy objectives that sought to "reinforce the cultural identity for Spanish-speaking students" while "developing leadership for the socio-economic and cultural development of the area affected by the university." Federal grants to combat unequal educational opportunities were flowing to the universities, and Willie Sanchez, the vice president for external affairs, and other administrators realized that Highlands was eligible to receive these new funds. With the new Highlands Board of Regents, a sympathetic interim university president, and increased federal funding, Chicano faculty were recruited nationwide and brought in. The aspiration of making this university an intellectual center of the Chicano movement was voiced. The fact that the first conference of the National Association of Chicano Studies (NACS) took place at Highlands in 1972 certainly exemplified this goal.

In the early 1970s, SASO changed its name to CASO (Chicano Associated Student Organization). The change responded to the increasing awareness within the student body and the community about their Indo-Hispano roots and better reflected the civil rights struggle in which they were involved. Two prominent women were instrumental in the activities of CASO: Adelita Medina, who collaborated on the newspaper *El grito del norte,* and Sylvia Gutiérrez, who had been in close contact with the Alianza Federal de Mercedes.[44]

In August 1971, the new Highlands Board selected a new president,

Francisco Angel. SASO took credit for the victory in spite of the fact that the search committee had overlooked the community's candidate, John Aragón. President Angel's tenure did not respond to all the expectations, yet he did manage to implement bilingual education and ethnic studies programs and support programs for minorities and faculty development programs on cultural awareness. Furthermore, Chicano faculty and administrators were hired until about one-third of all faculty members were Chicanos.

The first director of Chicano studies was Pedro Rodríguez, a professor of art. He assumed the position in 1971. Inspired by the Plan of Santa Bárbara, a blueprint for designing and implementing Chicano studies classes and programs at the post-secondary level, he sponsored the creation of a Chicano studies advisory body with representation from students, faculty, and community. Rodríguez brought in Chicano community elders such as Cleofes Vigil, a poet and composer of *alabados*, and an editorialist for *El grito del norte*. He also implemented an interdisciplinary program of courses in Chicano studies that involved three majors and three minors. As director, Rodríguez brought to Highlands the artistic and literary aspects of the Reconquista. Specifically, he brought mural art to Northern New Mexico. Rodríguez and his students painted at least six murals on campus. His paintings were influenced by the *maestros* of Mexican muralism, which explains his support for a summer exchange program in Mexico for Nuevomexicano art students to receive training from Mexican muralistas.

Rodríguez was also an activist. Along with Juan José Peña, Manuel Archuleta, and others, he promoted the creation of a chapter of the Raza Unida Party in Las Vegas. Several Chicano faculty and CASO members supported their effort, although others were deeply involved with the Democratic Party, controlled by "Tiny" Martínez. Eventually, Rodríguez was elected San Miguel County chairman of La Raza Unida—one of the most active chapters in the state. His militancy was, however, a factor in his tenure at Highlands. In late 1973, Rodríguez was forced to leave Chicano studies at NMHU because he was denied tenure. As he stated, "[T]here was a great deal of student activism at the time. Yet, there was a great deal of resistance from the firmly entrenched faculty at the time."[45]

A new period of mobilization started in late 1973. Students organized a takeover of the administration building. They managed to secure Las Vegas community support; thus, when Chicano students were arrested as a result of their mobilization, the response of the community was outstanding. The next day, $500,000 in property bonds were posted by Las Vegas community members to get students out of jail. In light of such an overwhelming response, the regents had to support Chicano student demands. It was in this atmosphere that Juan José Peña became the new director of Chicano studies. He expanded the course offerings in both Chicano and ethnic studies.

By 1975, the Chicano movement at Highlands had begun to decline. There were a number of reasons for the reversal of the movement's fortunes. In New Mexico, a new coalition of Republicans and conservative Democrats, "the cowboy coalition," took control of the state legislature. At Highlands, President Angel retired. The incoming president, John Aragón, who labeled himself a Chicano, pursued an anti-Chicano agenda once in office. He downplayed the growth of the ethnic studies programs with the argument that they should be part of mainstream departments. Funding became more scarce for Chicano studies. The lack of resources was one of the main reasons for the departure of Chicano faculty. Only Peña and Anselmo Arellano remained, and in the end, Peña left too. By this time, the student movement was weakened, and the majority of those who became activists had graduated and left Las Vegas to find employment or to pursue graduate work elsewhere. Others who were members of CASO and La Raza Unida were blacklisted and had to leave Las Vegas and even the state.[46]

A powerful anti-Chicano backlash, once latent, found full expression in Las Vegas. The university sought to erase all traces of the Chicano mobilization. Certain media were particularly helpful. A striking symbol of the new times was the destruction of the six murals painted during the height of the Movimiento on the NMHU campus. This vandalism occurred during a summer break in the 1980s.

Although there are currently Chicano faculty and administrative representation at UNM and NMHU, Chicano studies has not received the priority or support it deserves from policy makers and administrators. Given the history, tradition, and ethnic makeup of New Mexico, neglect of or even hostility toward Chicano studies might seem contradictory or difficult to understand. The explanation lies in the fact that Chicano studies reflects a more critical perspective of Nuevomexicanos in the state and nationwide, one that represents a clear challenge to the status quo by providing a critical viewpoint on the Nuevomexicano experience and even advocating the need to bring about a change in the power structures of the state.[47]

The movement in New Mexico inspired a cultural flowering throughout the state. The Academia de la Nueva Raza is a critical example. *Penitente, santero*, musician, and serrano sage, Cleofes Vigil became a symbol of the traditional culture and beliefs of New Mexico. His particular style and personality became an example of what would be named the Academia de la Nueva

Raza. This artistic Chicano think tank was founded in 1969 in Dixon. As part of its cultural endeavors, the Academia published the periodical *La resolana* and other booklets, such as *Entre verde y seco* and *El cuaderno de vez en cuando*. The writings were philosophical treatises on the nature and essence of Chicanismo. The membership of the Academia included Estevan Arellano, Amos Atencio, Tomás Atencio, Alberto Barros, Luis Jaramillo, Alberto Lobato, Alejandro "Jerry" López, Ernesto Antonio Mares, Vicente Martínez, Antonio Medina, Consuelo Pacheco, and Lorenzo Valdez. Instead of organizing demonstrations and other political activities, the core of the Academia generated conceptual ideas on Nuevomexicano culture in northern New Mexico and its historical roots. Academia members were interested in examining the ties between northern Nuevomexicano culture and other indigenous cultures in the Americas.

A $70,000 grant from the Presbyterian Church funded the Academia and kept it afloat for about twenty years. Its members recorded a great deal of oral history, which was a critical source for their writings. The purpose was to use the vernacular language and thoughts of the common people to develop a concept of cultural liberation similar to what the Penitentes had used during the Movimiento del Pueblo in the 1890s. Specifically, the idea was to use the concepts of agricultural societies as a bridge to a cybersociety. The Academia, however, was criticized by some for not using and printing in standard Spanish. At times, its members faced difficulties in getting their opinions accepted and discussed. Yet the contributions of the Academia were major, both in the preservation of cultural traditions and in the members' own creative work.

Through the efforts of the Academia to recognize the value of Nuevomexicano ideas and philosophy came an appreciation for the native arts of northern New Mexico such as weaving; painting; the carving of *santos, bultos,* and *retablos;* Penitente music; and dances such as *Los comanches, Los matachines,* and *Las inditas.* All of these artistic manifestations are now being acknowledged and displayed in museums all over the United States. In addition, the Academia encouraged the elders to play and record traditional songs accompanied by traditional instruments such as guitars, violins, and accordions. This institution was instrumental in capturing and maintaining the special essence and rich cultural traditions of northern New Mexico. The Academia indeed showcased the beauty and timeless nature of northern Nuevomexicanos with great sensitivity and reverence.

El grito del norte and other Raza newspapers were among the most important cultural manifestations to emerge from the Chicano movement. The newspapers carried the voices, soul, promise, and actions of the participants in the civil rights struggle to wider audiences. *El grito del norte,* founded by Elizabeth "Betita" Martinez in Española, was an important instrument for disseminating Movimiento issues and a vehicle for raising ethnic consciousness.

With great conviction and purpose, Chicano and Chicana reporters for *El grito* covered the principal questions that Nuevomexicanos addressed and fought for throughout the state. The intense activism, confrontations, victories, and defeats of the Chicano civil rights struggle are nowhere better captured than in the issues and pages of this newspaper. Specifically, *El grito* covered the activities of the Alianza Federal and the student movement. It publicized articles 2 and 12 of the New Mexico Constitution of 1912, which guaranteed Nuevomexicanos the protections of their rights under the Treaty of Guadalupe Hidalgo and the equality of Nuevomexicano children in schools, including the preparation of teachers in the Spanish language so that they could teach Spanish-speaking children.

History, labor, gender, politics, education, the Movimiento in other states, and Latin American and Third World social movements are but a few of the stories that appeared consistently in *El grito del norte*.[48] The newspaper also reported on Anglo, black, and Native American social movements in the United States. Reading *El grito*, Nuevomexicanos realized that they were not alone in fighting for social justice, but rather part of a worldwide struggle for justice and equality. The newspaper promoted the concept of *sin fronteras*—a struggle that knew no borders. Its "We Are Not Alone" articles emphasized that Chicanos were an integral part of the 600 million Latin Americans and that outside support would come for New Mexico's Chicano movement from Chicanos elsewhere in the United States and from the people of Latin America.

Newspapers were not the only educational and cultural manifestations. The political climate and struggles for social justice waged by Nuevomexicanos fostered and inspired a Movimiento literary generation that produced such writers as Rudolfo Anaya, who published one of the earliest and most revered Chicano novels, *Bless Me, Ultima*, in addition to a series of other novels, short stories, plays, and travel books. In theater, the Teatro Norteño would be followed by the prominent Chicano theatre group based in Albuquerque, La Compañia de Albuquerque, which has gained state and national renown. Furthermore, artists contributing to plastic as well as visual forms emerged in New Mexico and captured the struggles, history, and life of the community in murals, posters, graphic art, sculptures, lithographs, and graffiti.

When established publishing houses had no interest in including Chicano and Chicana authors or themes in their works, Nuevomexicanos—like other Chicanos across the country—founded their own presses and journals.

One important cultural outlet was *De colores: Journal of Emerging Raza Philosophies,* established by the journalist and writer José Armas in Albuquerque. This literary journal published numerous Nuevomexicano authors and included all literary genres in the issues. Various of its contributors began their publishing careers in the pages of *De colores.* El Norte Publications, a vestige of La Nueva Academia de la Raza, still publishes the occasional Nuevomexicano literary text.

A FINAL REFLECTION

By the late 1970s, the activist aspects of the Chicano movement had transformed noticeably, seeming to indicate a decline in energy. It had seen over a decade of continuous struggle, and these intense years of dedication and involvement in the civil rights movement had taken their toll. Numerous Nuevomexicanos, like other Chicanos, were worn out both physically and spiritually. Constant repression and harassment had affected them, and many changed their strategies, advocating the need to change the system from within or through the strengthening of community or political organizations. Others graduated from college or started families and faced new responsibilities. For a few, disenchantment caused by a failure to resolve the issues led them to drop out and let others continue the struggle.

The United States and the state of New Mexico had also changed. A conservative trend had emerged in reaction to the liberalism of the 1960s. The political climate affected individuals and policies in New Mexico; many began to follow national trends.

The Chicano movement in New Mexico also suffered and was severely limited by the class interests and assimilationist perspectives of established and conservative Hispanos as well as by powerful the Anglo forces that opposed it. Both of these groups perceived the civil rights struggle as a real threat to their privileges, and they did not desire a change in structure or power elite. They were the old guard—the gatekeepers—whose privileged positions were substantiated in large part by the workings of the status quo. These Hispano and Anglo elites had worked out their respective assigned roles. Even though Hispanos only alternated in positions of dominance, or at best had to settle for secondary appointments, they were nonetheless complacent and satisfied with this arrangement. The Hispanic voices and actions that opposed and even undermined the progress of the Chicano movement were particularly divisive and negative. The goals and ideology of the Movimiento went against the "so called harmonious inter-ethnic condition" of the state of New Mexico.[49]

Nevertheless, remarkable progress had been made, and the Chicano movement had indeed left an enduring mark. The Movimiento was a defining moment—a defining event—for Nuevomexicano history and society. As in greater Aztlán, the Reconquista in New Mexico raised ethnic consciousness, developed pride in Indo-Hispano roots and legacy, and heightened awareness of the deprivileged status of large segments of the Chicana and Chicano community. The land struggle under Reies López Tijerina was an inspiration and a symbol of defiance and valor for all. Chicano Studies programs were established at the University of New Mexico and New Mexico Highlands University and have expanded and matured. Civil rights leaders organized important coalitions. Political mobilizations took place, and Chicanos and Chicanas were elected and appointed to key state and local offices, including that of governor. A notable and creative cultural movement emerged and developed.[50]

The Reconquista in New Mexico forever changed the collective mentality and pride of Nuevomexicanos in their heritage and legacy. The fruits of the struggle can be observed in the Movimiento generations that are now practicing professionals, politicians, and community activists striving to carry out the promises and mission of Chicanismo in the post-Movimiento era.

NOTES

1. Juan Gómez-Quiñones, *Chicano Politics* (Albuquerque: University of New Mexico Press, 1990), 101–2.

2. See Leo Grebler et al., *The Mexican-American People: The Nation's Second Largest Minority* (New York: Free Press, 1970).

3. Richard Griswold del Castillo and Arnoldo de León, *North to Aztlán* (New York: Twayne Publishers, 1996), 129–30.

4. Gómez-Quiñones, 103–4.

5. On the aspects of the Chicano movement, see chap. 2 of Carlos Muñoz, *Youth, Identity, Power: The Chicano Movement* (New York: Verso, 1989), 47–73.

6. Richard Griego, interview by David R. Maciel, Albuquerque, N.M., June 23, 1997.

7. Practically all the general histories of New Mexico discuss the positive aspects of the Nuevomexicano experience. See, e.g., Susan A. Roberts and Calvin A. Roberts, *New Mexico* (Albuquerque: University of New Mexico Press, 1988).

8. David J. Weber, *Foreigners in Their Native Land* (Albuquerque: University of New Mexico Press, 1973), provides ample discussion of the land-grant question in the nineteenth century.

9. Reies López Tijerina, interview by Juan José Peña, Albuquerque, N.M., July 12, 1982.

10. Cited in Patricia Bell Blawis, *Tijerina and the Land Grants: Mexican Americans in Struggle for Their Heritage* (New York: International, 1971).

11. Ignacio M. García, *Chicanismo: The Forging of a Militant Ethos among Mexican Americans* (Tucson: University of Arizona Press, 1997), 32.

12. Cited in Richard Gardner, *Grito: Reies López Tijerina and the New Mexico Land Grant War of 1967* (Indianapolis: Bobbs-Merrill, 1970), 34.

13. Gómez-Quiñones, 115–16.

14. Elizabeth Sutherland Martínez and Enriqueta Longeaux y Vásquez, *Viva la raza! The Struggle of the Mexican-American People* (Garden City, N.Y.: Doubleday, 1974), 160.

15. Ibid.

16. Manuel P. Servín, *An Awakened Minority: The Mexican Americans* (Beverly Hills: Glencoe Press, 1974), 200.

17. Griswold and de Léon, 129–30.

18. Arturo Santamaría Gómez, *La política entre México y Aztlán* (Culiacán: Universidad Autónoma de Sinaloa, 1994), 73–77.

19. Cited in Blawis, 139.

20. Griswold and de Léon, 129–30.

21. Sutherland Martínez and Longeaux y Vásquez, 161.

22. Cited in Peter Nabokob, *Tijerina and the Courthouse Raid* (Albuquerque: University of New Mexico Press, 1969), 159–60.

23. Ibid., 12.

24. Griswold and de Léon, 129–30.

25. "Maestas for Governor," *El grito del norte*, Oct. 31, 1968.

26. See "Reies Sentenced," ibid.; "News of Tijerina from Jail," ibid., June 5, 1970; and "Tijerina to Be Freed," ibid.

27. *El grito del norte*, July–Aug. 1973.

28. Gómez-Quiñones, 117.

29. Ibid. See also "Tijerina Comes Home," *El grito del norte*, June 5, 1971.

30. See "Torture of Tijerina," *El grito del norte*, Apr. 26, 1971, and "A Story of Repression and Rape," ibid., Oct. 28, 1971.

31. "Congress of Land and Cultural Reform?" *El grito del norte*, Nov. 1972. See also Reies López Tijerina, *Mi lucha por la tierra* (México: Fondo de Cultura Económica, 1978).

32. David R. Maciel, *El bandolero, el pocho, y la raza: imágenes cinematográficas del chicano* (México: UNAM/UNM, 1994), has a detailed review and discussion of the film *Chicano*.

33. Ana Pacheco, "Reies López Tijerina: New Mexico's Revolutionary Revisited," *La herencia del norte* (Summer 1994): 39–41.

34. Juan José Peña, "The Chicano Movement in New Mexico," unpublished manuscript, 1997.

35. Eloy J. García Jr., "The Chicano Movement at New Mexico Highlands: An Interpretive History" (master's thesis, New Mexico Highlands University, 1997), 60.

36. Ibid., 74.

37. See "Bayonets at UNM," *El grito del norte*, May 19, 1970; and "The War Comes to Albuquerque," ibid., May 19, 1972.

38. Peña, 53–55.

39. Erlinda Gonzales-Berry, interview by David R. Maciel, Albuquerque, N.M., May 5, 1999.

40. Conversations with Tobías Durán, Director of the Center for Regional Studies, Albuquerque, N.M., 1996.

41. García Jr., 28.

43. Ibid., 33.

44. "Raza Expose Regents at Highlands U," *El grito del norte,* June 5, 1970. See also Garcia Jr., 35.

45. Pedro Rodríguez, interview by Juan José Peña, San Antonio, Texas, June 21, 1986.

46. Peña, 43.

47. García Jr., 53–54.

48. Peña, 46–47.

49. Richard Griego, interview by David R. Maciel, Albuquerque, N.M., June 23, 1997.

50. See *El grito del norte,* issues from 1968 to 1972.

Contributors

Benny J. Andrés Jr. is an assistant professor in the Department of History at Imperial Valley Junior College. His fields of teaching and research interest include Chicana/o history, the southwestern United States, and American ethnic and social history.

Anselmo Arellano is Vice President for Academic Affairs at L.V.T.I. Community College in Las Vegas, New Mexico. His fields of teaching and research interest are history, language, and the folklore of Nuevomexicanos and Chicanos in the Southwest.

María Rosa García Acevedo is an assistant professor in the Department of Political Science at California State University, Northridge. Her areas of teaching and research include Mexican and Latin American politics, immigration, and environmental issues of the U.S.-Mexican border.

Martín González de la Vara is an assistant professor in the Department of History at the Universidad Autonoma de Ciudad Juarez and a research professor at el Colegio de la Frontera Norte, Ciudad Juarez. His areas of teaching and research interests include the history of the U.S.-Mexican borderlands, Mexico, and Latin America.

Erlinda Gonzales-Berry is a professor and the chair of the Department of Ethnic Studies at Oregon State University. Her research and teaching fields include Chicana/o literature, cultural studies, and literary theory. In addition she is a published novelist and the coeditor of the UNM Press series *Pasó por Aquí: Nuevomexicano Literary Heritage.*

Carlos R. Herrera is a lecturer in the Department of History at San Diego State University. He has held an academic appointment at California State

University, Dominguez Hills. His fields of research and teaching interest include the borderlands in the colonial period, Chicana/o history, and Latin America.

David R. Maciel is a professor of history and chairperson of the Department of Chicana/o Studies at California State University, Dominguez Hills. His teaching interests and research fields include Chicana/o history, Mexico, modern Latin America, the southwestern United States, and film studies.

Gabriel Meléndez is an associate professor in the Department of American Studies at the University of New Mexico. His areas of teaching and research specialization are Chicano/a literature and Culture, modern Latin American literature, and the southwestern United States. He is coeditor of the UNM Press series, *Pasó por Aquí: Nuevomexicano Literary Heritage.*

John Nieto-Phillips is an assistant professor in the Department of History at New Mexico State University. His fields of research and teaching interest include Chicano/a history, the southwestern United States, and contemporary America.

Juan José Peña is a former director of Chicano Studies at Highlands University. Currently he is completing his doctorate in the Department of Spanish and Portuguese at the University of New Mexico. His academic interests include Chicano/a history, the Chicano/a movement, and the history of New Mexico.

Maurilio Vigil is a professor in the Department of Political Science at Highlands University. His areas of specialization are Chicano/Latino politics, American government, and the politics of New Mexico.

Index

Italic figure numbers (e.g., *fig. 13*) refer to figures in the unnumbered section following page 142.

Indian territories, 147
Indians. *See* Native Americans; Navajos;
  Pueblo Indians; Seminole Indians;
  Taos Indians
Indio bárbaros, 47, 48. *See also* Native
  Americans
Indios, 138n.69
Intermarriage, 20, 119, 240, 249

Knights of Labor: celebrations of, 68–69;
  and education, 69; and Gorras Blancas
  (White Caps), 70; growth of, 71; members of, 64; organizers of, 81n.48; as
  political force, 78n.8, 80n.22; racism of,
  71–72; and railroad workers, 64; support
  for, 66, 68, 69

La Mesilla, 38–39, 51–54
La Plaza Vieja. *See* Albuquerque
La Raza Unido. *See* Raza Unido Party
La Reconquista. *See* Reconquista
La voz del pueblo: and bilingual method of
  teaching, 182; editors of, 69, 70, 198;
  and Enabling Act, 187n.15; and Gorras
  Blancas, 67–68, 70; history of, 60; and
  Knights of Labor, 68; owner of, 76,
  78; and Partido de la Raza Unido, 282;
  and People's Movement, 59–60, 63;
  rival newspapers, 79n.17; and statehood,
  121–23, 140n.102; and United People's
  Party, 72
Labor movement: as "communist," 224;
  Nuevomexicanos in, 24, 91–92, 208; and
  Raza Unida Party, 281, 285; and Reconquista, 270, 281, 285; and strikes, 92, 224,
  285. *See also* Employment
Land: and Alianza Federal de Mercedes Libres, 272–75; and Alianza Federal de
  Pueblos Libres, 276–78; "community
  grants," 61; conflicts over, 16, 60, 61, 74,
  77, 105–7, 117, 242; and *diseños,* 16; and
  fencing, 61, 62, 65–66, 71; forged titles
  for, 62; and Gadsden Purchase, 53, 75;
  and La Mano Negra, 272; land grants to
  Nuevomexicanos repatriated to Mexico,
  47; land-grabbing, 61, 62, 63, 70–71,

77n.5, 264n.11, 271; land-grant movement,
  272–80; Pueblo land grants, 135n.6; taxation of, 17; Tierra Amarilla land grant,
  274; Tijerina and land struggle, 271–80;
  title disputes over, 16–17; and Treaty of
  Guadalupe Hidalgo, 43–44, 61, 62, 74,
  75, 77, 242, 271–80; and U.S. forest reserves, 17; and U.S. Office of Surveyor
  General, 135n.6; and water rights, 66. *See
  also* Fencing; and specific land grants
Language: and Americanization, 175, 178, 179,
  183–84; Constitution of New Mexico
  language clauses, 119–20, 173–74,
  187n.17, 187–88n.20; English as official
  language of New Mexico, 173; mandatory
  English fluency for state officials, 173;
  native-language rights, 175, 178–80, 185,
  189n.45; protection measures for, 172;
  Spanish as second language, 176–77;
  as statehood issue, 119–20, 133–34,
  140n.109, 147, 156–57, 172, 173, 175,
  187n.18; for teaching in schools, 119–20,
  122, 134, 169–85, 186n.10, 186n.11, 187–
  88n.20; and World War I nationalism,
  178. *See also* Spanish language
Las Vegas: civil rights protests in, 281, 291–
  95, *figs. 14–21;* ethnic demographics
  of, 291; and Gorras Blancas, 67; and
  Spanish-language press, 60, 147; and
  statehood, 124–25; and territorial politics, 59
Las Vegas land grant, 61, 62, 71, 75
League of United Latin American Citizens
  (LULAC), 87–89, 293

Manifest Destiny, 13, 25, 26, 27, 108
Maxwell land grant, 105–6
MECHA, 281
Memorials for statehood, 110–12, 159–60
Mestizos, 6–7
Mexican, use of, as term, 5, 137n.41, 263n.6
Mexican-American War: atrocities of, 32–33;
  Battle of La Cañada, 33; Battle of Taos,
  33; and bribery of New Mexico's officials,
  28–29; and California, 30, 31; causes of,
  13–14, 27–28; and December Plot, 31–33;